Writing in Focus

Trends in Linguistics

Studies and Monographs 24

Editor

Werner Winter

Mouton Publishers
Berlin · New York · Amsterdam

Writing in Focus

edited by

Florian Coulmas
Konrad Ehlich

Mouton Publishers
Berlin · New York · Amsterdam

Library of Congress Cataloging in Publication Data

Writing in focus.

(Trends in linguistics. Studies and monographs; 24)
Includes bibliographies and indexes.
1. Written communication. 2. Writing I. Coulmas, Florian.
II. Ehlich, Konrad, 1942–0000. III. Series.
P211.W717 1983 001.54'3 83–13095
ISBN 90-279-3359-6

Typesetting: Copo-Typesetting, Bangkok. – Printing: Druckerei Hildebrand, Berlin. – Binding: Lüderitz & Bauer Buchgewerbe GmbH, Berlin. – Printed in Germany.

Contents

Contributors

Florian Coulmas	The National Language Research Institute, Tokyo
Konrad Ehlich	Tilburg University
Peter Eisenberg	Freie Universität Berlin
Georg Elwert	Universität Bielefeld
Emilia Ferreiro	Instituto Politécnico Nacional, Mexico
Michael Giesecke	Universität Bielefeld
Jack Goody	University of Cambridge
Hartmut Günther	Universität München
William Haas	University of Manchester
Helen Harper	Amerikan Kiz Lisesi, Izmir
Marc L. Hazoumé	Centre Nationale Linguistique Cotonou
Angela Hildyard	Ontario Institute for Studies in Education, Toronto
Elmar Holenstein	Ruhr-Universität Bochum
Paul A. Kolers	University of Toronto
Otto Ludwig	Universität Hannover
Margaret Martlew	University of Sheffield
David R. Olson	Ontario Institute for Studies in Education, Toronto
Hanns J. Prem	Universität München
Berthold Riese	Proyecto Arqueológico Copán
Stanislav Segert	University of California, Los Angeles
Danny D. Steinberg	Rikkyo University, Tokyo, Japan
Toussaint Tchitchi	Centre Nationale Linguistique, Cotonou
Gernot Wilhelm	Universität Hamburg
Werner Winter	Universität Kiel

FLORIAN COULMAS and KONRAD EHLICH

Introduction

This book is concerned with writing and written language. The study of writing (cf. Gelb 1963) has a long history, a history that reflects the fundamental importance of this historical achievement. Written language, on the other hand, even though it has always been of great importance as an instrument of art and science, has hardly ever been made an object of scientific investigation. Moreover, the relationship between writing and written language has only rarely been seen as a problem in its own right.

Recently, however, an increasing number of scholars have become aware of the fact that there is more to the relationship between writing and language than a mere transposition from one medium to another. The study of writing in the historical context has usually concentrated on languages no longer in use and hence on speech communities where it is no longer possible to investigate spoken and written language as they coexist. Thus, the latter was only too often seen as simply a map of the former, and writing as an instrument of recording speech. The historian can only speculate on the effects that writing has had on languages such as, for instance, Sumerian, Chinese, or Greek. In order to better understand the historical and developmental relations between writing and spoken and written language and in order to overcome the simplistic view just mentioned, we must turn, therefore, to the cultural anthropologist who can observe the consequences of literacy (cf. Goody & Watt 1963) as they occur. To him/her it is quite clear that the adoption of a writing system by a traditional society has far-reaching effects not only on societal organization but also on the mode of communication and, eventually, on the language itself that has been reduced to writing. What are these effects, and what, indeed, are the changes that a language undergoes when reduced to writing, or as a consequence thereof? For some time, this has not been a respectable question in linguistic circles, because, according to the structuralist paradigm on both sides of the Atlantic (with the exception of the Prague school), the channel of its physical realization was not supposed to exercise any effects whatsoever on language. When Dwight Bolinger claimed in 1946 that it might be necessary to revise the dictum that language must always be studied without reference to writing, he voiced a very eccentric opinion, which is still not generally accepted. Yet, lately, more and more linguists have conceded that there are systematic distinctions between spoken and written language that are worthy of their attention, and some have begun to study them on a variety of structural levels. If there are any such distinctions it is clearly the linguist's obligation to account for them.

While it is true that speech and writing, on one level of analysis, are two physically different realizations of one and the same linguistic system, it cannot be denied that oral communication and literary communication differ in crucial respects, imposing very distinct conditions on the use of that system. The implications of permanent recording do have a bearing on the structure of linguistic expressions, affecting as they do (a) their syntactic complexity, (b) their relative semantic selfsufficiency, (c) their situational independence, and (d) the mode of their textual structuring. Thus the rules governing the production of linguistic utterances in speech and writing, respectively, only partly overlap. The extent to which they overlap is not necessarily the same for all languages and therefore has to be considered as an interesting parameter of interlinguistic and crosscultural variation. The extent of the overlap may vary with the literacy level of a linguistic community and with its literary history. Accordingly, the development of a written as distinct from the spoken variety of a language depends on a number of different factors.

One of these factors is, of course, the structural makeup of the respective writing system. Writing is a symbolic system for visually recording language; however, there are many different ways of doing that. Hence, determining the linguistic level of a script is an equally difficult and important task, a task which is not only linguistically interesting and revealing but also significant and challenging in a practical sense. When a language is reduced to writing and provided with a script for the first time, or when a given orthography is subjected to reform, the complex relations between language and writing have to be taken into account. For many language communities, the question of how to design an appropriate orthography is a pressing one. It can only be answered conclusively on the basis of a sound understanding of how language and writing can relate and interact. The complexity of this problem is not only indicated by the existence of typologically different writing systems but also by the fact that the alphabet, uniform as it is, allows for a considerable degree of variation in its application to a given language.

The alphabet has generally been considered as *the* revolutionary breakthrough in the development of writing and literacy and thus as the writing system that is superior to any other. The advantages of the alphabet seem obvious, indeed. It is easy to learn, because it has fewer units than any other writing system; and it is applicable to any language, thanks to its phonemic character. Yet the story of the alphabet is not as simple as that, as careful investigations clearly show. First of all, the alphabet did not come out of the blue, and there is evidence, some of which is presented in Goody's chapter, that the transition from pre-alphabetic literacy to the employment of a fully developed alphabet by the Greeks was not quite as dramatic and abrupt as has been widely assumed. Another important point is that the relative merits of the alphabet, in order to be justly assessed, have to be checked against a variety of purposes, i.e., ways of using it. With respect to some purposes, other systems are equally efficient, as is demonstrated in recent psychological studies such as, e.g., the one presented in Steinberg's chapter. Finally, alphabetic writing is subject to historical changes, and it is at least questionable whether or not the structural advantages of the alphabet are preserved throughout these changes and in the course of the historical development of the phonological and the orthographic systems of a language.

Some of these questions are for linguists to solve, others call for psychological testing, and still others can only be discussed in an historical perspective. It is evident, therefore, that a comprehensive understanding of the *development and use of writing systems* heavily depends on interdisciplinary cooperation. The fact that, thanks to its immense importance to mankind, writing is the common object of interest and investigation for a number of different scientific disciplines, seems obvious enough. Yet, academic departmentalization does not always favor interdisciplinary exchange, and, in spite of their shared interest, those disciplines concerned with particular aspects of the study of writing do not take too much cognizance of each other. Psychologists generally do not know much about what historians are doing, and the latter are not particularly concerned about problems of linguistic analysis. It is our contention that mutual openness with respect to the approaches of other fields is imperative for any discipline involved in the study of writing, if justice is to be done to its manifold nature. This aim is clearly impossible to achieve in a single book, but a step can be taken in this direction. Thus, the authors of this book have joined together in order to help overcome mutual indifference and ignorance and to stimulate cooperation across the boundaries of disciplines.

This book is divided into three parts, each of which is based upon and inclined toward the notions of one discipline, but at the same time is accessible to the reader whose background lies in other fields. The grouping of the papers reflects the respective center of attention of each one rather than its exclusive relevancy to an area of research.

The papers of the first part are centered around *linguistic aspects of writing.* While it is a matter of systemic differences which level of language the written sign connects to, it is also a matter of controversy. There are, in other words, factual as well as theoretical differences that have to be accounted for in determining what William Haas calls "the level of a script". A script, he argues in his paper, is derived on some systemic level from the spoken language. This derivational relationship, however, is not only a historical one but also a psychological one governing the operations of writing down and reading aloud, and these operations are what we have to consider in order to determine the systemic level of a script.

To characterize a script as logographic, syllabic, or phonemic is much too rough a distinction, one that cannot cover the interesting systematic relations constituting the makeup of a given writing system. Peter Eisenberg's paper is an example of what it takes to determine the systematic level of the alphabet as employed in a particular orthography. He presents a detailed analysis of the way morphological relations are represented in German orthography. He argues that "there is a mutual dependency of morphology and writing system", thus making the point that the graphemic system of a language ought to be considered as an integral part of its grammatical description.

Both Haas and Eisenberg are concerned with the relationship of the writing system to other parts of the language system as a whole. Otto Ludwig and Elmar Holenstein, by contrast, concentrate on more general and philosophically-directed problems. The focus of Ludwig's paper is on the relationship between the writing system and the written variety of language. He proposes some terminological distinctions in order to avoid the common confusion between instrument and product. Writing is an instrument of written language and a historical precondition of its emergence. However, there is a categorical difference between the two, and the historical precedence of writing over written language should not be mistaken as a logical relation of precedence. This, Ludwig claims, could be a misconception of the interrelations between writing and written language.

Granted that a writing system has to be analyzed as a relatively autonomous part of the overall language system whose status is not altogether secondary and derived, it is still important to find out exactly what kinds of properties a writing system shares with a language. Taking a semiotic approach, Holenstein discusses the question of whether and to what extent writing shares with language the important feature of double articulation. He maintains that this important characteristic of human language can, indeed, be detected in various scripts, and that it becomes increasingly important as the digitalization of writing advances.

Part Two of this book discusses aspects of the *history of writing and of writing systems.* It contains contributions that refer to one of the oldest and most outstanding fields of the scientific analysis of writing. The history of writing and the decipherment of hitherto unknown scripts has been one of the most fascinating aspects of philology and archeology for the past three centuries. The history of the great discoveries and of the continuous and – on the whole – highly successful efforts to decipher and interpret the written relics of the past have aroused the interest not only of the scholarly world but also of the general public. The decipherment of writing systems such as Egyptian, Sumerian, Akkadian, Hittite, Ugaritic, Cretan, of Aztec and Mayan hieroglyphs, cuneiform scripts, or other writing systems have provided us with a key to the understanding of forgotten languages which in turn have permitted insights into some of the most interesting and important cultures and societies at the very beginning of "history" in the strict sense of that term. Texts from the dawn of mankind speak to us and help us to understand the origins of traditions which are either still present in our own world or which reveal past worlds, showing the manifold ways in which mankind has developed thus far.

While the main developments of the history of writing are familiar to us through the results of past research efforts, it is now evident that we know as little about the internal course of this history as we do about the linguistic principles the decipherment was based upon. In other words, we must have more detailed background knowledge about the so painstakingly researched details and the so painstakingly described developments. This means that we must look into the linguistic, cognitive-theoretical, and social conditions and perspectives of these developments.

Jack Goody, in his article, investigates the role that literacy played in the ancient world. He offers insights slightly different from those he and Watt developed earlier. Literacy plays an important role in that, in contrast to oral tradition, the history of "false starts" is also reportable. The "erasure" of false starts, which appears as an unavoidable byproduct of oral reporting, gives way to a thinking process which reaches new exactness through recourse to explicit lines of reasoning. Not that there were no lines of argument in the pre-literate situation, but communication in the written mode made possible and even demanded increased reflection on the course of one's own thoughts. Thus the separation, the difference from the pre-literate societies is, on the one hand, less abrupt than was first suspected; on the other hand, the distance is reinstated through the degree to which the process can be operated in a new way to indicate future tendencies.

Literacy leads to written language, as Ludwig has pointed out; written language provides new forms which allow thinking to develop on a new level, proposing new problem solutions and submitting once-popular problem solutions to acute reexamination.

While the functionality of writing for social problem-solving is evident in Jack Goody's paper, Konrad Ehlich treats the development of writing systems in itself as one form of social problem solving. He takes the development of writing in the Near East as an example of a momentous development which has generated solutions up to the writing systems of today in the Western World. In his analysis, Ehlich reconstructs the main characteristics of the Ancient Near Eastern writing systems beginning with the Sumerian and Egyptian inventions and continuing through the Greek alphabet, with its full representation mode for both consonants and vowels. The transition from one form to the other proves to be the complex result of essential *and* contingent factors such as language structure, social needs for writing, the existence or lack of professional groups of scribes, and so on, which determined whether or not new inventions, new problem-solving strategies were developed. Far from being a homogeneous, straightforward process of development, the progress culminating in the alphabet shows a transition of the representation of spoken language through written means, a transition which was useful for the languages involved.

Stanislav Segert, in his article, compares, from a systematic point of view, two of the successful decipherment attempts of this century: that of the Ugaritic script, which was achieved shortly after the first finds in Ras Shamra around 1930, and the much more difficult one of Linear B. Segert's paper shows, on a micro-level, that essential and contingent factors significantly influence the success or failure of decipherment attempts. Since the languages in question, as well as the knowledge available on neighboring writing systems – a knowledge which is crucial for the development of sound working hypotheses – was very different in the two cases, the scientists' efforts also showed very different results. One of the surprising aspects of Segert's account of the decipherment of Ugaritic is that a less systematic approach proved to yield better results, in part, than a hypersystematic procedure that lacked essential intuition. The close cooperation between the scientists involved, in the one case, and its absence for a prolonged period of time, in the other, are shown to be among the most important reasons for the varying achievements in the two examples.

Gernot Wilhelm discusses another issue in the context of the Ancient Near Eastern writing systems and their analysis: the reconstruction of the phonology of "dead" languages from their writing systems, which also, in turn, usually had to be reconstructed. These two tasks of decipherment go hand in hand if there is no continuous tradition nor any form of *bilinguis* which allows the linking of the ancient finding to current knowledge of the phonology of a language. The case of Hurrian makes clear how highly complicated the reconstructive work of the phonologist of a "dead" language is, closely resembling the work of a criminologist who reconstructs the process of events from clues and evidence. The contradictions in the written tradition offer an especially outstanding means of discovering phonological traits and features of "dead" languages.

The Near Eastern area is only one of the main areas of the development of writing. Another such area is in the Far East, in China, which is the subject of the article by Florian Coulmas. The connection between language system and writing system is especially clear here. The Chinese script is logographically based. (The Western world, incidentally, has entertained the mistaken notion, since Leibniz, that Chinese has an ideographic – an idea – script.) The logographical structure of this script exhibits considerable advantages – advantages which have become painfully evident in connection with the current problem of romanizing the Chinese script. Thus it can by no means be assumed that romanization represents an improvement; rather, it has been introduced in China merely as an expedient.

One other area which is extremely interesting for the history of writing, from a systematic point of view, is the America of the Aztecs and Mayas. Here the transition from mnemotechnically motivated procedural representation to name representations to an actual hieroglyphic script is tangible – a process which can no longer be recognized in its full development in the scripts of Sumer and Egypt. The article by Hanns J. Prem and Berthold Riese describes the different forms developed in this area and shows, above all, how, on the basis of a practical starting point common to all, quite different degrees of development were achieved. The increasing conventionalization, abstraction, and standardization permitted the transition from boundaries which were no longer solely mnemotechnical – one could say, purely empractic – to a fully readable script.

While in the areas mentioned, there has been a largely unplanned development of writing and spread of literacy, the modern age has seen a number of attempts to provide languages with consciously planned writing systems. Werner Winter reports on such an attempt with the Walapai of Arizona. One of the most impressive results of this experiment is surely to be seen in the fact that the linguistically most rational form of writing is by no means the one which is most easily accepted by speakers and potential writers of the language. On the contrary, other factors, such as using writing as a membership device, as a means of indicating social identity, play a significant role which can also influence the structure of a script.

Many African countries are currently in the position of having to develop new writing systems for hitherto solely oral languages. Toussaint Tchitchi and Marc L. Hazoumé describe such an experiment in the Peoples' Republic of Bénin which involved the entire population of that nation. The way chosen for the development of a script in Bénin had as one of its main objectives the preservation of the linguistic varieties occurring within the national territory without "leveling" them in favor of a single language. The linguistic and practical problems arising in this connection are considerable. Tchitchi and Hazoumé describe the work of the committee entrusted with this task and the results achieved so far.

Georg Elwert took part in the self-help literacy campaign in the same country. His experiences offer interesting insights into the sociology of literacy in a situation which begins with the self-organizing of those who *want to learn*. These findings parallel, to an amazing degree, developments which, though they took place some centuries earlier, occurred in a sociologically very similar environment. Michael Giesecke offers details of this parallel movement: the spread of the knowledge of writing in Germany during the Reformation movement. The comparison of the two literacy programs shows the necessity of taking sociological categories into account in the analysis of writing development and dissemination.

Even the existence of a writing system in a country does not ensure that literacy is widespread throughout the population. In the article by Coulmas already mentioned, the Chinese situation is described from this aspect. The area in which Chinese is spoken encompasses nearly a billion people. The language, although it is called "Chinese", includes various dialects which differ considerably from one another. Writing represents a unifying bond – for those who master it. The fact that even the most elementary process requires over 2000 symbols obviously works against mass literacy. The Chinese writing reform attempts to solve this problem by means of a gentle reform in which the characters are simplified, and by the use of a romanized supplementary script. The general acceptance is, however, contingent upon a standard form of Chinese (Mandarin). Its propagation is being supported very carefully.

The range of the historical articles shows that we are ourselves part of history. The current problems of writing and literacy are of the utmost urgency for the greater part of mankind – for the spreading of knowledge depends essentially on the spreading of literacy, and these are absolutely necessary for the social as well as the economic development of humanity. History offers some cause for reflection and some suggestions for dealing with these problems in a purposeful way.

The six chapters of the last section of the book deal with *psychological aspects* of literacy, its acquisition and mechanics. Martlew, Ferreiro, Olson and Hildyard, and Steinberg and Harper all tackle particular problems connected with the development of individual literacy, mostly reporting on (various) experiments that were carried out under normal as well as abnormal conditions.

Margaret Martlew reports on the ontogenetic development of writing. Writing as a decontextualized mode of linguistic communication requires the integrated use of a variety of skills. They range from visuo-motor skills to conceptual skills of verbal planning. Awareness of the linguistic levels of word, sentence, and text is of crucial importance for the child's achievement in his/her learning process. At the end of this process, the child has acquired a complex capacity which makes it possible for him/her to generate and elaborate complex ideas. Martlew's description of the phases of development makes evident that there are important parallels in the ontogenesis and that part of the phylogenesis of writing has as its result the use of alphabetic writing systems. The parallels refer to the graphic and to the cognitive dimensions.

In her examination of the early stages of establishing a regular correspondence between sounds and written marks by preschool children learning an alphabetic orthography, Emilia Ferreiro takes a Piagetian approach, as does Martlew in her paper. Ferreiro argues that a proper understanding of the complex problem of the acquisition of writing can only be reached if this problem is put into the wider perspective of cognitive growth. The development of writing and reading skills, she suggests, presupposes a certain degree of meta-linguistic awareness – an observation providing a psychological counterpart to the fact that, historically, the development of writing systems depends on, as well as promotes, linguistic analysis.

An understanding of the difference between the meaning of a speaker and the meaning of a piece of written text seems to be one instance where the acquisition of writing and the development of metalinguistic awareness interact. David R. Olson and Angela Hildyard conducted a number of experiments on this topic, the results of which have led them to the conclusion that the possibility of differentiating between literal meaning and speaker's meaning, and hence the very notion of literal meaning, hinge on the existence and command of written language.

On one level of analysis, the claim that acquisition of writing presupposes some meta-linguistic awareness is quite straightforward, because it is just another way of saying that writing is usually taught as a system of signs whose elements refer to other signs that belong to a more basic linguistic sign system already familiar to the learner. The situation is quite different when this is not the case, that is, under conditions where the referents of written signs are *not* auditory-phonetic linguistic signs but concrete objects. Under such circumstances, written signs enjoy the status of a primary linguistic system. Under normal conditions, this does not usually happen; however, for congenitally deaf persons the primary use of written signs is one of the possibilities to make up for the defective auditory channel – hence the title of Danny D. Steinberg and Helen Harper's paper: 'Teaching Written Language as a First Language to a Deaf Boy', in which the authors describe how this possibility can be exploited, and what conclusions can be drawn about the psychological relations between language and writing.

Apart from the mode of acquisition, the most obvious difference between spoken and written language is in perception. Owing to the different sense modalities involved, the ways in which perceptual strategies and language processing on the cognitive level interact are bound to be different in spoken and written language. Some of the particular problems concerning visual language processing are investigated by Kolers and Günther. Representing the results of experiments with graphically manipulated pieces of written text, Paul A. Kolers stresses the significance of pattern analyzing operations. The results of Hartmut Günther's tachistoscopic and word recognition experiment, on the other hand, seem to give support to the view that meaning is the crucial factor in visual language processing.

The majority of the chapters in this volume have grown out of a conference on "The Development and Use of Writing Systems" held June 19–22, 1980, under the auspices of and at the "Zentrum für Interdisziplinäre Forschung", Bielefeld, FRG. Participants included linguists, psychologists, historians, anthropologists, and scholars representing various cross-sections of these disciplines. The conference was planned as a workshop in which discussions would play as important a part as prepared presentations. These discussions have encouraged us to believe in the possibility of interdisciplinary exchange. New aspects in the study of writing can emerge from applying the notions of one discipline to the well-established paradigm of questions of another, and it is our conviction that our understanding of the manifold problems of writing and written language can only profit from efforts to transcend departmental boundaries. This book includes revisions of most of the delivered papers as well as some invited papers.[1]

Note

1. The editors thank Constance Guhl (Universität Düsseldorf) for technical help in the translation and preparation of the manuscripts.

References

Bolinger, D.
1946 "Visual morphemes". *Language* XXII: 333–40

Gelb, I.J.
1963 *A Study of Writing.* Chicago, London: The University of Chicago Press

Goody, J.R. and Watt, I.P.
1963 "The consequences of literacy". *Comparative Studies in Society and History* 5: 304–345

Part One.

Linguistic aspects of writing

WILLIAM HAAS

Determining the level of a script

Abstract

The notion of the level of a writing-system is familiar. It is common practice to characterise a script as lexical (logographic) or morphemic or syllabic or phonetic-phonemic, or as a mixture of such levels. One might assume then that there are no problems about determining the level of a given script, ancient or modern. Yet, it happens frequently that even in instances where scholars are in perfect agreement about the definition of those descriptive terms and are equally agreed about the facts, they contradict one another, nevertheless, and ascribe different levels to one and the same script. Egyptian hieroglyphic writing has been described as logographic by some, and syllabic by others; the Semitic scripts have been made out to be syllabic by some, and phonemic by others; and doubts have been expressed about the phonemic character of the English orthography. Some clarification seems to be required, where at first sight everything appeared to be clear.

1. The level of a script is determined with reference to the spoken language from which the script is derived. The kind of writing we are concerned with, then, is 'derived' from speech in the sense that it represents determinate units – words or morphemes or syllables or phonemes – of the utterances of a specific language. To circumscribe our field of inquiry in this way is perhaps to state the obvious; 'being derived from speech' is often regarded as implicit to the very notion of writing. But writing, in this sense, is not co-extensive with written or graphic communication, and the boundaries of writing, in the usual sense of the word, are made clearer by looking beyond them. In particular, different *levels of derivation* become clearer when we view them as providing different ways of establishing a derived script, from out of all the possibilities of underived graphic communication.

We are constantly making use of graphic symbols that are *not* derived from the language we speak. Geographical maps or road-signs and scores of instruction-labels in common use are off-shoots of drawing or painting, rather than of speech.[1] The first beginnings of writing – 'pre-writing', as it is sometimes called – are of that independent sort; and some of our highly specialised notations, graphs and diagrams, continue to exploit the special virtues of underived graphic communication.

It is true, however, that every script that approximates the wide range and all-purpose use of spoken language has been derived from a spoken language. There is no logical necessity in this, but the fact is that no-one has ever gone to the trouble of freely inventing an entirely new lexicon and a new syntax of arbitrary signs to match the range of a spoken language. This is only reasonable. The derivation of a script from a given spoken language is difficult enough to achieve. It does not simply flow from any innate or universal human competence, but is a painstaking and slow achievement of scientific insight.

For a script to be derived, speech must first have been analysed. The unlimited number and variety of utterances must have been found analysable in terms of a limited inventory of recurrent units. The derivation of a script consists in the more or less regular assignment of written symbols to such units. The level of the underlying analysis determines the level of the script: the written symbols represent words or morphemes or syllables or phonemes. It is the choice of one of these that characterises a script as being derived on a certain level. A fairly obvious and important broader classification distinguishes (i) scripts that are derived on either the lexical or the morphemic level from (ii) those that are derived on either the syllabic or the phonemic level. Let us (with terms borrowed from L. Hjelmslev) call the former *pleremic,* and the latter *cenemic.*[2]

Spoken *units below the level of a script's derivation* are omitted; they appear only in re-translating the written text into speech. For example, *3 + 4 = 7* has nothing to *contract* correspondence with the syllables or phonemes that are made available in reading it aloud. On the other hand, correspondence with spoken *units above the level of derivation* is found in the text simply as an automatic consequence of lower-level representation.

There seems to be nothing contentious in the notion of the level of a script as I have tried to define it. It is familiar and seems clear enough.[3] Why then – we have to ask – should the application of that notion become the source of unresolved disagreements? Problems that are not foreseen in the familiar definitions seem to confront us as soon as we go on to apply the defined terms. Assessing the evidence is obviously crucial, in any given case, for that relationship of regular correspondence between, on the one hand, spoken units of a certain level and, on the other, the basic written units of a script. We shall have to look more closely, first, at applications of the two sides of the correspondence-relationship, and then at the operations that ascertain the presence of such a relationship.

2. When we consider the assignment of certain units of speech to a determinate level, we soon discover a possible source of confusion. It happens frequently that one and the same portion of speech may be assigned to more than one level. In *a book/əbuk/,* for instance, '/ə/' is a phoneme, a syllable, a morpheme, and a word; in *books /buk/* '/s/' is a phoneme as well as a morpheme. If we make a list of Chinese morphemes, it appears that almost every one of them is a syllable. Such overlaps have often been regarded as evidence for a mixed script. But it seems preposterous to say that *a* of *a book* is written in a syllabic or morphemic or lexical script, though it does of course serve to 'represent' a syllable, a morpheme and a word; and it is also wrong to regard the Chinese script as wholly or even partially syllabic.[4] The question is why.

We shall find that in order to determine the level of a script, it is not sufficient to ascertain the level of the units which the symbols of the script may represent; we have to ask about the *rules* by which units of a certain level are selected from given utterances. It will be clear then that the operative derivational rules of the English orthography which select '/ə/' to be represented by the *a* of *a book*, or '/-s/' to be represented by the *s* of *books*, is a phonemic-alphabetic rule; while the operative rules of the Chinese script assign its 'characters' to morphemes. Though units of different levels may overlap in the same portion of an utterance, the writing of that portion is still derived on just one of those levels: there is no overlap between different levels of derivation.

'Mixed scripts' are no exception. Here, different parts of a text may be derived on different levels. For example, in writing *fish & chips*, the ampers and, &, being assigned to a word, is written in a lexical script, while the rest of the written units select phonemes. Scripts of different levels mix in the text, but they do not overlap. Each part of a mixed text is derived on one level only.

If we now turn to consider the other side of a script's correspondence-relationships and try to identify the basic written units, we find again that we face problems that can be resolved only by reference to the script's constitutive rules of correspondence, the rules of its derivation from speech. Consider the *th* of *thin*. Is it one unit or two? It is obviously made up of two elements, *t* and *h*, which may each correspond to a different phoneme – for example, in *hit*. In matching the inventories of spoken and written elements, *t* and *h* will have to be listed as different graphemes. But in *θιŋ* there are no separate phonemes to correspond to the *t* and *h* of *thin*; *th* is said to be a 'digraph'. Something analogous is found in the majority of Chinese characters: each of them can be analysed into two graphemic elements: a 'silent' semantic marker or classifier (a 'radical') and a 'phonetic' complement. 'Silence' of the first element implies that the two co-occurring elements do not correspond to separate spoken units, though they contract separate correspondences elsewhere. Thus, the digraph 媽 (mā) 'mother' consists of (i) a grapheme 馬 which, when it occurs without a silent adjunct, means 'horse' /mǎ/ and is nearly homophonic with /mā/ 'mother' and (ii) a semantic marker 女 which means 'female' and is pronounced /nǚ/ elsewhere but is silent here.[5] There are good reasons for employing *t* and *h*, and also for employing 女 and 馬 as constituents of the digraph: *t* indicates the dentality and *h* the spirancy of the corresponding phoneme /*θ*/; 女 indicates the semantic class, and 馬 the pronunciation of the corresponding morpheme /mā/.

What then are the basic graphic units of a script? Only the constitutive rules of a script can tell us. These rules do not operate upon abstract inventories but upon *utterances* and *texts*, and they match texts with utterances by selecting written units to correspond to spoken units of a certain level. Let us call these units the *'characters'* of the script. Characters may be *simple*, i.e. not analysable into two or more potentially simple characters ('graphemes'), like the *t* or *h* of *hit*, or they may be *compound* (mostly 'digraphs'), like the *th* of *thin*, or the 女馬 'mother'.

The burden, then, of identifying the spoken and written units of a script falls upon stating its rules of correspondence. They establish a script and continue to control its use. The main burden of our task must be a closer examination of these rules.

3. We have seen that if we are to give an adequate account of that correspondence between writing and speech which constitutes a derived script, we must not view it as simply a match between two inventories. The rules of correspondence of a script cannot be stated as applying to isolated items in frozen lists; they concern *the use* of a script, the functions of elements, spoken and written, in utterances and texts. The regular correspondences which determine the level of a script are rules and tendencies that govern the derivation, on the one hand, of written records from utterances and, on the other, of spoken readings from written texts.

Every derived script is established and controlled by two kinds of rules:

(i) *rules of 'writing down'*: which, given units of a certain level (words or morphemes or syllables or phonemes), as they occur in actual utterances, govern the selection of appropriate written characters, to convert the utterances into texts, and

(ii) rules of *'reading aloud'*: which, given certain units of actual texts (characters), govern the selection of appropriate units of speech for converting the texts into utterances.

Correspondence, we may say, is determined by rules and tendencies of *glotto-graphic translation*: from speech into writing, and from writing into speech.[6] The units of speech, with which we are concerned in determining the level of a script, are source-units of translation in one direction ('writing down') and target-units of translation in the other ('reading aloud').

The relation between speech and writing, we shall say then, is essentially translatability. To recognise this is to be prepared for complexities which, though familiar to translators, are not anticipated by those who regard the matching of utterances and texts as secured by a simple matching of inventories. The most important point about rules of glotto-graphic translation is that the existence of such rules does not imply a one-to-one correspondence between spoken and written elements. Nothing of the kind is implied by rules of ordinary (interlingual) translation: on the contrary, one-many correspondences (like the translation of *know* by *kennen* or *wissen*) and many-many correspondences are the norm. It follows that the rules of translation will have to refer to the conditions that select one of the corresponding elements rather than another; and also that a rule for translating in one direction may be quite different from a rule of translating in the other direction. Thus, as both *kennen* and *wissen* have a straightforward translation into the English *know*, while an appropriate translation of *know* into German by either *kennen* or *wissen* requires more complicated rules that refer to categories of nouns (*Ich kenne Paul*) or to categories of sub-ordinate clauses (*Ich weiss, was er will/dass er kommen wird*) etc.; so the reading out, for instance, of *-al, -ol, -il, -el, -le* as syllabic /l̩/ in *refusal, symbol, pencil, marvel, battle* is perfectly straightforward in spite of the many-one correspondence between characters and phoneme, even though the rules for writing the syllabic /l̩/ by selecting one of those five characters are bound to be complicated. But since rules of translation – of glotto-graphic no less than ordinary translation – do not apply to isolated items in lists but always to units that are embedded in utterances or texts, the whole structures of those utterances and texts are available for the rules to refer to.

A rule of glotto-graphic translation will do two things: it will (i) identify the items that are to be matched and (ii) state the contextual conditions of that match. The two parts of a rule's operation must not be confused. It is the first that determines the level of a script; but the rule for the matching of a written character with a spoken element of determinate level may refer to co-occurring elements of *other* levels as contextual conditions of the match. (We are still matching words (and not clauses), when we translate *know* by *wissen* in the higher-level conditions of a following subordinate clause.)

3.1 A cenemic script does not cease to be cenemic when its matching rules operate under certain higher-level conditions.[7] To take a simple example, the English orthographic rule for the use of capital letters, which refers to the lexical category of proper names and to sentence boundaries, operates on the phonemic level (in selecting, say, *R* for /r/ in *Robert*), though it refers to lexical or syntactic conditions. Again, the rule for translating /l̩/ by *-al* in writing *refusal, approval, recital,* etc. is a rule for translating a phoneme, though it refers to the grammatical category of 'deverbal nouns'.

Most of the complications in the operation of a traditional orthography are due to the fact that changes in the spoken language have not been accompanied by corresponding graphemic changes. Since, however, most changes are regular, most correspondences will remain regular, too; we shall be able to state the relevant condition in terms of grammatical categories (such as 'proper names' or 'deverbal nouns'). But it may happen, especially when a phonemic distinction has disappeared from the spoken language, that the correspondence-rules for a written language which maintains that distinction will have to make reference to individual morphemes or words. Thus, the correct writing-down of /l̩/ as *-il* or *-el* in *pencil* or *marvel* can only be secured by reference to the individual words, though the correct reading-out of the words, with a syllabic /l̩/ to match the final *-il* or *-el* requires no morphemic reference at all. It is in such cases of individual morphemic or lexical reference that a phonemic-alphabetic script is felt to be *irregular.* English spelling involves quite a number of such irregular translations, though frequently only in one direction. The reading-out, for example, of *vain, vein, vane* relies on a perfectly regular match of the characters *ai, ei,* and *a-e* with the diphthong /eɪ/; but proceeding from speech to writing, we have to choose between those three characters and can do so only by referring to the individual words.

It would clearly be wrong to conclude that occasional reference, by the orthographic rules of English, to individual morphemes or words characterises written English as a mixed script, in the sense in which the deviant abbreviatory inscription *fish & chips* is mixed. In writing *fish & chips*, we are not only referring to a word ('and') but we match that word with a logogram (&): while in writing *vain*, we are referring to the word ('vain') in order to match the phoneme /eɪ/ with the character *ai,* to fill a gap between the regular phonemic correspondences of *v* and *n*. The lexical reference serves to supplement a regular but incomplete phonemic representation of the word by *v-n*. A cenemic script that relies exceptionally on reference to individual pleremic units is plagued by irregularities, but it is still a cenemic script.

3.1.1 It has been shown (Axel Wijk 1966) that "the vast majority of English words, about 90 to 95 per cent of the total vocabulary, do in fact follow certain regular patterns [of character-phoneme correspondence] in regard to their spelling and pronunciation." But let us digress a little and imagine an orthography where *all* the rules for character-phoneme correspondence ('letter-sound correspondence') involve reference to the individual lexical units in which the phonemes ('sounds') are embedded. Here, then, we should be referring to not just a few incomplete phonemic representations of words (such as /v-n/ for 'vain'): our imaginary orthography would have to rely on thousands of lexical representations, each unique for a specific lexical item, and it would, in addition, give us rules for relating these lexical representations to phonemes ('sounds'). Clearly, such a writing-system would be grossly inefficient. Being pleremic as well as cenemic, it loses the merits of both systems. By operating with unique lexical representations, it would fulfil the requirements of a pleremic script, but do so without omitting the representation of phonetic detail and, therefore, without gaining the distinctive advantages of a pleremic script. A pleremic script (like the Chinese) can serve a wide variety of phonologically divergent dialects and languages, precisely because it does not provide phonological information, leaving it up to the reader to supply this information from his knowledge of any one of those languages or dialects. Again, by providing a match of letters with phonemic-phonetic segments, our imaginary script would fulfil the requirements of a cenemic script and this, too, without achieving its advantages – that is, without the tremendous economy of allowing lexical representations to be just a consequence of 'letter-sound' correspondences. A script of such egregious inefficiency does not exist, in fact, but the fiction of one has been elaborated upon in some detail. Chomsky (1970) described the English orthography as if it were such a script – as if the conversion of written English into speech proceeded by an application of phonological rules to 'underlying lexical structures'. Our operations of reading an ordinary English text are, in fact, credited with all the 'derivational' processes which had been ascribed to the language in the Chomsky-Halle (1968) 'Sound Pattern of English'. But this is unreasonable. To describe a language is not the same thing as to describe the working-structure of a writing-system.

We may well accept it that as 'speaker-hearers' of a language we have some kind of global acquaintance with whole words, as well as some degree of analytic awareness of their phonetic constituents – in much the same way as we have global impressions of faces as well as more detailed perceptions of eyes, noses and lips, and we can expect a description of a language to give us an explicit account of both kinds of intuition, and of their connection. But a writing-system for a language is not designed to serve as a description of it. The technology of writing allows us to ignore many of the structures of spoken messages; indeed, it consists in selecting some of their elements only and relying on them for the conversion of speech into written texts. Progress in the technology of writing, from pleremic to cenemic scripts, has been made by progressively reducing the extent to which the system of a language is engaged in operations of glotto-graphic translation. The Chomsky-Halle interpretation of a cenemic script such as the traditional English orthography obscures the basic difference between cenemic and pleremic scripts, in terms of unique lexical representations.

There is, of course, nothing in the actual operation of reading, or of learning to read, to provide evidence for those processes ('sound patterns' or 'sound structures') the study of which is supposed to "clarify the relation of the conventional orthography to the structure of the spoken language" (Chomsky 1970: 4). Indeed, no such evidence is claimed. "Beyond. . . relative banalities", Chomsky (1970: 18) says, "I do not see what concrete conclusions can be drawn, for the teaching of reading, from the study of sound structure, although [he adds] this study may have profound implications for human psychology." 'Profound', here, appears to be the enemy of 'concrete'.

What shall we make of the alleged 'psychological reality' (p. 12) of those 'abstract lexical forms' and of the rules or 'processes' that convert them into a 'phonetic output'? Lexical representations, such as /korǽge/ (corresponding to *courage*) are said to be readily available to "the speaker-hearer who is acquainted with this word"; they are supposed to be "internalized, as part of his knowledge of English" (p. 11); and the system or rules of 'derivation' is similarly supposed to have been mastered before the learning process begins, as "part of the unconscious equipment of the non-literate speaker" (p. 16). We are warned at the same time that this valuable unconscious equipment of the speaker-hearer has nothing to do with the processes by which he learns to read. Indeed, his teacher must take care to keep it subliminal. He is told that "it would hardly make sense to introduce the beginning reader" (p. 15) to those abstract lexical forms or to the rules that convert them into speech. We will agree, of course, that it would be preposterous to try to teach, for example, the reading of *courage* by asking a learner first to convert the given string of letters into the abstract lexical representation /korǽge/ and then to apply, in successive stages, five rules (stress rule, velar softening, unrounding, e-elision, vowel reduction) in order to arrive at the pronunciation /kʌ́rəǰ/. But is it not worrying that an orthographic theory should exist, and especially one that claims psychological reality for all its ingredients, from which no conclusions of any importance can be drawn for the actual processes of using the orthography?

A more traditional account of the English orthography may be less profound in its implications for 'cognitive psychology'. Such an account will allow for the possibility that someone learning to read may have to discover things of importance that are not already in his mind. But the correspondence-rules of such an account will have the practical advantage of being descriptive of at least some important aspects of a reader's actual performance; and they will be directly relevant for the teaching of reading. *Courage,* for instance, which is one of the more difficult words, will still be found to translate into speech by character-phoneme correspondences which, with the sole exception of *ou,* are regular (see A. Wijk 1966: 85, 84, 66, 19, 56). The reader's knowledge of the specific word, of which he is given the regular but incomplete phonemic representation /k–rɪdʒ/ will only have to supply the 'irregular' /ʌ/.[8]

3.1.2 After this excursion, let us return briefly to what are genuine temptations to assume a pleremic admixture to a cenemic script. We encounter them, as already indicated, when a phoneme (or, in a syllabic script, a syllable) coincides with a morpheme or word – especially when that phoneme (or syllable) is picked out with reference to the very morpheme with which it coincides. For example, the final phonemes /s/, /z/, /ɪz/ correspond, in the present tense of verbs and in the plural of nouns, quite regularly to -*(e)s*; and they also coincide with the morphemes of present-tense or noun-plural. One might be inclined then to speak loosely of a representation of these morphemes by -*(e)s*. Strictly speaking, however, there is no good reason for regarding -*(e)s* as being written in a morphemic script. What we have here, besides regular phonotactic conditioning, is still nothing more than mere reference to the grammatical conditions which control the regular correspondence of -*(e)s* with the *phonemes* /s/, /z/, and /ɪz/. Glotto-graphic translation is still phono-graphic: from and into phonemes. The level of a script is the lowest level at which the matching-operation of glotto-graphic translation operates.

3.2 It remains to examine analogous problems in the characterisation of pleremic scripts – for it happens frequently that the correspondence-rules of a pleremic script make reference to elements of a lower level. Since, as we have seen, there is nothing in a piece of pleremic writing (in, for example, *£7*) to correspond to the phonological elements of its translation into speech, we might be inclined to assume that the only way of enabling a pleremic script, itself, to carry phonological information would be to add cenemic characters to it – as, for example, in the English orthographic convention of adding letters to the pleremic figures of dates: *1st, 2nd, 3rd, 4th . . . April.* This, however, is not what actually happened in the evolution of pleremic scripts.

The graphemes or characters of pleremic scripts that are commonly called 'phonetic' are not, themselves, cenemic – that is, not like the *st, nd, rd, th* which *are* a cenemic admixture to the pleremic 1, 2, 3, 4, etc. Invariably, they are graphemes already available for the representation of morphemes or words (such as the grapheme 馬 /mǎ/ 'horse' of the Chinese digraph 'mother'). Such graphemes seem to be used to refer to mere syllables, but they are doing this through homophony with a morpheme or word.

Again, the problem is how to interpret such reference to another level. We might be tempted to describe scripts like the Sumerian, the Chinese or the Egyptian, all of which do provide some lower-level information, as mixed scripts. But again, the temptation should be resisted. Where anything that may count as a lower-level unit is represented by a pleremic grapheme, it is unnecessary, and would therefore be wrong, to assume admixture of a lower-level script.

Precision about 'mixture' is no mere pedantry. It has, as we shall see, important implications for our understanding of the history of writing, but first, we should look more closely at some examples of homophonic reference in a pleremic script.

The Chinese write the name *Marx*, which they pronounce /mǎkèsī/, with three graphemes (i.e. with potentially simple characters) which, when they are not compounded, correspond to the morphemes /mǎ/ 'horse', /kè/ 'overcome' and /sī/ 'think'.[9] It is true that, of the three morphemes, only their syllabic values are left to correspond to this particular sequence of graphemes. But for a writer or reader to refer to the bare phonetic values of morphemes in that indirect fashion, i.e. by making *ad hoc* empty use of the corresponding pleremic graphemes, does not mean that the person is writing or reading a syllabic script. Similarly indirect are the 'phonetic' references of the Egpytian hieroglyphic script. Here, many of the native polysyllabic words are written as sequences of empty lexical graphemes. For example  (ms) 'brush' and  (dr) 'basket' make up a compound character (ms dr) 'ear'. But again, to recognize here the occurrence of voided lexical graphemes does not imply recognition of a syllabic or (as has sometimes been suggested) a phonemic-consonantal script.

The question we are asking about those voided pleremic graphemes is, in principle, similar to that of asking about an idiomatic phrase, such as *kick the bucket* in "He kicked the bucket", or about *pull* (*his*) *leg* in "They were pulling his leg", whether it consists of mere syllables, rather than words. For, clearly, those word-like constituents – *kick, bucket, pull, leg* – are here deprived of their lexical values. But would it not be strange, nevertheless, if those phrases were described as just sequences of phonemes and syllables? What we find in the empty idiomatic uses of words are *homophones* of them. We recognize them as belonging to our inventory of words, even when their semantic values no longer exist. In such contexts, we should call them 'pseudo-words', rather than describing them as syllables or as sequences of phonemes.

We shall distinguish two kinds of *homophony*: (i) between meaningful elements (as, for example, between the *bark* of a tree and the *bark* of a dog) – that is, *homonymy*, and (ii) between a meaningful element and a meaningless one (such as the *man* and *date* of 'mandate', or the *kick* and *bucket* of 'He kicked the bucket and was buried yesterday' – *idiomatic homophony*. Sequences of graphemes, such as those of the Chinese compound character for 'Marx' or of the Egyptian for 'ear' may be described as *idiomatic constructions*. In so describing them, we do not wish to conceal the fact that most idioms of spoken languages are not due to accidental homophonies (like those of *mandate* or *Măkèsī*) but have developed gradually from fully articulated semantic constructions. But this is a genetic difference. When an expression has become fully idiomatic, then there is nothing to distinguish it from accidental homophonies, and both are treated alike. There is a remarkable inclination to view them as vaguely suggestive of semantic constructions and to make all kinds of quasi-metaphorical or folk-etymological guesses, in order to endow the pseudo-lexical components with semantic values.[10] But this only goes to confirm that they are not taken as mere syllables or sequences of phonemes.

3.3 From a purely theoretical point of view, it is not immediately clear, how the homophonies of a language should affect a pleremic script or, indeed, whether they should affect it at all. (It would seem reasonable, after all, for two units such as the two words 'bark' to be represented by two different characters.) It comes as a surprise then for anyone new to the study of writing-systems, to discover the enormous and decisive role of homophony in the evolution of pleremic scripts.

Every pleremic script has developed gradually through homophonic extensions of what was originally a limited number of pictographic 'logograms'. Much of that homophony was homonymic. To select just two examples: the Chinese character whose present form is 扣 /kòu/ 'to strike' was constructed from two simple characters: 口 /kǒu/ 'mouth' (originally a picture of an open mouth ) and, preceding it, a graphic variant of 手 'hand' (originally a picture of an open hand ), the former to provide a phonetic indication (by homonymy), the latter a 'silent' semantic hint that the meaning is not 'mouth' but concerns manual action.[11] Similarly, the hieroglyphic pictogram  /wr/ 'swallow' has, in some contexts, the homonymic reading 'great'.[12] Very frequently, too, and especially in the representation of names (such as *Marx*) or of foreign words, the use of pleremic graphemes was extended in the manner of idioms, to mere parts of words which could be regarded as more or less homophonic with words or morphemes. There are languages (like Chinese) in which idiomatic homophony is very widespread; and it is such languages that offered the most favourable conditions for the development of a pleremic script.

Homophony is, of course, always only approximate, and what counts as sufficient for phonetic reference will differ from language to language. The Egyptian homophony-rules differ basically from the Chinese and from the somewhat similar Sumerian, in that they refer only to the consonantal constituency of words. This, as is well-known, is made possible by the morphological structures of the language. But it would be as misleading to ascribe to the Egyptian system of writing a representation of consonants, as it is to ascribe to the Chinese or Sumerian a representation of syllables. In either case, we are in danger of being misled by diachronic hindsight. All that we are entitled to say of the empty uses of the Egyptian, the Sumerian or the Chinese characters is that they refer to pseudo-morphs or pseudo-words. The scripts themselves afford no justification for crediting the writers or readers of it with operations of phonological analysis. Why should they expect the utterances of their language to be exhaustively analysable into sham-words? Even the most extensive use of idiomatic compounds in a language, spoken or written, does not imply any real awareness of phonological structure. In spite of all the references to phonetic form, the matching-operations of glotto-graphic translation are still performed on the level of morphemes or words.[13]

To us, with the hindsight that comes from our acquaintance with syllabic scripts (like the Akkadian or the Japanese) and with consonantal scripts (like the Semitic), the further steps that were required for the development of such scripts may appear to be negligible. But the transition from an idiomatically extended pleremic script to a cenemic one involved a momentous change of viewpoint. There had to be first a switch of attention: from the negative aspect of voided pleremic elements to the positive residue, from the semantic emptiness of some otherwise pleremic signs to their residual phonetic values. But this could only be the first step, and there could be no guarantee of the next being taken, for this next step implied a tremendous and revolutionary hypothesis about human speech: a suspicion or assumption had to emerge that hundreds or thousands of the available pleremic characters could be made redundant, because a very few of them, in empty use, would be sufficient by themselves to take over the whole business of communication.

Historical evidence suggests that this change of view was something extremely difficult to arrive at – more difficult, perhaps, than any of the other intellectual and technological achievements in the history of human civilization. The three great ancient scripts were pleremic, and all of them were tremendously stable. Lasting from two to four thousand years, they betrayed no tendency to change spontaneously into cenemic scripts. The impulse that was required for such a change seems always to have been the *borrowing* of a pleremic script – that is, its adoption by a language for which it had not been designed. It was then natural for the borrowed pleremic characters to be applied for the purpose of letting their phonetic values represent the alien words; and it was desirable to reduce such borrowings as much as possible – ultimately, to the minimum that was required for a syllabic or a consonantal-phonemic representation.

It is not unreasonable to suppose that Semitic consonantal writing developed from a borrowed Egyptian system of pleremic-idiomatic writing, just as the Akkadian syllabic writing developed from a borrowed Sumerian, and the Japanese syllabary from a borrowed Chinese system. The last step, however, of subjecting the borrowing language to an exhaustive syllabic or consonantal-phonemic analysis must have been very difficult even then; frequently, and for a long time, displacement of the pleremic tradition was patchy and incomplete.

It may be a sobering thought, for anyone interested in social institutions, that the institution of an efficient cenemic writing-system has not developed through sudden flashes of insight and leaps of imaginative thought, but that it emerged only very slowly, partly through happy historical accidents and partly by processes of laborious and piecemeal adaptation. This is obscured, when we insist on describing the scripts that existed at the beginning of those processes as if they had already anticipated an outcome of which the users of those scripts could not have had the slightest suspicion. These developments may have been pre-formed in the womb of history or the plans of Providence; but what we have to rely on when we describe a given script – all that we *can* rely on – are the operations it imposes on its users: the operations of writing down and of reading aloud.

Notes

1. I. J. Gelb (1952), who recognises this difference as basic, distinguishes the two kinds of 'writing' as 'semasiographic' and (somewhat misleadingly) 'phonographic', respectively. E. Pulgram (1976) replaced 'phonographic' by 'glottographic'.
2. As proposed by M. A. French (1976: 118), L. Hjelmslev's terms are formed upon the Greek *πλήρης* ('full') and *κενός* ('empty').
3. Disputes about the differences between 'broad phonetic transcriptions', 'phonemic analyses', and even Chomsky-Halle 'phonetic representations' are not relevant at this point. All these are intrinsically very similar, and they are all recognised as belonging to a 'level' of cenemic representation. Differences of opinion concern their status in the overall structure of a language and – with N. Chomsky and M. Halle, as we shall see – also their use in the design of a script.
4. Cp. P. Kratochvíl (1968: 155).
5. Cp. M. A. French (1976: 109).
6. I borrow the term 'glottographic' from E. Pulgram (1970). (Cp. note 1). For a more detailed account of a translational approach to the analysis of writing-systems, see W. Haas (1976) and, in application mainly to the English orthography, W. Haas (1970).
7. There are grammatical conditions (such as morphemic or lexical boundaries) which are present in *every* sample of speech. These should be recognised as implicit in the very constitution of a phonemic script (cp. W. Haas, 1967: 235ff).
8. It is, of course, important to realize that here, as in many other cases, *phonographic irregularity* serves a purpose: it ensures regular representation on a higher level. By writing *courage* and *courage-ous*, we provide recurrent representation for a recurrent morpheme, and this precisely by disregarding the phonological difference between /'kʌrɪdʒ/ and /kə'reɪdʒ(əs)/. The orthographic rules, here, which refer to a recurrent morpheme or word may, perhaps, be termed 'morphographic' or 'logographic' (as in W. Haas, 1970: 59f, 76f, or J. Vachek, 1973: 23ff, or 1981), as long as it is made clear that they are rules for a matching of written characters with phonemes (e.g. of *ou* with /ʌ/ and /ə/ in *courage* and *courageous*, respectively). If we were dealing with rules of a morphographic or logographic script, then the detailed lower-level information that is provided by an alphabetic orthography, would be simply 'left out'. It would, therefore, be less misleading to speak of '*hypercenemic*' *rules* in a *cenemic script* (cf. Haas, 1976: 192f).
9. I owe this example to M. A. French (1976: 111ff).
10. In describing the *pseudo-morphs* or *pseudo-words* of idiomatic expressions as 'meaningless', we do, of course, apply stricter criteria of 'constituent meaning'.
11. Cited from P. Kratochvíl 1968: 151.
12. See J. Friedrich 1966: 40.
13. In this, I am only expressing agreement with the views of many scholars who are, themselves, better qualified to judge about the particular pleremic scripts (cf. Y. R. Chao 1968, P. Kratochvíl 1968, or J. Friedrich 1966). For divergent views, see I. J. Gelb 1952. For a fuller discussion of the issues, W. Haas 1976.

References

Chao, Y. R.
1968 *Language and Symbolic Systems.* Cambridge: Cambridge University Press.

Chomsky, N.
1970 "Phonology and Reading." In H. Levin and J. P. Williams, eds., *Basic Studies on Reading.* New York: Basic Books, pp. 3–18.

Chomsky, N., and Halle, M.
1968 *The Sound Pattern of English*. New York: Harper & Row.
French, M. A.
1976 "Observations on the Chinese script and the classification of writing-systems." In *Writing without Letters*. Manchester: Manchester University Press, pp. 101–129.
Friedrich, J.
1966 *Geschichte der Schrift*. Heidelberg: Carl Winter.
Gelb, I. J.
1952 *A Study of Writing*. London: Routledge & Kegan Paul.
Haas, W.
1967 "Grammatical prerequisites of phonological analysis." In Josef Hamm, ed., *Phonologie der Gegenwart*. Graz and Vienna: H. Bohlaus, pp. 227–241.
1970 *Phono-graphic Translation*. Manchester: Manchester University Press.
1976 "Writing: the basic options." In W. Haas, ed., *Writing without Letters*. Manchester: Manchester University Press, pp. 131–208.
Kratochvíl, P.
1968 *The Chinese Language Today*. London: Hutchinson.
Pulgram, E.
1976 "The typologies of writing-system." In *Writing without Letters*. Manchester: Manchester University Press, pp. 1–28.
Vachek, J.
1973 *Written Language*. The Hague: Mouton.
1981 "English orthography. A functional approach." In W. Haas, ed., *Standard Languages, Spoken and Written*. Manchester: Manchester University Press, pp. 37–56.
Wijk, A.
1966 *Rules of Pronunciation for the English Language*. Oxford: Oxford University Press.

OTTO LUDWIG

Writing systems and written language

Abstract

The aim of this paper is to show that it is necessary both to differentiate between writing and written language and to investigate the connections between them. If a distinction is made between writing, written speech, written utterances, and written language, then the term "written language" may be taken to mean the following: the language that is appropriate for written utterances. Our investigation of the relationship between writing and written language shows that, although writing is a necessary precondition for the emergence of written language, the latter does not depend directly on the existence of the former.

1. *An Aristotelean tradition in linguistics?*

Let us assume that it is the function of written language to represent spoken language, just as it is the function of writing to represent sounds. Writing and written language can then be considered as having a derived or minor status: they are symbols of symbols, signs of second degree. This is how linguists, philosophers, teachers of rhetoric, and others view written language.

The first person to express this view was Aristotle. For this reason, the English linguist Angus McIntosh (1956: 40f.) talks about an "Aristotelean attitude". As Quintilian in the Middle Ages, followed by Ferdinand de Saussure, Leonard Bloomfield, and Charles Hockett agree with the Aristotelean view,[1] we have every reason to speak of a tradition, an Aristotelean tradition, that is, which is one of the many Aristotelean traditions that have shaped our intellectual life. This view has never been put forward so radically as in the first half of the 20th century when Ferdinand de Saussure spoke of the written language as being a "disguise" of language (1916/1967: 35); when Leonard Bloomfield (1939: 6) declared that there was no difference at all between written and spoken language and when, finally, Charles Hockett (1958/1967: 539) excluded written language from the realm of linguistics.

The hypotheses providing the foundation of this tradition were also formulated as early as Aristotle. Aristotle writes in his "theory of the sentence" (1958: 95):

> Thus, the sounds [. . .] arc symbols of ideas evoked in the soul and writing is a symbol of the sounds.

Here a link is established between the following two statements:

(1) The sounds are symbols of ideas formed in the mind.
(2) Writing, or to be more exact, letters are symbols of the sounds.

The combination of the two statements leads to the following conclusion: the letters are not just symbols of the corresponding sounds, but, since the sounds have a symbolic value by themselves, they are also symbols of the ideas formed in the mind. Writing (and written language) are thus symbols of symbols, symbols of second degree.

Ferdinand de Saussure (1916/1967: 28) took up these assumptions in his "Course" and expressed them more radically [my translation]:

> Language and writing are two different systems of signs; the latter only exists for the purpose of representing the former.

That means that writing exists only for the purpose of representing language. De Saussure continues:

> The subject matter of linguistics is not the connection between written and spoken word, but only the latter, the spoken word, is its subject.

Such a view is remarkable for several reasons: the written word (perhaps identical to "written language") is equated with writing. This view can also be traced back to Aristotle. The concept of "language" is not clearly distinguished from that of the "spoken word" (perhaps identical to "spoken language"). Language and the spoken word (spoken language) are the same thing. This leads to the following two equations:

writing	=	written language
spoken language	=	language in general

These equations result in assigning two different functions to the written and to the spoken language, as different as those of writing and language. Thus it becomes possible to regard language and writing as two different systems of signs. Just how much Ferdinand de Saussure emphasized the difference between the two becomes clear in the following:

> But the written word is so closely connected with the spoken whose

> picture it is that it is more and more taking over the main role. You finally arrive at the point where you credit the representation of the spoken symbols [i.e. the written word O. L.] with as much importance or even more as the symbols itself. It's like thinking it is better to see a photograph than a face in order to know somebody.

Written language is seen as a photograph of spoken language and therefore of language in general. This seems to me to be the clearest exposition of the Aristotelean tradition, mentioned above.

I would like to summarize the characteristic feature of this tradition in four parts:

(1) The only function of letters is to represent sounds.
(2) Sounds are symbols, symbols of ideas, formed in the mind or in the brain.
(3) Properties of letters are transferred to written language and are seen as properties of written language, that means that properties of the concept of "writing" become properties of the concept of "written language". Such a transfer presupposes an inadequate or lack of differentiation between writing and written language.
(4) The result of this transfer is the assumption that written language is not an expression of extra-linguistic facts, just like spoken language, but that it only represents the spoken language, or language in general, just like writing is the representation of speech sounds.

This view stands and falls with its underlying assumptions. In what follows, I will be concerned with the problem of drawing a distinction between writing and written language.

2. *Towards a distinction between writing and written language*

First of all, I would like to discuss the following two questions: (1) How can we interpret the equation of writing and written language? (2) Which concept of written language is presupposed by a given interpretation?

2.1 *Written speech*

In alphabetic writings, the characters have at least one function: they refer to certain sounds and represent them graphically. Since this is so, written texts can be translated into phonetic language; they can be read aloud. Talking about this, and only this, function of characters it is justified to say that they are derived from sounds, that they are symbols of symbols, so to speak.

There is sufficient support for the view that a character is only used in order to represent sounds in another medium. All attempts to transcribe spoken expressions or texts are – at least basically – visual, and are normally also written representations of spoken symbols. Phonetic transcriptions, however, do not provide the only support. I can imagine that a student just starting to learn how to write, first considers the characters as symbols of sounds. The situation will hardly be different in an illiterate society where a writing system is introduced for the first time.

Which concept of "written language" is presupposed in such a context?

If characters are only used in order to represent sounds, then the expressions and texts produced in this manner are written expressions and texts, however, the language expressed therein is not a written but a spoken language – with the exception that the level of representation, the level of phonetics, has changed. This level, indeed, has been put into writing. But this is not important. Even if spoken language was expressed by Morse signals, drum signals, tactile movements, odours or whatever, it still would be – apart from the level of representation – spoken language, never language drummed, smelled, or experienced on the skin – and certainly not written language.

In order to emphasize the fact that in such a case we have spoken language whose sounds are only put into writing and not written language, I will use the term "written speech" from now on.

2.2 *Written utterances*

One can also interpret the equation of written language and writing in such a way that the expression "written language" really means "written utterances". Ferdinand de Saussure speaks of "the written word" and, when Aristotle speaks of ideas evoked in the soul, to which first sounds and then characters are assigned, he seems to think about words, written and spoken. In this context, written language is thus what is recorded by means of characters: things written.

The basis of this view is the idea of different manifestations of one and the same language, the idea of the written and the spoken form of language. More explicitly, we have the following assumptions: (1) that there is a homogeneous natural language expressed in the same manner in written as well as in spoken utterances; (2) that, basically, all linguistic expressions used in spoken utterances can also be used in written utterances (and vice versa); (3) that the difference between spoken and written language – the only reason for speaking of two different forms of language – is just based on the frequency of occurrence, the difference, therefore, being solely a stylistic one. The basic assumptions to be made in order to analyze written language as the written form of linguistic utterances, are made explicit in the following quotation [my translation]:

> When examining written and spoken language it turns out [. . .] that the syntactically well-formed and semantically appropriate sentences appearing in the two media have the same grammar in principle [. . .]. This means that the abstract linguistic system of spoken and written language behind the various speech acts is the same. What is different in the two varieties of language is the distribution and frequency of occurrence of elements and rules of grammar and of the vocabulary in texts [. . .]. So, the differences are stylistic ones (H. Steger 1972: 196).

Other linguists have expressed similiar opinions.

I think it is quite sensible to regard written language as recorded language, as the written form of utterances, as language made manifest in a visual medium. One has to realize, however, that in this case the expression "written language" does not mean more than the more explicit expression "written utterance" and that therefore the expression "written language" would be really superfluous.

Like some other linguists I would like to assign an autonomous interpretation to the expression "written language", a meaning not yet covered by other expressions.

2.3 *Written language or language in writing*

By "written language" I do not mean written utterances, but the language appropriate for such utterances and available for this purpose in a speech community. This view implies:

(1) that generally we have a special variety of a language (the term "variety" in a lax sense of the word), and just in exceptional cases a special language (for example Latin in the European Middle Ages);

(2) that this variety is more or less conditioned by the medium, but not exclusively, since there are also other factors which may have influenced the creation of a written language (the important factor "writing" will be discussed below);

(3) that this variety is relatively independent of the spoken language: the extent of this independence cannot be determined in general (*in abstracto*), but has to be decided for each case and for every language.

Finally, the view stated above implies

(4) that written language is the result of an abstraction, not a real phenomenon, because written language itself consists of different varieties, just like spoken language, and has no homogeneous structure.

The interpretation of the term "written language" as "language in writing" is not new. A similiar view was proposed by the Prague linguist Josef Vachek, quite a long time ago (1939). Other linguists such as Aarni Penttilä (1970),

Hans Peter Althaus (1973), Ludwig Söll (1974), to name only a few, have expressed similar views.[2]

So far, I have given a few arguments in favor of drawing a distinction between writing and written language. Now I want to turn to another more difficult question, a question concerning the relationship between writing and written language.

3. *The connection between writing and written language*

There are good reasons for assuming that writing occurred prior to written language, both historically and logically. This assumption implies that the connection between writing and written language must be seen primarily as a dependence of the written language on writing.[3] What does "dependence of the written language on writing" mean exactly?

First of all, it means that writing is a *conditio sine qua non* for the existence of a written language. There would be no written language without writing. But such an interpretation is trivial.

Second, we may assume that not only the existence of a written language, but also its properties depend on properties of writing or a writing system. Such an interpretation is far from being trivial. If we intend to justify such an interpretation, we have to discover properties of written language which are due to properties of writing – and not to properties of other factors that could also have influenced the development of a written language, i.e. the process of writing and reading; the situation where a written communication takes place; and above all, properties that are part of the product of writing, the written utterance, or the written text.

The fact that properties of written language depend on properties of writing means several different things. To touch only on some aspects of the problem, we have to state that the written form of a language can depend on

(1) properties which are part of every writing system (universal principles of writing).

(2) It can also depend on properties which are only part of a particular writing system: the ideography, the logography or phonography.

(3) The written form of a language can be affected by properties developed in a special variety of a writing system, for instance in one of the various alphabetic writing systems.

Another difficulty is due to the fact that, at present, we know very little about the properties of writing and even less about the properties of written language. However, such knowledge is necessary if those aspects of written language are to be identified that depend on properties of writing and writing systems. Therefore, this problem can only be discussed in a very tentative way in this paper.

The aspects I would like to discuss are the following: the abstractness of written language and the abstractness of writing, the property of discreteness in writing and written language, the conservative character of written language and, above all, the systematic character of written language. All these aspects have to do with phonography, and with writing in general.

I anticipate that the result of the discussion will be the statement that, although writing is a fundamental condition of written language, the impact of writing on the written language is only indirect.

3.1 *The abstractness of written language*

A number of people have drawn attention to the abstract character of written language as compared to spoken language. The well-known psychologist Lew S. Wygotski (Lev S. Vygotsky) says [my translation]:

> Written language presupposes [. . .] for its development [. . .] a high degree of abstractness. It is a language without intonation, without musical elements, without expressiveness, without any phonation. It is [. . .] a language that lacks the essential property of spoken language, the phonetic substance (1934/1969: 224).

Notice that it will hardly be possible to derive the abstractness of written language solely from writing. Ludwig Söll (1974: 22) is right in linking the rationality of written language to its specific functions. Wygotski, on the other hand, refers to the abstractness of the situation in which writing takes place:

> It is a language without a partner to talk to [. . .], the conversation with a white sheet of paper, with an imaginary communication partner (1934/1969: 225).

In talking about the abstractness of written language in connection with writing, one usually refers – as, for example, Wygotski in the first quotation – to the fact that writing – or rather letters – make an abstraction of all the musical properties of sounds: accent, intonation, tone of voice, as well as the other prosodic characteristics of spoken utterances. As far as letters are concerned, we may agree with this opinion. Letters (graphs) are indeed more abstract than sounds (phones).[4] But difficulties will arise when we try to apply this statement to a written utterance as a whole. Though it may sometimes be hard to find expressions in written language that can represent the prosodic features of spoken language, it is not impossible. There are forms in written language that are at least functionally adequate, for example variation in word order, verbal descriptions of prosodic features, the design of hand- or typewriting and so on.

In short, it is not justified to say that written language is abstract because of the abstract character of writing. All we can say is that the abstractness of writing is a condition beyond other conditions that may have an impact on the abstractness of written language.[5]

3.2 *The discreteness of written language*

Every language is composed of discrete units: phonemes or graphemes. This feature of language appears much more clearly in the graphs (letters) of alphabetic writing systems than in phones (sounds). Sometimes, sequences of graphs are written continuously, often – as for example in typewriting – discontinuously. Even if the graphs follow each other continuously, it is always possible to separate them without any difficulty (cf. E. Pulgram 1976: 2ff.). The segmentation of sequences of phones is more difficult. Often, it is very difficult to decide where one sound segment ends and the other one starts. In other words, discreteness, a fundamental principle of language, is more manifest in graphs than in phones (cf. R. Langacker 1967: 70).

This property of graphs seems to be a precondition not only of certain properties of written utterances but also of certain properties of written language.

Anyone who has ever tried to transcribe utterances from a tape knows how difficult it is to identify words, sentences or paragraphs. This is much easier with written utterances. In most cases, a segmentation is given by means of punctuation. Words are separated by spaces, sentences by spaces and punctuation marks, paragraphs by spaces, punctuation and indentation. No doubt, the discrete character of the graphs favors the easy segmentation of written utterances.

The fact that the basic units of written utterances are easy to distinguish seems to be of importance for written language. Some students have assumed that the units of written language have to be defined in a different way from those of spoken language. Manfred Bierwisch says with respect to the category of the word [my translation]:

> One has to be aware of the fact that words in the sense of combinations of graphs separated by spaces are the reflex of certain syntactic conditions which are projected into written language by relatively complicated rules. The concept of a "word" as a "combination of graphs between spaces" is first acquired with the acquisition of the writing system. Besides this, a normal speaker has a phonologically, a syntactically and a semantically-based concept of a word. That these concepts

> are not identical with the concept "word" given by the graphemic rules, is shown by such cases as *zu kommen* beside *anzukommen* etc. (1972/1976: 73).

As regards the category of text, Konrad Ehlich pointed out [my translation]:

> that texts are identified by the separation of verbal activity and the direct space of activity. This means: they are separated from the hearer by presupposing a hearer who is not co-present with the speaker (1979: 513).

In the same way it would be possible to give definitions for the categories of sentence and paragraph. In all cases, units of written language are defined by separability. This fact indicates that there is a relation between the discreteness of graphs and the discreteness of the basic units of written language. This is a fundamental difference between written and spoken language. Due to the transitory character of the acoustic medium, spoken language is organized by continuity, connectivity and integration – to mention just the suprasegmental features in addition to intonation. By contrast, because of the visual medium, written language is organized by discreteness, separability and segmentation.

4. *Conservative elements and the systematic character of written language*

The symbols of all writing systems are characterized by the fact that they can be inscribed on objects that are perceptible, three-dimensional and have a certain stability (i.e. wood, leather, clay, stone, but also paper). Because of this property, characters or symbols are also perceptible, they can be spatially ordered (from left to right, from right to left, from top to bottom etc.) and they stay so for some time.

These statements are trivial. Less trivial are the conclusions to be drawn from them.

The first conclusion concerns an aspect of written utterances. In written utterances, language confronts man in an objectified form. It appears to have become an object itself or at least part of an object: perceptible, three-dimensional and constant.

The second conclusion concerns the people who read and write, who use such utterances. Language, whose manifestations become so obvious for the human eye, can be looked at, reflected upon, modified, looked at repeatedly, shown to others etc. It impinges upon the consciousness of man in a different way than oral manifestations: particularly as a spatial and perceptible object. This means that man's relationship to language will change, too. He will become conscious of language, at least more conscious than would normally be possible with spoken utterances alone.

The third conclusion concerns written language itself, more precisely, two of its most prominent features: its conservative and its systematic character. Not only does the written form of language affect man's awareness in a way that differs from the spoken form, it also has a different impact. Because it does not fade away immediately, it is preserved better in the memory. Furthermore, it can be read a long time after it was recorded. In this way, it is possible for linguistic expressions that have become rare in the spoken language, or that have disappeared altogether, to be preserved in the written language. The conservative elements in the morphology of written language are well-known: the passé simple in French, the subjunctive in German, the preterite tense in written narratives of South German etc. Especially obvious is the conservative trend in the vocabulary. W. Zengel, for instance, in an investigation of Latin vocabulary of juridical texts demonstrated that many of the words had been preserved for thousands of years.

Man, who is able to adapt a sophisticated relationship to language with the help of writing and written utterances, is capable of noticing and being aware of features of language which can hardly – if at all – be detected in spoken utterances. Above all, he has thus detected the systematic relationships of language. In this way, we may explain the fact that the systematic character of language is more apparent in written than in spoken language: in phonography, whenever it deviates from the so-called phonetic principles, but also in morphology, in syntax and word-formation.

Our attempt to demonstrate the dependence of written language on writing has not yielded many concrete results. However, we could perhaps make the following two generalizations:

(1) Writing is a necessary precondition for the evolution of written language. Yet, the influence that writing had on the development of written language does not seem to have been very substantial. Properties of the medium and, more importantly, properties of written utterances had a more direct influence on the development of written language.

(2) If a connection between writing and written language could be established, this would always lead to the conclusion that written language is not directly dependent on writing. It is quite simple to demonstrate the influence of writing on properties of written utterances. Such properties of written utterances seem to determine the consciousness and behavior of people who read and write, and it is only through the consciousness of people that written language is influenced by writing.

Appendix

Supplement to the list of McIntosh 1956, p. 14 f. footnote 1:

Marcus Fabius Quintilianus: *Institutionis oratoriae* I, 7, 31: hic enim est usus litterarum, ut custodiant voces et velut depositum reddant legentibus, itaque id exprimere debent, quod dicturi sumus. hae fere sunt emendate loquendi scribendique partes.

Johann Wolfgang Goethe: *Werke*, Hamburger Ausgabe, Band 9, Hamburg 1967, S. 447: Schreiben ist ein Mißbrauch der Sprache, stille für sich lesen ein trauriges Surrogat der Rede.

Rudolf Hildebrand: *Vom deutschen Sprachunterricht und von deutscher Erziehung und Bildung überhaupt* 3. Auflage Leipzig und Berlin 1887, S. 44: Das ist das Leiden, an dem unsere Sprache krankt, auch in der Schule: die schwarzen Striche auf dem Papier sind unserer Zeit das Wesentliche des Wortes, das Zeichen ist uns zur Sache selbst geworden, die Schale gilt als der Kern.

Hermann Paul: *Prinzipien der Sprachgeschichte* 6. Auflage Darmstadt 1960, S. 374: Die Schrift ist nicht nur nicht die Sprache, sondern sie ist derselben auch in keiner Weise adäquat.

Lew S. Wygotski: *Denken und Sprechen.* Stuttgart 1969, S. 225: Es ist natürlich, daß die Sprache ohne realen Klang, die [. . .] eine Symbolisierung der Lautsymbole, d.h. eine Symbolisierung zweiter Ordnung fordert, in dem gleichen Maße schwieriger sein muß als die mündliche, wie die Algebra für das Kind schwieriger ist als die Arithmetik.

Notes

1. Other examples are mentioned in A. McIntosh 1956: 14f., footnote 1. Supplements to his list are included at the end of this article.
2. A question they never discussed, in spite of its importance, is the following: Where is the border-line between spoken and written language? In my view, written language begins where verbal expressions are based on principles other than the principles you find in spoken language. I suspect that the border-line has to be drawn at the phonographic level. Written expressions that are based only on the so-called phonetic principle represent spoken language. Written expressions that are based on the morphological principle, for example, represent written language. Naturally, drawing the line between the two will be a matter of definition.
3. This statement does not exclude, of course, the possibility that under certain circumstances written language might in turn influence the writing system.
4. Cf. Y. R. Chao: "To one, who is used to an alphabetic system of writing, it seems to be the simplest thing to talk about the sound" e", the sound "l" (el), the sound "b" (bi), or even the sound "w" (dublju:). But to one used to a logographic system like the Chinese or a syllabic system of writing like the Japanese, the nature of sound segments in the forms of consonants and vowels is not at all obvious and even seems highly abstract" (quoted in W. Haas 1970: 37f.).
5. A further argument for the abstractness of writing is this: It is well-known that the graphemes and phonemes of a language stand in a complex relationship. Groups of graphemes can stand for groups of phonemes and vice versa. This relationship is a symmetric one. The question is whether or not there is an additional, and asymmetric, relationship. William Haas (1970) contested just that. McIntosh (1961) adopted this opinion. He gives the graphemes a referential meaning. Graphemes refer to phonemes. Graphemes are signs, phonemes are not. Let us assume that McIntosh is right. What consequences does this have? Phonemes are the result of an abstraction. If graphemes refer to phonemes, then they are not only the result of an abstraction (as phonemes are) but they would also refer to abstractions. They would be abstract in a double sense of the word.

References

Althaus, Hans Peter et al.
1973 *Lexikon der Germanistischen Linguistik.* Tübingen: Niemeyer.

Aristotle
1958 *Kategorien. Lehre vom Satz.* Hamburg: Meiner.

Bandle, O., Klingenberg, H., Maurer, F. (eds.)
1972 *Festschrift für Siegfried Gutenbrunner.* Heidelberg: Winter.

Bierwisch, Manfred
1972 "Schrifstruktur und Phonologie." In *Probleme und Ergebnisse der Psychologie*, pp. 21–44. Reprinted in Adolf Hofer, ed., *Lesenlernen: Theorie und Unterricht.* Düsseldorf: Schwann, 1976.

Bloomfield, Leonard
1939 *Linguistic Aspects of Science.* Chicago: The University of Chicago Press.

Ehlich, Konrad
1979 *Verwendungen der Deixis beim sprachlichen Handeln* 2 vols. Bern, Frankfurt, Las Vegas: Peter Lang.

Haas, William
1970 *Phono-graphic Translation.* Manchester: Manchester University Press.
ed. 1976 *Writing without letters.* Manchester: Manchester University Press; Lotowa, N.J.: Rowman and Littlefield.

Hockett, Charles
1958 *A Course in Modern Linguistics* 1st edition 1958. 2nd edition 1967. New York: Macmillan.

Langacker, Ronald W.
1968 *Language and its Structure.* New York, Chicago, San Francisco, Atlanta: Harcourt, Brace & World.

McIntosh, Angus
1956 "The analysis of Written Middle English." *Transactions of the Philological Society:* 26–55.
1961 "Graphology and meaning." *Archivum Linguisticum* 13: 107–120.

Penttillä, Aarne
1970 "Zur Grundlagenforschung der geschriebenen Sprache." *Acta Societas Linguistica Upsalliensis Nova, Series 2.* 2: 21–55.

Pulgram, Ernst
1976 "The typologies of writing systems." In W. Haas, ed., *Writing without Letters.* Manchester: Manchester University Press: Lotowa, N. J.: Rowman and Littlefield, pp. 1–28.

Saussure, Ferdinand de
1916 *Grundfragen der allgemeinen Sprachwissenschaft.* 1st edition 1916, 2nd edition Berlin 1967: de Gruyter.

Söll, Ludwig
1974 *Gesprochenes und geschriebenes Französisch.* Berlin: E. Schmidt.

Steger, Hugo
1972 "Gesprochene und geschriebene Sprache. Ein Essay." In O. Brandle et al, eds., *Festschrift für O. Gutenbrunner* Heidelberg: Winter, pp. 195–202.

Vachek, Josef
1939 "Zum Problem der geschriebenen Sprache." *Travaux du Cercle Linguistique de Prague* (*TCLP*) 8: 94–104.
1976 "Geschriebene Sprache. Allgemeine Probleme und Probleme des Englischen." English edition 1973, German in edition K. Horalek, J. Kuchar, J. Scharnhorst, E. Ising, eds., *Grundlage der Sprachkultur. Teil 1.* Berlin (GRD): Akademie Verlag, pp. 240–295.

Wygotski, Lew S.
1934 *Denken und Sprechen.* First edition 1934, German transl.: Frankfurt/M.: S. Fischer 1969.

Zengel, M.
1962 "Literacy as a factor in language change." *American Anthropologist* 64: 132–139.

ELMAR HOLENSTEIN

Double articulation in writing*

Abstract

Apart from the genetic code, double articulation seems to be a privilege of human signs. It implies a specific cognitive competence, the use of tools to build other tools. Generally, in nonlinguistic sign systems with a double articulation, the signs of the second articulation are metaphorically used signs of an old first articulation – signs that were originally sense-determinative are transformed into sense-discriminative signs. In scripts, one finds in addition to this kind of origin, transformations of genuinely senseless elements into sense-discriminative signs. In this case, well-shaped geometric figures are favored. The double articulation of this kind has primarily an economic motivation. This motivation gains in significance with the technicalization of scripts.

1. *The anthropological relevance of double articulation*

A system of signs is called doubly articulated when it consists of two levels of organization, a first level of signs with a *sense-determinative* function (morphemes, words, sentences) and a second level with a *sense-discriminative* function (distinctive features, phonemes, syllables). Hjelmslev suggested that these be termed respectively *plerematic* and *kenematic* signs. The older generation of linguists considers this special kind of double articulation to be a peculiarity of human language (Benveniste 1952: 62; Hockett 1963: 12; Jakobson 1973: 44). Lévi-Strauss (1964: 37f.) treats double articulation as the criterion according to which a system of signs may be given the title 'language'. When the discovery of the genetic code revealed a non-human sign system that undeniably had a double articulation – four nucleotide bases fulfilling an exclusively discriminative function and triplets of such nucleotide bases ('words') along with hierarchically higher-order units ('sentences') transmitting determinative chemical information – Jakobson (1973: 52), master of the search for invariants, promptly found a common denominator: The genetic code, the primary manifestation of life and language, the primary manifestation of humanity, are the two fundamental transmitters of information from generation to generation: the molecular and the verbal legacy are two indispensable presuppositions of cultural tradition.

Younger semioticians (Prieto 1966; Eco 1972) contest an exclusive ascription of double articulation to language (in the narrow sense of the word). The cleavage between these standpoints makes a different orientation of the camps evident. Linguists of the older school take double articulation to be a criterion distinguishing human from animal languages; the younger semioticians, on the other hand, when they attack the linguistic "myth of double articulation" as being "obstructive" – which it is, in fact, on superficial analysis – have other human sign systems in mind, which equally are featured by double articulation. This view can be accommodated without further ado by the linguists cited above, since they see in double articulation (disregarding the genetic code) a peculiarity not so much of language as of the human. Double articulation distinguishes human from all animal languages as far they are now known, and also from most, but not all other human sign systems.

The creation and use of signs that are not intended to designate non-semiotic entities, but rather to produce other signs, presupposes a cognitive competence, the ability to produce tools to produce other tools, which anthropologists still consider as being a mark of the human (cf. Jakobson 1973: 58). The epistemological, not to mention anthropological implications of double articulation are an invitation to investigate non-linguistic sign-systems that exhibit double articulation, especially those that permit us to investigate double articulation in the nascent state, such as some recently developed writing systems. These newly developed systems stand in evocative contrast to those nonverbal sign-systems to which double articulation has been attributed in semiotics until now.

2. *Functional conversion of sense-determinative into sense-discriminative signs*

Until now the debate has one-sidedly taken account of those secondary sign systems of which the second, or kenematic (quasi-phonematic) articulation occurs in sign units that in their original use had a sense-determinative rather than a sense-discriminative function. This is so of the examples adduced by Prieto and Eco, just as of Bühler's old example of the sailor's flag code (1934: 70f.). The elements of the traditional seaman's code – round ball, triangular penion, and a quadrangular flag – represent geometrical figures. This original iconic meaning is dropped in the flag code. Neither the single elements nor subgroups of them have a constant and positive meaning. Their only function is to distinguish the complex signals from each other when they occur in different positions.

○ △	You are running into danger.
△ ○	Shortage of provisions.
□ ○ △	Do you have messages for me?

In the case of six-digit telephone numbers, of which each pair of numerals (digits) designates successively a neighborhood, a street and a block of houses, the single numerals making up a sense-determinative pair have themselves only a sense-discriminative function. Likewise, each of the numerals of the two-digit numbers designating the various bus lines of a city functions only to distinguish meaning. Bus line *23* has nothing in common with other lines whose first numeral is *2,* nor with those whose second is *3*. The numbers do not mean that all buses with the same numeral in the same position run in the same direction, serve the same neighborhood, or belong to some special class for speed and comfort. Their sole function is rather to distinguish one bus line from all others with different numerals. The example of the bus numbers shows clearly that the usage of their components is an extended, metaphoric one. Signs that had a sense-determinative function in their original usage (as signs of natural numbers) come to have secondarily, in another sign system (that of public transport), a merely sense-discriminative function. They are now metaphorical signs, also in the sense that the echo of their original meaning is more or less latently heard in their new usage, according to the sensitiveness and attitude of the receiver. These examples of double articulation do not present a simple case of the production of tools for the production of other tools, as is the case in spoken language. Tools already available – with a sense-determinative function – are rather converted into tools with a new, now sense-discriminative function.

3. *Structural and functional anisomorphism of speech and alphabetical writing*

Before going on to present newer writing systems as an illustration of non-linguistic sign systems with a second articulation of originally, not merely secondarily kenematic signs, it might be helpful to reflect on the rationale that deterred leading phonologists from describing writing analogously to speech as a doubly articulated system (in which the letters, styled as graphemes, might assume the part of the phonemes). Their reason was not the lack of structural isomorphism, nor the conspicuous fact that there is no one-to-one correspondence between letters and phonemes so that a grapheme often corresponds not to a phoneme, but to a morphophoneme, and conversely that a single phoneme often corresponds to a whole group of letters (Ger. *sch, ch*; Engl. *th*), nor that the internal structure of phoneme and letter are not congruent. In the case of the letters

d b
q p

the binarily structurable constituent parts – a vertical line extended upwards or downwards; a semicircle open to the right or to the left – do not correlate to distinctive features of the corresponding phonemes (say to the oppositions acute–grave and tense–lax). Their point was also not that alphabet systems are of non-uniform, heterogeneous origin, nor that the perception of letters is only in part digital, but predominantly holistic, by means of *Gestalten*: a heterogeneous origin does not preclude the selective coalescence into a unitarily ordered system; the perception of sounds, too, may be a mixed process, both digital and holistic. Furthermore, it is possible to analyze each *Gestalt* by means of a grid, so that in principle each figure can be registered either holistically or digitally, as the need may be. The need, and therewith also the factual extent of the hierarchically ordered digital analysis of written symbols that was originally holistically conceived, increases to all appearances with the increasing number and complexity of these signs.

The decisive reason for the disjunction of speech and writing was rather the absence of a functional isomorphism. Whereas the phoneme *m* has a purely diacritical, relational, negative function, and evinces mere 'otherness', the letter *m* has a determinate, constant and positive meaning: it is the sign of the phoneme *m,* which takes its place in the oral rendering of the text. Letters are, so to speak, metasigns, "signs of signs", namely of sounds, whereas phonemes are special kinds of signs, sense-discriminative or diacritical "signs on signs", namely on morphemes (Jakobson 1939: 296). The introduction of letters brings with it a different sort of conversion of signs, not a transmutation of signs with a sense-determinative function into signs with a sense-discriminative one, but rather a conversion from signs for units of sense (*Sinneinheiten*) into signs for units of sound (*Lauteinheiten*) and therewith from objective to metalinguistic signs. This modification is generally appreciated as such on the phylogenetic level, where it manifests itself in the step from semasiography (in a wide sense including ideography, phraseography and logography) to phonography (in a narrow sense restricted to syllables and alphabetical writing). It is less well known that a similar step is just as manifest in the ontogenesis of writing. A child finds it much easier to correlate graphemic structures with senseful units than with elemental phonic units

(Gleitman & Rozin 1977). A child learning to write has functional, not structural, difficulties. He has more trouble correlating written signs to sense-discriminative phonic signs instead of to sense-determinative signs than with the specific figuration of alphanumerical signs and the specific graphomotoric skills connected therewith.

What distinguishes *au fond* speech and writing is not their differing physical media, an acoustic and an optical medium, respectively: that would be a too culture-specific, perhaps also a too species-specific view of the matter. Deaf-and-dumb languages are quite genuine languages, and meet all the specific criteria of languages (multimodality, grammaticality, productivity, semantic universality – and double articulation). Telegraphic messages can be transmitted just as well acoustically (by key-sounds or drumbeats) as optically. On the other hand, there are signs in formalized languages for operations that are carried out primarily optically, and of which spoken designations have become secondary. Finally, there is the recent phenomenon of 'noise-writing', of the noise, specific even to the trade brand, that each key punch on a typewriter produces, and which is said to be used by intelligence services (at least in science fiction) to decode the letters typed.

The difference between speech and writing is also not primarily structural. As regards structure, artificial writing systems are extremely flexible – in contradistinction to natural speech, they are capable of giving an exceedingly polymorphous performance. It is possible in principle to develop a writing system that duplicates the structure of the spoken language (see phonetic alphabets and spectrograms).

What motivates and legitimates the distinction between speech and writing as two categorially different sign systems is the difference between their specific functions: speech is a sign system that immediately symbolizes meaning; writing is a sign system that symbolizes another sign system, and this either in another medium (thus our current visual writing system) or only in another structure (thus morse code, insofar as it is implemented by key punches). This specific, functional difference also immediately gives rise in normal cases – so long as isomorphism is not the intended goal, as in the case of the phonetic alphabet – to specific structural differences, which are common to writing systems and to other adaptations of language to various media of communication: for example, to pidginization, metricization (cf. Justeson 1976: 78f.) and, we can add, to its internalization, to the so-called 'inner speech' (cf. Holenstein 1980: 126 ff.). These transformations reveal regularities of simplification, for example in the reduction of marked phenomena in contrast to the conservation of unmarked phenomena, and also in the tendency to introduce similar operations to represent the same phenomena, for example reduplication to indicate extension (plurality, size, intensity, and so on).

The functional disjunction of speech and writing does not preclude the possibility that a sign system that was originally introduced as a (secondary) writing system can assume the function of a (primary) sign system that immediately symbolizes senseful units, thus becoming, according to definition, a genuine language. In special cases (such as that of deaf and dumb), this change of function can be a complete transformation, in other cases (such as that of our normal usage of writing) only partial. Functional conversion and plurifunctionality are a universal possibility, not just semiotic, but also ontological (Holenstein 1979).

In fact, the "mediation theory of word recognition", the theory of the indirect access to the meaning of a word via its sound shape, has already become a classic topic in experimental reading research. Meaningless, but pronounceable, combinations of letters are not readable in cases of phonemic dyslexia. Rhymes based on homophones (*hope–soap*) are not recognized. Concrete or figurative nouns, on the other hand, are readable. Errors that do occur are semantically *canal–river*) and not phonically motivated. Here, clearly, the sequence of letters takes over the function of, or circumvents the sequence of, phonemes as the immediate carrier of the meaning of the word. (The pronunciation is derived from the rightly or wrongly apprehended meaning.) It may be assumed that, in such cases, the letters function as (senser-) discriminative signs and not, as is usual, as (sound-) determinative.

The fundamental possibility that a normal, skilled reader has direct access to the meanings of words is now generally admitted – just as the fact that even fluent reading is never completely free of phonemic mediation. Research has gone on to clarify the factual extent, the conditions and the roles of the two modes of access. Direct access occurs mostly in the case of the more common words. It increases with the ability to read and, conversely, has the function of increasing precisely this ability along with the speed of reading; these two phenomena are best explained in relation to a context inferred by direct access and to the expectation of meaning that thereby arises. The complementary task of verifying the expected meaning "from the bottom up" devolves upon the mode of indirect access. The reader understandably takes recourse to this mode mostly when faced with unfamiliar expressions, but he also uses it to make precise and to confirm his direct understanding when this is required, when more than just the approximate meaning of a text is of interest, and when the exact sequence of words matters just as much as the literal meaning.

Philosophers make a great fuss about the deficient categorial distinction in the designation of phenomena that belong to different categories, and view this deficiency as being responsible for the worst of all mistakes – the worst in a philosopher's eye – the category mistake. The use of similar lexical categories to designate both (independent) substances and (dependent) properties in alternative sentences such as "The wall protected the inhabitants from the enemy missiles" and "The height of the wall protected the inhabitants from the enemy missiles" seems to imply that 'wall' and 'height' are things and causes in similar ways. But it should be philosophically just as fruitful not only to decry the disadvantages but also to consider the advantages of this peculiarity, characteristic of so many sign systems, of not systematically and pedantically rendering categorial differences of the signified entities with exactly corresponding signifiers; and also to consider the ontological and cognitive conditions which keep the man of good common sense in general and the man of philosophical perspicacity in particular from being confused in his use of signs by the lack of categorial differentiation. The under determinateness of structure relative to function and interpretation should also be considered at this point, in view of it being, in addition to its role in banning monotony, the basis of linguistic creativity.

4. *Functional conversion of graphemes from sound-determinative to sense-discriminative signs*

There are, however, words in which some graphemes have a sense-discriminative function, even though the decoding of the words concerned is phonemically based. These are phonemically ambiguous German words such as: *Mal–Mahl; Lid–Lied; Stil–Stiel; Laib–Leib; Saite–Seite; Waise–Weise; Meer–mehr; du reist–du reihst*. The range of examples in English (*knight–night; know–no; pane–pain; lane–lain; to–too–two* is so abundant that one wonders if perhaps English has made the turn back towards the logographic principle (cf. Gleitman & Rozin 1977: 21, 33, 35f.). The *h* in Ger. *Mahl* does not designate a sound that is to be pronounced in its place, and it is redundant as a sign for the lengthening of the preceding vowel. It does, however, immediately distinguish the meanings of *Mal* [mark] and *Mahl* [meal] just as the phoneme *e* in the place of *a* distinguishes between *Mahl* and *Mehl* [flour]. Here, too, the previous remarks about the examples of doubly articulated sign systems hold good: The discriminative signs were originally determinative signs that have been converted to fulfil a new function. It is sometimes even a case of a second functional conversion of these signs. Both letters *h* and *e* normally designate phonemes. In the course of the development of the German language they came to be used in certain contexts as signs of a distinctive feature, namely of the length of the preceding phoneme. Finally they came to be signs that immediately distinguish meaning.

Features indicative of a tendency to give graphemes a discriminative function are also to be found in the use of groups of letters to designate a single phoneme, say, in the German usage of *ch* [x] and *sch* [ʃ]. The single graphemes in such combinations no longer have a constant and positive meaning. They serve only to distinguish from each other groups of letters that designate different sounds.

What is striking in such examples of a nascent double articulation is the anisomorphism of the signifier and the signified. Signifiers of one and the same category are used to render signified entities of widely different categories. The same grapheme *e* is not only used to designate two different sounds in *elend*, but also to designate a distinctive feature, the length of the vowel in *siech* [sick] (vs. *sich* [himself]), and to distinguish the meaning of *Stiel* [shaft] from that of *Stil* [style]. This neglect of categorial differences is even clearer in the cases of the morse alphabet and the genetic code. The delimitative devices or 'punctuation marks' here have the same type of structure as the other plerematic signs. In morse code, in addition to the punctuation marks, the signs for a special category of words, the numerals, have the same type of structure as the signs of the single letters.

J	• — — —
colon	— — — • • •
2	• • — — —

5. *Functional conversion of senseless into sense-discriminative elements*

The interpretation of letters as plerematic signs conforms with the fact that the majority of alphabetic characters can be most simply analyzed not directly into distinctive features (which do not have an independent existence), but rather into independent units, comparable to phonemes, which are then resolved into distinctive features. This conformity is merely a factual one, not a necessary one, which might be derived from the plerematic status of graphemes. Certainly a system of letters is possible of which the units determining sounds could be resolved directly into distinctive features: for example, a system consisting of lines drawn with differing length, color, brightness and position. The fact that the logically most simple realization was not taken up is in part grounded in the same way as redundancy in general (which is an adaptation to the needs of reception and production), and in part, as in printing, in the necessity of establishing a recognizable kinship to traditional alphanumeric systems.

At least three starting points can be discerned in the decomposition of traditional alphanumeric writing systems into sense-discriminative features. The first was the upshot of the concern to standardize printing type, the second of the advent of illuminated writing, and the third of the development of electronic reading machines. The first of these tendencies reached both its technical and its ideological zenith in the *Bauhaus* between the two World Wars, and coincided with the world-wide establishment of phonology. The *Bauhaus* and the establishment of phonology had in common the aim of analyzing the respective phenomena on which they are based – spatial shapes and colors in the one case, speech sounds in the other – into abstract fundamental elements, and of combining these elements in complex structures, according to the nature of the material requirements, while preserving at the same time the 'organic relations' between the elements (cf. Kandinsky's lectures on form and color in the *Bauhaus*, Wingler 1969). The task of coping with the flood of vouchers for financial and goods transactions gave a much greater impetus to the third movement than did the humanitarian aim of providing reading machines to the blind. Waybills thus provided the basis for the Near-Eastern origins of writing, but also for the most advanced (electronic) mode of reading.

The standardization of sign systems is made up of three processes:

1. the decomposition of articulated as well as of inarticulated, continuous wholes into uniform constituent parts that may be artificial and abstract; the stencil lettering of Albers (Fig. 1) breaks up the vertical bars of b, d, p and q into three squares. In illuminated lettering (Fig. 4 & 5), the vertical bars of *1* and *7* are resolved into five or more dots.

2. the reduction of *allo*-forms, that is of context-sensitive variants that exclude each other in any one context; hence the reduction of so-called complementary distributions; in illuminated lettering, slanting lines are rendered as vertical lines (for example, in the numerals *4* and *7* in Fig. 4), or slanting and vertical lines are both rendered with the same minimal slant (following the example of italic type). Similarly, round figures are recast as angular; or, as a compromise solution, the corners are left out, so that all figures are rendered essentially alike, with a slightly round looking form (see the numerals *5* and *8* in Fig. 4).

3. the reduction of redundant signs; printing type omits as redundant the transverse bar in the middle of the numeral 7, which, together with a somewhat longer, horizontal rather than slanted line at the top, distinguishes this numeral from the numeral *1*. Zealots of unity among the reformers of German writing are also opposed to the superfluous use of capital letters to single out nouns: "we use only small letters, and thus save time" (*Bauhaus* maxim).

In the stencil lettering of the *Bauhaus* collaborator Joseph Albers (Fig. 1 & 2),

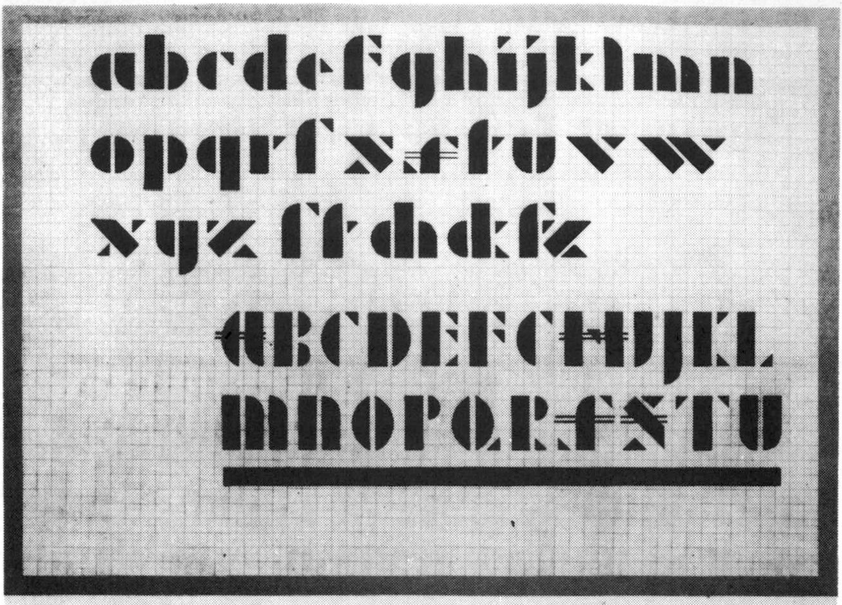

JOSEF ALBERS: Schablonenschrift

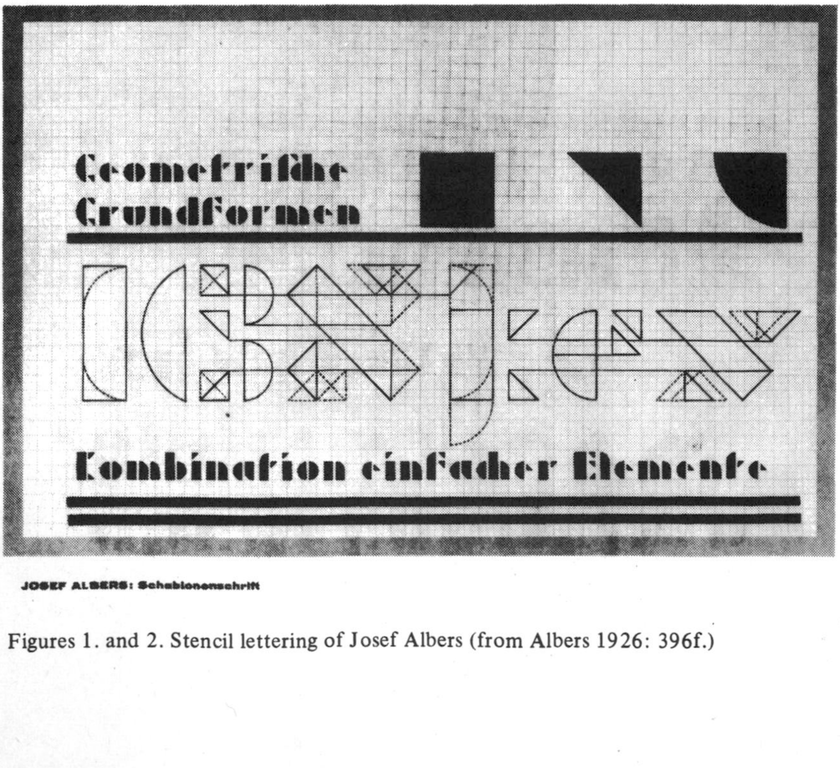

JOSEF ALBERS: Schablonenschrift

Figures 1. and 2. Stencil lettering of Josef Albers (from Albers 1926: 396f.)

the letters are constructed out of basic geometrical shapes, in fact, of only three shapes (or more strictly speaking two): the square, the triangle (half a square), and the quarter circle. The same or almost similar shapes served more than ten thousand years ago as ideograms in the Near-Eastern precursors of writing. Later, they were used as sense-discriminative signs in an early modern non-phonic sign system, in the sailor's flag code cited by Bühler. Now they turn up again in the construction of graphemes as sound-determinative signs. Recent research shows that not only concrete pictograms but also – even primarily – abstract geometric figures are to be considered as the earliest forerunners of abstract writing systems in the Near East. Aside from stylized animal shapes and, later, in the cities, also the forms of vessels, various abstract figures such as spheres, discs, cones, cylinders, triangles, rectangles and the like also functioned as counting tokens imprinted first on clay envelopes and later on earthenware tablets, and these made up the origin of the succeeding letters (cf. Schmandt-Besserat 1978; Fig. 3)

Irrespective of the fact that the three fundamental elements of the stencil letters can be isolated as independent figures which are not inherently dependent components of the letters, it is also more economical to coordinate them in the analysis with the phonemes themselves, rather than with the distinctive features of the phonemes. If they themselves were treated as distinctive features, the quarter circle would have to be treated as two (unanalysed) complex distinctive features (a quarter circle rounded to the left *vs.* one rounded to the right; the curvature upwards and downwards is irrelevant because of complementary distribution in that system). Albers' stencil lettering resolves accordingly into three graphemes analogous to the phonomes of the spoken language, and into a larger number of distinctive features. The position of the grapheme on the ground to be filled out by the characters, also functions as a distinctive feature in most visual writing systems; the ground to this end is usually imagined as being subdivided into cells. The use of the triangle may suffice here to illustrate the major principles of organization in the system of Albers. Beyond the position of the triangle in the figure, the position of the right angle and the doubling of triangles are distinctive features.

c vs. *e*	- right angle top right vs. bottom right (this is no minimal distinction; the contrast between top vs. bottom, or moving the triangle half a space would suffice)
i vs. *r*	- triangle to the right vs. top
i & *r* vs. *n* & *m*	- a combination of bars composed of two squares with triangles vs. quarter circle(s) above square(s)

f vs. *s* vs. *f*	- two triangles vs. one triangle top right vs. one triangle middle right
ss vs. *v* & *w* vs. *x*	- top right: one triangle with the right angle top right vs. top left vs. two triangles; bottom: one vs. two vs. no triangles
k vs. *b*	- two triangles vs. two quarter circles
β vs. *z*	- the triangles are redundant

The invention of electronic illuminated lettering made it possible to represent various letters without changing the basic hardware (say in the form of movable metal leaves, each imprinted with a different letter).

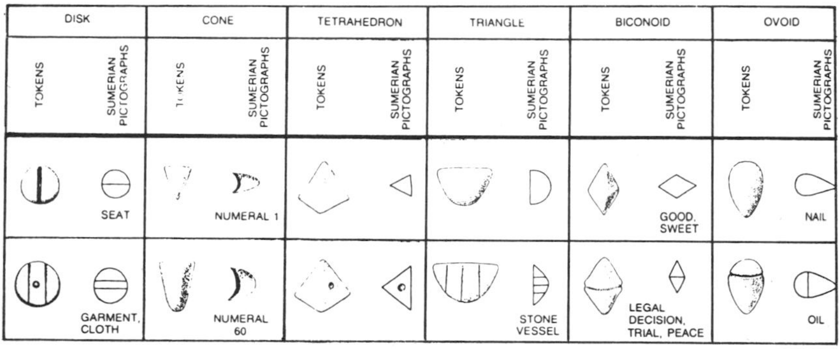

Figure 3. Non-iconic precursors and early forms of writing. From *The Earliest Precursor of Writing* by D. Schmandt-Besserat.

The illuminated letters consisting of vertical and horizontal lines (Fig. 4), such as are found on pocket calculators, can be most easily analyzed as ten sense-determinative signs with seven distinctive features or elements – lines distributed over seven cells or positions. The verticality or horizontality of their position is redundant in an analysis from the point of view of electronic production. The introduction of two independent kenemes (vertical and horizontal lines) with seven distinctive features, the seven cells or positions of the lines, however, meet better with the requirements of human perception. The discrimination is based on the presence or absence of the lines. Of course, the fact that they can be further analysed in terms of the antitheses right vs. left, top vs. bottom, inside vs. outside, opens up the possibility of alternate analyses. It is not exceptional, that distinctive features which occur as the final functional features can still be analyzed. The distinctive features of phonemes, too, can be subdivided into the properties of sonority, tonality and duration.

The complementary distribution of vertical and horizontal lines can be reduced by the choice of dots (Fig. 5). This standardization requires, however, that the number of sense-discriminative elements be increased from seven to fifteen. The redundancy of qualitative differences (vertical vs. horizontal lines) is eliminated in favor of a uniform quantitative redundancy. The noteworthy feature of this model is that the atomic scanning of the fifteen discriminative elements is, not only for the human receptor but also for the computer, not the most economic method. The human receptor resolves the figures most simply into vertical and horizontal, partially overlapping lines, each consisting of three dots. The electronic use of luminous figures, too, can be simplified by the integration of single dots into groups of three, whereby the terminal dots can belong to two neighboring groups. Furthermore, some dots imply others: dot *1/2* does not light up unless the dots *1/1* and *1/3* light up, so that the operation of the dots *1/1* and *1/3* can be coupled with that of *1/2*. The operation of all fifteen dots can be reduced to that of seven coupled with the rest, that is, the model represented in Figure 5 can be reduced with respect to production to the model of Figure 4.

An increase in the number of cells from fifteen to thirty-five suffices to render the capital letters of the Latin alphabet as illuminated letters in a form that is easy for the human eye to recognize and discriminate (Fig. 6).

Since the function of these systems of letters and numerals is not simply and directly to signalize speech sounds and numbers, but to do this while preserving a recognizable similarity to known alphanumeric characters, their shape is in great measure redundant. A comparison with telegraph codes (Fig. 7), which are based on the same dot system as illuminated writing, can illustrate this point. The international telegraph alphabet restricts itself to five cells, the Van Duuren Code to seven. The two-dimensional field of illuminated letters is here reduced to one dimension. The discovery of mistakes in the Van Duuren 7-Unit Code is made easier by an invariant property of the 'letters' of this code; the regular manner in which they are composed out of three positively and four negatively (zero) marked compartments. The control function of redundancy now becomes a principle of organization. Four of the seven 'letters' of the Van Duuren signals are zero-signs (blank compartments). On the level of distinctive features, the frequent presence of zero-signs is a characteristic of sign systems in general, and of technical sign systems in particular.

In the case of printing and illuminated lettering, the development of a double articulation is motivated primarily by considerations of production. The decisive factors are technique and economy of production. The aesthetic aspect, concerning the reception of the signs, should of course not be suppressed. Unity in plurality and geometrical formation, too, are aesthetic moments. In

Figure 4. Illuminated numerals I

Figure 5. Illuminated numerals II

Figure 6. Illuminated letters

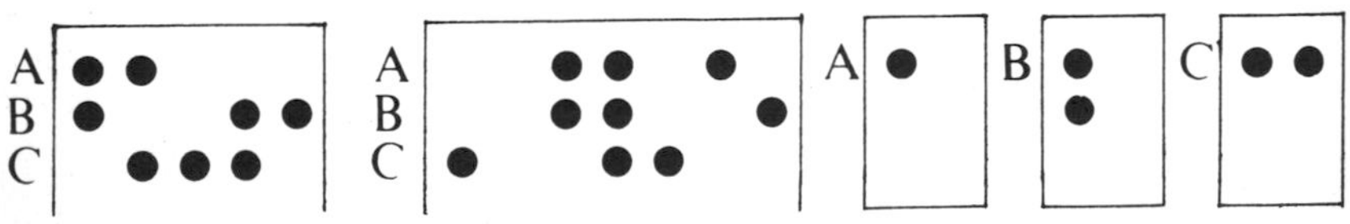

Figure 7. (i) International Telegraph Code
(ii) Van Duren 7-Unit Code
(iii) Braille Code for the blind

the case of reading machines, however, the doubly articulated analysis is determined exclusively by considerations of reception. The writing systems, however constructed, whether holistically or digitally, exist. There is a machine that is projected and already in use (cf. Kurzweil 1978; Eckmiller 1969) that can decipher about three hundred current fonts and transpose them into another medium (either acoustic or haptic) which is accessible to the blind, that is, into speech or Braille. The success of such an "omni-font reading machine" is dependent upon the establishment of the invariant properties of each unit of the alphabet, as well as of the variations that are dependent upon factors such as the position and size of letters, continuous combinations of letters, ellipsis in the case of the fusion of two letters (cf. the *ch* in the case of Albers' stencil lettering, Fig. 1), and the quality of the printing materials and the printing itself.

Considering the range of possible variations discussed above, it is useless to fix on an absolute similarity of tokens of any one type. Where light and dark are distinctive features, it is misleading to orient oneself to an absolute range of lightness. In a grey and black composition the light part can be as dark as is the dark part in a white and grey composition. The figures for the number *7* in the Anglo-Saxon writing style and for the number *1* in the Continental-European are so similar as to cause confusion. Whether a given figure is a *1* or a *7* can be decided by the omni-font reading machine by no other means than those used by the human reader, that is, on the basis of the occurrence of the alternative figure in the context (say of a continental 7 with a transverse bar in the middle, or of an Anglo-Saxon *1* without a nearly horizontal bar at the top), or on the basis of some other kind of indication (say English text).

6. *Concluding remarks*

Double articulation has, in the case of writing, a predominately economic rationale, to which ever-increasing importance has been attributed in the wake of mechanization. Aside from aesthetic considerations, which should not be underestimated, the clarity, and hence also the ease and reliability of discrimination are also important factors (seaman's code, writing for the blind). With the increasing number of signs, and the diversity connected therewith, it becomes impossible to focus on a disordered multitude of holistic key features: an at least partial digital analysis, taking account of originally senseless elements, becomes indispensable (cf. the Far Eastern logograms and the omni-font reading machine).

The sign systems adduced by opponents of the linguistic "myth of double articulation" are in many respects different from the writing systems presented here. Their examples show new sign systems consisting of composite signs constructed by making use of already given signs. The signs are converted from a sense-determinative to a sense-discriminative function. Signs that already have a current metaphorical function are preferred here, for example, numerals, playing cards (hearts, clubs, spades, diamonds), and the like, which, similarly, have been adduced as examples (Eco 1972: 239). In the case of the newer kinds of writing (printing and illuminated lettering), however, we are dealing with given sign systems, which in their traditional forms can be considered as being only in part doubly articulated, say in the case of single letter groups such as b, p, d, g. They are now broken down into discriminative elements which only partly and more or less by chance correspond to the given, normal shape properties that, in the traditional forms, function as the key features. Shapes are developed that are precise, though abstract, and are known not only in geometry but also for their diversified use in other sign systems. They stand, moreover, in a clear relationship to each other, in a relationship plausible also in terms of *Gestalt* theory. Three dots yield a continuous line in the morse alphabet, but a discontinuous line in the cited illuminated lettering.

The seaman's flag code cited by Bühler seems to hold an intermediate position. Despite the partial identity of its discriminative elements with those of Albers' stencil lettering, it was classed with the first group. In this code, the geometrical figures all occur in isolation and in a prototypical position and shape, that is, they occur in such a way that they are generally familiar as iconic representations of themselves. In the stencil lettering, on the other hand, they occur in a non-prototypical position, in configurations that depict non-prototypical figures – overly long rectangles, for example – so that they are sometimes not recognizable as such at first glance.

However much one is inclined to segment such squishes, so usual in semiotics, it should be beyond dispute that it is a matter not of a gradual, but, more radically, of a qualitative displacement: from sense-determinative to senseless units in order to obtain sense-discriminative units, from concretely iconic signs to more abstract (often geometrical) figures; and amongst these figures, from complex multidimensional shapes (sphere, square) to their elemental components (line, point); and this indeed both in the development of alternative sign systems (from the seaman's flag code to the morse alphabet, from James Gills' triangular modification of the ordinary alphabet for the use of the blind to Louis Braille's writing for the blind), and also in the standardization of traditional alphanumeric systems (from stencil to illuminated lettering).

Restricting the examination to the last two centuries, one could conjecture that universal regularities are at work in these *prima facie* plausible displacements, just as the development from semasiography to phonography is reflected also in the ontogenesis. But such a conjecture might be ethnocentric and rash. The counting tokens, which are the likely precursors of Near-Eastern writing systems, are not only, for the most part, abstract symbolic ideograms. As they increase in number and become more differentiated, it appears that there is an immediate emergence of abstract symbols, in addition to the concrete iconic signs on the tokens – dots and lines drawn in various directions, which function as sense-discriminative elements, that is, as signs lacking a constant and positive meaning. Abstract symbolization, such as the sense-discriminative function of signs, is not a prerogative accruing exclusively to the unconscious origin of natural languages, much less to the intense reflexion and formalization of the last two centuries. The Near-Eastern origin of writing also reflects and confirms the development from multidimensional to elemental forms.

Note

* Slightly revised version of "Doppelte Artikulation in der Schrift", *Zeitschrift für Semiotik* 2. 1980, Translation with the help of Donald F. Goodwin.
Thanks are also due to the editors of the *Zeitschrift für Semiotik* for their permission to include the article in this volume.

References

Albers, J.
1926 Zur Ökonomie der Schriftreform. In *Offset-Buch-und Werbekunst* Heft 7, 1926. Leipzig: Der Offset-Verlag, pp.395–397.

Benveniste, E.
1952 "Communication animale et langage humain". *Problèmes de linguistique générale I*. Paris: Gallimard (1966), pp. 56–62.

Bierwisch, M.
1972 "Schriftstruktur und Phonologie". *Probleme und Ergebnisse der Psychologie* 43: 21–44.

Bühler, K.
1934 *Sprachtheorie*. Stuttgart: Fischer (1965).

Eckmiller, R.
1969 "Maschinen zur optischen Zeichenerlernung". *Studium Generale* 22: 1026–1045.

Eco, U.
1972 *Einführung in die Semiotik*. München: UTB.

Gleitman, L. R. & Rozin, P.
1977 "The Structure and Acquisition of Reading I-II". In A. S. Reber & D. L. Scarborough, eds., *Towards a Psychology of Reading*. New York: Wiley, pp. 1–141.

Hockett, C. F.
1963 "The problem of universals in language". In J. H. Greenberg, ed., (1966) *Universals of Language*. Cambridge, Mass.: M. I. T. Press, pp. 1–29.
Holenstein, E.
1979 "Von der Poesie und der Plurifunktionalität der Sprache". In R. Jakobson *Poetik*. Frankfurt: Suhrkamp, pp. 7–60.
1980 *Von der Hintergehbarkeit der Sprache: Kognitive Unterlagen der Sprache:* Frankfurt: Suhrkamp.
Jakobson, R.
1939 "Zur Struktur des Phonems". In *Selected Writing I*. The Hague: Mouton (1971), pp. 280–310.
1973 *Main Trends in the Science of Language*. New York: Harper Torch Books.
Justeson, J. S.
1976 "Universals of language and universals of writing". In *Linguistic Studies Offered to Joseph H. Greenberg I*. Saratoga, Cal.: Anma Libri, pp. 57–94.
The Kurzweil Report 1
1978 No. 2. Cambridge, Mass.: Kurzweil Computer Products.
Levi-Strauss, C.
1964 *Mythologiques I: Le cru et le cuit*. Paris: Plon.
Prieto, L. J.
1966 *Messages et signaux*. Paris: PUF.
Scheerer, E.
1978a "Probleme und Ergebnisse der experimentellen Leseforschung". *Zeitschrift für Entwicklungspsychologie und Pädagogische Psychologie* 10: 347–364.
1978b Review of A. S. Reber and D. L. Scarborough, eds., (1977), *Toward a Psychology of Reading*. Hillsdale, N.J.: Lawrence Erlbaum. In *System: A Journal for Educational Technology and Language Learning Systems* 6: 187–193.
Schmandt-Besserat, D.
1978 "The Earliest Precursor of Writing". *Scientific American* 240 (6): 38–47.
Weigl, E.
1974 "Zur Schriftsprache und ihrem Erwerb – neurophysiologische und psycholinguistische Betrachtungen". In W. Eichler and A. Hofer, eds., *Spracherwerb und linguistische Theorien*. München: Piper.

PETER EISENBERG

Writing system and morphology. Some orthographic regularities of German

Abstract

There are detailed orthographic rules for most alphabetic writings, which tell us in nearly all cases how to write correctly. Yet it is not very well known, to what extent these rules correspond or even coincide with the linguistic rules underlying the writing system of the language in question.

The approach outlined here presupposes that the graphemic part of a grammar is to be considered as an integral part of the overall language system, and that it has to be investigated by the same linguistic methods as the other subsystems. Support is given for this thesis by an examination of the relation between morphology and graphemics in German. It is argued that there is a close mutual dependency between the morphology and the writing system.

1. *Remarks on the linguistic level of alphabetic writings*

There is some agreement among linguists working on problems of writing systems, that these systems have to be considered as proper subsystems of language systems and that it should be desirable, therefore, and possible, to treat the graphemic part of a grammar as one of its components in the usual sense, i.e., to fully integrate it into an overall grammar of the language under description. There is much less agreement about the linguistic level on which the graphemic component should be based, and this paper is not intended to make any substantial contribution to this problem. Nevertheless, I would like to make some remarks about my own view of the present situation. These remarks serve the purpose of clarifying what is intended by the proposals made in Sections 2 and 3, and thereby of avoiding counter-arguments which do not meet the point I want to make.

With respect to the linguistic level of alphabetic systems, the most debated question is whether, and to what extent, these systems are phonologically or phonetically based, and it has been shown several times that much confusion exists concerning this problem.[1] In my opinion, most of this confusion originates from the simple, if not trivial, fact that there is much discussion about the principles of orthography without sufficient agreement about the concepts of phonology and phonetics used in these discussions. But even if it is clear what should be understood with respect to phonology vs. phonetics, people sometimes tend to generalize certain observations, regarding them as 'proof' of the fact that the whole system should be taken to have this or that property as its basic property. So we read statements like „daß die deutsche Orthografie sich direkt auf die Phoneme/Grafeme bezieht und nicht auf phonetische Varianten, ist am velaren Nasal [ŋ] nachzuweisen" (Müller 1978: 28), where the velar nasal is taken as evidence for the 'phonemic principle' in German orthography. I think William Haas (1975 and in this volume) has argued quite convincingly that it is not justifiable to place existing writing systems on one linguistic level in such a way that it could not have access to information from other levels. On the other hand it does not, according to Haas, alter the level of a script if it takes into account information from any other level. A syllabic script remains syllabic even if it depends in part on the phonetic level and vice versa. Similar conclusions can be drawn from what still appears to be the most conclusive approach to graphemics, especially its integration into an overall grammar, namely the one outlined in Bierwisch 1972.

Bierwisch presupposes a generative phonology of the Chomsky/Halle 1968 type. The relation between the sound level and the graphemic level is realized by so-called grapheme-phoneme-correspondence rules (GPK rules). These are context-sensitive rewrite rules which formally resemble very much the usual phonological rules. They differ essentially from phonological ones in not containing units from any sound level on their right side, but units from the graphemic level. Each GPK rule allows for the rewriting of a sequence of sound units by a sequence of graphemic surface units, i.e. letters. Bierwisch is able to show that in German not all GPK rules can operate on the deep phonological level. Some of these rules can only operate after certain phonological rules have been applied, but as it is not possible to give any generalized criteria for the graphemic relevance of phonological rules, it follows that it might only be possible to follow certain GPK rules after all phonological rules have first been applied, i.e. on the phonetic level.

Despite the fact that Bierwisch uses – and given his approach has to use – a fully elaborated generative phonology, it is not at all clear whether we should speak of our writing system as 'phonological'. The reason for this is what has just been said about the level of application of GPK rules. There is no level on which they operate, and *a fortiori* it is not the phonological level.

Even though the following arguments will show that I have largely adopted Bierwisch's way of thinking about the writing system, I want to stress, nevertheless, the term 'morphological', and do not make any attempt to integrate what I have to say into a generative phonology. There are essentially two reasons for this. First there are facts to be handled which cannot be handled, as far as I can see, in a reasonable way within generative phonology. As an example, let me mention the relevance of the morphological distinction productive/non-productive for graphemics. Secondly, there seems to be a tendency, at least in the lexicalist quarters of the generative camp, to establish a morphological component within the grammar, and to pay more attention to the morphological and, especially, to word formation rules in their own right, than was the case in earlier periods. This would mean that approaches of the Chomsky/Halle type, which did not leave much room for morphology between syntax and phonology, should be abandoned (see for instance Aronoff 1976 and Booij 1977). The design of the morphological part of the grammar then follows the still more general tendency not to separate the different subsystems completely, but to provide the possibility of mutual interaction. It seems to be the case, furthermore, that practically all components of the grammar do heavily rely on information from the surface level (with respect to morphology cf. Motsch 1977 and especially Plank 1980).

The graphemic subsystem of German gives us some hints pointing in the same direction. So it can easily be shown that for the purpose of grasping the regularities of graphemics one should use not only phonemic and morphosyntactic, but also graphemic information itself which, in turn, serves morphological purposes (see Section 2). This certainly has to be taken into account if one reflects the possibilities to integrate graphemics into the grammar. It is not our goal to do this here. By discussing some examples, we only want to show what kind of influence of morphology on writing one has to be aware of.

2. *The principle of greatest similarity*

It is one of the most obvious properties of our writing system that the graphemic representations of different units from a paradigm are made as similar as possible to each other. This fact is normally accounted for and explained by stating that graphemic representations are in many cases not derived from phonetic, but from some deeper structures. Therefore, certain phonetic differences between units of the same paradigm might be neglected within the written forms of these units. Since the mechanism in question does not provide in all cases *identical,* but very often only *similar,* graphemic representations, we propose to call it the *principle of greatest similarity* and not the principle of identity, as one could first be inclined to do. Some relevant examples that come immediately to mind are given below.

The principle of greatest similarity has a systematic and a historical aspect. According to a widespread opinion, it is this principle which is to some extent responsible for the growing influence of written language on the native speaker's knowledge about his language. Since, by this principle, the writing system directly reflects the morphological structure of the language, and since writing systems seem to be more conservative than sound systems, it follows that one can expect a direct interaction between the functioning of the writing system and morphological change. More specifically, one can expect that the writing system tends to prevent certain morphological changes since it keeps alive the native speaker's knowledge about those derivational relations, which could easily be lost if this knowledge had to be based on the sound system alone. Examples of this kind are available from the morphological literature. Plank, for instance, (1980: 95ff.) demonstrates that morphological reanalysis, which is one of the most important mechanisms of morphological change, would occur more often than it does if we did not have a writing system of the kind we have.

Let us now illustrate some of the effects of the principle of greatest similarity in German orthography. In German, as in English, a suffix *iv* is used to derive adjectival stems from noun stems, as, for example, in *extensiv, kooperativ, massiv, produktiv.* For the stem of these adjectives, one could think in principle of three different graphemic representations with respect to the suffix *iv,* which would all be in accordance with the principle of greatest similarity, namely:

(1) a. *massiwer–massiw*
b. *massifer–massif*
c. *massiver–massiv*

(1a) would be the 'normal' phonological spelling in German. Since this is a case of final devoicing, and since this rule is generally neglected by the GPK rules (i.e. the voiced consonant is the only one which appears on the graphemic level), one could expect ⟨w⟩ for both [v] and [f].[2] (1b) could be motivated by the French writing. This would mean that we had taken over the French form ⟨*massif*⟩ and maintained this form in German, though it would not fit the German system. Yet it is clear that we often accept foreign spellings which do not fit our system when we accept foreign words. (1c) could be motivated by similar reasons, since in French we do have ⟨*massive*⟩ as well as ⟨*massif*⟩.

The reason why the German system in fact selects (1c) seems to be the following. We do not have a phonological rule of final devoicing which replaces /v/ by /f/, though this would be possible with respect to the phonetic values of these segments. /v/ and /f/ constitute one of the two or three pairs of consonants in German which meet the phonetic conditions of final devoicing, but which, nevertheless, are not related to each other by this rule. Therefore, the system cannot accept (1a). Similar for (1b): there is no case in German where a voiceless consonant could be read as voiced. Originally, this was also true for ⟨v⟩, which has as its usual reading a voiceless consonant such as the ⟨v⟩ in *Vater, viel, Gustav, verlieren.* Yet in another group of words, namely foreign words, ⟨v⟩ as a historically younger reading has also the value /v/, as in *Version, Vene, Verdikt.* This means that ⟨v⟩ is the only one of the three letters for which we have a voiced and a voiceless reading, though these readings are never related to each other by final devoicing. This seems to be the reason why the writing system accepts ⟨v⟩ for all forms of the paradigm. In doing this, another regularity must clearly be neglected, namely the one which says that in case of final devoicing, the writing system is based on a deeper phonological level, i.e. it chooses the letter which normally stands for the voiced consonant. This example illustrates that the principle of greatest similarity is even maintained in certain cases where other important rules are canceled.

From the following examples, it can be seen that our principle is indeed one of similarity, not of identity. In these cases, morphological alternations correspond to differences in spelling, but these differences are smaller in the written form than in the phonetic and phonological form. We are concerned with vowel alternations in German, which are conventionally divided into the subclasses Umlaut and Ablaut. As far as I can see, this terminology is not motivated phonetically but graphemically, since I do not know any phonetic criteria which would allow the introduction of a special class of pairs of phonetic units, consisting each of 'Laut' and 'Umlaut'.

The principle of greatest similarity is realized with respect to Umlaut by introducing new letters into the alphabet which constitute a formal similarity between units not existing on the phonological or phonetic level. For the diphthong [oi] this even means that a graphemic representation ⟨äu⟩ is introduced, which has the same phonetic counterpart as the ⟨eu⟩ used 'normally' and which is only used to establish a formal similarity with respect to ⟨au⟩. In other words, ⟨äu⟩ is only used within units which are (by inflexion or derivation) morphologically related to units with ⟨au⟩ in the corresponding position, such as in *Haus–Häuser, Auge–äugen.* ⟨äu⟩ is never used in any other position, therefore it never occurs in words such as *euch, Efeu, Freund*. It should be clear that in cases of this kind, graphemic similarity goes beyond similarity on any level of sound.

There are other means of expressing similarities with respect to Ablaut, because we find them in the occurrences of vowels within the forms of so-called strong verbs and mixed verbs. Problems of economy would arise if the system used similar letters to express the paradigmatic relations between forms such as *trinke–trank–getrunken*. It would cause an inflation of graphemic ambiguities and lead to a very complex system of graphemes if we invented special letters to express the fact that [i], [a], and [u] appear in the same position within the forms of a paradigm. But the possibility for expressing similarity does exist with respect to the graphemic realization of vowel length as it is expressed by the occurrence or non-occurrence of the so-called 'Dehnungs-*h*'.

The rules about where the Dehnungs-*h cannot* appear are pretty clear and well-known. These rules are based on purely phonetic and graphemic conditions. In contrast to this, we do not have any rule which tells us, where the Dehnungs-*h must* appear. Nevertheless, it always holds that if the Dehnungs-*h* appears in one form of a verbal paradigm to mark a vowel as [+tense], it will also be used in all other forms of that paradigm if a tense vowel occurs in that position, even if we have different vowels. The same holds if the tenseness is not expressed by the Dehnungs-*h*. So we have *stehlen–stahl–gestohlen, fahren–fuhr, befehlen–befahl,* but *gebären–gebar–geboren, gären–gegoren, küren–gekoren.* I know of no exception to this principle.

The consequence of this regularity is especially impressive in the case of [i:]. In many orthographic books we find a rule saying that ⟨e⟩ has a similar function with respect to ⟨i⟩ as has the Dehnungs-*h* with respect to the other vowels, i.e. [i:] is graphemically realized as ⟨ie⟩ instead of ⟨ih⟩. This does not hold for those cases which we are considering. The Dehnungs-*h* is *always* found in forms with an [i:] (i.e. a tense vowel) if it appears in other forms of the paradigm too, and of course it then never appears only in forms with [i:]. As a consequence, we get three graphemic representations of [i:]. We write *Igel* and *viel* as we write *Abend* and *kahl:* [i:] is represented as ⟨i⟩ and as ⟨ie⟩ just as [a:] is represented as ⟨a⟩ and ⟨ah⟩. We then have, of course, ⟨ie⟩ according to the principle of greatest similarity where [i:] is in the relation of Ablaut to another tense vowel represented without Dehnungs-*h*, such as in *verlieren–verlor, rufen–rief.* On the other hand, we have ⟨ieh⟩ as graphemic representation of [i:] only in those cases, where [i:] is in the relation of Ablaut to another tensed vowel which is represented graphemically by vowel plus Dehnungs-*h*, as such in *befehlen–befiehlt, empfehlen–empfiehlt, stehlen–stiehlt.* In this respect, ⟨ie⟩ behaves like a simple letter. There are very few cases in German where [i:] is represented as ⟨ieh⟩ for other reasons than the ones just stated, such as in *Vieh* and its derivatives. These are not just exceptions to our rule, but there are special etymological reasons for such spellings which we cannot go into here. There is a fourth graphemic representation for [i:], namely the one such as ⟨ih⟩, in, for example, *ihr, ihn.* It has an interesting, but very limited distribution and is not our concern here.

From this example, it can be seen how consistently paradigmatic relations are expressed by the writing system. Graphemic similarities of this kind seem to be very resistent to historical change, and, of course, do not have any direct correspondence at the sound level.

3. *Morphological determination of graphemic ambiguity*

Before we try to explain why certain types of graphemic ambiguities occur in our writing system, it seems to be useful to comment briefly on the concept of graphemic ambiguity itself. When we use the term 'graphemic' in this paper, we always refer to the surface level of written texts. On the surface level, we are concerned with the letters of our alphabet and the rules for their combination. It is not our aim to contribute to or make use of a 'graphemic theory', which classifies letters and sequences of letters, the 'graphs', into classes called 'graphemes'. A theory of this kind would have to consider graphemic structures not as surface structures, but as structures on some deeper level of description. I do not want to discuss any of these theories here, but only want to make clear that we are always talking about the surface of scripts, considered as consisting of sequences of letters.

It seems reasonable, then, to base the concept of graphemic ambiguity entirely on the surface level, i.e. to relate the surface of written texts to the surface of spoken texts and not to any deeper phonological level. By doing this, we are following Bierwisch (1972: 75), who considers a *phonetic* representation as being *graphemically* ambiguous, if and only if it has at least two graphemic representations. According to Bierwisch (ibid.), there might be two different kinds of reasons for this kind of graphemic ambiguity. A phonetic form might be graphemically ambiguous

a. because the sound structure allows for the application of competing GPK rules (*mahlen–malen, Vetter–fetter, das–daß, Meer–mehr, du reihst–du reist*)

b. because phonemic distinctions, which are expressed graphemically, are removed by phonological rules (*Hund–Hunt, Tod- tot, (K)ranich–(t)ranig, du reist–du reißt*).

From a systematic point of view, there is a substantial difference between both types of ambiguity. Type (b) can be considered to be fully explained within the presupposed framework. The different graphemic representations are derived in a completely normal way by the application of phonological rules and GPK rules. Type (a), by contrast, is based on the notion of markedness. At a certain stage of derivation, it is possible to apply two or more GPK rules to the same unit. In Bierwisch's approach, the choice between these rules is controlled by a system of markings. In a case like *Fuchs* vs. *Jux,* one form is considered as marked, i.e. not as the standard case. A GPK rule for these exceptions is only applied to those units which are marked for this rule. In our example, the marked GPK rule would convert /ks/ not to the normal ⟨chs⟩ but to ⟨x⟩ for marked units such as /juks/.

To use the concept of markedness is sometimes nothing more than a way of producing a correct solution by completely mechanical procedures. From the general theory of markedness, we know that the *real reasons* for units to be marked are of a very different nature. So we have to ask whether we are able to find out why certain units are marked with respect to the rules of the writing system and why others are not, and we will thereby find out what could be the reasons or some of the reasons for graphemic ambiguities. In what follows we will propose some preliminary answers to this question by showing how the choice between different GPK-rules is determined by the morphological properties of the units in question.

Example 1.

In our first example we are concerned with the relevance of inflexion vs. word formation (including composition) for writing. Even though it is not always easy to draw a sharp line between inflexion and derivation, this distinction is taken to be well-established in traditional and modern morphology. In most cases it appears to be irrelevant for the writing system, as can be seen from examples such as *Kinder–kind–kindlich* or *Könige–König–königlich*. As an example of where this distinction is relevant for spelling we will consider the phonological rule of geminate reduction in German (Geminatenvereinfachung), which was formulated and discussed in some detail in Wurzel 1970.

Roughly speaking, geminate reduction deletes certain phones in case they meet identical phones at a morpheme boundary. As Bierwisch has shown, this rule is relevant for writing. There are GPK rules which can only apply after the application of geminate reduction. So we write *du reist, du reißt, du reizt, du feixt* and not *du reisst, du reißst, du reizst, du feixst.* Now in Kohrt 1978 (63f.) it is argued that in some cases the GPK rules are working independently of geminate reduction. Whereas /t/ is deleted in forms such as *er rät* (from *raten*), it is not deleted in *er lädt* (from *laden*). In this case the relevance or irrelevance of the rule simply appears to be determined morphonologically, but for other cases such as *er wird* from *werden* (not *er wirdt*!) this apparently does not hold. In general, there does not seem to be a simple criterion for the relevance of the rule and Kohrt states (ibid.) "daß die Grafemrelevanz bzw. -irrelevanz der Geminatenvereinfachung nicht durch einen bloßen Bezug auf bestimmte Klassen von Flexionsmorphemen gekennzeichnet werden kann."

In the original formulation of geminate reduction by Wurzel, the necessity for this rule is demonstrated by the following list of phenomena (1970: 221f.):

I. die 'endungslosen' Pluralformen bestimmter *ge*-Kollektiva (*die Gebirge, Gelege, Gestade*), deren zugrundeliegende Repräsentation /ge+STAMM+e+e/ ist;
II. die Dativ-Plural-Formen der schwachen Nomina wie *den Buben, den Augen, den Straßen,* die aus /būb+n+n/ usw. abgeleitet sind;
III. die Konjunktivformen wie *ich komme* und *du kommest,* die auf Repräsentationen /kom+e+e/ und [kom+e+est] (aus /kom+e+st/) zurückgehen;
IV. Flexionsformen der 3rd. Person Singular wie z.B. *er rät* und *er brät,* in denen jeweils ein stammhaftes /t/ steckt (vgl. /rät+t/);
V. Flexionsformen der 2nd. Person Singular wie z.B. *du heißt, du reißt, du mißt* (/rejs+st/ usw.).

It is immediately clear that in all these cases geminate reduction is relevant for writing. Furthermore these are all definitely cases of inflexion and not of derivation.

Wurzel then states (1970: 222), that geminate reductions "auch über die Begrenzungen von 'orthografischen Wörtern' (. . . vgl. *das ist tief* [istīf]) und sogar von 'phonologischen Wörtern' im Sinne Chomskys und Halles (. . . vgl. *Schiff fahren* [šifar(ə)n] hinaus operieren. Ihre Domäne ist die phonologische Phrase (und damit manchmal der ganze Satz). "Although this is certainly correct for geminate reduction itself, it does not hold for its graphemic relevance. Instead I would like to claim that the maximal domain for GPK rules lies in general word forms.[3] We will give another example later to support this claim. If it is correct, most cases of geminate reduction have no automatic consequences on the graphemic level. Furthermore it seems to be the case that geminate reduction is never relevant in cases of word formation, no matter whether these are cases of derivation (2a) or composition (2b).

(2) a. *Schrifttum, unnachgiebig, ummodeln, annehmen, einnehmen, enttarnen*

b. *Stahllunge, Skatturnier, Tiefflieger, Waldessaum, heillos.*

It is not necessary to discuss the effect of the different forms of geminate reduction on spelling in order to be able to state that *all* cases of geminate reduction in writing are cases of inflexion. I would even claim that with inflexion, geminate reduction is *always* relevant for graphemics, at least if it has the effect of deleting one of two identical letters. If not, we get special rules which rely on special conditions, as in the case of *lädt.* Kohrt's *wird* instead of *wirdt* is not a real counter-example since the conjugation of *werden* is not completely regular anyway.

If our analysis is correct, then geminate reduction shows how different kinds of morphological facts can be directly relevant for spelling.

Example 2.

As is the case with word formation vs. inflexion, it is not always easy to decide whether a morphological unit or a morphological rule which makes use of that unit is productive, active, or neither, at any given time. Nevertheless, it is useful and even necessary that these terms in morphology exist simply because they refer to significant differentiations within the morphological system. Moreover, it seems to me that this distinction may also be of significance for the rules of spelling. We will illustrate this by referring to an interesting story told by Mark Aronoff and by complementing it by some further observations.

Aronoff, 1978, is concerned with the Latin suffix *-or,* its English and American descendents and their graphemic representations. In Latin,*-or* is used to nomnalize intransitive verb stems, as in *error, tremor,* and for agent nominalizations on the basis of the supine, as in *censor, victor, factor.* The counterparts of both suffixes *-or* were homographs in Middle English as well as in Anglo-French, where it was written as *-our.* In the sixteenth and seventeenth century, the etymologically correct form *or* was introduced into English. It then happened that the agent nominalizations were easily adapted to the new spelling, whereas the other type of nominalization was fairly resistent against it. That is why we now have *behaviour, rigour, labour, favour,* on the one hand, and *mediator, oppressor, supervisor* on the other. In American English this differentiation in spelling, which developed in English during the last three hundred years, was lost. The only written form was *-or.* Now there is also in English a suffix *-er* in addition to *-or* which has one function in common with *-or,* namely that of forming agent nominalizations from verbal stems such as in *writer.* Aronoff draws attention to the interesting fact that there is now a tendency in American English to write *all* agent nominalizations with *-er* and the other nouns with *-or.* Thus we fund nomina agentis such as *adviser, sponser, adjuster,* but never **coler,* **behavier* etc. This would mean that within the system of American English, a pair of suffixes *-or*–*-er* is developing which is to some extent an analogue to the English *-ou*–*-or*. The morphologically and semantically well motivated differentiation in English is reintroduced into American English, yet with the effect of a simplified orthography.

In German we have *-or* (*Direktor*) as well as *-er* (*Programmierer*) and *-eur* (*Konstrukteur*) in agent nominalizations. For reasons of space, we will not discuss the distribution of these suffixes here.[4] Instead we will elaborate a little on the use of a letter specific to German (and some other) system, namely the occurrence and nonoccurrence of ⟨ö⟩ ([ø]) in some classes of foreign words.

In foreign words, the French suffixes (*i*)*eux* and *eur* are written partly with ⟨ö⟩ and partly in the original way:

(3) a. *muskulös, seriös, monströs, mirakulös, amourös, mysteriös, Likör*
   b. *Ingenieur, Hypnotiseur, Dekorateur, Friseur, Masseur.*

It can be seen immediately that the difference in spelling must depend on the different status of the affixes *-ös* (*-iös*) on the one hand, and *-eur* on the other. The former suffix is not productive in German, in some cases it is not even recognized as a suffix at all. Even though the function of *-ös* as derivator of adjectival stems from noun stems is immediately recognizable in most cases, it is at least doubtful whether and in what way this regularity can be understood within the German morphological system. In many cases, the noun stems are not stems of German (not 'eingedeutscht'), as can be seen from examples like *muskulös, seriös, amourös.* These stems are not morphological units of the German system. That this construction is rather demotivated can also be seen from forms like *porös.* For many speakers, this word is not a derivative at all, but is a morphological simplex, in contrast to the form *porig* which uses the productive suffix *-ig*.

The situation is different with *-eur,* which first of all has preserved one of the meanings it has in French. With this meaning (deverbal nominalization referring to persons ('actors')) it is productive in German. The nouns with *-eur* are derived from verbs with *-ieren* (*massieren–Masseur, hypnotisieren–Hypnotiseur, frisieren–Friseur*) or from nouns with *-ion* (*Dekoration–Dekorateur, Konstruktion–Konstrukteur*) which in turn are derived from verbs with *-ieren*. This difference is probably motivated by phonetic facts (vowel or liquid in the terminal position of the stem in the latter cases). Furthermore, the nouns with *-eur* can themselves serve as the basis for derivations such as in *Masseuse, Friseuse, Ingenieurin, Dekorateurin.* Thus the suffix *-eur* seems to be well integrated into the German system. I am taking this fact as the reason for the stableness of its written form. If a morphological unit is actively used within a language, and if there are no special reasons to change it (as in Aronoff's example), then it is reasonable to expect that this unit will be more likely to preserve its form than those units which are about to loose their morphological status. This could, for instance, explain why, despite many attempts to introduce the written form *Frisör,* we still write *Friseur.* On the other hand, we should write *Likör* and not *Likeur,* as we do, because this *-ör* has nothing to do with the *-eur,* neither morphologically nor semantically. Therefore [œ:] is written here as in most French loan words ⟨ö⟩ (*Möbel* etc.), even though there is a significant phonetic difference between the French form [œ:] and the German form [ø:]. This difference does not cause any problem because ⟨ö⟩ in German stands for both [œ] (*Spötter, Mörder*) and [ø] (*schön, möglich*).

Once again, this reflex of morphological facts in the writing system does not seem to have any counterpart at the sound level.

Example 3.

We will now consider in some detail the graphemic representation of the voiceless alveolar spirant [s]. As a separate letter or sequence of letters it is represented as ⟨s⟩, ⟨ss⟩, and ⟨ß⟩ in German. I am especially interested in finding out the rules which control the distribution of ⟨ß⟩.

The letter ⟨ß⟩ ([estset]) was introduced into the alphabet of German in the fourteenth century as a replacement of ⟨sz⟩. Its original function can roughly be understood as serving the purpose of avoiding the homography of two different [s]. To be more precise, ⟨ß⟩ was used as the graphemic counterpart of the [s] which originated from [t] by the Second Consonant Shift and then merged with the older [s] phonetically (cf. Müller 1978: 32f.). The role of ⟨ß⟩ in the writing system of present day German is not quite clear. There are many different proposals to formulate the distribution of ⟨ß⟩, but I know of none which comes to the conclusion that this distribution is at least approximately regular or even linguistically motivated. A typical statement to this effect is the one from a prominent orthography book by Mentrup which says that "In *many* cases there are reasons for choosing between ⟨s⟩ and ⟨ß⟩" (Mentrup 1968: 82; my translation, my italics). As a starting point for the analysis, we will present the rules for the distribution of ⟨ß⟩ according to Eichler 1978, 16ff. We have changed the presentation of the rules and translated them into English to make them easier to read, but we have not made any substantial change.

(4) [s] is represented graphemically

a. as medial sound between long vowels and vowels always as ⟨ß⟩ (*rußen, Maße*)

b. as medial sound between short vowels and vowels always as ⟨ss⟩ (*hassen, Nüsse*)

c. as medial sound between vowels and consonants

α. as ⟨ß⟩ only if [s] also appears in the forms of the paradigm where the position in question is followed by a vowel (*spaßt–spaßen, paßt–passen*)

β. as ⟨s⟩ in all other cases (*Rast, Rost, Ast*)

d. as medial sound between consonants as ⟨s⟩ if there are forms within the paradigm without [s] (*magst–mögen, hackst–hacken*)

e. as final sound after vowels

α. as ⟨ß⟩ only if [s] also appears in those forms of the paradigm where the position in question is followed by a vowel (*Ruß–Rußes, Haß–Hasses*)

β. as ⟨s⟩

1. if [z] appears in the same position (*Maus–Mäuse, Gas–Gases*)
2. in foreign spellings (*Bus,* though we have *Busse*)
3. in the suffix *nis* (*Finsternis,* although we have *Finsternisse*)
4. exceptions (*aus, bis*)

f. as final sound after consonants as ⟨s⟩

1. if [z] appears in the same position (*Gans–Gänse*)
2. as suffix *s* (genitive, plural) (*Abschieds, Muttis*)
3. exceptions (*stets, bereits, allerdings).*

It should first be mentioned that this is one of the most complete and explicit statements of the rules under discussion. Its structure is imposed by the distinction between medial sound and final sound and by paradigmatic relations between word forms.

To reconstruct these rules in order to grasp more of the real structural conditions underlying the distribution of ⟨ß⟩, we first have to introduce the notion of morpheme boundary (#) and to understand the concept of medial sound as "not at the morpheme boundary".

The only subrule from (4) which we are not going to change is (4b). We only reformulate the condition for the context. Instead of a short vowel, we speak of a vowel with the feature [–tense]. We do this because in other cases it is correct not to speak of long vowels but of tense vowels. So we will avoid speaking of long or short vowels altogether. The rule for ⟨ss⟩ from (4b) is now found as (5a). It seems to be important that [s] in German is *always* written as ⟨ss⟩ independently of any morphological conditions, in the context specified in (5a). That is to say that

$$
\begin{array}{lll}
\text{(5) a.} & & \langle ss \rangle \ / \ [-\text{tense}] \quad [+\text{voc}] \\
\text{b.} & & \quad\ \ / \ [+\text{tense}] \quad [+\text{voc}]/-\# \\
\text{c.} & [s] \rightarrow & \langle ß \rangle \ / \ [+\text{tense}] \quad \#\text{St}+ \\
\text{d.} & & \quad\ \ / \ [-\text{tense}] \quad \#\text{St}+ \left\{ \begin{array}{l} [-\text{voc}]_{\text{Af}} \\ \emptyset \end{array} \right. \\
\text{e.} & & \langle s \rangle \ \text{else}
\end{array}
$$

⟨ss⟩ is completely determined by phonetic conditions. It occurs both at morpheme boundaries (*hassen, Nüsse, gegossen*) and in the medial position (*Wasser, Kessel, Russe*).

Now ⟨ß⟩ behaves completely differently in this respect. With rule (5b) we first handle ⟨ß⟩ in the medial position. Our notation /— # says that a position *within a morpheme* is required. We understand the concept of morpheme in the Bloomfieldian sense as "minimal form". We have to fulfill this condition if we want to refer to a medial sound in the sense stated above. We specify the preceding vowel as [+tense] because ⟨ß⟩ occurs after long vowels (*Straße, Muße*) as well as after diphthongs (*Meißen*, perhaps *außen*. I will come back to this example later).

With (5c) and (5d) we cover the occurrences of ⟨ß⟩ at morpheme boundaries. In (5d) it is specified that [s] is not written as ⟨ß⟩ at all morpheme boundaries but only in the final position of stems (St). The category St is a morphological constituent category. It is not possible to go into the presupposed morphological approach here (cf. Lieb 1977). I only want to mention that in this morphology, only three constituent categories are used, namely stem (St), affix (Af), and form (Fm). All other specifications such as stem "of a verb", suffix "to derive nominals from verbs" etc. are not given in the constituent structure, but in what we call the marking structure. For the time being, it is only important that the constituent categories St and Af are sufficient to formulate the subrules (5c) and (5d): it is not important which kind of St or Af we have. By the notation St+ we mean "a stem which has always an [s] in final position", as in *fließen, Maße*. Thus, St – is "a stem which can have [z] in final position" as in *reist, Maus, Gas*. Rule (5c) then states that [s] is written after tense vowels as ⟨s⟩ in the terminal position of stem morphemes, if [s] is preserved as terminal sound in all derivational and in flexional variants – in generative terms: if the underlying stem has an /s/ in final position. It can easily be shown that with (5c) we cover all cases from (4a) which are not covered by (5b), plus all cases from (4c, α) and (4e, α) with tense vowel, i.e. *spaßt, spaßen, rußen, Ruß* etc. The remaining cases are covered by (5d). This rule says that [s] is written as ⟨ß⟩ in the final position of stem morphemes if it is preceded by a lax vowel and if the following affix begins with a consonant, or if a suffix does not occur at all. The rule handles expressions such as *paßt, ißt, Haß*.

There are some problematic cases with respect to (5), a few of which I should like to discuss very briefly. Forms such as *außer, außen, draußen, außerhalb* can be understood as being handled in two different ways by (5), depending on whether or not one wants to postulate a stem ⟨aus⟩. This is a difficult question, especially for *außer* and its derivatives. But we always get the correct spelling by (5), independently of the morphological analysis.

A different problem arises in connection with expressions such as *reist* from *reisen* as related to *reißt* from *reißen.* Here we have two different forms of geminate reduction. The contiguity of the final [s] and the suffix *-st* has different graphemic consequences. For *reist* it is again without consequence whether we consider the first or the second [s] as being deleted. We always get the correct spelling. But for *reißt* we have to postulate a stem ⟨rais⟩ because otherwise (5c) could not be applied. From the standpoint of morphology this is not an unreasonable commitment, I think.

As far as I know there exists only one expression which is not covered by (5). It is the conjunction [das], written ⟨daß⟩. Here we have an example of an effect of the so-called semantic principle of orthography by which in German homophone forms are sometimes discriminated graphemically.

What conclusions can be drawn about the writing system from a rule like (5)? First we have to state that – contrary to what our orthography books tell us – there seem to be practically no irregularities in the graphemic representation of [s]. This appears to be an important fact if one remembers that orthographic rules are the basis for teaching children the writing system. A linguistic analysis can prove that things are regular which normally are believed to be not at all regular or only partly regular.

Second, (5) seems to be much simpler than (4), although it is even more complete in the sense just indicated. This greater simplicity is quite substantial and is not primarily caused by the more restrictive language we have used to formulate the rules. There are other reasons for this simplicity.

First, we do not try to specify all cases positively as was done in (4). Instead we consider ⟨s⟩ to be the standard representation of [s] and we then specify the conditions for ⟨ss⟩ and ⟨ß⟩. By this we follow Bierwisch's proposal as to the difference between marked and unmarked cases. Yet we do not just mark some lexical entries for certain rules, but we specify the structural conditions for certain spellings.

As for the substance of (4) and (5) it seems to me that the main difference consists in our readiness to use morphological terms for formulating the rules.[5] Since it would take too much space to comment on this in detail, I want to discuss only one point at some length.

Take the spelling of [us] in *Bus* (4eß2). This spelling is unusual according to (4) since the plural form *Busse* also has an [s], so we would have to write

Buß. The explanation would be that *Bus* is a foreign spelling. This explana tion seems to be reasonable since indeed we have many words with *us* which are marked morphologically as 'foreign'. This can be concluded from the fact that these words have an unusual plural, i.e. a plural without Umlaut (see 6a), as we normally have it (see 6b).

(6) a. *Omnibus–Omnibusse, Autobus, Fidibus, Habitus, Praktikus, Physikus, Krösus*
    b. *Kuß–Küsse, Schluß, Guß, Fluß, Nuß*

in (6a), *us* or *bus* are morphologically analyzed (and partly reanalyzed) as nominative singular affixes with the plural counterpart *usse*. So the forms in (6a) are certainly marked as foreign, but they are integrated into the morphological system in a way that differs from other words with *us* eg. those from scientific terminologies like *Kasus, Genus* etc.

This could be an argument for understanding the *us*-writing as 'foreign'. But, on the other hand, we also have many foreign words with an ⟨ß⟩, where ⟨ß⟩ is used in accordance with our orthogaphic rules. The forms in (7) show that ⟨ß⟩ is indeed used in foreign words if the structural conditions are met.

(7) *Prozeß, Streß, Abszeß, Stewardeß, Narziß, Expreß*

In my opinion, the spelling of the nouns in (6a) is not irregular, but fits the system very well. We write *nisse–nis* exactly like *usse–us,* and this too is not an exception, according to the orthography books. Quite generally, we seem to have the simple regularity that [s] is never writen as ⟨ß⟩ in an affix.[6] One can easily check this by considering all so-called exceptions in (4). The distribution of ⟨ß⟩ is then determined by the following facts (stated partly in morphological terms).

(8) a. in medial position, ⟨ß⟩ is determined phonetically
    b. in final position of stem morphemes, ⟨ß⟩ is determined morphonologically
    c. ⟨ß⟩ normally occurs *only* in stem morphemes
    d. if ⟨ß⟩ occurs outside stem morphemes, there are special reasons for this ('semantic' principle for *daß*).

These results clearly indicate that certain regularities of our writing system are stated in the most simple and adequate way if one refers to morphological categories or, more generally, to genuinely morphological distinctions. As the greatest unit relevant for the writing system, we have word forms. All structural phenomena which go beyond word forms are irrelevant for the writing system, as far as spelling is concerned. Within word forms, we have to rely on morphological categories such as stem and affix. I am pretty sure that there are many other rules of orthography which make reference to this distinction, e.g., rules for the doubling of consonants. Although this hypothesis cannot be confirmed at present, it should not be too surprising if it turned out to be true. With respect to their internal structure, affixes form a separate class of morphological units anyway, by what are called morpheme structure conditions, cf. Booij (1977: 22ff.)

Notes

1. With respect to German, consider for instance the collections of quotations from the literature given in Müller 1978 and Kohrt 1979.
2. In what follows, '[a]' denotes the phonetic segment *a*, '⟨a⟩' denotes the graphemic segment *a*, and '/a/' denotes the phonological segment *a* or simply 'the sound segment' *a* without specification of level of representation. Where no misinterpretations can arise, '⟨ ⟩' will often be omitted.
3. The word form as the domain for GPK rules can be exceeded if this is marked by a special character like the apostrophe. It is then possible that a rule for vowel reduction, which is a close relative of geminate reduction, is relevant for graphemics (see for instance French *Avenue d'Espagne, l'eau*).
4. With respect to spelling, things are completely different from English anyway since there is a clear phonetic difference in German between *-or* [o:ə̯] and *-er* [ɐ].
5. This seems also to be the main difference with respect to the most comprehensive study about the graphemic representation of [s] in German, which is found in Müller 1978. Like Eichler, Müller (1978:11) speaks of 'medial position', 'final position', etc., without referring to any other morphological units than word forms. Therefore, he is not able to systematically separate the distribution of ⟨s⟩ and ⟨ß⟩. Furthermore, Müller always states necessary conditions for the distribution of ⟨s⟩, ⟨ss⟩, and ⟨ß⟩, not sufficient ones. On the other hand, he gives some informal hints as to the relevance of morphosyntactic categories for the distribution of ⟨s⟩ (1978: 26).
6. Forms like *Stewardeß, Baroneß* are no counter-examples to this regularity since *-eß* should not be considered as a German affix, despite the fact that we also have *Steward* and *Baron* (cf. Plank 1980:113ff.).
   The form *Bus* has to be treated as analogous to the forms in (6a), though it certainly does not contain two morphemes.

References

Aronoff, Mark
1976 *Word Formation in Generative Grammar.* Cambridge, Mass.: MIT Press.

Aronoff, Mark
1978 "An English spelling convention." *Linguistic Inquiry* 9: 229-303.

Bierwisch, Manfred
1972 "Schriftstruktur und Phonologie." *Probleme und Ergebnisse der Psychologie* 43: 21–44. Also in A. Hofer, ed., *Lesenlernen.* Düsseldorf: Schwann (1976), pp. 50–81.

Booji, G.E.
1977 *Dutch Morphology. A Study of Word Formation in Generative Grammar.* Lisse: De Ridder.

Chomsky, Noam and Halle, Morris
1968 *The Sound Pattern of English.* New York: Harper & Row.
Eichler, Wolfgang
1978 *Rechtschreibung und Rechtschreibunterricht.* Königstein: Scriptor.
Haas, William
1970 *Phono-Graphic Translation.* Manchester: Manchester University Press.
1975 'Writing: the basic options.' In W. Haas, ed., *Writing without Letters.* Manchester: Manchester University Press, pp. 131–208.
Kohrt, Manfred
1978 Generative Phonologie und deutsche Orthografie. *Münstersches Logbuch zur Linguistik* 1: 49–76. (University of Münster).
Kohrt, Manfred
1979 "Rechtschreibung und 'phonologisches Prinzip'." *Osnabrücker Beiträge zur Sprachtheorie* 13: 1–27. (University of Osnabrück).
Lieb, Hans-Heinrich
1977 *Outline of Integrational Linguistics.* Fachbereich 16 der FU Berlin (= *LAB 9*).
Mentrup, Wolfgang
1968 *Die Regeln der deutschen Rechtschreibung.* Mannheim: Bibliographisches Institut.
Motsch, Wolfgang
1977 "Ein Plädoyer für die Beschreibung von Wortbildungen auf der Grundlage des Lexikons." In H. Brekle & D. Kastovsky, eds., *Perspektiven der Wortbildungsforschung.* Wuppertal: Bouvier, pp. 180–202.
Müller, Rolf
1978 "Die *s*-Zeichen in der Linguistik und Didaktik der deutschen Schriftsprache." In *Laut und Schrift in Dialekt und Standardsprache.* Wiesbaden: Steiner, pp. 7–54 (= *Zeitschrift für Dialektologie und Linguistik,* Beiheft N.F. 27).
Plank, Frans
1981 Morphologische (Ir-)Regularitäten. Aspekte des Wortstrukturtheorie. Tübingen: Narr. (Diss. Hannover 1980)
Wurzel, Wolfgang Ulrich
1970 *Studien zur deutschen Lautstruktur.* Berlin (GDR) (= *Studia Grammatica VIII*).

Part Two.

Historical aspects of writing

JACK GOODY

Literacy and achivement in the Ancient World

Abstract

The 'literacy thesis' attempts to relate, in specific ways, certain of the achievements of 'civilization' to changes in the means and mode of communication, and in particular to the acquisition of different forms of writing. One important change was the introduction of the alphabet, which various scholars have linked to features of Greek culture. Recent research, however, suggests that the Proto-Canaanite consonantal alphabet, invented c. 1500 B.C., had almost as great potentialities as the vowel plus consonantal alphabet of the Greeks. Moreover, some of the Greek achievements themselves must be related more strongly to the work of their predecessors, including that done by means of the clumsier logographic system of cuneiform writing.

Lloyd's work on the origins and development of Greek science attributes those achievements to the adoption of general scepticism, to the use of specific forms of proof and demonstration, and to the modes of argument employed in a political-legal context. An example from Babylonia is taken to suggest that these modes of proof were already in use at an earlier period and that they were closely linked to the development of writing, as was the extension of 'scepticism'. We need to modify not only the idea of the uniqueness of the Greek alphabet but also the uniqueness of their intellectual achievement. Both rested firmly on earlier developments in the Near East.

I want to have a further look at what is crudely known as the 'literacy thesis' in relation to the Ancient World. The phrase is crude because the variable that one is interested in investigating relates to a series of changes in the way human beings communicate with one another, and the effect these have upon the content and style of communication, and upon social life in general. So that we should not think of a simple binary shift between oral and literate, but a whole sequence of changes that have to be defined in terms of the means of communication (or what I have also called the technology of the intellect) and the mode of communication, if by that sybylline phrase I can cover elements of social organisation and ideology that may inhibit or favour the adoption of a specific technology, the realisation of its full potential, and the opportunity for its further development.

It has been suggested that in placing so much emphasis on literacy in an attempt to face up to the differences between what have been described as primitive and advanced, traditional and modern societies, we are simply replacing one dichotomy, one set of binarisms, by another. That is not the case; we are concerned with a whole set of changes, from clay to papyrus, for example, as well as with what in a Popperian way I am going for the moment to call closed and open, religious or ideological systems.

In any case I would argue that even if I were simply replacing one set by another, at least this dichotomy attempts to offer some kind of general explanation; it implies a statement of a causal rather than simply a descriptive kind. It points to a mechanism by which the difference came about, not simply in Greece or Babylonia, but elsewhere.

By the phrase 'pointing to a mechanism' I don't mean that I am offering a mechanistic, deterministic, explanation. Those who work in the humanities and social sciences are too apt to talk in such terms, in monocausal terms, because their mode of discourse (linear exposition by the written word) makes it difficult to present a multifactorial analysis except in a vague and eclectic manner. But essentially we should be involved in weighting one variable against another – it is our techniques and data that inhibit us from going very far in this direction.

In considering this thesis, there are at least two important developments since the article by Watt and myself, published in 1963, and since the work by Havelock, and these suggestions ought to be considered, if not accepted. Both are the results of the work of Semitic scholars. One should remember that it was the Afro-Asiatic languages (which include Semitic) that were widely used in the early development of writing in the Near East (apart of course from the very early use of Sumerian).

The first point has to do with the date and origin of the Greek alphabet. Received opinion, which we earlier followed, has it that the Greeks adopted the Phoenician alphabet around 750 B.C. This date fits with local archaeological evidence, that is, with the material from inscriptions recorded by Jeffrey (1961). It fits with certain historical data, and with the idea of a Dark Age between the loss of Linear B c. 1100 and the adoption of the alphabet, a period of some 350 years, equivalent to the gap between the time of Shakespeare and the present day.

But the hypothesis does not fit with certain other data. First, the distribution of Phoenician throughout the Mediterranean is held by some to have occurred at least a century earlier, possibly more. According to F. M. Cross (1974), a fragmentary stele from Nora in Sardinia (*not* the Nora Stone of the 9th century B.C.), "can be no later than the eleventh century B.C." (1974: 492).

Second, the hypothesis does not fit with the supposedly archaic features of the Greek script which looks to many Semiticists as though it has been borrowed much earlier. We can put the technical arguments in the following way. Many modern scholars of the ancient Greek script have followed Rhys Carpenter who, on the basis of the similarity of the letters, argued for a Semitic script borrowed during the eighth century (Carpenter 1933; Jeffrey 1961: 15). Negative support for this date was provided by the absence of earlier Greek texts, obviously an important consideration. Nevertheless, Semiticists like Albright, Cross, Driver and Gelb advanced the date by a century because of the wide diffusion of the Phoenician alphabet throughout the Mediterranean in the ninth century (Albright 1949: 195–6; Gelb 1963: 180–181; Cross 1967: 23; McCarter 1975: 123ff.). More recently a study by Naveh makes a much more radical claim, dating the Greek borrowing as early as 1100 B.C. because of the paleographic similarity between the Greek script and the Proto-Canaanite letters of the Late Bronze Age, at a time when the script was not fixed as to direction. The major difficulty in this thesis has been the absence of a long-legged *kaf* in Proto-Canaanite which could serve as the archetype for the Greek form (1973: 7), for a suitable *kaf* had made its appearance only in the second half of the ninth century. The recent discovery of the twelfth century sherd at 'Izbet Ṣartaḥ in Palestine has removed this obstacle; the sherd is inscribed with 87 letters, making it a long alphabetic text of the period, and including an abecedary of 22 letters, one of which provides a suitable model for the missing form (Demsky n.d.).

We have treated the alphabet here (as Diringer and others have done) as a unique invention. There are good empirical reasons for such an assumption, in terms of its known history and present distribution. But there are also good theoretical ones, since the alphabet is a very abstract device; it consists of (in the case of English) 21 stops and 5 voiced elements. It also represents a terminal point in a scheme of 'logical' development. One reaches that point of high abstraction by starting with

i. logograms ('word signs')

ii. moving to syllables, signs for BA, BE etc.,

iii. then proceeding to the further break-down by using the initial (or other) letter to stand for the common phonetic element in a group of syllables; the alphabet may only emerge when the whole range of syllables are put together in a matrix, that is, in a graphic form consisting of the combination of x and y coordinates.

It is possible for a society to go straight to a syllabary as its first system of writing, and this type has many advantages for the process of learning to read. Even so, all the examples we know of appear to have been stimulated by contact with literate societies outside. But to go straight to a new alphabet, on the other hand, means jumping to a level of abstract analysis which only earlier literate operations appear to allow. This step is not a matter of invention *de novo*, nor does it follow automatically from earlier ones. However, it is implied in those steps and is not possible without them.

Before we ask what difference these developments make not simply to our earlier hypothesis but to an assessment of the role of changes in human communication, there is another point that needs to be considered. In arguing for the pre-eminent character of the Greek contributions to the alphabet, Watt and I were following a line of thought that was clearly congenial to the European experience and to the role of a classical education. Following Gelb, we accepted the term 'alphabet' as appropriate only to the Greek script, which provided signs for consonants and vowels, but not for the parent script that represented consonants alone. That position needs to be reconsidered. Current opinion would certainly modify the radical distinction in modes of writing, suggesting that the breaks between the logographic, syllabic, and alphabetic system are less clear cut than the terminology implies. The nature of a logographic system, in particular the number of signs involved, leads, at an early stage, to some kind of phonetic representation, signs signifying the sound rather than directly representing the semantic reference of a word. Such was the history of developments in the Near East. Since phonetic signs were additions to, rather than replacements of, other signs, their introduction added to the complexity of the script itself. Nevertheless, the phonetic principle was embedded in these scribal systems and the second millennium saw the development of an alphabet consisting of consonantal signs alone. Development is often a matter of shedding non-phonetic elements, of the gradual domination of the alphabet as the simplest and most efficient system. In this process of shedding non-alphabetic constituents, which makes possible the 'describalisation' of culture and lays the basis for an 'unrestricted literacy', social as well as technical factors play an important part.

The first systematic transcription of consonants was used to write down one of the Semitic languages all of which give great weight to consonantal roots. Should this be described as an alphabet? The point is arguable. It was only the later Greek alphabet that systematically provided graphemes for vowels as well as for consonants, and its comprehensive character was surely one element in making it such a versatile instrument for writing, and especially for reading. On the other hand the Greek alphabet is closely linked to the consonantal alphabet that was developed long before, from 1500 B.C. onwards. First used by scribes, that is to say, by the advocates and practitioners of a restricted literacy, these consonantal systems were adapted for scripts that became as flexible as the Greek, for another great branch used for writing down Aramaic gave birth to written Arabic as well as to all the alphabetic scripts of the Indian subcontinent, of South East Asia and much else besides. It was the adoption of these scripts that formed the background of that intellectual revolution of the East, the development of Sanskrit in the form in which we know it, as well as constituting the prerequisite and tool of Brahman authority, and at a later stage leading to the rise of Buddhism, Jainism, and of alternative modes of Hinduism.

The notion that the gap between the Greek and earlier 'alphabets' is less wide than many have assumed derives partly from the extensive diffusion of the consonantal alphabet, the Phoenician version in the West and the Aramaic in the East. These forms of writing exploded rapidly over a large part of the Eurasian continent in a manner very different from the impact of earlier systems. Their impact is indicated by the continuity of their form, for it is a remarkable fact that the purely arbitrary ordering of letters in the Roman alphabet, which, once memorized, gives us such a formidable power of recall of and control over information, has remained relatively constant from 1500 B.C. to the present day, that is, over a period of 3500 years. This ordering has no 'rational' justification, except that continuity, once established, pays off. Change the order to a more logical one, vowels first, then consonants, and you upset the organisation of every dictionary and telephone directory that has ever been produced. The arbitrary order ABC is basic to our understanding of the universe we have created.

But there is a third point. Not only may the Greek alphabet be earlier than we suspected, not only may it be closer in form to consonantal alphabets, but the previous types of writing may have had some of the liberating effects that certain authors (including Watt and I) attributed to alphabetic literacy. The point is obvious in the Chinese case. The logographic script inhibited the development of a democratic literate culture; it did not prevent the use of writing for achieving remarkable ends in the spheres of science, learning and literature. The same point seems to hold for the Ancient Near East. If so, we may need to modify our ideas not only about the uniqueness of the techniques available to the Greeks (i.e. their alphabet) but also of the uniqueness of their achievements in some other respects.

The question of the relationship between the achievement of the Greeks and the development of writing systems has been raised in G.E.R. Lloyd's distinguished work *Magic, Reason and Experience. Studies in the Origins and Development of Greek Science* (1979). To put a sensitively phrased thesis in simplistic terms, Lloyd argues that what happened in Greece constituted a defeat for magic and the victory of reason. Greek society developed a general scepticism which was related to the growth of specific methods of proof; and he suggests that since the consonantal alphabet was invented at an earlier point in time, we should not look there for the cause of this development but rather to the use of argument that characterized the judicial and political process.

My comments are directed to qualifying some aspects of the idea of the uniqueness of 'Greek science', specifically its procedures and assumptions; secondly, to relating the growth of science to growth in the development of more abstract writing systems; and thirdly, to relating the growth of Greek science to the freeing of literacy not only in a technical sense (through its possession of the first C.V. alphabet, a fact that seems to be of less importance than we had earlier supposed) but also in a wider sociological sense (that is, in the relative freedom from ecclesiastical or scribal control). At the same time, I do not wish to imply that everything is due to a unique causal factor; it is a matter of weighing one element against another. While accepting much of Lloyd's argument, including the importance of the argument itself, I would want to redress the balance in another direction.

The general problems that face us are encapsulated in the title of the book itself. Lloyd writes of the origins of Greek science. Yet he is also dealing with the origin of all science and its dissociation from magic. From the standpoint of explanation and fact, two different situations need to be distinguished. Are we trying to account for the origins of a form of knowledge (if we can agree for the moment that science is a form of systematized knowledge) or are we trying to account for the adoption of those forms in a particular place at a particular time, for example, the transfer and adaptation of Western Science to West Africa?

Lloyd is clearly concerned with the more general problem, and this he relates to criticisms directed at magic and to the growth of a general scepticism. At the same time, he is aware of the fact that to speak of 'the emergence of philosophy and science' in Greece is to use a shorthand phrase which requires some modification; first, because 'magic' still persisted, even among the scientists and philosophers (indeed the very concept was perhaps a shifting one), and second because science had already begun in Babylonia and Egypt. In this context, he talks of the continuities, and even the comparability of achievement, in the fields of medicine and astronomy; "in both cases, the production of *written* records transforms the situation as regards the preservation, diffusion and utilisation of the knowledge in question" (p. 232).

What earlier societies lacked, however, was "the notion of proof" (p. 230); they failed to acquire "a notion of rigourous demonstration" or "self-conscious methodologies" (p. 233). The Greeks, he recognizes,

> were certainly not the first to develop a complex mathematics – only the first to use, and then also to give a formal analysis of, a concept of mathematical demonstration. They were not the first to carry out careful observations in astronomy and medicine, only the first – eventually – to develop an explicit notion of empirical research and to debate its role in natural science. They were not the first to diagnose and treat some medical cases without reference to the postulated divine or daemonic agencies, only the first to express a category of the 'magical' and to attempt to exclude it from medicine (p. 232).

One of the problems lies in the use of the term 'magical' as an analytic tool. The title of Lloyd's book, *Magic, Reason and Experience*, provides a kind of counterpoint to Evans-Pritchard's famous empirical study of the Azande, *Magic, Witchcraft and Oracles*. The terms 'magic' and 'magical thinking' are common tools of discourse in the social sciences, in philosophy and in history, but they are concepts that require some elucidation.

In the language of the LoDagaa of Northern Ghana, there appears to be no equivalent that one can reasonably translate as 'magic'. Indeed the notion does harm to their own categories or forms of knowledge, for it cross-cuts their way of understanding the world. It is sometimes the case that a person will comment *o tera tĩĩ*, "he has medicine", referring to an individual's powers that we would describe as 'magical'. On the other hand, the same term is used for curative medicines, whether in the local or in the European repertoire (Goody, 1962).

Where and how did the term arise? As Lloyd explains, for Herodotus the *magoi* were a distinct tribe.

> But already in the fifth century *magos* and its derivatives came to be used pejoratively – often in association with . . . other words for vagabonds, tricksters and charlatans . . . – for deception, imposture and fraudulent claims for special knowledge . . . Thus these texts already exhibit what was to remain a prominent feature of the words from the *mag-* root (and of their Latin equivalents . . .). They were never clearly defined in terms of particular beliefs and practices, but were commonly used of such activities or claims to special knowledge as any particular author or speaker suspected of trickery or fraudulence. Pliny, for instance, attacks the 'magical art' at length . . . But that does not prevent him from including in his work a mass of homeopathic and sympathetic remedies,

> amulets and the like, which he is half inclined himself to believe to be efficacious; he often mentions, for example, the special, ritualistic procedures to be used in their collection and preparation . . . (1979: 13).

Even at this stage, the term 'magic' was used of the beliefs and predictions of other people, and hence of ideas and procedures that were foreign to one's own. The Coming of the Magi was the visit of non-Christians, of non-Jews, to pay homage to Christ. Already the concept had a slighting implication of beliefs that were not worthy to be held and practices not worthy to be undertaken; later on it designated beliefs and practices that lay outside the Church and were condemned by it. I would argue, therefore, that the LoDagaa have no concept of magic, not because they lack the necessary scepticism, but because they lack the bounded system of beliefs that excludes 'magic', or defines it as being 'other'. This lack is not so much a matter of 'tribe' (since, in West Africa, beliefs and practices cross the often shaded boundaries of groups in the same way as kola nuts, cloth or salt) but of the definition of a boundary between systems of belief that literacy encourages, even if this feature is not tied in any absolute way to religions of the Book.

The problem of magic is linked to that of scepticism. Examining the Presocratic texts, Lloyd is concerned with the growth of general scepticism and hence of rationality. He rightly points out that Keith Thomas remarked upon the sceptical approach to astrologers in sixteenth and seventeenth-century England, where the recognition that some were charlatans and quacks "only served to buttress the status of the system as a whole" (1971: 401). He recognises too that this attitude was not confined to 'rationalising' Europe in the throes of developing capitalism. Joseph Needham presents an account of the sceptical tradition in Chinese thought, on which Lloyd comments, "there are some admittedly rather limited signs of critical and rationalistic attitudes towards divination in two third-century writers . . . 'Today all the artful and foxy magicians of small talent, as well as the soothsayers, disseminate and reproduce diagrams and documents, falsely praising the records of prognostication. By deception and misinformation, by greed and dishonesty, they lead the ruler astray. How can we fail to suppress and banish such things?' ". The criticism of another Chinese writer is "strikingly similar" to that of Lucretius, while a third claims that, "As a matter of fact. diviners do not ask Heaven and Earth, nor have weeds or tortoise shells spiritual qualities"; at the same time this last writer rejects the idea that dead men become ghosts, although, in a different form, the notion is still part of many world religions.

However, Lloyd claims that while scepticism existed before the Greeks, as well as among other peoples, there is a significant difference between general and specific scepticism. He quotes the well-known passage from Evans-

Pritchard's study of the Azande where the author points out that, while individual witchdoctors might be frauds, there was no scepticism about witch-doctoring in general. "I particularly do not wish to give the impression that there is any one who disbelieves in witchdoctorhood. Most of my acquaintances believed that there are a few entirely reliable practitioners, but that the majority are quacks" (1937: 185). Evans-Pritchard went on to remark that "faith and scepticism are alike traditional. Scepticism explains failures of witchdoctors, and being directed towards particular witchdoctors even tends to support faith in others" (p. 193).

The difference, Lloyd claims, can be seen in the work of the Greek author of *On the Sacred Disease* who is against *all* purifiers, and against the idea that ritual purification can influence natural phenomena. The difference, moreover, constitutes "a paradigm switch". . " the Hippocratic writer rejects the notion of supernatural intervention in natural phenomena *as a whole*, as what might even be called a category mistake. Even when we have to deal with the divine, the divine is in no sense *super*natural. ." (1979: 26–27).

The last point can be most easily cleared away. The concept "supernatural'' is clearly one derived from the observer's point of view. It is difficult to see, despite the insistence of Levi-Strauss on the divide between nature and culture, or of other writers between the natural and the supernatural, that these concepts have any widespread or universal roots in the notions of the actors themselves; like 'sacred' and 'profane', they are analytic tools.

Returning to the difference between specific and general scepticism, on which great importance is placed, we should nöte that society as a whole did not reject intervention of supernatural agencies. Moreover any scepticism must be related to a particular universe, which is in essence a matter of definition. The common anthropological argument, expressed by Evans-Pritchard, that you can reject diviners without rejecting divination has something to be said for it. But only a limited amount. It is difficult so see why worries about the morality of a particular pope do not raise doubts about the papacy in general, do not lead to the asking of other questions. What is critical here is the way of recording these doubts, as well as the way of accounting for failures in divination, since the question of the nature of the evidence impinges on the question of scepticism. The certain knowledge that a notebook shows that my dreams have come true in only 5 out of 100 cases must modify my attitude towards dreams as indices of future events. In oral memory the many failures tend to get forgotten in favour of the occasional hits. It is the systematic recording (or even the possibility of so doing) rather than an attitude of mind that allows us to be "generally sceptical". In other words there is perhaps not the radical division between particular and general scepticism that the theory demands. Those differences that do exist need to be related to literacy (to recording), as well as to other specific factors.

It is to one such specific factor that Lloyd relates the general scepticism of the Greeks. This he connects with the nature of argument, especially as it appears in legal dispute. He concludes his book with the following remark:

> The sterility of much ancient scientific work is . . . often a result of the enquiry being conducted as a dispute with each contender single-mindedly advocating his own point of view. This is easy to say with hindsight: but an examination of the Greek evidence suggests that this very paradigm of the competitive debate may have provided the essential framework for the growth of natural science (p. 267). [It is related to] the experience of radical political debate and confrontation in small-scale, face-to-face societies (p. 266).

The argument is an interesting one. It is similar to that propounded by Robin Horton in replacing the open-closed dichotomy which he had used in an earlier discussion of the difference between Western science and African thought (1967; 1979), with the idea that certain circumstances bring about the opposition of theories, leading to cumulative learning. Horton sees 'science' as emerging in situations where there is a confrontation of theories, a clash of cosmologies, which produces the kind of ferment to which Lloyd refers. Similar arguments apply, in my view, to both formulations.

Undoubtedly the political situation in Greece was an important element in intellectual development. Even more important, perhaps, was the relatively free religious life, to which Lloyd refers in his opening chapter. There he writes,

> These texts show that in the sixth and early fifth centuries it was, within broad limits, perfectly possible both to criticise existing religious ideas and practices and to introduce new ones. To put it negatively, there was no dogmatic or systematic religious orthodoxy. Although there were certain widespread and deeply held beliefs, there was no common sacred book, no one true religion, represented by universally recognised spokesmen-priests or prophets and backed by an organised religious authority such as a church. The expression of new and quite individualistic views on god and the divine was, as our examples show, not only possible but quite common, and by the end of the fifth century we have evidence of a series of rationalistic accounts of the origin of religion (1979: 13–14).

The argument is convincing. Greece was on the periphery of the Ancient World, both politically and religiously. Just as the alphabet developed on the periphery of the great civilisations – if not in Sinai then at least in Syria – so too the freedom from the constraints of the great empires and their accompanying cults gave speculation a freer rein.

But the development of science is not simply a matter of speculation, of which there is often much evidence. As Lloyd repeatedly insists, it is also a matter of proof, evidence, of *recorded* scepticism that builds upon the thoughts of more than one man, of more than one doubter, and creates a body of new knowledge, a tradition of cumulative scepticism.

Clearly, ideas of evidence and proof are already present in oral societies, not to mention the Ancient Near East. In his account of Barotse jurisprudence (1955), Gluckman provides us with an excellent analysis of the use of evidence in an oral society. This use is different from that of European courts, with their restricted ideas of 'factual' relevance. Concepts of relevance are differently phrased in multiplex situations where people interact with one another in a variety of contexts, any one of which may be relevant to any other. I would again suggest that the differences in the nature of evidence in these societies is related in a fairly direct way to the absence of written codes; and, furthermore, that the forms of refutation linked by Lloyd to this politico-legal activity are again closely associated with the development of writing, including that used before the Greeks.

In his account of the early work *On the Sacred Disease*, the account which displays a general rather than a specific attack on purifiers, Lloyd points out how the author, who makes only a rare use of empirical evidence, supports his thesis by deploying "critical and destructive arguments to defeat his opponents" (p. 24). The first of these weapons is an implicit form of the argument later known as Modus Tollens: 'if A, then B; but not B; therefore not A'. This "powerful technique to refutation" was being utilized long before it was stated in general terms by Aristotle and formally analysed by the Stoics in the early Hellenistic period.

I would suggest that these forms of refutation are in many respects not so very different from the forms of argument found in oral societies. Proof, evidence, witnesses, forms of argument, all these are present. But they do not take the same shape; there is not the same degree of formalisation, largely because the Greek versions were developed in a written medium, which, partly because it operated in a single communicative channel, necessarily introduced an element of formalisation. The clue, or rather one clue, lies in the use of the letter A, an alphabetic sign, in the procedures themselves. These are signs of high generality, high abstraction, but considerable power. Try to formalise a general proposition using concrete data instead of, as in the present case, appealing to arbitrary data, to nonsense.

Try, too, expressing ideas in the form of the syllogism. Try comparing versions of the same story and perceiving the diversity and contradictions.

Try formulating opposition and analogy, in which both opposition (across) and analogy (down) exist in the same time-frame, let alone exist in the 'de-contextualised' way that is characteristic of the work of Pythagoreans and of anthropologists. Try all this *without* writing, without the use of graphemes.

In one sense this type of formalisation is implicit in writing. Certainly it seems to have appeared before the Greeks, with simpler systems of writing than the alphabet. One example is given in a recent article by J. Bottéro entitled "Les noms de Marduk, l'écriture et la 'logique' en Mésopotamie ancienne". The author analyses two tablets found in the Library of Assurbanipal, which consist of a 'commentary' on the fifty names of Marduk, listed in parallel form, the Sumerian and Akkadian terms side by side in columns. Here the process of offering equivalents, of adopting a translation procedure, has interesting consequences. "Dans cette culture, comme qui dirait diplopique, essentiellement enracinée dans la monde sumérien et épanouie dans l'univers accadien, de telles Listes ne formaient pas seulement l'armature de la lexicographie, mais, pour les lettres au moins, la propre assise de la pensée" (p. 15).

The procedure was essentially a literary one, if only because Sumerian was a 'dead language' and could hardly be anything else. . . . "dans le but d'obtenir, en partant du Nom, autant de sumérogrammes qu'il leur était necéssaire pour retrouver l'intégralité du texte de l'*En. el.*, les auteurs de notre pièce ont traité Iedit Nom en procédant suivant les règles de leur propre *écriture*" (p. 16). They proceeded by decomposing words, using of course determinatives which were written but not pronounced.

These lists produce a series of equations, of polarities and analogies, which the commentator tries to explain [my translation]:

> So we suggest that all the rare equivalences, unused (*inusuelles*), unknown, between the sumerograms in the first column and the Akkadian words in the second, have been in a way demonstrated and 'acquises', even 'conquises', either by our authors, or else before them by their lexigraphic authorities, by means of real modes of reasoning which employed, in essence, the procedure of analogy and successive equations of one term and another, ending up by placing in a relation of equivalence the first and last of the series: 'si A=B et si B=C, donc A=C' (p. 24).

These are the procedures by which our 'commentators' came to draw from the different names of Marduk the "integralité du texte consacré par l'*En. el.* à leur paraphrase", showing the way that, just as the universal encloses the particular, each of these names contains "la totalité des attributs, des qualités, des mérites et des hautes-faits de ce dieu: bref, de sa *Nature* telle que le Poème la détaille" (p. 24).

The argument is very similar to the one Lloyd is making about proof in connection with Modus Tollens. It is an argument that is correct but requires supplementation. I would suggest that:

(i) this particular formalisation is a product of writing, at whatever specific moment of historical time it may appear;

(ii) it appeared before the Greeks;

(iii) it was critical to science and to all systematic knowledge.

The earlier existence of such procedures would support Neugebauer's contention that we can speak of the development of science in the Ancient Near East. But what sort of science? He himself argues for the creation of "ancient science" in the Hellenistic period, "where a form of science was developed which later spread over an area reaching from India to Western Europe" and remained dominant until the creation of "modern science in the time of Newton" (1969: 1). But there was a yet older science, if by that expression we mean systematised knowledge, stemming from earlier Oriental civilisation. Of course, knowledge that is systematised to a certain degree existed and exists in oral cultures. I refer here to the kind of systematisation, developed before the Hellenistic period, whose nature is indicated by the titles to the chapters of Neugebauer's book on the exact sciences in antiquity: "Babylonian Mathematics", "Egyptian Mathematics and Astronomy", "Babylonian Astronomy". In addition, we find developments in the fields of medicine and the natural sciences, in the study of drugs, plants and stones. The first advances are critically dependent upon recording natural phenomena, while the formal classification of the constituent elements of the world seems implicit in the whole use of lists that dominates Sumerian and Akkadian literary work to such an extent that it gave birth to a branch of knowledge known as *Listenwissenschaft*. But it is astronomy that Neugebauer regards as "the most important force in the development of science since its origin sometime around 500 B.C. to the days of Laplace. . ." (1969: 2). Significantly, astronomy which had been closely connected with divination (1969: 101–102), was developed on the basis of a series of mathematical operations (the early texts dating from 1800 B.C.) and observational records (from 700 B.C.), producing a consistent mathematical theory around 500 B.C. These developments gained little from the invention of the alphabet; indeed, mathematics rests on universal logographic symbols rather than restricted phonetic ones.

I have used the opportunity to comment upon part of the discussion in Lloyd's important book in order to rectify some aspects of the argument put forward by Watt and myself respecting the Greek achievement. The invention of the Greek alphabet, while clearly marking an important advance, was a less dramatic technical event than we claimed. But then some aspects of the Greek achievement were also less unique, as researches into earlier literacy can only make increasingly clear.

Of course, other important factors in the Greek situation led to the development and use of this type of proof or demonstration at this particular time. Here the periphery argument seems to me strong, so does the related argument concerning the nature of political legal and religious institutions. But without wishing to fall into the jargon of necessary and sufficient causes, these developments are all linked to communication in the written mode. Moreover, these changes did not all occur at once; the struggle against 'magic' did not only take place in Greece: it occurred in China, among the Romans (Christian and pagan), and also at the time of the European Renaissance (Thomas 1971). It was a continuous struggle, for reasons to do with the God who failed ('magic' at times representing an alternative as well as a rejected belief) and the gradual adoption of more complex modes of discrimination among 'theories'.

The struggle continued long after the decline of Greece; the battle wasn't won there and then, nor perhaps even now. Indeed, was there ever a general change of the kind that most theorists want to explain? Was there really a sudden change in modes of *thought*, just like that, as distinct from ways of thinking?

The Greek achievement has to be seen in the context of other achievements, other attempts to systematise knowledge. In these achievements, writing was the *sine qua non*. It made possible a special kind of debate, not, I think, based exclusively on a particular political system, nor upon the clash of cultures in a general sense, but upon the framed opposition of theories which writing makes possible. Writing renders contradiction and proof explicit – the ideas themselves are certainly present in oral societies – and it not only makes possible a particular type of formalised proof (e.g. Modus Tollens), it also accumulates and records these proofs for future generations and for further operations.

References

Albright, W.F.
1949 *The Archaeology of Palestine.* Harmondsworth, Middlesex: Penguin Books.
Bottéro, J.
1977 "Les noms de Marduk, l'écriture et la 'logique' en Mésopotamie ancienne." *Ancient Near Eastern Studies in Memory of J.J. Finkelstein.* Connecticut Academy of Arts and Sciences, Memoir 19: 5–27.
Carpenter, R.
1933 "The antiquity of the Greek alphabet." *American Journal of Archaeology* 37: 8–29.
Cross, F.M.
1967 "The origin and early evolution of the alphabet." *Eretz-Israel* 8 : 8–24.

1974 "Leaves from an epigraphist's notebook: the oldest Phoenician inscription from the Western Mediterranean" *The Catholic Biblical Quarterly* 36: 490–93.

Demsky, A.
n.d. A Proto-Canaanite ABECEDARY dating from the period of the Judges. MS.

Evans-Pritchard, E.E.
1937 *Magic, Witchcraft and Oracles among the Azande.* Oxford: The Clarendon Press.

Gelb, I.J.
1963 *A Study of Writing* (2nd ed.). Chicago, London: The University of Chicago Press.

Goody, J.R.
1962 *Death, Property and the Ancestors.* Stanford: Stanford University Press.

Goody, J.R. and Watt, I.P.
1963 "The consequences of literacy". *Comparative Studies in Society and History* 5: 304–345.

Gluckman, M.
1955 *The Judicial Process among the Barotse of Northern Rhodesia.* Manchester; published on behalf of the Institute for Social Research, University of Zambia, by Manchester University Press.

Horton, R.
1967 "African traditional thought and western science". *Africa* 37: 50–71, 155–187.

Jeffrey, L.H.
1961 *The Local Scripts of Archaic Greece.* Oxford: Clarendon Press.

Lloyd, G.E.R.
1979 *Magic, Reason and Experience. Studies in the Origins and Development of Greek Science.* Cambridge: Cambridge University Press.

McCarter, P.K.
1975 *The Antiquity of the Greek Alphabet and the Early Scripts.* Missoula (Montana): Scholars Press.

Narveh, J.
1973 "Some Semitic epigraphical considerations in the antiquity of the Greek alphabet". *American Journal of Archaeology* 77: 1–8.

Neugebauer, O.
1969 *The Exact Sciences in Antiquity* (2nd ed.). New York: Dover Publications.

Thomas, K.
1971 *Religion and the Decline of Magic.* London: Weidenfeld & Nicolson.

KONRAD EHLICH

Development of writing as social problem solving*

Abstract

The Ancient Near Eastern writing systems give a good example of the development of writing systems in general. Writing systems are the result of social efforts to overcome the transient character of speech acts. Starting from ancient "count stones" (9000-2000 B.C.), the Sumerian cuneiform script was created as a complex, mainly logographic, system of language representation. The strategy of problem solving which was applied by the inventors of the cuneiform script can be analyzed semiotically. The complex nature of the linguistic signs proved the logographic system to be insufficient. In consequence, the phonic dimension of the linguistic sign was made use of to establish better writing systems. The Akkadian syllabic script was a first but unsatisfactory solution which followed this line of development. The Semitic consonant script constituted a qualitatively new solution which was further elaborated with the type of the Greek consonant-vowel alphabet.

1. *The development of writing systems in the Near East*

The "fertile crescent", which extends from Egypt through Palestine to Mesopotamia, is an area which produced the earliest of mankind's highly-developed cultures. Associated with the emergence of these cultures was the development of a number of writing systems in this area – systems which exhibit the most diverse structures and the influence of which can be seen to this day in the writing of a large part of the world's people. If we include the Iranian area on the one hand, and the Mediterranean (partly colonized by the Phoenicians and partly captured by the Greeks and Romans) on the other hand, as the border of this Near Eastern cultural center, we have a region providing examples of the fundamental structures of writing systems in general, and of the transition from one structure to another. Thus it lends itself to an investigation of principal characteristics in the development and dissemination of writing systems.

In the following, I single out one aspect of this subject, namely the systematic ways in which writing systems were developed and modified. Thus I am not concerned with the facts as such (facts established in a series of discoveries and deciphering efforts),[1] but rather with tracing their internal relationships. I will focus on writing as 'social problem-solving';[2] a working out of a means of overcoming certain limitations of speech activity, in particular its evanescence (see Section 2). The various writing systems of the Near East attempt to solve this problem in different ways, and the diverse forms these problem solutions take are the result of complex, intertwined, systematic *and* random historical impulses.

As a means of reconstructing the complex history in its internal order, I am asking how the evanescence of language became a problem for the speakers of various languages, and how they tried to solve this problem.

2. *Overcoming the evanescence of speech*

Speech is evanescent in that speech acts are bound to speech situations (Bühler 1934). The evanescence of spoken language runs counter to any need for promulgation. However, while speech acts are bound to speech situations, language contains a *potential* that transcends the immediate speech situation, a potential which is made use of in the linguistically mediated organization of memory. This organisation brings to the level of consciousness linguistic possibilities far beyond the immediate use of language. These possibilities become mobilized upon the emergence of a need for their use. This is exactly the case with all attempts to promulgate speech acts and knowledge in a way which overcomes the immediate *origo* of the *hic et nunc* (Bühler 1934). The need for promulgation creates its own linguistic form, and the form in which the speech situation is transcended is the *text.* Thus, the release of language from the immediate speech situation is an analytical stipulation for the process known as the production of texts (cf. Ehlich 1979, Section 6). Texts, then, are not tied to writing. Oral tradition makes texts out of speech acts, as do any acts of writing. Those texts which were essential for a society were long preserved orally for re-application across speech situations, as for example cultic enactions, etc. The problem of making speech permanent is thus partially solved. The solution is a partial one for a number of reasons and is adequate only as long as there is a comparatively small number of texts to transmit.

3. *On the threshold of writing: "count stones"*

The oral problem solution is adequate for those speech acts which are integrated into repetitive speech situations. However, it is not applicable to occasional, contingent speech acts (acts which are often repeated as "type" but in each case are different as "token") which nevertheless need to be preserved. At this very point, the oral procedure breaks down – and here lies one important motivation for inventing writing.

I am speaking of simple economic transactions such as became necessary under the more highly developed social and economic conditions of the centralized high river cultures which had developed the division of labor to a relatively great extent. The delivery of tribute to the representatives of the society, priests or kings, required certification; markings were necessary to record the status of the accounts. It appears that, over thousands of years, a primitive "bookkeeping system" developed. From this, according to all we know at present, the first written characters originated in Mesopotamia.

Denise Schmandt-Besserat collected and systematically analyzed in minute detail (cf. as overview Schmandt-Besserat 1978) a large number of individual documents from throughout the Near East. The fascinating result of this research is the working out of a system of pre-writing bookkeeping using small geometric and abstract representations, figures that first appeared in the 9th millennium B.C. and that were used in Sumerian cities such as Kish up to the 2nd millennium B.C. They were known as "count stones". Minute examination of the individual finds and some texts, found, for example, in Nuzi, allow reconstructions of the way these count stones were used:

> In addition to the scribes' elaborate cuneiform records the palace administration had parallel tangible accounts. For example, one token of a particular kind might represent each of the animals in the palace herds. When new animals were born in the spring, the appropriate number of new tokens would be added; when animals were slaughtered, the appropriate number of tokens would be withdrawn.
> (Schmandt-Besserat 1978: 40)

This "bookkeeping system", admittedly, does not yet represent a system of writing. The individual count stones are above all simple representations of objects. They are *simple symbols* which satisfy in a direct way the classic definition of a symbol, that "something" stands "for something". This directness is abandoned only in a second step. Assuming the analyses made by Schmandt-Besserat prove to be correct, this process itself can be read out of the finds. Namely, in addition to the simple count stones complex forms for their storage were developed at a later time, so-called *"bullae"*, earthen vessels in which the count stones were collected. The vessels were sealed in order to prevent their contents from being tampered with. In this way, however, a new problem arose, namely, that it was impossible to tell from the outside of the vessel what it contained. To solve this, the clay, while still damp, was stamped with impressions of each of the count stones that were subsequently deposited in the vessel (Schmandt-Besserat 1978).

This led to an interesting development. The new form of representation raised the whole procedure to a qualitatively new level: the symbols on the outside of the hollow vessels were no longer symbols standing in direct representative relation to the objects (sheep, goats, grain, etc.), but were symbols that stood *for symbols* (namely, for the count stones in the vessel). In this way, the symbolic system as a whole was released from the directness of the pictorial representation. The symbols now were second-order symbols and therefore set the stage for a further development of which Schmandt-Besserat rightly observes:

> The bulla markings were clearly not invented to take the place of the token system of record keeping. Nevertheless, that is what happened. One can visualize the process. At first the innovation flourished because of its convenience: anyone could 'read' what tokens a bulla contained and how many without destroying the envelope and its seal impressions. What then happened was virtually inevitable, and the substitution of two-dimensional portrayals of the tokens for the tokens themselves would seem to have been the crucial link between the archaic recording system and writing. (1978: 47)

Through this substitution in a two-fold symbolic representation process, the prerequisite for a fundamental generalization was established: a *problem-solving potential* that allowed considerable expansions. They were advanced in the *Sumerian* writing development.

The count stones comprised, on the one hand, *object* representations (such as dog, stone vessel, cow, mat) and, on the other hand, representations of certain *numerical values* (especially in spherical form (see Fig. 3 in Holenstein,[3] this volume)). Numerical concepts are more than the representation of mere sensory perceptions, they include a mental processing that transcends the morphology of real entities, the form (or "gestalt") of things which can be perceived and reproduced in symbolic form. In that respect, an abstraction similar to (albeit not identical with) the transition from symbol to symbol-of-symbol can be seen in the numbers and their representation by means of counting symbols, though this problem solving strategy apparently had no direct effect on the other strategy. As the writing systems developed further, the system of numbers preserved its own individual structure (cf. Coulmas 1980).

Both developments – object representation and the representation of numerical values – were taken up when the early Sumerian writing system was developed. They can still be seen in the oldest preserved forms of writing. Morphologically (in the sense of the graphic-optical gestalt) the connection can be identified directly by comparing the oldest Sumerian written symbols and the count stones, as shown in Fig. 1 of this article and Fig. 3 in Holenstein *op. cit.* – the illustrations show, in juxtaposition, the count stones (left) and the corresponding Sumerian written symbols from the oldest epoch (right).

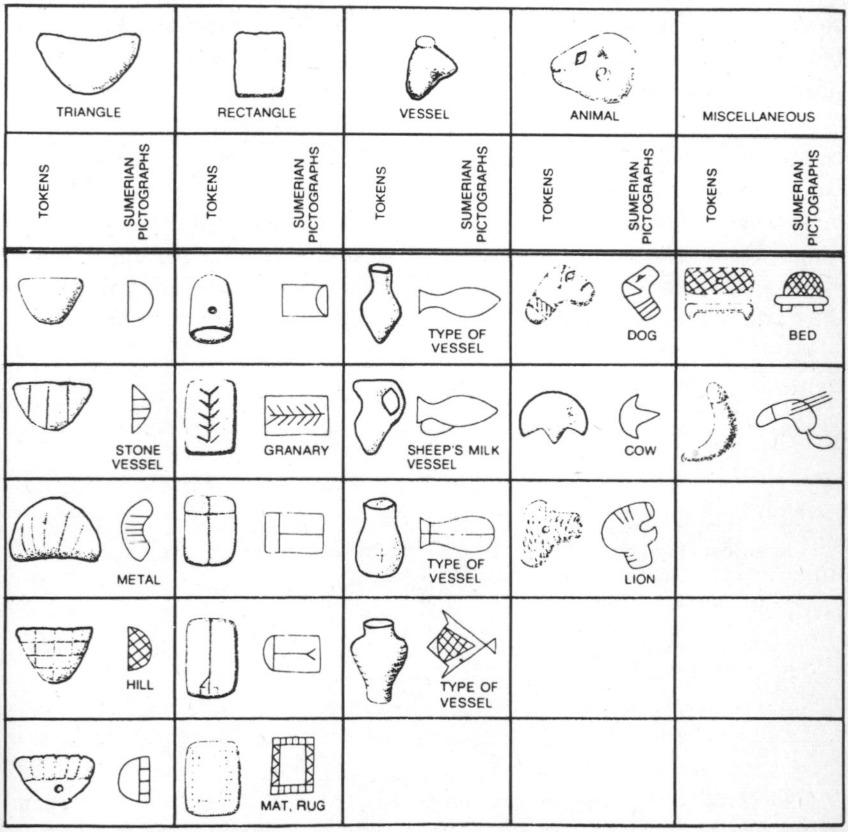

Figure 1. Count stones

4. *Systematic aspects of the transition to writing*

The relationship between symbol and object, as far as it has been discussed up to now, can be reconstructed as follows: an object O (an entity of reality) has a certain gestalt (or morphological structure in the visual, but not in the linguistic, sense) M_o. This gestalt is figuratively represented by means of an "image" A (primary visual symbol, "count stone"). The image itself can be duplicated as representation A′ of representation A. In this way, complex symbols are produced. Their connection with language, though, has not yet been explained. It is also complex. Roughly speaking, we can say that in the process of language development, the object O is transformed into the linguistic symbol S, which, for its part, represents the object O within discourse (the sigmatic aspect of symbols according to Klaus 1972; more generally speaking, the representational function of symbols according to Bühler 1934). Both representational forms, the pictorial- (or graphic-)symbolic and the linguistic, are not directly connected with one another. Nevertheless, just as the primary object O can be linguistically transformed, so can the images A and A′ of the object be linguistically transformed ("linguistically" not in the meta-sense in that the images are spoken of as images), but directly, in that the symbolic process of "standing for" is, in a way, reversed and that the object O is referred to by means of the images A or A′). Figure 2 illustrates the relationship mentioned.

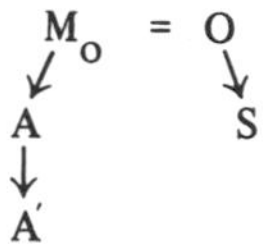

O = object of reality
A = count symbol
A′ = proto-written symbol
S = language symbol
M = visually perceivable gestalt
a→b a is transformed into b
O = M_o O has M

Figure 2.

Of interest here is the connection that is established between the graphic representation, especially in the form A′, and the language symbol S. While the image A is a relatively direct form of representation because of its homomorphy with M_o, both A′ and S are comparatively complex and 'indirect'. This communality of A′ and S will be an important condition for the subsequent step in development: A′ and S are brought into relation with one another (Figure 3).

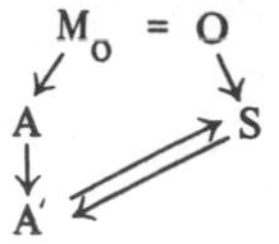

Figure 3.

The image A′, which owed its existence to the derivational connection with the gestalt of the object, is, for the observer, recognizable as a representation of the object. In that way it becomes – in an elementary sense – "*readable*". On the other hand, this relation is inverse: the linguistic symbol is transformed into images of the structure A′. This means, then, that spoken language becomes *writable*: *the conditions and the strategy for establishing a writing system are given.* Only the mutuality of the relation R (A′, S) constitutes the beginnings of writing in the true sense. When this reversal from "readability" (in the elementary sense) to writing is carried out, readability in its full sense is also effected.

With that, a qualitatively new method for solving the problem of the evanescence of speech has been discovered. Instead of speech acts being preserved and made transmittable by means of mental processes (especially memorizing) and by means of the use of corresponding linguistic forms (oral text forms), the storage is externalized, reified in an object, namely, the material written upon, which overcomes time and space and places the permanence of its own materiality in opposition to the impermanence of the speech event.

With this discovery, the transmission of speech events arrives at a new level. Generation upon generation has continued on the course once adopted, and has found further solutions which, however, are almost all based on the elementary discovery which is visible in Sumer's early history.

This problem solution became an enormous force. It gained such significance that, in time, it replaced the old solution in many areas – not without opposition and serious objections, but, generally speaking, with a growing intensity which appears to be losing strength only now, in our era, with the invention of new methods of visual representation (cf. Goody and Watt 1968).

5. *New problem situations: The complexity of the language symbol*

5.1 *The sound-meaning-writing unity*

The first epoch in the development of writing, then, found a *solution* for the elementary *problem* of transmission. The problem solution went qualitatively beyond the already found solution of *simple representation.* But it was in the idea of simple representation that all necessary prerequisites for the new problem solution were already present.

That new problem solution, however, did not prove to be the ultimate one. On the contrary, it contained a *potential for further problems.* The expression "potential" is to be understood here in the philosophical sense of the Latin "*potentia*" or the Greek "*dynamis*". The problems are inherent in the problem solution, but further circumstances are required to actualize them, to allow them to become real.

The main problem, once the mutual relationship between the proto-written symbol A′ and the language symbol S is established, lies in the *internal structure* of the linguistic symbol, which owes its communicative efficiency to a complex structure, the unity of sound and "meaning". Linguistically speaking, this problem is perhaps taken up most precisely in the psychological interpretation of this unity described by de Saussure et al. 1915, as "sound-image", and "concept" or "meaning image". I do not want to go into these problems here, especially that of the comprehension of meaning. "Meaning", in this sense, refers to de Saussure's differentiation, because it contributes to a better understanding of the further processes of the development of writing.

To begin with – on the systematic level of writing development shown in Figure 3 – the development of the simple practical use of the mutual relation of A′ and S could be regarded as being sufficient. The problem solution then appears to be *adequate.* Its result was a system of *visualizations of language relations.* A *language sign*, consisting of a *sound image* and a *meaning image*, corresponding to a *graphic symbol.*

One can speak of a system of *word-writing* or also – with regard to the representation of meaning – of an ideo-graphic system. Indeed, the complex language-writing unity shows a marked imbalance in favor of the *meaning* side of the language symbol. The language symbol describes the direct relation to the object represented; the *graphic* representation also reproduces qualities of the object. In this way, they resemble one another. On the other hand, the *phonic* aspect is unyielding in relation to the object; it conforms to its own rules.

5.2 *Abstraction and pictoriality*

In the *Sumerian tradition*, the previous development had already involved a considerable reduction regarding the transformation of visual characteristics of the objects into the written symbol, or, in other words, an abstraction from the gestalt M_0; the abstraction being especially dependent upon the aim of the entire representational process – that of facilitating the ephemeral purposes of "bookkeeping". This is also reflected in the further history of the Sumerian-Akkadian writing development. Falkenstein writes [my translation]:[4]

> For a writing system such as the Babylonian, which from the beginning was conceived as a serviceable writing system for the recording of economic transactions, the briefest way of writing was the best. The sign forms already underwent considerable changes in the 'archaic' era. This was due to the use of a thicker stylus which, although it produced more distinctive impressions, no longer permitted the production of the curved lines often found in the oldest writing period. These now had to be replaced by impressions which were at an angle to one another. At the same time, however, a conscious striving towards a cursive form of writing is noticeable. This tendency is so pronounced that, around 2500 B. C., in the texts from Suruppak (now Fara), it is already hardly possible to find symbols whose pictorial character is immediately recognizable. (1959: 7).

The early forms of Sumerian writing can be seen in Figure 4 (the so-called

Figure 4. The Hoffmann Tablet

Hoffmann Table, in D. Barton 1913: vii) and, in the comparison, Figure 5 in the left column. The other two columns reproduce examples of later developments which demonstrate, on the one hand, the process of the trans-

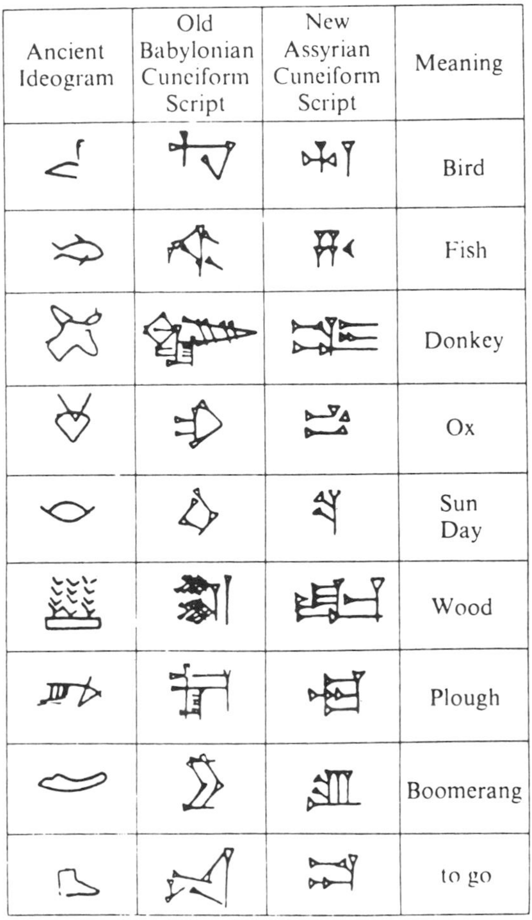
Ancient Ideogram
Old Babylonian Cuneiform Script
New Assyrian Cuneiform Script
Meaning
Bird
Fish
Donkey
Ox
Sun
Day
Wood
Plough
Boomerang
to go

Figure 5. Development from Early Sumerian writing to New Assyrian cuneiform script.

From *Die Schrift in Vergangenheit und Gegenwart* by H. Jensen.

formation into cuneiform writing and, on the other hand, the trend to simplification on the part of later writing reformers.

The *Egyptian* form of writing, or hieroglyphic writing, did not take this course. It maintained the pictoriality to a greater degree than did the Sumerian symbols. The word symbols, or ideograms, have a more obviously pictorial character: they are picto-grams. Thus they are much more closely related to the gestalt M_0 of the object to be represented and make a strong attempt to maintain its characteristics.

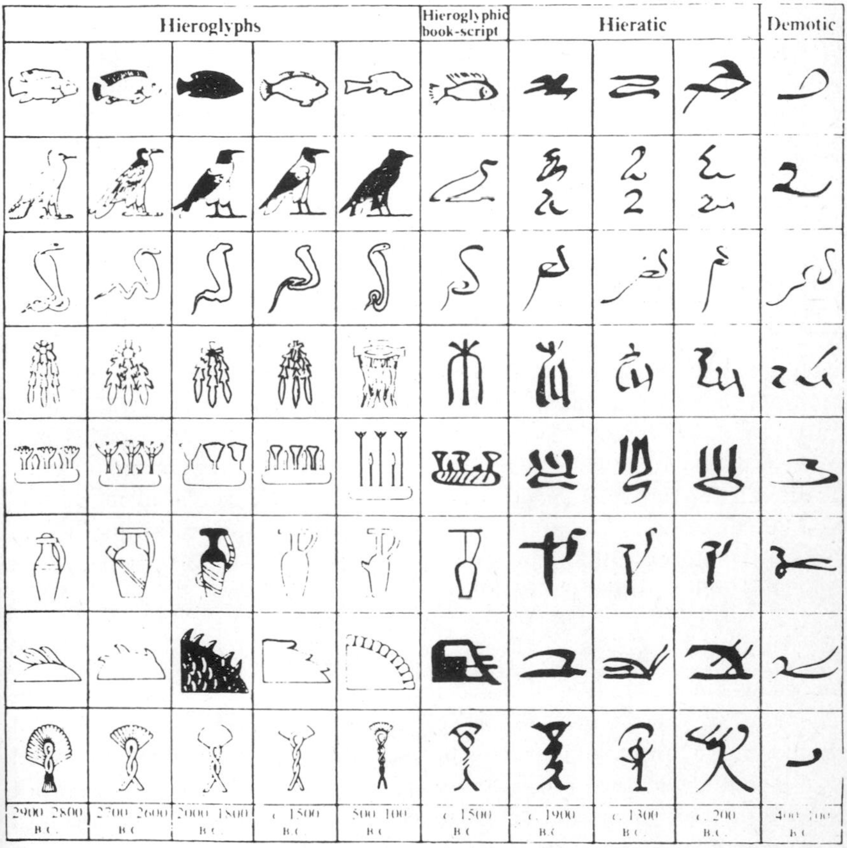

Figure 6. The development of Egyptian hieroglyphic writing

From *Die Schrift in Vergangenheit und Gegenwart* by H. Jensen, Copyright © 1958, VEB Deutscher Verlag der Wissenschaften. All rights reserved.

In Figure 6 we can distinguish the development of different Egyptian writing forms. The gestalt of the objects is recognizable right up to the latest Egyptian epoch (column 5). Although abstraction also appeared from the beginning of the second millennium B. C., it only occurred in the more strongly cursive form of Hieratic, up to the late Demotic script (cf. for a summary of the development, Jensen 1970: 54–81). Because of the nature of the writing materials (for example, ink and papyrus) the cursive variety developed in a completely different way from cuneiform. Its type bears more resemblance to the Chinese writing symbols, which were produced using similar materials (cf. Coulmas 1980: Part 2). Some of the reasons for the stronger orientation towards the gestalt may have to do with the different social aims of writing in early Egypt as compared with the Sumerian aims of "bookkeeping". However, we have little information on this subject. Following the pattern of Figure 2 and 3, the difference can be represented in Figure 7:

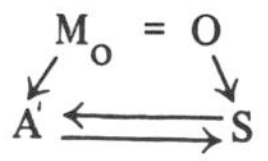

Figure 7.

The more marked abstraction in the Sumerian writing development proved to be a new *solution potential* for the further history of writing. But in their initial styles, both forms of writing development, cuneiform and hieroglyphic, offer in principle the same types of problem solution: they depend on an indirect relation between language sign and differently produced representations of the object. The same problem solution is displayed in the Chinese system (cf. Coulmas this volume). The similarity of the solutions includes a similarity with regard to the *problem potentials*.

5.3 *The written reproduction of nonvisual parts of reality*

Ideograms are relatively well suited to represent objects that, as "*res extensae*", (1) have visual-optical forms, (2) are lasting, and (3) can be reproduced by the "static" means of (partially abstracted) drawing, i.e., of symbolization in the above-mentioned sense. But there are aspects of reality that are not covered by the characterization of "res extensa". Languages provide means to "reproduce" them as well. The main classes are as follows:

(a) qualities;
(b) abstract ideas and positions;
(c) movements and conditions;
(d) complex facts and relations.

(e) In addition, a series of operative units is required to facilitate the processing of linguistic activity, to enable language to be an effective means for representation and communication.

Once the mutual relation of image A or A′ and the language sign S is established, the five classes (a) through (e) offer new problems that prove to be impediments to the course of the problem solution underway.

The ideographic writing systems reacted to these problems in very different ways. In part, the problem solutions are determined by the languages. It is well-known that languages are by no means identically structured (cf. Brettschneider 1980). On the contrary, very different methods are used in the various languages for the *linguistic* representation of the classes (a) through (d) and for the aims of class (e). These problem solutions now regain significance for the development of writing.

Sumerian is, much more than Egyptian, a language with oligosyllabically structured individual words and agglutinatingly structured formatives (Falkenstein 1959: 15). It thus lies between the isolating type, such as Chinese, and the inflecting type, such as Semitic. The Egyptian language, typologically situated between the Semitic and the Hamitic, is closer to the inflecting languages.

Oligosyllabic structures apparently favor the maintaining of logographic scripts. This proves to be just as much the case for Chinese as for Sumerian. If the logographic problem solution is maintained in principle, there follow a number of individual strategies which provide a means of approaching the problems relating to (a) through (e).

In a first phase (systematically speaking), the problems are scarcely relevant, namely, as long as the writing pertains to an extremely limited linguistic area. The writing needed for commercial transactions hardly requires those parts of language named in the classes (a) through (e) – with the exception of the abstract representation of numerical relationships discussed above, and the linguistic activities arising from their context, which give the writing a solidly *empractical* character: The "empraxy" is thus of major importance not only for speech acts (Bühler 1934) but also for elementary forms of writing. This constitutes, admittedly, a contradiction to the potential overcoming of the situational binding of speech acts which makes up the essence of writing. In consequence, as long as the graphic empraxy exists in this form, writing cannot fully develop its potential for transmitting language from one speech situation to another.

Clear answers to the questions mentioned were only necessary when there was a gradual release from empraxy. The answers were generally sought in the utilization of certain *analogizations* which abstract and transfer features of the primary writing form, i.e., the ideograms. Thus the problem solution consisted in systematically guiding the reader's association (with a certain degree of arbitrariness): Guiding the reader's associating aims towards standardized indentification patterns which enable the reader (a) to recognize that the pictogram or ideogram does not stand for what it directly represents and (b) to choose, in an appropriate way, a related alternative.

Figure 8. Egyptian Hieroglyphs

Figure 8 shows such a process: "cool" is represented by a pitcher with water flowing out of it (class (a)), "south" by a lily, the symbol for Upper Egypt (class (b)); motions are represented by selecting a characteristic moment from the process as a whole (class (c)). This last method uses accurate analytical observation; for example, "flying" is shown by means of a bird at the moment of lifting off from the ground, or "beating" by means of the stick in a man's raised hand. But the main problem which remains with this solution, is that many of the signs become equivocal. Over and above the pictorial convincingness, therefore, it is the *conventionality* of written symbols which is indispensable for their practical application. This is even clearer in the case of complex situations and relations (class (d)) such as, for example, "ruling", which is represented by a scepter, or "age" (a man with a staff), to say nothing of abstractions on higher levels.

In Sumerian, (Figure 9) combinations of two different symbols are often found, e.g., those for "mouth" and "bread" become the symbol for "eating": an additional facilitative strategy. The combination has the advantage, in con-

Figure 9. Compound sign information in Sumerian

From *Die Schrift in Vergangenheit und Gegenwart* by H. Jensen. Copyright © 1958, VEB Deutscher Verlag der Wissenschaften. All rights reserved.

trast to the other strategies, that it is already possible to recognize in its form the complex associational achievement.

6. *The reproduction of operational language units and the utilization of the sound aspect of the language sign*

6.1 *Use and disadvantage of phonically oriented writing symbols*

Whereas there are strategies to find writing symbols for classes (a) through (d), the situation is much more complicated with (e), the operative units of language such as, for example in Sumerian, the affixes (postpositions, prefixes and suffixes) and "particles". For some time, this difficulty was "solved" by simply not indicating these units in written texts (Falkenstein 1959: 21).

When this solution appeared to be no longer adequate, a completely new strategy was required. The strategies which led to the extension of symbols for the more complex relationships discussed so far had concentrated on the *meaning side* of the language sign, and on linking it with the graphic-pictorial representation of the visual form of the object as well as on the transfer of visual features by means of standardized sign recognition procedures which steer the reader's associations in a fixed way.

Thereafter, it was no longer the semantic but much more the *phonic* dimension which became important, and which was extracted from the complexity of the linguistic sign for the further production of writing. This change of solution strategy was made easier by the fact that the Sumerian language includes, among its monosyllabic words, words consisting of a single vowel. This oligosyllabic or, even more, the strongly monosyllabic character of Sumerian made possible a shift in emphasis: it was no longer the meaning side but the *sound side that was isolated* in order to work consecutively to the symbol that, uncoupled from the meaning side, was interpreted only phonetically.

The process of isolating the phonic side within the complex unity of written symbol, sound, and meaning was additionally eased by the fact that Sumerian includes a number of *homonyms* (which were possibly differentiated, however, by means of tones (cf. Falkenstein 1959: Section 6d)). To some extent, they could be substituted for one another: in this way, for example, the symbol for *ti* ("arrow"), an arrow, was used to write the homonym *ti*(*l*) ("life"). This process made it easy to functionalize symbols for the representation of the operative language units.

However, the problem solution generated a considerable new problem; namely, it led to an extraordinary degree of ambiguity in written documents. One written symbol allowed, in principle, several readings:

(a) a reading which refers to
   1. the original unity of the sound and meaning sides of the linguistic sign,
   2. its graphic representation form,
   3. the gestalt of the object named in the linguistic sign;

(b) a reading in which the connection between the meaning side and the gestalt of the object is dissolved and a second meaning is suggested by means of associative inference;

(c) a reading which eliminates the original meaning side while retaining the phonic side and which substitutes a new meaning that, however, usually has no illustrational gestalt of its own (as in the case of "*ti*" ("life"));

(d) a reading following the same procedure as in (c) but referring to an operational unit of language which is homonymous to another phonic item.

The possibilities are summarized in Figure 10.

Type	Object		Written Sign	Language Sign		
	Extra-linguistic	Gestalt		Meaning		Sound
				Referential	Intra-linguistic	
(a)	e	e	e	e		e
(b)	d	(d)	e	d		d
(c)	d		e	d		e
(d)			e		d	e

e = elementary d = differentiated

Figure 10.

This complex situation is the result of the attempt to make up for the shortcomings of the procedure which, originally, had presented itself as such a reasonable form of writing. Despite the unsatisfying state resulting from the new strategy, the transition to the phonic side is of considerable *fundamental* significance, since the course entered upon here involves a great solution potential for the further development of writing.

6.2 *Auxiliary solutions*

First, however, the resulting situation proved to be so problematic that new solutions had to be sought. They were not found in a fundamental reorientation but in the development of auxiliary solutions. The two most important were the expansion of *phonic writing* and the introduction of *determinatives.*

Once the possibility of a separation of the phonic-graphic complex from the total relationship of the symbolic unity was recognized, it was increasingly used to achieve phonic specification.

In this way, e.g., the symbol 𒀭 can be read either as "*an*" ("heaven") or as "*dingir*" ("god") (semantic multiplicity of type (a) vs. (b), whose construction, considering the religious ideas of the Sumerians, can easily be understood). In order to show which one of the two possible readings is meant, a second cuneiform symbol. e.g. that of "*na*", is added in the first case. The ambiguity is thus resolved for the reader, who knows that he should read "*an*", that is, the word that ends with the first consonant of the following symbol (Jensen 1970: 92). Or, with the addition of type (d), the reader has to read "*ana*", namely, "*an*" ("heaven") plus "*a*" ("in"), "in heaven" (Falkenstein 1959: 19f.; the doubling of the "n" which results from writing "*an*" plus "*na*" is, as far as can be discerned, of no consequence phonologically, Falkenstein ibid.). If, on the other hand, the reader finds a syllable symbol for "*ri*", then he, in the same way, knows that he should read "*dingir*" ("god").

Thus the difficulty arising through the introduction of the phonic reading is countered by the same strategy which led to its creation.

The case of the second auxiliary strategy, the *determinatives*, is different. These are symbols which indicate the semantic class membership of the preceding or following word. Thus, for example, the already mentioned "*dingir*" stands as a determinative next to the names of gods, "*lu*" ("man") next to the names of tribes, "*giš*" ("tree") next to the names of trees and wood products, and so on. The determinatives serve purely to assist in the better recognition and easier classification of the symbols. They thus give a sort of "reading instruction" which makes clear that they perform a mere auxiliary function that is supposed to help solve the problems of the previous problem solution.

7. *Old problem solutions and a new language type: Akkadian*

7.1 *An inconsistent syllabic writing system*

The Sumerian writing system next experienced a developmental impulse that came from without. The gradual conquest of Sumer by Semitic tribes which adopted the culture of those they defeated led to the application of the Sumerian writing forms to a language of a fundamentally different type, namely, the Semitic language of the Akkadians (later developed further into Babylonian and Assyrian). Like all other Semitic languages, Akkadian is an inflecting language with a very rich verbal morphology. Essentially, the meaning elements are fixed upon the *consonants* of the roots; the variety of concrete lexical and morphological units is created by means of *vocalic changes* and *affixes* (prefixes, affixes in the strict sense, suffixes, and a few infixes).

The writing forms created by the Sumerians were relatively ill-suited for such a language. Monosyllabism plays a completely subordinate role in the Semitic languages. Much more important is the clear recognition of the consonant patterns. In spite of this, the Akkadians adopted the Sumerian script and attempted to adapt it to new ends. This adaptation, however, was restricted to the limits of the Sumerian type of writing and did not lead to a fundamentally new problem solution type. This meant that the last mentioned way of phonic writing was considerably extended: The *syllabic writing* system was increasingly improved. Thus the Akkadian appropriation of cuneiform resulted in a writing system with a mainly syllabic character.

Along with this expansion, however, the limits were reinforced, thus new problem solution strategies were not possible. Besides the syllabic writing characteristics, the other presyllabic methods of writing remained in full force; indeed, they were broadened in that not only were the Sumerian expressions used for the readings, but the corresponding Semitic ones as well (thus, for example, as well as "*dingir*" ("god"), "*ilu*" ("god"), etc.). The development is very similar to that in Sino-Japanese (cf. Coulmas 1980, Section 3).

The result is a still stronger state of diffusion than was exhibited by the Sumerians. Each symbol now had such a variety of possible readings that the comprehension of the text was made extremely difficult. The situation can be made clear by means of an example from an Akkadian syllabary (Figure 11, based on Labat 1963: 48f.).

The five columns in Figure 11 on the left show the writing of the symbol in various epochs (the first column shows the oldest form, cf. Figure 3 above); the sixth column shows the symbol in its classic (Neo-Assyrian) form. In addition to the already described possibilities of reading (Section 6.2) for "*dingir*" and "*an*" ("heaven") the corresponding Semitic forms "*ilu*" ("god")

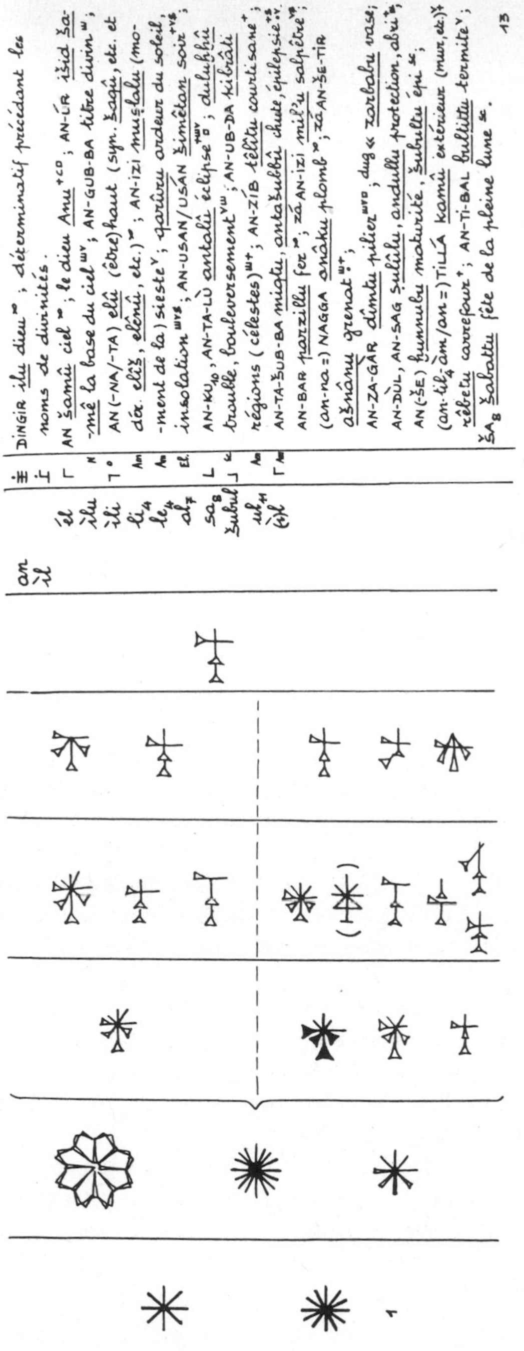

Figure 11. Entry from a Sumerian-Akkadic syllabary

From *Manuel d'épigraphie akkadienne* by R. Labat. Copyright © 1963, Imprimerie Nationale, Paris.

and "*šamu*" ("heaven") appear. From these, a series of additional syllabic readings of a phonic nature can be derived (column 7). Furthermore, the writing symbol appears in a number of additional readings with, in each case, a Sumerian and an Akkadian reading (column 9).

Thus the Akkadians attempted to approach the problem situation with a purely quantitative increase in the use of the already worked out problem solutions. On the whole, this method was not effective. Instead, the problem was made even more acute.

7.2 *Interim result: The Sumerian-Akkadian and the Egyptian situation*

The solution course taken in Egypt was similar to that in Sumer, but here the problem situation was aggravated by the fact that the linguistic structure was more in contrast to the uniform sound-meaning-writing symbol formation: Egyptian, as a language very like the Semitic, also works by means of the attachment of meanings to the root consonants. In addition, it is inflecting. Specifically, the Egyptians also managed to develop an elementary phonic script that comes close to the alphabet. Only the method of formation is somewhat different. It is not entire syllables (= words) that are used for the phonic writing, for, because of the language structure, monosyllabic expressions play too small a part for that. Instead, another problem solving procedure enters the picture. It is not that whole words, standing for themselves, are weakened on the meaning side in order to serve as phonic substitutes, but that the *initial sound* of an expression is separated from the rest of the word body (acrostychic method); the symbol that serves the written reproduction of the whole word is used as the symbol for that sound. This results in a "pseudoalphabet", as is shown in Figure 12.

But, just as in Sumer-Akkad, the existence of such a phonic writing possibility had no germinal consequences. Rather, the whole historically developed conglomeration of problem solving methods persisted, in that the individual procedures were used side by side and in combination with one another.

In both cases, therefore, the result of the solutions was a large number of new problems. This less than satisfying situation was apparently perceived by the users as being not so pressing that new solutions *had to* be sought. On the contrary, they contented themselves with the status quo already achieved and attempted to manage with it as well as possible.

That is a not wholly atypical phenomenon. Only when an elaborated alternative appears are the problem situations perceived anew. Otherwise, things remain as they are with the established solution refined, canonized and taught.

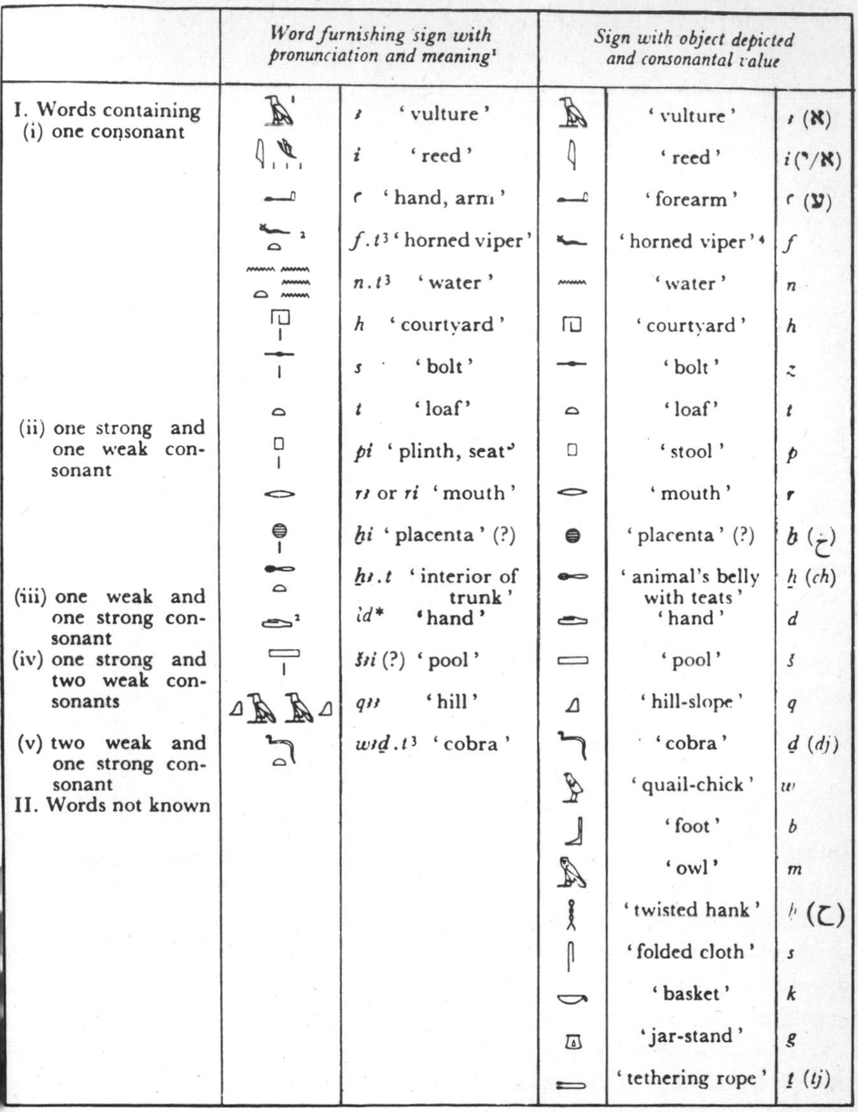

	Word furnishing sign with pronunciation and meaning[1]		Sign with object depicted and consonantal value		
I. Words containing (i) one consonant		ȝ 'vulture'		'vulture'	ȝ (א)
		i 'reed'		'reed'	i (י/א)
		ʿ 'hand, arm'		'forearm'	ʿ (ע)
		f.t[3] 'horned viper'		'horned viper'[4]	f
		n.t[3] 'water'		'water'	n
		h 'courtyard'		'courtyard'	h
		s 'bolt'		'bolt'	z
		t 'loaf'		'loaf'	t
(ii) one strong and one weak consonant		pi 'plinth, seat'		'stool'	p
		rȝ or ri 'mouth'		'mouth'	r
		ḫi 'placenta' (?)		'placenta' (?)	ḫ (خ)
		ḥȝ.t 'interior of trunk'		'animal's belly with teats'	ẖ (ch)
(iii) one weak and one strong consonant		ỉd* 'hand'		'hand'	d
(iv) one strong and two weak consonants		šȝi (?) 'pool'		'pool'	š
		qȝȝ 'hill'		'hill-slope'	q
(v) two weak and one strong consonant		wȝḏ.t[3] 'cobra'		'cobra'	ḏ (dj)
II. Words not known				'quail-chick'	w
				'foot'	b
				'owl'	m
				'twisted hank'	ḥ (ح)
				'folded cloth'	s
				'basket'	k
				'jar-stand'	g
				'tethering rope'	ṯ (tj)

[1] Taken from the most primitive known writing.
[2] Form not actually found but inferred.
[3] Final *t* indicating feminine gender (s. p. 158 n. 1).
[4] Or perhaps rather *wfi* 'horned viper'.

Figure 12. Egyptian 'pseudo-alphabet'

7.3 *"Conservatism" of writing*
Thus, the state of problem solutions then reached was unsatisfying – but it was, apart from a few exceptions, not unsatisfying enough to provoke drastic change.

The complex problem situation was not overcome in the writing system itself, but in the societal personnel who made use of the writing system. In both Sumer-Akkad and Egypt, the traditional needs of the entire society were taken care of by a specific class of the populace, the priests, officials, and especially the subgroup of "scribes" (cf. Driver 1976: 62–64). The early Sumerian "bookkeeping" was already handled in the temple, where the central organization was based. The members of these groups used the medium of writing, and it was especially made up for their professional activities. They received instruction in it at an early age. The acquisition of writing skills took place, therefore, with a view to later activity in connection with membership in such a group. In this way, the ability to write had a marked technical aspect related to the professional requirements of the scribe as an official; writing was, above all, professional knowledge. This coupling of writing with particular professional groups apparently had repercussions on the status quo at any given stage of the problem solution of writing development. Through the professional-linked transfer of writing ability, the continuity in the passing on of the problem solving strategies, once reached, was guaranteed. The often observed "conservatism" of writing systems probably had its roots here.

8. *Semitic consonant writing*

Up to the end of their history, the Sumerian-Akkadian and the Egyptian writing types retained the complex form described above. A qualitatively new step occurred, neither in the one nor in the other area, but on their borders, namely, in Palestine and in the Sinai region. It appears that the development took place in various locations. Unfortunately, the finds relating to the beginnings of the transition from the ideogram and syllable writing to the new type of writing are very incomplete and, furthermore, not always clearly interpretable. This is the case, above all, for the *protosinaitic* script (cf. Albright 1966). While, for example, Driver 1976, expresses in principle a positive opinion with regard to the decipherability of this script, Friedrich 1954, is extremely sceptical. This is not the place for an extensive presentation of the controversy. If the protosinaitic language is to be seen as Semitic in the sense of the readings of Gardiner, Grimme, and Sethe (cf. Friedrich 1954: pp. 140–142; Driver 1976: pp. 94–96), then we have in the protosinaitic inscriptions a significant link between the *Egyptian* system of writing

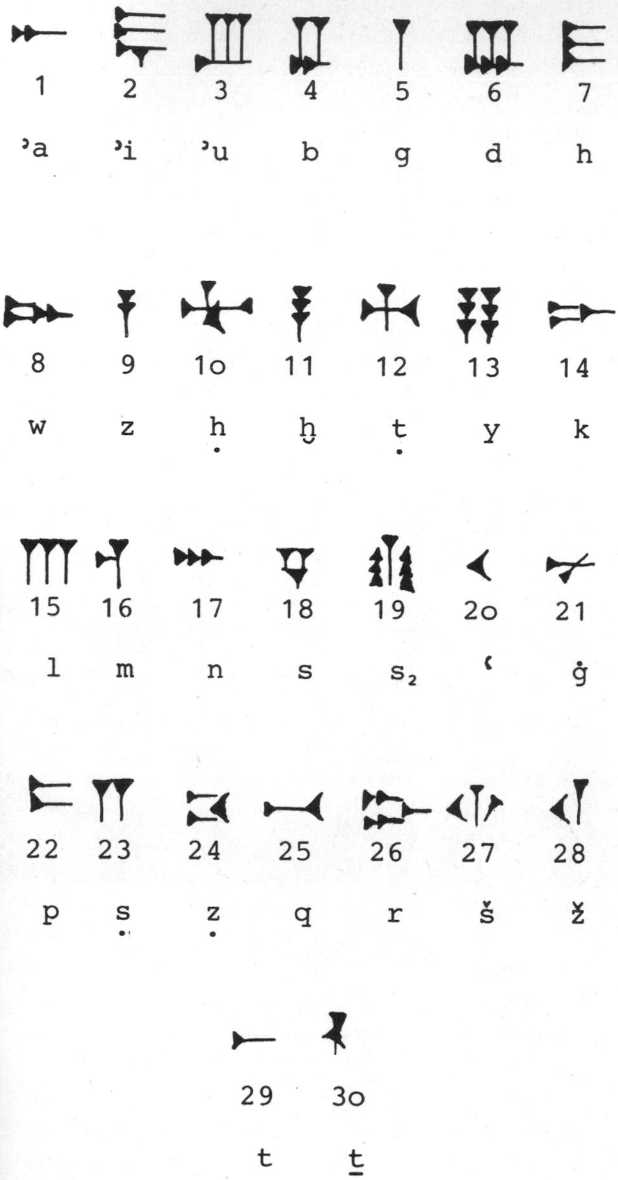

Figure 13. The Ugaritic Alphabet

and the later *Semitic consonant writing system.* We have no documentation of any kind for the *transition* of *cuneiform* from a syllabic to a consonant writing system. Only the completed result is documented in the texts, discovered in 1929, from *Ugarit* (a city on the North Syrian Mediterranean coast which existed until around 1400 B.C.).

The texts from Ugarit are produced with only 30 cuneiform signs. This already shows one of the central characteristics of the new writing system: its sign economy. The signs reproduce the *consonants* of the Ugaritic phoneme inventory. This corresponds to the general Semitic phonology. In the case of the Aleph (the glottal stop, which counts as a consonant in the Semitic languages), three vowel distinctions were undertaken even beyond that (q.v. Figure 13), Figure 14 shows the oldest surviving written alphabet, a small tablet from Ugarit upon which (perhaps as a learning exercise?) the cuneiform alphabet was imprinted (from Druet 1976: 11).

Figure 14. The oldest surviving written alphabet

The texts of the Ugaritic cuneiform tablets that have been found up to now illustrate the most varied text types, from simple economic/commercial texts through Ugaritic-Akkadian parallel lists to numerous mythological texts. The language of Ugarit is a Semitic language of the northwestern type (related to Hebrew and Phoenician-Punic). The problem posed in connection with the writing of Akkadian, namely the confrontation with an unsuitable writing system which had been developed for another type of language, was solved here in a *new and radical way*. The solution proved to be very effective, as most of the texts show. While the Akkadians, in a series of compromises, tried to adapt the inflexible representational means to their language and, at best, found a system of syllabic writing with numerous redundancies, the people of Ugarit (or their predecessors, who are unknown to us) changed the problem solving strategy; they recognized that the reproduction of central structural characteristics of their language was the *main problem* to be dealt with in seeking an adequate writing system. From the phonic writings of the Sumerian-Akkadian cuneiform script, the concentration on the phonic course was known to them as a *possible* solution which was not, however, worked out. In that way it was relatively easy for them to drop the reliance on both the meaning side of the linguistic sign and the visual gestalt of real objects when they established their writing system. Instead of getting lost again in the no longer viable problem solution from the early stages of the discovery of writing, they were able, through the concentration on the phonic side, to break through to a new solution. This led to a practical insight into the phonological side of the language. This, in turn, is suggested by characteristics of the Semitic language type itself. The known peculiarities of Semitic already demand of its speakers/hearers a comparatively analytic approach to the production and comprehension of utterances. The identification of the consonant structure is absolutely necessary, especially in order to recognize the meaning of the word or root semantics. Use could be made of this in the further development of the phonic-syllabic problem solution type. The consequence is the construction of *consonant alphabets.*

In this way, the history of writing is enhanced by a new and independent type containing a considerable potential for further problem solutions. Although its development was made possible by specific characteristics of the language type that was to be written, its use was not limited to that language type. On the contrary, it proved to be extraordinarily useful for other languages.

To conclude this section, let us ask about the linguistic-theoretical significance of the "Semitic discovery". The concentration on the phonic side was made at the expense of the material gestalt qualities of reality which were contained in the type A′ representations and entered into the written symbols. The release of cuneiform symbols from this relationship paid, on the form side, the same price. On the one hand, the writing symbols were developed into a system of a specific kind. On the other hand, however, this system was not consistently developed further. It inherited, as a kind of historical "birthmark", a variety of forms which now appeared only randomly. It was reproducible only through considerable mnemotechnic activity. The abstraction was advanced with the discovery and systematic development of single-sound symbols. To the same degree as this development was effected, the demands on memory could become less. Both were possible after the phonic syllable writing dissolved the complex unity of meaning-sound-symbol-form. The further development of the phonic representation led, as a result, to the written symbol being produced – from a systematic point of view – at another place. Writing made itself master of the internal mechanism of the formation of signs: The sound side of the language sign is, of course, the expression of a complex and abstract representation formation. In the development of the language system itself, the process of a simple analogization between reality characteristics and representational means (onomatopoeia) was abandoned at an early stage. A dissociation of "meaning" and material substratum (sound), which through abstract-artificial associational relationship were newly connected to one another, took its place. This solution formed the basis for the efficiency of language signs. In terms of linguistics, one can speak of the "double articulation" or "double organization" of language (Martinet 1963; Holenstein this volume).

Consonant writing proved to be an important step in the development of writing systems because it, in its own way, made writing *more linguistically adequate.* In effect, with the "Semitic discovery", writing caught up with the knowledge man had gained in the "double articulation". This does not mean that the consonant or consonant-vowel writing system is the most suitable for all languages (cf. the introduction to this volume). It is certainly already clear that the efficiency of writing systems in individual cases is determined by very diverse factors. But even for languages that have a pictographic or ideographic writing system, the consonant or consonant-vowel writing system is, at least as an auxiliary writing system, applicable if only because of its "language proximity".

The Semitic consonant writing system underwent, in the course of its history, an elaborate development. The cuneiform symbols were soon abandoned, other forms succeeded them. The Phoenician-Punic, the Hebrew, the Aramaic, the Arabic, and the Ethiopian writing systems are the most important later forms of the Semitic consonant writing system. In some cases, they developed from one another. With the exception of the Phoenician-Punic, they are still in use today. The Arabic and Hebrew scripts were even transferred to languages of other types (Persian, Turkish, and Urdu on the one hand; Yiddish, on the other).

9. *Outlook: alphabetic writing systems*

The consonant writing system, on the basis of its comparatively simple structure, made writing substantially easier. But even this far-reaching problem solution did not yet lead to a fully satisfactory result. Restricted by its starting point, the Semitic language structure, this writing system in general did not provide a means for the representation of *vowels*. Because of this, the individual reading of the written symbols retained considerable uncertainties which had to be (and still must be) compensated for through context and by the readers' general knowledge. Only with the migration of the Semitic writing system into the Greco-Roman area did this problem fully come to light. (Within the Semitic writing systems themselves, only auxiliary solutions were developed which, however, will not be discussed here.)

The previous problem solutions already contained within themselves the elements of the further solution: On the one hand, the procedure for finding means of representation of phonemes was already given. It only needed to be carried over to the total phonological system of the language, including the vowels. On the other hand – and this is more a coincidental condition – because of different consonantization, the Semitic writing system proved to have more symbols than were needed to represent the Greek consonants. Just these surplus writing signs were used to expand the phoneme labeling principle. Thus, the aleph symbol became the symbol for /a/, the yod symbol the symbol for /i/, and so on (cf. Figure 15).

The result of this development is at hand in the consonant/vowel writing system that, for example, the reader of these lines is utilizing. In principle, the structure has not changed from that of the Greco-Roman writing system. For most of the Indo-European languages in which alphabets with vowels and consonants are used, they prove to be relatively effective; and languages of other typcs such as Turkish or Basque can be reproduced well with it.

There are, however, languages that require additional writing strategies, especially tone languages (cf. Fromkin 1978). The problems connected with the identification and written reproduction of tones or tone-like phenomena in the German language (cf. Ehlich 1983) can perhaps give us an insight into the problem situations which confronted the inventors and developers of writing systems in general. They were not able to refer to previous problem solutions, because the problems they faced were often so new that not even the problem structure was recognizable.

Surmises and tentative solutions led to elementary results, problem solutions, the (not to be underestimated) achievements of which contained the fact that the problem structure itself was more clearly contoured. Thus in subsequent phases of writing development other and more exact solutions

Figure 15. Development from Old Phoenician to the Greek alphabet

could be found: The old solutions often provided an "over-supply" that was able to lead beyond the state reached. At the same time, many solutions involved new problem potentials. The development of writing systems, like other undertakings of the human species, did not proceed in a single line, nor can it be evaluated linearly. Gains on one side bring drawbacks on the other. The history of the development of writing in the Near Eastern area, and further afield, shows itself to be a process that is determined by many factors, some of which are merely coincidental, some of which have systematic status. The total process generated a series of problem solutions that, for hundreds and hundreds of years, have satisfied society's need to make speech permanent.

The confrontation with new requirements and relationships proved to be a concrete negation and "Aufhebung" of already found solutions that, as a whole, have stimulated the development of writing. The process of writing is still an essential condition for the transmitting of complex speech acts and knowledge systems. New writing systems are constructed for non-written languages – or their speakers develop them themselves. The development of writing systems as social problem solving is still going on. Its history permits the solutions to be found more easily today, however, than in the times in which the first steps had to be taken. The strategies are related to possibilities in language itself that remain actualizable and that are ontogenetically reproducible in the process of learning to write. (cf. Weigl 1979).

Notes

* I would like to thank Angelika Redder and Florian Coulmas for critical comments, Constance Guhl for her translation into English of an earlier German version (*Zeitschrift für Semiotik* 2, 1980), and Gail Jefferson for an intensive discussion and many improvements of the English text. Thanks are also due to the editors of the *Zeitschrift für Semiotik* for their permission to include the article in this volume.

1. For factual information, mention should be made of the great monographs on writing upon which I have based my work, especially Jensen, 1970; Gelb, 1952; Cohen, 1958; Friedrich, 1954; Driver, 1976; Diringer, 1948/49.
2. Weigl (1979), in an article on "Lehren aus der Schriftgeschichte für den Erwerb der Schriftsprache", has likewise discussed the history of writing under the aspect of "problem solving methods". The similarity between his and my approach, developed independently of one another, in my opinion can be seen as a confirmation of its usefulness. In particular, Weigl draws in other aspects that it is not possible, for reasons of space, to discuss here.
3. Holenstein (this volume) refers more to the numerical representations in the count stones; examples for these are reproduced in his Figure 3. I do not go into details of the writing of numbers here; cf., however, page 57 on this question.
4. "Babylonian" is used here as a comprehensive term for the Mesopotamian (thus, the Sumerian and the Akkadian) form of writing.

References

Albright, W. H.
1966 *The Proto-Sinaitic Inscriptions and their Decipherment.* Harvard.
Barton, G. A.
1913 *The Origin and Development of Babylonian Writing.* Leipzig: Hinrichs, Baltimore: Johns Hopkins Press.
Brettschneider, G.
1980 "Sprachtypologie und linguistische Universalienforschung". *Studium Linguistik* 8/9: 1–31.
Bühler, K.
1934 *Sprachtheorie.* Jena: Fischer. 2nd ed. (1965), Stuttgart: Fischer.
Cohen, M.
1958 *La grande invention de l'écriture et son évolution.* (3rd. ed.). Paris: Imprimerie Nationale/Klincksieck.
Coulmas, F.
1980 "Schriftentwicklung, Schriftverarbeitung: Herkunft und Funktionsweise der japanischen Schrift". *Zeitschrift für Semiotik* 2: 361–374.
Diringer, D.
1948–49 *The Alphabet. A Key to the History of Mankind.* London: Hutchinson.
Driver, G. R.
1976 *Semitic Writing. From Pictograph to Alphabet.* 3 Vols. London: Oxford University Press.
Druet, R. et al. (eds.)
1976 *La civilisation de l'écriture.* Paris: Fayard et Dessain & Tolra.
Ehlich, K.
1979 *Verwendungen der Deixis beim sprachlichen Handeln.* Frankfurt: Lang.
Ehlich, K.
in prep. *Interjektionen.* Tübingen: Niemeyer.
Falkenstein, A.
1959 *Das Sumerische.* Leiden: Brill.
Friedrich, J.
1954 *Entzifferung verschollener Schriften und Sprachen.* Berlin: Springer.
Fromkin, V. (ed.)
1978 *Tone: A Linguistic Survey.* New York: Academic Press.
Gelb, I. J.
1952 *Von der Keilschrift zum Alphabet.* Stuttgart: Kohlhammer.
Goody, J. and Watt, J.
1968 "The Consequences of Literacy". In Goody, J. (ed.) (1968) *Literacy in Traditional Societies.* London: Cambridge University Press, pp. 27–68.
Holenstein, E.
1983 "Double Articulation in Writing". This volume.
Jensen, H.
1970 *Sign, Symbol and Script.* London: Allen & Unwin.
Klaus, G.
1972 *Semiotik und Erkenntnistheorie.* (3rd. ed.). Berlin: VEB Deutscher Verlag der Wissenschaften.
Labat, R.
1963 *Manuel d'épigraphie akkadienne (Signes, syllabaire, idéogrammes).* Paris: Imprimerie Nationale.
Martinet, A.
1963 *Grundzüge der allgemeinen Sprachwissenschaft.* Stuttgart: Kohlhammer.
Saussure, F. de, et al.
1915 *Cours de linguistique générale.* de Mauro (ed.) (1978), 3. ed, Paris: Payot.

Schmandt-Besserat, D.
1978 "The Earliest Precursor of Writing". *Scientific America 6:* 38–47.
Weigl, E.
1979 "Lehren aus der Schriftgeschichte für den Erwerb der Schriftsprache". *Osnabrücker Beiträge zur Sprachtheorie 11:* 11–25.

STANISLAV SEGERT

Decipherment of forgotten writing systems: Two different approaches

Abstract

The paper compares the decipherment of the Ugaritic cuneiform alphabet (§ 2.) and of the Linear B syllabary (§ 3.) from a systematic and a methodological point of view. Both cases are characterized by the fact that there was no bilinguis which could be used for decipherment. Though there are some similarities in both decipherments, the strategies which were successfully applied also differ in many respects. The systematic evaluation of the methods applied shows that the most methodical ways need not necessarily be the most effective ones. In both cases, close cooperation of scholars from various backgrounds proved to be one of the most important means for arriving at good results. The comparison leads to a critical evaluation of decipherment strategies, and of scientific discussions with regard to them, which can be useful for further cases in which unknown writing systems might come up (§ 4.).

1. *Two forgotten writing systems from the Late Bronze Age*

1.1. The comparison of two successful decipherments of written texts using graphic signs of unknown function and meaning shows both similarities and differences. There are similarities in external circumstances. Both Ugaritic cuneiform records and Greek documents in Linear B writing were written mostly in the 14th and 13th centuries B. C. The civilizations supporting these writing systems in the Late Bronze Age did not survive the upheavals introducing the Iron Age into the Eastern Mediterranean basin. The city of Ugarit was destroyed around 1200 B. C.; its remains were found under the hill called Ras Shamra, in Northern Syria, only in 1929. The cities overwhelmed by the Dorian invasion – Knossos on Crete and Pylos and Mycenae on the Peloponnese – were not forgotten in Greek tradition, but it is only since 1900 that they have begun to yield in significant numbers the documents of the most ancient writing system used by Greeks.

1.2. Both decipherments compared here were accomplished recently: that of the Ugaritic alphabet fifty years ago (1930), that of Linear B more than a quarter of a century ago (1952). Detailed accounts by all the decipherers are available. Charles Virolleaud, Hans Bauer, and Paul (Édouard) Dhorme published both reports about the progress of their attempts and final accounts. The progress of the decipherment of Linear B can be closely traced in the publications by Michael Ventris and John Chadwick.

1.3. The decipherment of Ugaritic alphabetic writing and of Cretan Linear B syllabary belongs in principle to the same category. Using the classification of I. J. Gelb, the work started in both instances with an unknown writing system and unknown language (Gelb's type III), and in both cases, during the decipherment, the language was either identified or found to be closely related to a known language. It was recognized that the language of the cuneiform texts found at Ras Shamra in Syria was closely related to Phoenician and Hebrew, and, similarly, that the words in the Linear B texts from Crete and Peloponnesus belonged to an archaic dialect of Greek. The decipherment continued according to Gelb's type I: a known language began to be used to aid the definitive decipherment of unknown writing.

1.4. There is a considerable difference between the decipherment of the Ugaritic cuneiform alphabet and that of Cretan Linear B syllabary: All Ugaritic letters were determined by comparison of words with words of related Semitic languages. During the decipherment of Cretan Linear B writing, grids containing a considerable number of syllabic values were constructed by Michael Ventris, and only then were some words recognized as belonging to an archaic Greek dialect. The use of later Greek dialects served to extend and to verify the results of decipherment reached by application of the combinatory method.

1.5. From the external viewpoint, some characteristic differences deserve to be mentioned. The script of the text from the ancient city of Ugarit was deciphered in a very short period of time (within one year after the texts were made available) almost independently by three scholars known for their achievements in the field of ancient Semitic languages. Half a century elapsed between the first publication of the Knossos texts and their decipherment by Michael Ventris and John Chadwick. Ventris, an architect by profession, had been interested for many years in the decipherment of this unknown writing. Chadwick, a classical scholar, contributed his skills to further the study of the archaic stage of the Greek language.

1.6. There was no *bilinguis* or any closely similar set of graphical signs available for either of the two decipherments compared here. During the work on decipherment, some proper names and some pictorial renderings of objects were used to a limited extent for the primary identification of the signs of the unknown writing. To a larger extent they were used, however, for the verification of results.

1.7. In the following, the methods used for the eventual decipherment of Ugaritic cuneiform letters and of Cretan Linear B signs will be presented. Due attention will be given to those approaches which eventually led to an impasse. Various methods of verification of the results will also be presented and evaluated.

2. *The decipherment of the Ugaritic cuneiform alphabet*

2.1. The decipherment of Ugaritic writing was accomplished by three scholars who were in some kind of, but mostly indirect, contact. Each of them at some point made use of some of the results achieved by the other decipherers. The relative merits of these three scholars were discussed in various accounts of the decipherment. Without minimizing the role of two outstanding Semitic scholars, Hans Bauer, Professor at the University in Halle, Germany, and Paul (Édouard) Dhorme, Professor at the École Biblique in Jerusalem and later in Paris, the decisive role played by Charles Virolleaud deserves not to be forgotten. It was Virolleaud who, in his function as the Director of Antiquities of the French Mandate of Syria, sent Léon Albanèse to conduct the first archaeological research in the Ras Shamra region, and it was Virolleaud who rightly determined the function and the value of the first letter of the Ugaritic alphabet, which served as a clue for the other two decipherers. Virolleaud also deserves full recognition for the prompt publication of 51 texts in an unknown cuneiform script found during the excavation conducted by Claude Schaeffer at Ras Shamra in May 1929. If Virolleaud had retained for himself the newly found texts of the first and second excavation seasons, he would undoubtedly have been able to decipher them.

2.2.1. At first, Virolleaud supposed that the texts found at Ras Shamra were written in an unknown, foreign language, perhaps related to that used on Cyprus.

A West Semitic text from the Late Bronze Age, found in Northern Syria on the Mediterranean coast, would be more likely written in a linear alphabetic writing of the Phoenician type.

2.2.2. Virolleaud observed that the group of six signs occurring on a bronze adze also appears at the beginning of one of the tablets (18: 1), but preceded by another sign. He concluded that this sign, consisting of three vertical wedges, indicated the preposition before a name or title, corresponding to Akkadian *ana* ("to"). Since the corresponding West-Semitic preposition is written with a *l-*, the first clue to the decipherment was provided.

2.2.3. From this starting point, Hans Bauer, Paul Dhorme and Virolleaud proceeded to determine other cuneiform letters. All three decipherers accepted the affinity of the language of the Ras Shamra texts to Phoenician and Hebrew. As there were about 26 or 27 different cuneiform signs, they assumed an alphabetic writing with letters that indicate consonants only, as in Phoenician and Hebrew. These two languages were accepted as a model by all three decipherers. There was no bilinguis immediately available, but the considerable repertory of Phoenician words attested in inscriptions, and especially the large corpus of Hebrew Biblical and epigraphical texts provided enough comparative material.

2.3.1. The role of the decipherers was not made easy by the small quantity and poor quality of the texts available to them after the first excavation season of 1929. In addition to five bronze adzes – four of them with identical texts consisting of six letters only and one showing four more signs in front – and a short inscription on a cylinder, there were 48 clay tablets, many of them quite fragmentary. It was later found that no fewer than nine were written in Hurrian, a quite different, non-Semitic and still not completely understood language. The use of dividing wedges between the words has proved to be a great help for the decipherment, but the inconsistency of their use led the most methodical of the decipherers, Hans Bauer, to some wrong identifications which temporarily blocked further progress. In general, the texts from the 1929 season remain among the most difficult Ugaritic texts, and some of them were not satisfactorily interpreted in the subsequent fifty years.

2.3.2. Two basic methods were used for identifying Ras Shamra cuneiform letters: All three decipherers attempted to find words containing two identical letters, or two or more letters in a characteristic combination occurring in several words. Bauer also tried to utilize the distribution of letters – or functions of graphemes – in typical morphemes. He suspected that certain letters would occur – frequently or less frequently – in prefixes, certain letters in suffixes, and a small set of certain letters in prepositive particles indicated by one letter only. From the two combinations of two letters tentatively established by this approach, one was proved to be correct and yielded two very frequent letters: *n* and *t*. The other alternative did not bring correct results: the signs supposed by Bauer to be *w* and *m* were later determined to be *k* and *š*.

2.3.3. All three decipherers reached partial results which were later confirmed as being correct, but none of them was able to complete the decipherment on the basis of the texts found in 1929. While working alone, Bauer and Dhorme identified some frequently occurring letters incorrectly. Only after using the results achieved by the other decipherer, were Bauer and Dhorme able to continue and to reach further satisfactory results. Virolleaud continued only after he had obtained the texts excavated at Ras Shamra during the second season, in 1930; first, an atypical tablet containing some numerals, then the well-preserved large tablets with literary texts.

2.3.4. The following survey concentrates not so much on the individual merits of the three decipherers, but rather on the usefulness and reliability of the methods used by them. However, in the early stages of the decipherment, even some identifications and interpretations which were later proven to be partially or totally wrong were helpful.

2.4.1. The decipherment started with Virolleaud's determination of the letter consisting of three vertical wedges as being a preposition, written in West Semitic languages with the letter *l*. All three decipherers then proceeded to search for words containing this letter. Bauer, and in a later stage also Dhorme, used Virolleaud's observations that the four letters at the beginning of the longer inscription on the bronze adze indicate the name of the object. This presupposition was much later proven wrong; these letters give the name of the high priest, *ḫrṣn* /ḫarūṣānu/, derived from the word for "gold", but the damage to the progress of the decipherment was not too serious, since in the supposed word for "adze" *grzn* (cf. Hebrew *garzēn*) two common letters are identical and two others indicate consonants which are somewhat related phonetically.

2.4.2.1. Bauer succeeded in finding the word "son" *bn*, which occurs more than fifteen times in text 10. The other frequently occurring word, *bt*, yielded another frequently found letter, *t*. With the help of letters *b* and *l* he identified the frequently occurring name of god *b^{c}l*, "Baal". The word with identical consonants both before and after *l* was identified by Bauer as the numeral "3", and the new letters as *š*. Only later, when he applied the Arabic model of a Semitic language with a richer inventory of consonants, was Bauer able to see in the first and third letter of this word signs for a consonant different from the Phoenician and Hebrew *š*, and corresponding to the Arabic interdental *ṯ*. Characteristic combinations of more letters led Bauer to the identification of two names of godesses, *aṯrt* "Athirat" (Hebrew "Ashera") and ^{c}*ṯtrt* ("^{c}Athtart"). The word *arb*^{c} was recognized as the numeral "4".

2.4.2.2. In addition to these and other correct identifications of letters, some misinterpretations hampered Bauer's first effort. With the help of his three sets of letters indicating characteristic morphemes, Bauer tried to identify a three-letter word containing the middle consonant *l* which was expected to be – and, in fact, is – relatively frequent in these texts: the word for "king", written in Phoenician and Hebrew as *mlk*. This attempt was hampered by the inconsistency of the Ugaritic scribes, who sometimes did not divide the word for "sheep", written as one single letter *š* (cf. Hebrew *śæ*), from the preceding names of gods *il, b*^{c}*l, dgn*. Bauer, therefore, read this letter erroneously as *m*, which occurs very frequently as the pluralic or other morpheme at the end of words. The word which Bauer read as *mlk* ("king") was in reality another frequently encountered word *šlm* ("peace (-offering)"). What was presumed to be the same word provided with a suffixed pronoun written as the consonant identical with the last consonant of the noun, *mlkk* ("your king"), was in reality the plural *šlmm* ("peace-offerings"). Instead of the correct *khnm* ("priests") (2: 10, 18), Bauer read *mhnš*. Another source of errors was the incorrect reading *grzn* instead of the correct *ḫrṣn* in the longer inscription on the bronze adze. The letters incorrectly determined as *z* and *m* – actually *ṣ* and *š* – then led to the incorrect identification of the letter consisting of two horizontal wedges as being *q*, instead of *p*; *p* was sought in the letter which was actually *s*.

Bauer also considered some other possibilities, which were later proven correct, but he rejected them, as he did not find the resulting words adequate.

2.4.2.3. Even so, in his first attempts made from April 22 to April 27, 1930, Bauer was able to identify correctly no fewer than 17 letters. He recognized two different letters for the glottal stop, in *arb*^{c} ("4"), and in *il* ("god, Il").

2.4.2.4. Paradoxically enough, it was Bauer's more sophisticated method, with respect to the functional distribution of phonemes or letters, which led him to incorrect conclusions, while a less sophisticated method for identifying groups of letters with known West Semitic words resulted in findings which were eventually proven to be correct.

2.4.3.1. Dhorme's first attempt started with the letter *l* and continued with identification of the name *b*^{c}*l* ("Baal") in text 14. Another valid result was the correct identification of the word *mlk* ("king"). In his report, Dhorme did not give any particular reason why he preferred this combination over other words consisting of three different letters with *l* in the second position. Perhaps its relatively high frequency was decisive. With the knowledge of the letter *b*, Dhorme tried to identify the common words *bn* ("son") and *bt* (which can indicate both "daughter" and "house").

2.4.3.2. Although Dhorme correctly identified *mlk*, he did not succeed with *bn* and *bt*. The confusion between two letters as frequent and functionally loaded as *n* and *t* temporarily prevented further progress in the decipherment.

2.4.4. According to his account, presented only after the decipherments of Bauer and Dhorme were published, Virolleaud proceeded in his first attempts in much the same way as the other two scholars. Starting with his own identification of *l* (18: 1), he recognized in *mlkm* (17: 1) the plural "kings". This interpretation is perhaps not entirely correct, because in a list of gods this word may indicate a god with a name similar to Milkom, attested in Hebrew, but the identification of all the letters in this word was correct. Virolleaud was able to identify the names of the god *bᶜl* ("Baal") and of his female counterpart *bᶜlt* ("Baalat"). With the help of this *t* he found the frequent and ambiguous word *bt* whose identification eluded Dhorme. In a way similar to Bauer's, Virolleaud recognized in *l* flanked by identical letters, the numeral "3"; he also identified this new consonant as *š* in *šlš* ("3") and *šlšm* ("30"), according to the Phoenician and Hebrew model.

2.5.1. The results of the independent work of all three scholars were promising and would probably have led each of them individually to a satisfactory decipherment. The decipherment was speeded up by the communication of results between Bauer and Dhorme.

2.5.2.1. After Dhorme was informed by William F. Albright of Bauer's partial solution, which was already published, he was able not only to correct his own identification of *n* and *t* but also to improve on Bauer's erroneous identifications. Dhorme proposed to read *m* and *š* instead of Bauer's *k* and *m; k* instead of *w; p* instead of *q*. Subsequent study proved that Dhorme was correct.

2.5.2.2. Dhorme was also able to establish a tablet of the Ugaritic alphabet based on the Phoenician or Hebrew model of 22 letters. Only two letters are incorrect, due to the fact that the alleged word for "adze" was read as *grzn:* instead of *g* there should be *ḫ*, instead of *z* there should be *ṣ*. While no letter for *ṭ* was found, Dhorme supposed that there were two signs each for aleph, ᶜain and shin. Since, for the Ras Shamra language, Dhorme did not reckon with the possibility of a richer consonantal inventory than that found in Phoenician or Hebrew, some relevant letters such as *ḥ* and *ḫ*, ᶜ and *ǵ*, *š* and *ṯ*, were not clearly distinguished. A few rather rare letters remained non-determined, such as the variant *ŝ* and *ẓ*.

2.5.2.3. Dhorme reached his results by continuing the method of identifying the words on the tablets with the known Phoenician and Hebrew words. He proceeded even further in identifying and translating combinations of words, such as *lrb khnm* (18:1) ("to the High Priest") or *bt mlk* (5: 2) ("the house of the king") and – with not as yet exact identification of letters – *bᶜl zpn* – correct *ṣpn* – (9: 14) ("Baal Saphon"), *bym ḫdš* – correct *ḥdṯ* – (3: 48) ("on the day of the new moon").

2.5.3.1. As Dhorme used results reached by Bauer, Bauer corrected some of his own identifications with the help of Dhorme's proposals and was also able to provide a corrected list of Ugaritic letters – on October 5, 1930.

2.5.3.2. Bauer's advantage was the distinction of two letters, corresponding to the proto-Semitic *ṯ* and *š* and of the variant to emphatic *ṣ*, which was then recognized as an emphatic interdental, usually transliterated by *ẓ*. Bauer also kept apart three different signs for the glottal stop (aleph) combined with different vowels.

2.6.1 All these results reached by combined efforts of Bauer and Dhorme were based on 48 tablets and three other texts excavated in 1929 and were promptly published by Virolleaud. Virolleaud himself was able to use the results of the 1930 excavation at Ras Shamra.

2.6.2 The first text which he received was a tablet written from right to left – other Ugaritic tablets being written from left to right – in a simplified alphabet, in which the letter *š* indicated the equivalents of both *ṣ̌* and *ṯ*, while *ḫ* was also used instead of *ḥ*. Interestingly enough, the not quite correct conclusions presented by Virolleaud did not affect the decipherment too seriously. Virolleaud correctly recognized several numerals written in this sub-standard text with *š* which are comparable to those in Hebrew: *šš* ("6"), *ḫmš* ("5"), *ᶜšr-* ("10"). The word considered by Virolleaud to indicate the numeral "8", written *šmn*, instead means "oil", a word with a close parallel in Hebrew.

2.6.3. More important results were reached by Virolleaud on the basis of extensive literary texts from the 1930 season containing some 800 lines. Again continuing the combinatory method – e.g., *dgn* ("Dagon"), *gpn* ("vine") – he was able to identify the letters *g, z, ṭ, p, ṣ, q*. Virolleaud rendered, according to the Arabic model, the letter *š* rather as *ś*, correctly recognizing that it was related to Hebrew śin. He also recognized that words with a letter corresponding to Hebrew shin are related to those with *ṯ* in Arabic. Virolleaud was also able to distinguish *ḥ* and *ḫ* and to recognize that a letter later identified as *ǵ* is related to Hebrew ḥeth. He also distinguished the vocalic elements in three different signs containing the glottal stop (aleph): in the first he correctly saw *a*, in the second *e* – which is actually at most a subphonemic variant of the correct *i* – and in the third a variant to *e*, while the correct vowel of this relatively rare sign is *u*.

2.6.4. These results of Virolleaud's gave both Bauer and Dhorme the opportunity to supplement and correct their identifications.
2.6.5. The identification of the three remaining letters was hampered by their low frequency and by the irregular correspondence to their equivalents in other Semitic languages. Eventually the values of letters *ẓ*, *ǵ* and *ḏ* were determined. The letter transliterated as *s̀* was recognized as a variant to the more frequent *s*.

2.7.1. It was only later that several means became available for verifying the decipherment of the Ugaritic cuneiform alphabet; in the longer coherent epical texts excavated in later seasons, the interpretation already provided sufficient verification.
2.7.2. In general, as methods of verification, the following may be mentioned here: bilingual texts in which the wording in a better-known language confirms the interpretation; identification of names known from other sources; alphabetic lists of graphical signs which may indicate the number and thus the completeness of decipherment; external identity or similarity of some graphical signs.

In the case of Ugaritic, all became available only after the decipherment was done by other methods.
2.7.3. The first of these verifications was provided by Bedřich Hrozný in 1932, on the basis of a Hurrian text from Ras Shamra published by Charles Virolleaud, with the help of Virolleaud's list of letters. Hrozný recognized several names of Hurrian gods followed by a post-positive datival particle, and related them to the names known previously from syllabic cuneiform sources: *ṯmg-nd*–Šimegi, *pḏḏpḫ-nd*–Piša(i)šapḫi, *ḫbt-d*–Ḫepat. Hrozný was also able to provide readings of the names of the gods which were eventually proved to be correct: *ddmš*–Dadmiš, *nbdǵ-d*–Nupatig. He also found the name of the god Kumarbi in a text from the first season (4:6): *il kmrb*. Hrozný also identified the names of foreign peoples in the Ugaritic text 2: *ḫry*–Hurrian; *ḫty*–"Hittite"; *alṯy*–"Alashiote".
2.7.4. A sufficient number of previously known names of Canaanite gods was found in the Ugaritic text from 1929 by Virolleaud, Bauer and Dhorme.
2.7.5. The number of letters in the Ugaritic alphabet was eventually determined by several alphabet tablets found only in the later excavation seasons. The number of letters (graphemes) is 30. Other different forms are no more than graphical variants.
2.7.6.1. The very last letter in the sequence, usually transliterated as *s̀*, is an imitation of the letters s (samek) of the linear West Semitic alphabet. This may support its identification. But attempts to derive simple forms of cunei-

form Ugaritic letters from the phonologically and graphically related Akkadian syllabic signs did not succeed.
2.7.6.2. One of the alphabet tablets, found in 1955 and published in 1957, presents Ugaritic letters accompanied by their phonetic renderings in Akkadian syllabic signs. If this tablet had been known sooner, it might have provided considerable help for the decipherment.
2.7.7. There are a few texts which can serve as a *bilinguis*. The closest to a bilinguis is the list of gods, the so-called "Pantheon of Ugarit", which had been already found in a fragmentary Ugaritic version in 1929; a complete Ugaritic version was published in 1976, and the Akkadian version in syllabic cuneiform in 1968. Lists of geographical names in alphabetic and syllabic writing provide the opportunity to compare the names and values of the signs. Corresponding formulae in the letters and in the contracts occur in both the Ugaritic and Akkadian versions.
2.7.8. All these means of verification were available many years after the decipherment was reached by comparing Ugaritic words to words known from related Semitic languages, Phoenician and Hebrew.

2.8.1. It is clear not only that the West Semitic language of Ugarit was very close to Phoenician and Hebrew – the differences have become more apparent after more detailed comparison – but also that the graphic systems were nearly identical. The consonantal alphabet was used for all these languages. The Ugaritic cuneiform alphabet graphically represented sounds of a language which was both older and relatively archaic and therefore exhibited a richer inventory of consonants.
2.8.2. The presence of additional consonant letters, such as those for interdentals *ṯ* and *ẓ* and for postvelars *ḫ* and *ǵ*, was originally considered by Bauer and Dhorme to be inconsistent and redundant. But after their function had been determined by Bauer and Virolleaud, these additional consonant letters came to be recognized as giving reliable evidence of a richer consonantal system, very similar to the systems of Classical Arabic and of Epigraphic South Arabic.
2.8.3. Another difference between the Ugaritic and Phoenician alphabets was the use of three different letters for the glottal stop (aleph), according to whether it was followed or preceded either by /a/ or by /i/ or by /u/.
2.8.4. Both these sets of differences slightly delayed the decipherment of the Ugaritic alphabet, but later even these features helped toward a better understanding of Ugaritic texts, as they indicated their more differentiated consonantal system and helped to determine some vowels. The archaic phonological and inflectional systems were then successfully determined by

using a model of a Semitic language which is attested from much later periods but which preserved some original features, Classical Arabic.

2.9.1. Some specific features and characteristics of texts excavated in 1929 from Ras Shamra, which served as a basis for the decipherment of the Ugaritic alphabet, were of some help. A very helpful feature was the use of a word divider. But the inconsistency of its use caused serious difficulties for Hans Bauer. The variety of types of Ugaritic texts from 1929 – rituals, letters, administrative texts, even one literary poetic text – was probably helpful, as it offered the opportunity to find a greater variety of names and words. On the other hand, the homogeneous structure of the texts excavated in 1930 provided a safe basis for the complementation and verification of the decipherment, probably more because of the great number of well-preserved lines than of the actual homogeneity of the texts.

2.9.2. It is interesting that the more systematic approaches have proved to be less effective than a less methodical way of identifying isolated words. The attempts of Hans Bauer to use the distribution of certain consonants in suffixes and prefixes were only of limited success. But the distributional method, already applied by Virolleaud, provided the first clue to the decipherment by determining the function and the value of the preposition *l-*.

2.9.3. The role of chance in the decipherment of the Ugaritic writing was considerable. In determining the word *mlk* ("king") Dhorme was lucky, while Bauer failed. But luck deserted Dhorme in his attempts to correctly distinguish the very frequent combinations *bn* and *bt*. Good luck worked in realizing Virolleaud's methodically sound hypothesis that the first four letters in the longer texts on the bronze adze would yield the word for "adze"; eventually, after many years, it was found that the word is a personal name, *ḫrṣn* – derived from *ḫrṣ* ("gold"), but, luckily, this word is very similar to the supposed word for "adze", *grzn*, the two more frequent letters being identical and the other two phonetically not too far apart. This incorrect identification actually provided a positive step in the process of decipherment.

3. *The decipherment of the Linear B syllabary*

3.1.1. In the following account of the decipherment of Linear B writing of the documents found on Crete and in Southern Greece, the similarities and the differences between their decipherment and that of the Ugaritic alphabet will be referred to from time to time. The content and style of Ugaritic administrative texts, indicating the origin of persons by an adjective derived from geographical names, was taken into consideration by Michael Ventris as a possible analogy for the content and style of some Linear B tablets.

3.1.2. While the Ugaritic alphabet was partly deciphered in less than one year after the first tablet was found at Ras Shamra, the interval of time between the finding and the deciphering of Cretan Linear B text exceeded fifty years. Many Linear B texts were found at Knossos as early as 1900. Only a few were published in the same year, and about 120 more in 1909. A. J. Evans, who was responsible for the excavation, not only delayed the publication of the texts – most of them were published only after his death, in 1951 – but he even tried to impede the study of these texts by other competent scholars. The publication of the tablets of Pylos on the Peloponnese, which were excavated by the American scholar C. W. Blegen in 1939, was delayed until 1951, but here the delay was caused by World War II. Blegen considerably helped the verification of results by promptly sending the copy of the tablet P641, found in his excavation in 1952, to the British decipherers.

3.2.1. The Linear B material available to the prospective decipherers since the beginning of the twentieth century represented thousands of tablets. The quantity considerably surpassed the narrow basis used for the decipherment of Ugaritic writing, but this material was not so diverse.

3.2.2. The relatively large number – more than eighty – of graphic signs on the Linear B tablets indicated a syllabic system. The use of word dividers in the form of short vertical strokes eventually proved very helpful. Also helpful were pictorial signs for various categories of words contained in the tablets. With hindsight, it is clear that very few attempts to decipher Linear B presented since the beginning of the 20th century were of any consequence; many of the proposed decipherments were presented by amateurs. The validity of some previous attempts at decipherment can be assessed only from the perspective of the successful decipherment presented in 1953 by two British authors: architect and cryptographist Michael Ventris and classicist John Chadwick. Some observations made by A. J. Evans, A. E. Cowley and Johannes Sundwall were recently confirmed as being correct. But only the attempts to find in similar groups of letters different grammatical forms of certain words, presented by the American scholar Alice E. Kober, were directly used in the successful process of decipherment.

3.3.1. The relevant work on decipherment started only fifty years after the first Linear B texts were excavated on Crete. While all three decipherers of Ugaritic writing were experienced Semitic scholars, the decipherer of Linear B writing was a young architect. He became interested in these texts when he was a teenager, and wrote an article about them at the age of eighteen.

3.3.2. After a very short period of uncertainty the decipherers of Ugaritic started working under the supposition – soon to be confirmed – that Ugaritic texts were written in a Semitic language closely related to Phoenician and Hebrew, the linguistic character of the texts in Linear B, however, remained unclear until a relatively late stage of decipherment. Ventris himself expected a language considerably different from Greek, and during his work on the decipherment rejected several tempting partial results simply because they pointed to Greek. Of course there were other scholars – such as Emmett L. Bennett, who was in charge of publication of the texts from Pylos excavated by Blegen – who supposed that these texts were written in an archaic dialect of Greek.

3.3.3. Lacking a bilinguis, the only method of decipherment of an unknown language in unknown writing – Gelb's type III – was combinatory. Relations between certain combinations of signs had to be established. Here the observations presented several years earlier by Alice E. Kober proved helpful. She put together several groups of words whose initial signs were identical, while the differing final signs supposedly indicated different endings, presumably of gender (masculine or feminine), number (singular or plural, possibly even dual), grammatical cases, or derivative affixes. Some support for the differences of gender of these words was given by pictorial signs for MAN or WOMAN.

3.3.4. Observations of variants indicating some phonetic or phonological connections, and of corrections which left the originally written sign visible on the clay revealed some similarities between signs. Ventris put together these two kinds of connections between the signs. He used both their original graphical form and the convenient system, introduced by Bennett, whereby individual signs were given two-digit numbers. In these preliminary operations no connection between a sign and its phonetic or phonological value was established.

3.3.5. A general statement can be made at this point: A connection between a sign of whatever kind and the phonetic reality can be reached only by using a known sign of a different system: either a sign of a different writing system for the same language or for another language, or a sign of the same system used for rendering a sound of a different language. Pictorial signs alone cannot provide this connection.

3.3.6. Ventris tried to establish phonetic values for the presumably syllabic signs of Linear B. Since the signs were grouped into words with the help of word dividers, he used this distribution of signs as an indicator of their character; the signs occurring with very high frequency at the beginning of words were presumed to indicate syllables consisting of a vowel only.

Another useful observation concerned the repetition of signs at the ends of words; they were considered to be characteristic inflectional endings.

3.3.7. Another possible method is to find similarities to a known writing system. The shapes of several Linear B signs are very similar to those of certain signs of the Cypriot syllabary, a writing system used in inscriptions of the Greek dialect of Cyprus of the 7th-3rd centuries B. C., deciphered in 1877. Ventris supposed – and this supposition was later confirmed – that the values *pa, na* and perhaps *ti* can be ascribed to Linear B signs on the basis of their similarity to Cypriot syllabic signs. He also used the high frequency of the Cypriot *a-* at the beginning of words as a helpful – and correct – analogy for the use of the Linear B *a-*.

3.3.8. On the basis of these observations, Ventris was able to establish grids in which the syllabic signs were arranged in columns according to vowel, and in rows according to initial consonant, under the supposition that these signs – as in the Cypriot syllabary – consisted of a consonant followed by a vowel; the signs expressing a vowel only were especially important in the process of decipherment.

3.4.1. The progress of Ventris' decipherment can be followed in the Notes 1 to 20 which he sent in 1951 and 1952 to scholars working in the field. The decisive stage came in June 1952, shortly after he sent out Note 20, in which he denied the possibility of finding a Greek language in Linear B texts. Only then was the decisive step taken; it consisted in relating some names of cities on Crete known from Greek sources with the words in Linear B. This was made possible by applying a device used in the Cypriot syllabary. In this syllabic writing, which had no signs for isolated consonants, it was necessary to indicate clusters of two consonants by signs consisting of the consonant and the vowel of the following consonant (i.e., $-V_1 C_1 C_2 V_2-$ was written as $-V_1-C_1 V_2-C_2 V_2-$). The first name found in Linear B was Amnisos, known from Homer, appearing as *a-mi-ni-so*. In a similar way, the name of Knossos was recognized in *ko-no-so*, of Tylissos in *tu-li-so*. A noun, presumably of non-Greek origin, was also determined: *ko-l/ri-ja-to-no* indicated a word for a spice, written in Greek as *koriandros* or *koriainon*.

3.4.2. The first genuine Greek words which were found by Ventris in Linear B with the help of his grid were *ko-wo* and *ko-wa*, related words for "boy" and "girl". The meaning of these two words, but not their phonetic value, had already been recognized by Archibald Sayce in 1927. The archaic Greek forms *korvos* and *korvā* could be reconstructed on the basis of the Homeric *kouros*, Attic *koros* and *kora*, and the Doric *kōros* and *kōra*. A frequent Greek word was the one indicating "total", *to-so* for masculine and *to-sa* for feminine, corresponding to the Greek plurals *tosoi* and *tosai*. In the light of these words, the conjecture rejected by Ventris in his Note 11 – to relate *do-we-lo* to the Classical Greek *doulos*, "slave" – appeared to be correct. Ventris originally supposed that this word was a loan-word borrowed by the Greeks from an unknown Minoan language.

3.4.3. A combination of words recognized by Ventris as being Greek – but accepted as such only later – appeared on a tablet in which a schematized picture of a chariot indicated the general orientation of the meaning; the Greek equivalent *araruiai haniaphi* then gave the appropriate meaning "fitted with reins".

3.4.4. Already, in this early stage of decipherment, some characteristic features of Linear B syllabary were recognized: The liquids /l/ and /r/ were not distinguished, the aspirated consonants /th/, /ph/ and /kh/ were not distinguished from their non-aspirated counterparts; the consonants *-s*, *-n* and *-r*, when they closed the syllable, were not expressed in this writing. These ambiguities made the identification of words of this archaic Greek dialect – used in Knossos and on the Peloponnese in the 13th century B.C. – with the Greek words, as attested since the 8th century in the alphabetic writing, considerably difficult.

3.4.5. Some other Greek words were recognized in tablets whose character had been determined previously; e.g., some of them contained the names of trades. Further assistance was provided by the previously established sets of declensional or derivative endings. The word for "shepherd", nominative *po-me*, genitive *po-me-no*, classical *poimēn* and *poimenos*, and the words for "priest" and "priestess", *i-(e-)re-u* and *i-je-re-ja*, classical *hiereus* and *hiereia* were determined.

3.5.1. At this stage, Michael Ventris obtained effective cooperation from a classical philologist, John Chadwick of Cambridge. Chadwick's cooperation helped to clear up many problems connected with the archaic character of the Greek language in Linear B tablets. It was strange to find the sign for *-qe* instead of the Greek post-positive conjunction *-te* ("and"), though this had been postulated previously for the older stage of Greek; the Latin equivalent of this word is *-que.*

3.5.2. The close cooperation between Ventris and Chadwick led to the determination of hundreds of words and even of complete sentences which could be clearly understood. This was especially the case with connected texts on the tablets from Pylos.

3.5.3. Ventris and Chadwick had the opportunity to present the decipherment of Linear B without delay in the *Journal of Hellenic Studies.* Their report was written in November 1952 and appeared the following year.

3.6.1. Nevertheless, the lack of a bilinguis which could verify the decipherment gave some critics the opportunity to express their disapproval. They were not satisfied with the coherent system of grammar, with identification of a great number of vocabulary items (both general words and proper names), and with the coherence of translated passages, supported by their agreement with pictorial signs.
3.6.2. Only with hindsight was it possible to use no fewer than nine of the Cypriot syllabic signs of the same or nearly the same graphical form and identical syllabic values to verify the results.
3.6.3. The opportunity for a conclusive and impressive verification was provided by C. W. Blegen, who communicated to the decipherers the tablet found by him at the excavation of Pylos in 1952 but made legible only in 1953, after the decipherment of Linear B was reached (Pylos 236 = Ta 641). It is a list of various ceramic instruments and vessels. Two tripods are marked there, by a dual form *ti-ri-po-de*, classical *tripode.* The numeral "4" is indicated there by both a numeric sign (this system had already been determined by E. L. Bennett in 1950) and by a word in an archaic form *qe-to-ro-we* (cf. Classical Greek *tettares*). A vessel depicted as having no handles is described as *a-no-we*, classical *anous*, "without handles".

3.7.1. The similarity between the Linear B syllabary and the Cypriot syllabary is substantial: both these systems are composed in principle of signs consisting of one consonant and one vowel, or one vowel only – the clusters of consonants at the beginning of some Linear B signs can probably be interpreted as monophonemic – and they also use the values of vowels identically, *a, e, i, o, u.* Also, the way of indicating clusters of consonants with redundant vowels is shared by both these systems. But the consonants /-s/, /-n/ and /-r/ at the ends of words are omitted in Linear B, while in the Cypriot syllabary they are indicated by a syllabic sign consisting of the appropriate consonant and vowel *-e*, e.g., *-no-se* for /-nos/.
3.7.2. It is obvious that the syllabic system of Linear B was taken over from another language and does not adequately express Greek phonemes and their combinations. Therefore, many words contained in Linear B Greek texts – which number many thousands – have not been satisfactorily interpreted. Even some texts whose individual words are known do not give a satisfactory meaning.
3.7.3. While the Ugaritic language of cuneiform texts from the 14th and 13th centuries B.C. is commonly considered as being a language separated from Phoenician and Hebrew, the archaic dialect evidenced by the Linear B documents in Knossos and on the Peloponnesos, and used during approximately the same period, is considered to be a dialect of the Greek language.

Thus, the evidence for Greek language was extended several hundreds of years back. From the linguistic viewpoint, the difference between the Greek of Linear B and even the later Greek dialects of the classical period, such as Arcado-Cypriot, which are closer to it than Attic Greek, appears to be greater than that between the above mentioned Semitic languages. The use of the terms "dialect" and "language" obviously varies from discipline to discipline.

4. *Results of decipherments*

4.1. The cuneiform script of Ugarit and Linear B both appeared to be purely phonetic writing systems without any logographic or ideographic elements. In both these systems, the principle of expressing one phonological unit, whether one phoneme or a combination of two phonemes by one sign, is consistently applied. Neither of these systems indicates all the phonemes of the given language with sufficient exactness and completeness. On account of this, after a gap of three thousand years, a safe reconstruction of the languages and a perfect understanding of all the preserved texts is not possible.
4.1.1. No phonetic type of writing can be deciphered without an ultimate reference to a language whose phonetic system is known. This principle was very clearly formulated by Alice E. Kober. Phonological values of Ugaritic letters were determined using Hebrew, which has been used in an uninterrupted tradition of sacred texts since antiquity; the phonemes not represented in Hebrew were supplied from the tradition of Classical Arabic and from observation of conservative contemporary Arabic dialects. All these identifications were made under the supposition that the structure of the phonological systems of ancient Semitic languages corresponds closely to those of the modern Semitic languages and dialects.
4.1.2. The phonological values of both consonantal and vocalic phonemes contained in the syllabic signs of Linear B were determined according to ancient Greek dialects, whose phonological systems have been partially reconstructed on the basis of Greek scholarly traditions and of the modern Greek language, with the additional help of the information provided by some ancient Greek authors. For some features not represented in any Greek dialect, the comparison with related Indo-European languages such as Latin, Hittite, and Sanskrit was used. Even if the character of some rare phonemes and their position within the phonological system could be determined, their actual pronunciation remains unclear.
4.1.3. The Ugaritic cuneiform alphabet, in principle, expresses one phoneme by one letter. This principle is to some extent violated – perhaps only from the viewpoint of modern scholars – by the use of three different letters for the glottal stop combined with the vowel that follows or precedes them.

These letters basically indicate the character of the vowel, /a/ or /i/ or /u/. The glottal stop is, from a phonetic viewpoint, the cessation of the phonic stream, not a sound. It is therefore not expressed; only the positive value, the vocalic sound, is indicated. The doubling of consonants is a significant feature in the Ugaritic language, but no graphical device is used for indicating doubled letters.

4.1.4. Those Linear B signs which have been determined conclusively enough indicate the consonant and the following vowel (CV). The signs that indicate the vowel only (V) can be considered a sequence of zero consonant and a vowel. This uniformity of signs is inconvenient for the rendering of closed syllables (CVC) and of clusters of consonants at the beginning of a syllable ($C_1 C_2 V$-).

4.1.5. The decipherment of the Ugaritic writing system was verified by the coherent system of Ugaritic language, a system that was similar to those of other Semitic languages, especially Hebrew and Arabic. The critics' voices against the validity of decipherment were of no consequence. The only other attempt at decipherment offered by Ferdinand Bork as an alternative to that reached through the combined efforts of Virolleaud, Bauer, and Dhorme was easily proved to be inadequate.

4.1.6. More substantial criticisms were voiced against the decipherment of Linear B as presented by Ventris and Chadwick. Further work on the numerous unresolved problems of Linear B texts redirected the criticism away from the results of this decipherment, which clearly and convincingly established the phonological values of the frequently used signs as well as the rules for their combinations, towards the deficiencies of this writing system itself, and towards its inadequacy for expressing the Greek language. Many words remain uncertain, while their phonemes and their meanings cannot yet be clearly determined, because of the omission or ambiguity of many significant consonants.

4.2.1. The validity of the decipherment of an unknown writing system has to be evaluated in relation to its adequacy for the respective language. If the writing system does not express the phonemes – and in many instances the significant suprasegmental features – of a language distinctly enough, the problems that remain in the interpretation of the texts should not be exploited as objections against the decipherment. A comparative examination of the writing systems with respect to the system of languages may promote understanding of the nature – and often also the persistence – of the problems.

4.2.2. Linguistic typology has to be taken into consideration. Different functional utilization of consonants and vowels has to be observed. For

Semitic languages – in spite of some recent criticisms – the traditional distinction may be used at least as a working hypothesis: the consonants, most frequently combined in groups of three, indicate the roots, which express the basic meaning of the words. Vowels – and a limited number of consonants – modify these basic concepts.

4.2.2.1. In Greek, the structure of both the bases of words and of inflectional morphemes is similar: both of them consist of consonants and vowels. While certain patterns can be found in both the formation of words and in the inflectional morphemes, the relative functional load of consonants and vowels cannot be clearly separated.

4.2.3.1. The consonantal letters of the Ugaritic alphabet express the consonantal phonemes exactly. Even the archaic features and the trend toward simplification of the consonantal system are adequately reflected. The relatively high number of 27 consonantal letters corresponds to 27 phonemes represented in archaic and classical stages of Ugaritic.

4.2.3.2. The capability of the Ugaritic alphabet to directly express vowels is limited to three vocalic vowels /a/, /i/, /u/ in certain positions, if they are preceded or followed by the glottal stop. Thanks to the consistent system of Ugaritic inflection and word formation, it was possible to extend by analogy the information about these basic vowels to many slots in the Ugaritic words of various categories. These three Ugaritic vowel letters indicate only basic values; they do not distinguish short and long vowels. Their opposition is phonologically relevant and functionally significant. The necessary information has been provided through comparison with other Semitic languages. It was possible to determine the values /ē/ and /ō/, for which the related letters *i* and *u* are used.

4.2.3.3. Both open (CV) and closed (CVC) syllables can be indicated in the Ugaritic alphabet. Of course, only consonants are directly expressed, while vowels in general are not indicated. An open syllable is rendered by one consonant sign, a closed syllable by two consonant letters.

4.2.3.4. A writing system directly indicating only consonants, which are the bearers of the basic concepts of words, and omitting vowels, which serve mostly to modify these concepts, can be considered adequate for a Semitic language. Such systems were and are used for most Semitic languages. The rigidity of their systems helps to overcome the lack of direct information from the writing by the possibility to supply vowels from analogical forms and even from related languages.

4.2.4.1. The consonantal components of Linear B syllabic signs in the basic grid directly indicate only 10 different values. The other rare and therefore not clearly determinable signs and values are not taken into consideration here. The comparison with consonantal phonemes reconstructed on the basis of later Greek dialects shows the inadequacy and ambiguity of this system. From the 10 consonantal components, only five serve to indicate one phoneme only: /w/, /j/, /s/, /z/, and – at least from the synchronic viewpoint inconsistently – /d/. Two other components are used to express two different phonemes each: one for /t/ and aspirated /th/, one for liquids /r/ and /l/. Three components can indicate any of three members of a series, unvoiced, voiced, and aspirate: *p, k* and *q* (for labiovelar consonants). There were no special devices to indicate doubled consonants in Linear B.

4.2.4.2. Many consonants closing the syllable after a vowel are omitted in Linear B. Since many important inflectional morphemes contain /-s/ or /-n/ at the end of the syllable, the character of many words remains unclear. Another omission affects first components /s-/ and /v-/ in a cluster of two consonants beginning a syllable ($C_1 C_2$ V-).

4.2.4.3. The number of vocalic qualities in the Linear B syllabary is five: /a/, /e/, /i/, /o/, /u/. This number seems to be sufficient for determining the character of morphemes and words, even if their length is not indicated.

4.2.4.4. Diphthongs are treated differently in Linear B. While the /-u/ as second component is regularly indicated by the *u* sign, the second component /-i/ is usually not indicated at all. The relevant and frequent inflectional morphemes /-oi/ and /-ai/ are not adequately expressed in most instances.

4.2.4.5. In Linear B there is a redundant feature in many clusters of two consonants at the beginning of the syllable. The first syllabic sign indicates not only the first consonant, but also the vowel which is pronounced after the second consonant. It may be supposed that this is only a redundant graphical device, not an attempt to express an anaptyctic secondary vowel.

4.2.5. The deficiency of both the Ugaritic and the Linear B systems may be shown by comparing the texts with their phonological reconstructions. It would be possible to give an approximate estimate of the number of phonemes which are directly indicated compared with the number of all phonemes in a written text, but such simple numerical statistics give only distorted results, since the functional load of the missing phonemes would not have been taken into account.

4.2.5.1. In the Ugaritic alphabet, all consonantal phonemes are exactly expressed. The number of missing vocalic phonemes is lower than 50%; since the proportion of closed syllables (CVC) may be about 10%, the proportion of vocalic phonemes not expressed directly may amount to about 45% of all phonemes. This proportion is slightly diminished by taking into consideration vocalic phonemes directly indicated by three vocalic signs related to the glottal stop, *a, i,* and *u.* The resulting percentage of directly expressed phonemes may be around 55%.

4.2.5.2. The percentage of consonantal phonemes expressed directly in the

Linear B syllabary can be estimated, admittedly on the basis of quite a small sample, to 80% or even a little more; therefore, nearly 20% of phonemes are omitted altogether. But among the phonemes which are directly expressed by the first consonantal component of the syllabic sign, many are not distinguished exactly. If we count the unvoiced members of the stop series and /r/ from the liquid series as basic or most frequent, the proportion of the less frequent phonemes which are not expressed exactly would reach nearly 5%. The redundant use of signs for consonant and vowel (CV) for the first consonant of a cluster also contributes to the ambiguity; this redundancy appears in nearly 5% of all signs. Since vowels are expressed, apart from the few exceptions such as /-i/ as the second part of diphthongs, their percentage approaches 100%. The resulting percentage of directly expressed phonemes may well exceed 90%, but about 5% of all phonemes is not expressed exactly.

4.2.5.3. The simple percentages indicate that Linear B renders directly a relatively much larger number of phonemes than the Ugaritic alphabet, but since many of the phonemes are omitted in very sensitive positions, the determination of many words and inflectional morphemes is made uncertain. The greater variety in Greek word formation and in inflectional systems of both nouns and verbs in Greek explains this apparent difference. While in Ugaritic there is only one system of case endings with a slight difference between masculine and feminine nouns, in Mycenaean Greek at least three different paradigms appear with relatively great frequency. Since there are few Greek verbal forms in the Linear B texts, the difference between the variety of Greek verbal paradigms as contrasted to the uniform system of the Ugaritic verb does not appear conspicuous.

4.2.5.4. Characteristic examples of ambiguity caused by not expressing some important Greek phonemes are given by Ventris and Chadwick: *pa-te* can indicate the Greek *patēr* ("father") or *pantes* ("all") (plur. masc.); *pa-si* can mean *phāsi* ("they say") or *pānsi* ("to all"). Similar ambiguities can be observed in those West Semitic alphabets which indicate consonants only, as in Ugaritic: *bt* can be read as /bittu/ ("daughter") or as /bētu/ ("house"), the end vowel /-u/ indicates a nominative, but words with genitive ending /-i/ or accusative ending /-a/ are written in the same way in this writing system.

4.2.5.5. The comparison of these Greek and Semitic samples shows, in spite of their small extent, that the omissions and ambiguities of Linear B affect the identification of Greek words much more strongly than the lack of vowels affects the analysis of Ugaritic words. The possible choices in Ugaritic are much more limited both in the grammatical category and form and in the basic meaning. This considerable difference is caused by the character of the language. The writing systems contribute in different ways to uncertainties of reading and interpretation of texts forgotten for three thousand years.

4.3.1. Beyond comparison of writing systems and of the structures of the language, the character of the texts may affect our comprehension of them. Here again the Ugaritic texts provide more information.

4.3.2. Even though the number of Ugaritic tablets does not exceed 1400 – and many of them are fragmentary and short – the longest tablets give coherent literary texts. Their poetic character is very similar to the most ancient Hebrew poetry known from the Bible. The interpretation of the Ugaritic poems was aided considerably by this similarity of prosodical patterns, by the application of so-called *parallelismus membrorum*, as well as by the use of corresponding poetic devices of a semantic character. Many non-literary texts in the Ugaritic script and language, especially letters and contracts, were successfully interpreted with help of formulae found in Akkadian texts from Ugarit.

4.3.3. The Linear B texts are all of a non-literary character: lists of persons, animals, instruments, commodities, etc. Parallels from other areas of the Mediterranean, even from Ugarit, are not close and frequent enough to be of any great help for their interpretation. The lack of connected literary and non-literary texts is evidently a hindrance for the comprehension of both the linguistic features and the scribal devices of Linear B.

Notes

For general information about Ugaritic writing and its decipherment cf. de Langhe 1945: I, 221-263; Driver 1954/1976: 148–152, 252, pl. 46–48: Friedrich 1954: 69–72; Gelb 1963: 129–130; Diringer 1968: I, 150–152; II, 144, 146–147; Gordon 1968: 104–114; Röllig 1969: 289–291; Pope 1975: 117–122.

For general information about Linear B writing and its decipherment cf. Ventris and Chadwick (1956) 1973: 3–91; Chadwick (1958) 1967; Gelb 1963: 91–97; Gordon 1968: 115–132; Diringer 1968: I, 116–119; II, 123–127; Grumach 1969: 234–235, 244–248, 254–267; Pope 1975: 159–179; cf. Friedrich 1954: 130–135.

Notes to Paragraphs:

1.1: Drower 1975; Saadé 1979; Dow 1973; Chadwick 1973.

1.2: Virolleaud 1929; 1931; 1936: 67–77; Bauer 1930; 1932; Dhorme 1930b.

For an exact chronology of steps in the decipherment of the Ugaritic writing cf. Bauer 1932: 41–56.

Ventris and Chadwick 1953; (1956) 1973: 3–91; Chadwick (1958) 1967.

1.3 and 3.3.3: Gelb 1975: 73–74.

2.3.1: cf. CTA 166, 168–170, 175, 180, 183.

2.6.2: Virolleaud, Syria 15, 1934: 103–104; UT 57; CTA 207; KTU 4.31.

2.7.3: Hrozný 1932a; Virolleaud, Syria 12, 1931: 389–390; UT 50; CTA 172; KTU 1.60 (cf. 1.26; 1.135). – Hurrian names are given according to Hrozný 1932a. Professor Gernot Wilhelm (Saarbrücken) kindly gave me (in his letter of August 27, 1980) forms according

to recent standard transcription systems for Hurrian: either (rendering of syllabic signs) Šimike, Ḫepat, Nupatik, Kumarpi, or (considering allophonic voiced consonants) Šimige, Ḫebat, Nubadig, Kumarbi.
2.7.6.2: RS 19.159; Virolleaud, Le Palais Royal d'Ugarit, II (MRS VII), 1957, nr. 189; UT 1189; KTU 5.14.
2.7.7: Nougayrol 1968: 42–64, nr. 18. – Virolleaud 1929 (and UT): nr. 17; CTA 29; KTU 1.47 (and 1.118). – Cf. de Langhe 1945: I, 232–233.
4.1.5: Bork 1938. Cf. de Langhe 1945: I, 228–234.

References

The references contain only items directly related to the paper. There are excellent detailed bibliographies available (which were gratefully used for compiling this paper):

For the Ugaritic writing etc.:
Index bibliographiques de Langhe 1945: I, XV–LVII.
Bibliographie générale. Herdner, CTA 1963: 293–331; Addendum à la bibliographie, 333–339.
Ugaritische Bibliographie . . . Dietrich 1972 – (arranged according to the years of publication, since 1928).

For the Linear B:
Bibliography. Ventris and Chadwick. 1973. 595–605. – (References to current bibliographical lists on p. 595.)

Ugaritic texts (1–48) are quoted according to numbers in the first edition by Virolleaud 1929, accepted by Gordon, UT. 1965. For the numbers in other systems, cf. CTA p. XXXI–XXXII; KTU 489–490.

Abbreviations

AJA *American Journal of Archaeology*
AOAT *Altes Orient und Altes Testament.* Kevelaer: Butzon & Bercker, Neukirchen-Vluyn: Neukirchener Verlag
ArOr *Archiv Orientální*
CAH *The Cambridge Ancient History.* Third Edition. Vol. II, part 1, 1973; part 2, 1975. Cambridge University Press.
CTA see Herdner 1963
KTU see Dietrich et al. 1976
MRS *Mission de Ras Shamra.* Paris: Imprimerie Nationale – P. Geuthner
RB *Revue Biblique*
UT see Gordon1965

Bauer, H.
1930 *Entzifferung der Keilschrifttafeln von Ras Schamra.* Halle: Niemeyer.

1932 *Das Alphabet von Ras Schamra. Seine Entzifferung und seine Gestalt.* Halle: Niemeyer.

Bennett E. L.
1950 "Fractional quantities in Minoan bookkeeping". *AJA* 54: 204–222.

1955 *The Pylos Tablets: Texts of the Inscriptions Found 1939–1954.* Princeton: Princeton University Press.

Bork, F.
1938 *Das Ukirutische, die unbekannte Sprache von Ras Schamra. Die Grundlagen der Entzifferung.* (Mitteilungen der altorientalischen Gesellschaft, XII, 1). Leipzig.

Chadwick, J.
1958 2nd ed. 1967. *The Decipherment of Linear B.* Cambridge: Cambridge University Press.
1973 "The Linear B Tablets as historical documents." *CAH* II/1: 609–626, 805.
1975 "The prehistory of the Greek language." *CAH* II/2: 805–819, 1028–1029.

Corré, A. D.
1966 "Anatomy of a decipherment." *Wisconsin Academy of Sciences, Arts and Letters* 55: 11–20.

De Langhe
1945 *Les Textes de Ras Shamra et leur Rapports avec le Milieu Biblique de l'Ancien Testament, I–II.* Gembloux: J. Ducujot; Paris: Desclée de Brouwer.

Dhorme, P. (É).
1930a "Trouvailles sensationelles en Syrie." *RB* 39: 152–153.
1930b "Un nouvel alphabet sémitique." *RB* 39: 571–577.

Dietrich M. and Loretz, O.
1972 *Ugaritische Bibliographie der Jahre 1928–1966.* (*AOAT* 20/1–4).

Dietrich M., Loretz, O. and Sanmartín, J. (KTA)
1976 *Die keilalphabetischen Texte aus Ugarit.* (*AOAT* 24/1).

Diringer, O.
1968 *The Alphabet: A Key to the History of Mankind. I–II.* (1948) Third ed. 1968. New York: Funk & Wagnalls.

Doblhofer, E.
1957 *Zeichen und Wunder: Die Entzifferung verschollener Schriften und Sprachen.* Wien etc.: Neff.

Dow, S.
1973 "Literacy in Minoan and Mycenaean lands." *CAH* II/1: 582–608.

Driver, G. R.,
1948 *Semitic Writing: From Pictograph to Alphabet.* 1954/1976. London: Oxford University Press.

Drower, M. S.
1975 "Ugarit." *CAH* II/2: 130–160, 932–938.

Evans, A. J.
1909 *Scripta Minoa, I.* Oxford: Clarendon Press.
1952 *Scripta Minoa, II,* J. L. Myres (ed.). Oxford: Clarendon Press.

Friedrich, J.
1954 *Entzifferung verschollener Schriften und Sprachen.* Berlin &c.: Springer.

Gelb, I. J.
1963 *A Study of Writing.* (1952, revised ed. 1963). Chicago & London: University of Chicago Press.
1975 "Records, writing, and decipherment." In H. H. Paper, ed., *Language & Texts: The Nature of Linguistic Evidence.* Ann Arbor: University of Michigan, pp. 61–86.

Gordon, C. H.
1965 *Ugaritic Textbook.* Roma: Pontificium Institutum Biblicum.
1968 *Forgotten Scripts.* New York: Basic Books.

Grumach, E.
1969 "Die kretischen und kyprischen Schriftsysteme." In U. Hausmann, ed., *Allgemeine Grundlagen der Archäologie.* München: Beck, pp. 234–288.
Herdner, A.
1963 "Corpus des tablettes en cunéiformes alphabétiquee découvertes à Ras Shamra-Ugarit de 1929 à 1939." (*MRS* X).
Hrozný, B.
1932a "Une inscription de Ras Shamra en langue churrite." *ArOr* 4: 118–129.

1932b "Les Ioniens à Ras Shamra." *ArOr* 4: 169–178.

1949 *Les inscriptions crétoises: Essai de déchiffrement.* Praha: Orientální ústav.
Kober, A.
1944 "The 'adze' tablets from Knossos." *AJA* 48:64–75.

1945 "Evidence of inflection in the 'chariot' tablets from Knossos." *AJA* 49: 143–151.

1946 "Inflection in Linear Class B: 1. declension." *AJA* 50: 268–276.

1948 "The Minoan scripts: fact and theory." *AJA* 52: 82–103.
Lejeune, M.
1958 *Mémoires de Philologie Mycénienne. Première série (1955–1957).* Paris: Centre National de la Recherche Scientifique.
Nougayrol, J.
1968 "Textes suméro-accadiens des archives et bibliothèques privées d'Ugarit." *Ugaritica* V: 1–446. (*MRS* XVI).
Pope, M.
1975 *The Story of Decipherment: From Egyptian Hieroglyphic to Linear B.* London: Thames and Hudson.
Röllig, W.
1969 "Die Alphabetschrift." In U. Hausmann, ed., *Allgemeine Grundlagen der Archäologie.* München: Beck, pp. 289–302.
Saadé, G.
1979 *Ougarit: Métropole Cananéenne.* Beyrouth: Imprimerie Catholique.
Schaeffer, Cl. F.-A.
1929 "Les fouilles de Minet-el-Beida et de Ras Shamra (Campagne du printemps 1929)." *Syria* 10: 285–297.
Segert, S.
1979 "Ugaritic poetry and poetics." *Ugarit-Forschungen* 11.

1981 *A grammar of the Ugaritic language, I–II.* Berkeley-Los Angeles-London: University of California Press.
Ventris, M.
1940 "Introducing the Minoan language." *AJA* 44: 494–520.

1953 "A note on decipherment methods." *Antiquity* 27: 200–206.
Ventris, M. and Chadwick, J.
1953 "Evidence for Greek dialect in the Mycenaean archives." *JHS* 73: 84–103.

1956 2nd ed. 1973. *Documents in Mycenaean Greek.* Cambridge: Cambridge University Press.

Virolleaud, Ch.
1929 "Les inscriptions cunéiformes de Ras Shamra." *Syria* 10: 304–310, pl. LXI–LXXV.

1931 "Le déchiffrement des tablettes alphabétiques de Ras Shamra." *Syria* 12: 15–23.

1936 *La légende phénicienne de Danel. MRS* I.

GERNOT WILHELM

Reconstructing the phonology of dead languages

Abstract

This paper is concerned with the phonology of dead languages. On the basis of correlations between written and acoustic signs, some possibilities of historical reconstruction are examined. The focus of our considerations is on the phonology of Ancient Near Eastern languages written in cuneiform. The adoption of a given writing system to a hitherto unwritten language requires certain modifications of that system. The analysis of such modifications allows us to establish phonemes which were not part of the original inventory of signs. It is to be stated, however, that in the case of Akkadian a complete phonology could only be established on the basis of comparison with closely related languages.

"Dead" languages are written languages, the corresponding sign-systems of which – spoken languages – are no longer in use. The description of a "dead" language cannot automatically choose the phonological system as its lowest level. Since the sign-system to be described is constituted by graphemes and not by signs, the reconstruction of the oral sign-systems of any level depends on the determination of the linguistic level of the script (cf. the contribution of W. Haas in this volume). If the written message matches speech only on the level of a whole utterance, there is no way at all to draw any conclusions about the linguistic structure. The opposite extreme, the one-to-one correspondence between graphemes and phonemes, which allows application of linguistic descriptional patterns without prior investigation, is very rare, and – at least in modern times – it is influenced by linguistic considerations (Vachek 1973: 21 sq.). Most writing systems, however, combine phonological and morphological information.

Since the grammar of "dead" languages cannot be reconstructed with the aid of a competent speaker, but only by analysis of written messages, the investigation of writing systems from the point of view of correspondences between graphemes (and grapheme combinations) and lingual signs (phonographic, morphographic, logographic) is a prerequisite.

One might argue that the grammar of dead languages could disregard the reconstruction of phonology, because decoding written messages does not require the ability to read the text in a phonetically correct way or to segment the text on the phonological level, as is proven by exclusive reading knowledge of foreign languages (Artymovyč 1932). In this case the reader has a command of information about linguistic phenomena of all structural levels beyond that of phonology, about which he may have only vague ideas. One might assume that in a similar way the description of the morphology of dead languages could be based on the notation of recurrent meaningful grapheme sequences.

This comparison, however, is not fully adequate. Reading knowledge is attained on the basis of existing grammars which are based on a background of comprehensive linguistic data, whereas the student of "dead" languages has to derive the linguistic structure of a language only from the texts at his disposal (leaving aside the possibility of reaching conclusions from comparative linguistic material). As long as the relations between script and the different levels of language are not classified, a grammar of a "dead" language will only be correct and complete to the extent of how close the script comes to the principle of pure phonography. Under- or over-differentiation of the grapheme inventory as compared with the phonological system correlates with a deficit of phonological and morphological insight, unless its phonological or morphological significance is determined. Consequently, the reconstruction of the phonological system, on the basic level with the most limited inventory of signs, is an indispensable objective of the study of dead languages.

A language is conditioned by its phonological system, but the phonological system can only be deduced from the language itself, as is evident from the technique of minimal pairing. It follows that the reconstruction of the phonology of a "dead" language cannot depend exclusively on a study of the script employed for writing messages in that language. Additional linguistic data are needed, especially semantic data. In the course of the history of the great decipherments of ancient scripts and the subsequent reconstruction of the respective languages, these data were provided by bilingual or quasi-bilingual inscriptions, the latter being texts with numerous recurrent elements out of a corpus well defined by content, e.g. a diplomatic correspondence between certain rulers on identical or similar subjects. Loan words and names may serve the same purpose. The approaches to the reconstruction of the phonological system of several Ancient Near Eastern languages, which will be subject to further examination in this paper, show methodological differences which depend on whether a language is closely related to a group of well-known and at least partially still spoken languages or whether it is isolated.

A language of this latter group is Sumerian, the oldest known language of the accusative-ergative type (oral communication by K. Heger, Heidelberg, and, independently, P. Michailovski, Philadelphia), which was spoken in Southern Mesopotamia during the 3rd millennium B.C. and became extinct no later than the beginning of the 2nd millennium B.C. Another virtually isolated Ancient Near Eastern language is Hurrian, an ergative language which recently received some attention from linguists because there is evidence for the rare anti-passive construction (Thiel 1975: 200, 204; Anderson 1976: 17). Hurrian is related to the poorly attested Urartian which was spoken in Eastern Anatolia in the first half of the 1st millennium B.C.. Diakonoff (1971: 157–171; 1978) has put forward arguments in favor of a relationship with North Caucasian languages. Hurrian became extinct at the end of the 2nd millennium B.C., except in a few remote areas in the Kurdish mountains, where it may have survived for another 500 years, finally to be superceded by Kurdish.

Akkadian, on the other hand, is a language belonging to the closely inter-related Semitic group. It was spoken in Mesopotamia beginning in the 3rd millennium B.C., when it underwent strong Sumerian influence, and survived until the end of the 1st millennium B.C., gradually being replaced by Aramaic.

All these languages were written with cuneiform writing, the earliest script coming into existence in Persia and Southern Mesopotamia around the turn of the 4th millennium. In the course of time, this writing system changed considerably. Since the primary purpose of the script was not to represent human speech but to serve as a device for recording economic data, the significative potential of the oldest cuneiform system was rather limited. In the terminology of W. Haas (1976) this system would be called "pleremic" with both "motivated" and "arbitrary" graphemes. It is widely accepted that cuneiform writing was originally designed to write the Sumerian language, though it must be admitted that evidence for this assumption is still very scant. Various reasons such as the necessity of writing names (Gelb 1963) and especially the impact of borrowing the script in order to write other languages (Haas 1976: 202–204) led to the most important achievement of ancient writing, the insertion of syllabic signs into the logographic system. Cuneiform writing continued to be a mixed system of logographic and syllabic signs until its very end in the 1st century A.D. It is noteworthy that there were nearly pure syllabic cuneiform systems in use during the 2nd millennium B.C. (e.g. Old Assyrian, Hurrian), but apparently they were not perceived as a breakthrough in communicational development. It is generally assumed that the strong esoteric traditions of scribalism interfered with the ideal of a pure syllabic writing that is easy to learn, but it might very well be that a mixed system of logographic and phonographic signs in a given cultural environment better fulfilled the need to "speak quickly and distinctly to the eyes, so that the proper idea can be mobilized without any difficulty" (Frinta 1909, cited and commented by Vachek 1973: 13).

The phonological system of a "dead language" affiliated with a still spoken group of languages such as Akkadian is usually reconstructed on the basis of comparisons (Diakonoff 1980). Rules of correspondences are established which serve for attributing readings to cuneiform sign in addition to those readings reached in the primary decipherment. But the reconstructed Akkadian phonological system is not at all unequivocally represented by cuneiform signs. According to *communis opinio,* it took the Akkadians about a millennium to assimilate the borrowed writing system into their own language. It was not before the 14th century B.C. that the basic phonemic distinctions of the Akkadian phonological system (voiced, unvoiced, "emphatic") were at least partially rendered in writing.

The most ancient Akkadian syllabary used the signs for stops and sibilants without any discrimination of voicedness, unvoicedness, and "emphasis". Though there were many homophone signs in Sumerian, the Akkadians apparently felt no need to attribute new phonetic values to them in order to achieve a better correlation between phonemes and graphemes. They used, e.g., the two signs later spelled /gi/ and /ki/ indiscriminately for phoneme sequences which we define, because of etymological considerations, as /gi/, /ki/, or /qi/.

It was Gelb (1961: 33) who offered the explanation that the Sumerian phonological system did not share the opposition 'voiced' versus 'unvoiced' but the opposition 'aspirated' versus 'unaspirated'. Since the latter does not exist in Akkadian, the Akkadians, according to Gelb, used the Sumerian signs for aspirated and unaspirated consonants indiscriminately for their voiced, unvoiced, and "emphatic" consonants.

This explanation tries to keep in line with the once established Akkadian phonological system implying the "triadic" groups (voiced, unvoiced, "emphatic"), which are a characteristic of the alleged Proto-Semitic consonantal system (Moscati 1964: 24). Here the limits of the comparative method are clearly visible. The phenomena could easily be interpreted in a different way. One could argue, e.g., that Proto-Semitic had only two sets of stops (and fricatives?) which were not distinguished according to sonority but, e.g., to intensity ('tense' versus 'lax'). In the framework of such a hypothesis, the opposition 'voiced' versus 'unvoiced' would have been inserted into the system at a later time. This would have to be described as a process of phonemization of primarily allophonic features, since the phonemic opposition 'tense' versus 'lax' is often combined with non-phonemic differences of sonority. The emergence of the opposition 'voiced' versus 'unvoiced' would cause the tense consonants to change their phonetic realization and to become velarized, pharyngalized, or even glottalized as in Ethiopic. There are many data which could be used in favor of such a model, but it is beyond the scope of this paper to elaborate on this point. It has to be stated, however, that the postulated change would have taken place between the Old Akkadian and the Old Babylonian period, i.e., at about 2000 B.C., and it might be assumed that the language of the Amorites who settled in Mesopotamia at that time played a role as catalyst (Krecher 1969: 161 fn. 7).

The attempt to describe the phonology on the basis of comparative considerations only yields satisfactory results when there is corroboration from the writing system, as is the case for the younger stages of Akkadian. This method cannot be applied, of course, to isolated languages such as Sumerian or Hurrian. In reconstructing the phonological systems of these languages, we start from the phonetic values which have been attributed to the syllabic cuneiform signs on the basis of the language suitable for comparison with well-known languages, in this case Akkadian. It is evident that the chance of establishing correct definitions of sign-values employed in writing phonologically "unknown" languages depends on the degree of reliability of the values fixed for the "known" ones. Another point which has to be taken into account is the direction of borrowing. The Akkadians borrowed the Sumerian writing system, whereas they conveyed their own system to the Hurrians, which means that the Hurrian syllabary, as opposed to that of Sumerian, was somehow developed from the Akkadian. In order to reconstruct Sumerian phonology, we have to examine the way the Akkadians borrowed Sumerian writing. In many cases this does not yield results at all, because the Akkadians did not restrict themselves to adopting the syllabograms used in Sumerian or to employing Sumerian logograms as syllabograms by divorcing them from their semantic content; they also defined new syllabograms on the basis of the Akkadian correspondence of Sumerian logograms. The cuneiform sign, e.g., which we read /á/ meaning "arm" in a Sumerian context, is used as a syllabogram with the value /id/ in Akkadian, because "arm" is *idum* in Akkadian. A further difficulty is the limited number of Sumerian syllabograms, which are basically restricted to writing bound morphemes, whereas the lexemes are written logographically. Only a few rather late Sumerian texts are written syllabically throughout. In reading Sumerian logograms we depend on the phonetic renderings which the scholarly work of Akkadian scribes of the 2nd and 1st millenia B.C. handed down to us. These phonetic renderings, however, are based on the younger Akkadian phonology, not the Sumerian one. The recent discoveries at Ebla, which yielded Sumerian syllabic texts from a very early period, will certainly contribute to our understanding of Sumerian phonology, but nevertheless some scepticism is indicated regarding the chance to reach comprehensive and unequivocal results.

The situation of Hurrian is somewhat different. Hurrian texts are written virtually exclusively by syllabograms. The orthography of the most important Hurrian document, the so-called "Mittani-letter" giving nearly 500 lines of text, is very consistent. The syllabary of this text ultimately goes back to the Old Akkadian syllabary, though there is some later Babylonian influence, too. We may assume that this Mittani syllabary has been in use to represent the Hurrian language for quite a long time, during which it apparently underwent some adjustments by Hurrian scribes. The discrepancies between the Akkadian forerunner and the Mittani syllabary itself are supposed to correlate to differences in the phonology of the two languages which the scribes felt to be essential to render in the script.

The careful notation of such regular deviations may yield clues for the reconstruction of the Hurrian phonology, as will be shown by the following examples.

The Old Akkadian syllabary used indiscriminately the signs later spelled /ku/ or /gu/ for any velar stop plus /u/. The syllabary of the Mittani-letter employs both signs, but here ⟨ku⟩ and ⟨gu⟩ are not interchangeable as they are in Old Akkadian. Apparently, what were allographs in Old Akkadian, have been defined as graphemically opposed in Hurrian. The same phenomenon occurs in the Babylonian syllabary, where the two originally interchangeable signs are fixed to represent the unvoiced as opposed to the voiced velar stop plus vowel /u/. Evidently, the Babylonian scribes found it necessary to introduce the category of voicedness into the inherited sign inventory to which this category was originally alien. In Hurrian, the two signs have been newly defined in a different way, which can be analyzed by paying attention to graphemes combined with the two signs in question. In Hurrian orthography, the vowel of an open syllable is very often repeated by signs which are the only alphabetic element in cuneiform writing and which only represent vowels. The Akkadian syllabary has two signs for the vowel /u/, the use of which differs according to period and place. In the Hurrian syllabary they represent different vowels which can be shown to fall into the phonetic range of [u] and [o]. If the vowel of the sign KU is repeated, it is consistently U_1 (/o/), whereas the vowel of GU is iterated as U_2 (/u/). So we may say that regardless of what the exact quality of the consonant was, the allographs KU and GU have been defined in the Hurrian writing system as velar stop plus /o/ versus velar stop plus /u/. We may conclude that, deviating from Akkadian, Hurrian had two back rounded vowel phonemes.

A parallel case is the pair of signs KI and GI. In the Old Akkadian syllabary they are allographs for the phoneme sequence velar stop plus /i/. In the Babylonian syllabary they are distinguished according to voicedness of the consonant; in the Hurrian syllabary they differ in vowel quality: KI represents velar stop plus /i/, wheras GI represents velar stop plus /e/. This differentiation leads to the conclusion that Hurrian had two front, unrounded vowels in the phonetic range of [e] and [i]. It is true that the phonemic distinction between /e/ and /i/ also existed in Akkadian. But Akkadian /ĕ̄/ is historically derived from /ă̄/ or /ĭ̄/ and in some positions the phonemic opposition /ĭ̄/: /ĕ̄/ is neutralized. This may be the reason why the Akkadian syllabary never reached a consistent opposition between signs containing i and signs containing e.

The writing system of the Mittani-letter consequently distinguishes five vowels: a, e, i, o, u, whereas the original Akkadian system represents the three vowels a, i, u and, in addition to that, rather imperfectly, e.

There may be even a further indicator for more variation of the vowel system. As mentioned before, the vowel of a syllabic sign already ending in a vowel may be repeated by a vowel sign ("plene-writing"). In the Babylonian writing system, this pattern indicates vowel length, which is phonemic in Akkadian. In Hurrian orthography, plene-writing may serve the purpose of indicating the quality instead of quantity of the vowel of the preceding CV-sign. The sign NI, e.g., may be read /ni/ or /ne/, and it is only by addition of the vowel-signs I or E that the reading becomes unambiguous. But in contradiction to this explanation, there are many plene-writings which apparently have a different meaning, e.g., the sequence ŠE-E. ŠE alone can only be read /še/, not /ši/, because there is a different sign ŠI. In addition to that, there are many plene-writings in A, though all syllabograms containing a are unambiguous. Presumably plene-writings represent another phonetic phenomenon, which very likely has phonemic status, because Hurrian-speaking scribes found that it required connotation. This may be vowel length, as it is in the Babylonian system, but scholars disagree about this point (cf. the latest discussion by Thiel 1975: 99 sqq.). In any case, the plene-writings may lead to the necessity of doubling the minimal vowel system of five vowels.

Hurrian texts have not only been written by Hurrian but also by Semitic and Hittite scribes, who wrote down Hurrian rituals and incantations which were readily adopted beyond the borders of the Hurrian realm. These texts, as well as single Hurrian words and names showing up in Akkadian and Ugaritic texts, are extremely helpful for analyzing the Hurrian phonology. The foreign scribes wrote down what they heard in terms of their own phonological system. Thus, it is very likely that their texts do not care for oppositions alien to Semitic. But, on the other hand, they represent Hurrian allophones as long as they more or less coincide with Semitic phonological oppositions. Texts of this kind can be regarded as imperfect phonetic transcriptions, which may yield important results when matched with basically phonemically written texts of Hurrian scribes. Hurrian texts written in the Ugaritic alphabetic script are particularly valuable, because this writing system has a much more extended inventory of unambiguous consonantal signs than the syllabic cuneiform system.

It has been shown that Semitic scribes distinguished voiced and unvoiced stops and fricatives in their transcriptions of Hurrian texts. Hurrian scribes, on the other hand, employed signs for voiced and unvoiced consonants without any phonetically or phonemically relevant distinction ("Hurro-Akkadian syllabary") or they used a reduced system of signs without such variation ("Mittani-Hurrian syllabary"). By means of texts written by Semitic scribes, positional rules for voicedness can be established which may be described in the following way: Stops and fricatives are voiced in final position and in contact with m, n, r, l; they are unvoiced in all other positions except intervocalically, where they are either voiced or unvoiced.

These data could be interpreted in the following way: Hurrian has a phonemic distinction between voiced and unvoiced stops and fricatives, but this opposition is neutralized in all positions except the intervocalic. This is basically the approach of the first comprehensive Hurrian grammar (Speiser 1940/41). The objection must be raised, however, that in the case of the foregoing interpretation it seems strange that the Hurrian syllabary does not make use of the possibilities of the Babylonian system to choose different signs for voiced as opposed to unvoiced consonants. One might argue that the tradition of the Old Akkadian syllabary, which had no distinction of sonority, was strong enough to prevent innovations deriving from the younger Babylonian system. But this would at best explain the Mittani-Hurrian syllabary, whereas the chaotic interchangeability of signs for voiced and voiceless stops in groups of texts from environments strongly influenced by Babylonian scribal traditions points to the fact that the distinction of sonority was non-phonemic in Hurrian. Another interpretation is supported by the observation that the orthography of the Mittani-letter gives double consonants, where Semitic scribes use voiceless ones, and single ones corresponding to voiced consonants, both in intervocalic position. Several scholars (Bush 1964, Diakonoff 1971) postulate phonemic consonantal length, which according to them only occurs in intervocalic position. Thiel (1975), however, posits a phonemic distinction of intensity. According to Thiel, tense and lax consonants do not only appear in intervocalic, but also in initial position. Their phonetic realization depends on their position within what he defines as an expiration-group, in such a way that the realization of a tense consonant in one position might be phonetically identical with the realization of a lax one in another position.

But why are tense consonants in intervocalic position represented in writing by geminated consonants? Thiel thinks that in this position, consonantal length is a non-phonemic characteristic. This explanation takes for granted that reduplication of consonants in script represents double or long consonants in speech. This, however, is only true in the Babylonian writing system. In the Old Akkadian, the Old Assyrian, and to a certain extent even in the Old Babylonian script, geminated consonants usually do not get a different treatment from single consonants. In Old Akkadian, double consonants are sometimes represented by so-called "broken graphics", which means a sequence of signs of the form (-C)VC-VC.

Reduplication of consonants in Old Akkadian writing quite often represents the combination consonant plus open juncture or glottal stop. If we assume that the Mittani-Hurrian orthography maintained this practice, we are allowed to draw the conclusion that the formally reduplicated intervocalic consonants of the Mittani-letter are not only unvoiced, but that they are also glottalized. The latter characteristic might be the allophonic realization of tense consonants in a certain position. It should be noted, however, that phonemic glottalization has been postulated for Urartian and that it is a common feature in Caucasian languages.

There is a phenomenon, however, which interferes with the results reached so far. In different Hurrian and Hurro-Akkadian groups of texts, double consonants correspond to homorganic nasals plus voiced consonants. In Hurro-Akkadian texts, *paǵrošše*, e.g., alternates with *paǵronze*, etc., the Akkadian name of the Euphrates, Purattum, appears in the form Purandi, the Akkadian verbal form *inaddin* becomes *inandin*. It is hardly possible that the phonetic realization of tense consonants as unvoiced and glottalized alternates with that of voiced, pre-nasalized consonants. The aforementioned study by Thiel sketches some possible patterns of explanation, but unfortunately they cannot be substantiated with the material at hand.

We have gone into some detail to illustrate the problems of phonological reconstruction of dead languages. It must be stated that, despite some results achieved in particular areas, it has not been possible to reconstruct comprehensively the phonology of any Ancient Near Eastern language except that of (younger) Akkadian, which is closely related to other Semitic languages. The fact that we nevertheless do understand texts written in most of these languages, perfectly or at least rather well, is caused by the restrictions which are put on written messages by function and tradition, and by the property of written characters not only to be "symbols of symbols", but to acquire to a varying extent "the status of signs of the first order" (Vachek 1973: 37).

References

Anderson, Stephen
1976 "On the notation of subject in ergative languages." In Charles N. Li, ed., *Subject and Topic.* New York, San Francisco, London: Academic Press, pp. 1–23.

Artymovyč, Agenor
1932 "Fremdwort und Schrift." *In Charisteria Guilelmo Mathesio quinquagenario . . . oblata.* Pragae, sumtibvs "Pražsky linguistický Kroužek" (Cercle linguistique de Prague).

Bush, Frederic W.
1964 *A Grammar of the Hurrian Language.* Ph.D. dissertation, Brandeis University. Ann Arbor: University Microfilms 64–12, 852.

Diakonoff, Igor M.
1971 *Hurrisch und Urartäisch.* Münchener Studien zur Sprachwissenschaft, Beiheft 6, N.F. München: Kitzinger.
1978 "Hurrito-urartskij i vostočnokavkazskie jazyki." *Drevnij vostok* 3: 25–38 (English summary p. 260).
1980 "Towards the pronunciation of a dead language: Akkadian." *Assyriological Miscellanies* 1: 7–12.

Gelb, Ignace J.
1961 *Old Akkadian Writing and Grammar.* (Materials for the Assyrian Dictionary 2). 2nd printing. Chicago: University of Chicago Press.
1963 *A Study of Writing.* 2nd printing. Chicago: University of Chicago.

Haas, William
1976 "Writing: the basic options." In W. Haas, ed., *Writing without Letters* (Mont Follink series 4). Manchester: Manchester University Press: Rowman and Littlefield, pp. 131–208.

Krecher, Joachim
1969 "Verschlußlaut und Betonung im Sumerischen." In W. Röllig, ed., *lišān mitḫurti. Festschrift Wolfram Freiherr von Soden.* (Alter Orient und Altes Testament 1) Kevelaer: Butzon & Bercker; Neukirchen-Vluyn: Neukirchener Verlag.

Moscati, Sabatino, et al.
1964 *An Introduction to the Comparative Grammar of the Semitic Languages. Phonology and Morphology.* Wiesbaden: Harrassowitz.

Speiser, Ephraim A.
1940/41 *Introduction to Hurrian.* (Annual of the American Schools of Oriental Research 20). New Haven: Pub. by the American schools of Oriental research under the Jane Nies publication fund.

Thiel, Hans-Jochen (undated)
1975 "Phonematik und grammatische Struktur des Hurrischen." In W. Haas, ed., *Das hurritologische Archiv . . . des Altorientalischen Seminars der Freien Universität Berlin.* Berlin: 98–239.

Vachek, Josef
1973 *Written Language. General Problems and Problems of English.* (Janua Linguarum, Series Critica 14). The Hague/Paris: Mouton.

HANNS J. PREM AND BERTHOLD RIESE

Autochthonous American writing systems: The Aztec and Maya examples

Abstract

Many ethnic groups in Pre-Columbian Mesoamerica employed graphic systems that were capable – to different degrees, however – of transmitting verbal messages, making use in the first place of the ideographic way of representation. Most writing systems applied the phonetic principle as well, in order to reduce the ambiguities of ideograms. Aztec writing is presented as an example of this type of script. The most sophisticated system of ancient America, in which phonemic writing had been largely expanded on the morphemic and syllabic level, was employed to a very great extent by the writers of Classic Maya more than a millenium before the arrival of Europeans.[1] *On account of a number of factors this writing system is, however, only poorly understood.*

1. *Writing systems of pre-Columbian Mesoamerica*

There has been a long controversy over the question of whether or not the American Indians had developed autochthonous writing systems. It is evident that many ethnic groups in pre-Columbian America employed graphic systems that were capable – although to different degrees – of transmitting verbal messages. That some or all of these systems can be traced back to transoceanic stimuli or wholesale importation from the Ancient World, has often been claimed but cannot be sustained. On the other hand, whether these graphic systems of ancient America can be called "writing" depends primarily on one's definition of "writing".

Although the existence of writing systems is considered as an important diagnostic trait of civilization in ancient America and elsewhere[2] (Kirchhoff 1952:25), only two of the many different American scripts have been investigated in detail: Maya writing and Aztec writing. During the last decade

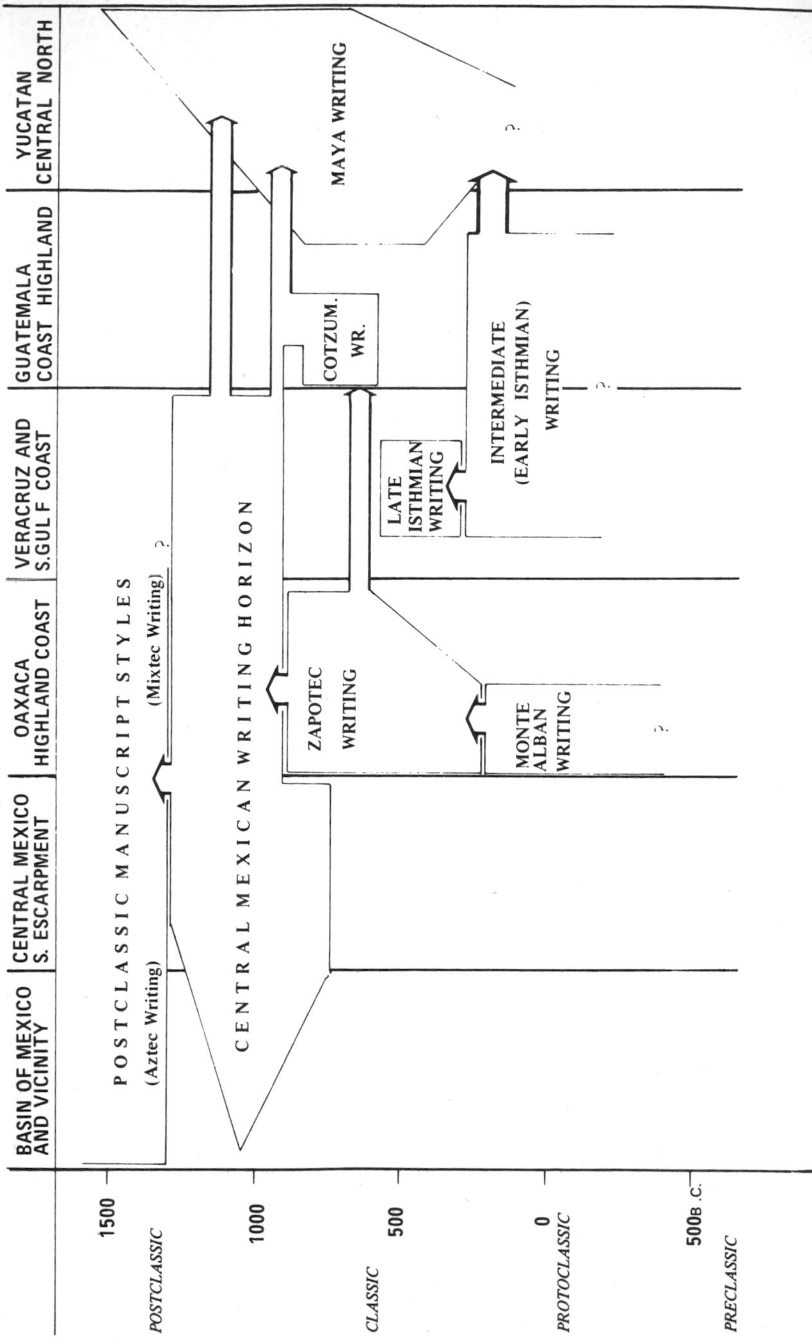

Figure 1. Development and regional distribution of autochthonous American writing systems.

some important investigations have been carried out with respect to Mixtec writing (Smith 1973, Marcus 1980) and the systems preceding it.

All writing systems of pre-Columbian Mesoamerica (between the Basin of Mexico and the eastern border of Guatemala approximately) seem to be genetically related. Lack of thorough investigations of inscriptions in many regions of Mexico, however, permits only a hypothetical reconstruction of a genealogy of Mesoamerican scripts (Fig. 1). In many cases, especially in pre-Classic times, the spatial and temporal extension of a certain writing system can be traced only through a few, more or less isolated, often even incomplete or damaged, inscriptions on stone monuments (Prem 1973). Writing on manuscripts, made of deer hide or certain plant fibers probably existed as well, but only very few of them, dating from the last centuries before the Spanish conquest, have survived.

The languages which correspond to the pre-Classic and even most of the Classic writing systems are completely unknown, with the single exception of Maya writing (see below).

Of all Mesoamerican writing systems only Aztec writing is really well-known. This does not mean, however, that Aztec inscriptions or manuscripts can be read without any difficulty, but the reasons for the remaining ambiguity are certain peculiarities of the writing system itself. On the other hand, Maya hieroglyphs, which certainly are much more elaborate, are still only poorly understood.

2. *Aztec writing*

Nahuatl, the language of the Aztecs and many of their neighbors in Central Mexico, pertains to the Uto-Aztecan stock. Nahuatl is characterized by an ample use of suffixes and prefixes which controlled both inflection and derivation. It has frequently been cited as a standard example for incorporating languages (Bloomfield 1950:241). Most interesting for the purpose of our discussion is the habit of compounding which was extensively used, especially in the refined speech of the urban elite of the Aztec capitals, but which in general constituted the main device for amplifying the basic vocabulary as well (See Table 1). The favorite style of educated Nahuatl speakers was ornate, highly metaphoric and often reduplicative.

The themes of Aztec writings can be grouped into three main categories: historical, religious-divinatory, and administrative. While the religious-divinatory and the administrative manuscripts contain isolated textual (verbal) data, correlated with other information conveyed by means of tables and the like, the first group of manuscripts is based on continuous textual information, i.e. historical accounts. Each of these categories had its own characteristic set of graphic modes of representation, many of whose constituents were used in one or both of the other categories as well.

Table 1. Examples of Nahuatl (Aztec) compound nouns

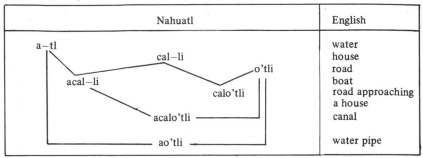

Nahuatl	English
a–tl	water
cal–li	house
o'tli	road
acal–li	boat
calo'tli	road approaching a house
acalo'tli	canal
ao'tli	water pipe

Note: In compounds the singular number suffix -tl, tli or -li is truncated.

The Aztecs and their Nahuatl-speaking neighbors in post-Classic times produced an impressive historical literature. But they lacked any method by which their textual information could be recorded word by word; rather, they were forced to employ two mutually complementary methods, which were used according to the specific requirements. The basic facts of a story were recorded by "narrative pictography" – a graphic depiction of the event by its more or less self-evident portrayal. To facilitate drawing as well as recognition as much as possible, conventionalization was necessary. In Aztec historical manuscripts the degree of conventionalized representation was low, restricted more or less to the omission of confusing details and to the adoption of the principle of the most characterizing view (not necessarily the most natural one!). In comparison, Mixtec manuscripts show a highly formalized representation, raising the density of information but rendering the text, at the same time, less easily intelligible to an untrained reader.

The transmission of a certain message, say the history of the ruling dynasty, could be accomplished easily by pictographic representation – if the reader was more or less familiar with the outlines. But certain details of the message, which tend to elude even a well-trained memory, especially names of persons and places and, of course, historical dates, required more precise recording. In order to achieve this and for this purpose alone Aztec (and other Central Mexican) "hieroglyphs" were employed. Interspersed in the flow of pictographic narration they were used as explanatory glosses. Because of this task they were only capable of transmitting isolated fragments of information; which, in spoken language, corresponded to substantives, including deverbative nouns and (in compounds) nouns with adjectival meaning and numerals. Hieroglyphs thus never correspond to verbs and other word classes on account of their restriction to names and dates. Therefore, hieroglyphs were unsuited for transmitting texts – and this, consequently, was never attempted.

Sign	Explanation	Nahuatl	Mixtec (day sign)
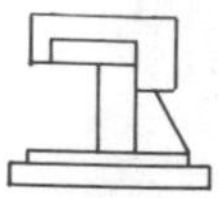	house (3rd day) (cross-section of a temple building with flat roof)	calli	huahi (cuau)
	water (9th day) (vessel with splashing water)	atl	nduta (tuta)
	flint (18th day) (ceremonial flint knife with decoration)	tecpatl	yuchi (cusi)
	mountain (cross-section of hill, protuberances indicating "stony")	tepetl	yucu
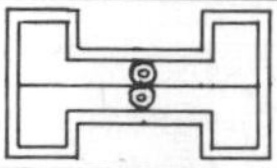	ball court (bird's view of ball court with markers)	tlachtli	yuha
	stone (?)	tetl	yuu

Note: Drawings according to standard forms. In Mixtec a different set of words is used for the everyday use and the calendrical use. (Smith 1973:23).

Figure 2. Examples of signs used in Aztec and Mixtec manuscripts

Aztec hieroglyphs – and the same applies to Mixtec hieroglyphs – cannot be called a system in the strict sense of the word. There was neither a defined corpus of signs that had to be used nor a body of strict rules that had to be observed in every case, but, rather, a considerable latitude obtained, which enabled every writer to find his own solutions according to the requirements of the given occasion. Every hieroglyph except the frequently used calendaric ones, is an individual composition, based on free invention but employing conventionalized signs and standardized arrangements where possible. The signs are often used in narrative pictography also as qualifiers according to their conventionalized semantic designatum. So it cannot be decided whether they were derived from standardized representations in narrative pictography or vice versa. Despite standardization, however, only a reduced number of hieroglyphs showed a high degree of abbreviation and graphic transformation. In most cases the depicted object remained recognizable even to an untrained reader.

As Aztec hieroglyphic writing never possessed a clear-cut corpus of signs, only a minority of the signs that were normally employed had standardized forms: a few plants, animals, parts of the human body, natural phenomena and the like, and some cultural artifacts. An even smaller number of signs had, apart from other semantic contexts, an unambiguous lexemic designatum. This applies especially to the signs and names for the 20 days which were among the most frequently used signs. Only this group of signs (certainly far fewer than 100) can be called logograms (see Fig. 3, "B").

The standardized signs with a conventional designatum, especially the twenty signs, were not restricted in usage to one particular language only. They can be found with but minor stylistic variations of their graphic forms in pre-Spanish manuscripts composed by speakers of various languages as different from each other as Nahuatl and Mixtec, for example. These standardized signs functioned as logograms, whose lexemic realization was, however, clearly defined only within one specific language. In other languages they could be understood and read as well, but with quite different lexemic designata (see Fig. 2). Aztec writing, its conventional graphic signs and their semantic designata were thus not restricted to the Aztec (or Nahuatl) language, but covered a considerable spectrum of Central Mexican indigenous languages – the extent of this coverage, however, remains obscure due to the lack of documents in many regions.

Aztec signs, of traditional (standardized) form or designed in more or less free rendering, were not identical as far as their mode of functioning is concerned. Even within the so-called "ideographic" mode of writing, where signs had only, or in the first place, a semantic designatum, important differences can be discerned in the details (Fig. 3). The differences are located within the pattern of correspondence between sign and (semantic) designatum. The most characteristic type of ideographic writing (Fig. 3, "A") is also the most frequent. In this case, the sign designates an item of semantic information only. The phonetic realization (pronunciation) is not indicated, it has to be supplied by the reader – the result of which is a certain degree of ambiguity. Usually there is a considerable number of words (lexemes) that fit the semantic designatum of a single ideographic sign. Many of these words are synonyms, but other associative linkages between semantic designatum and verbal message can be found – and it was left to the reader to re-discover the writer's meaning. On the other hand, one single concept could be the semantic designatum of different signs – where different modes of association were employed (Fig. 3, "E").

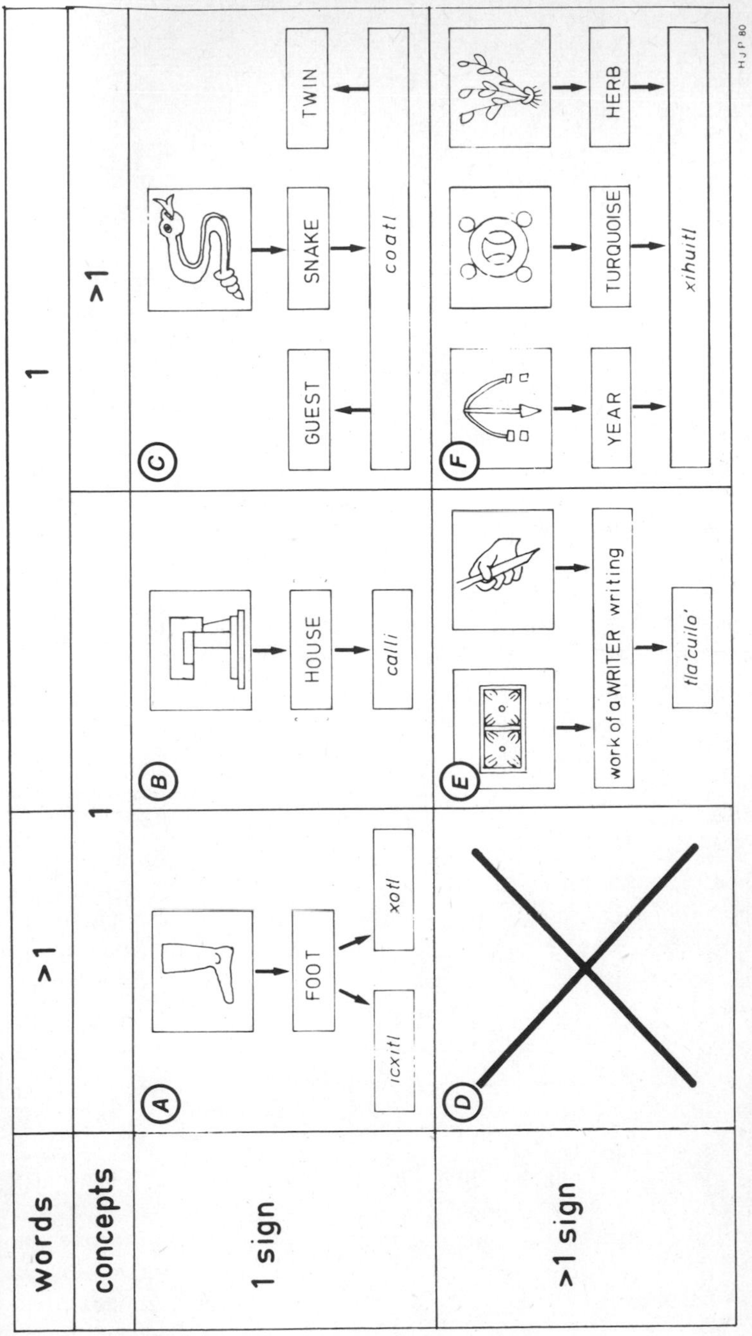

Figure 3. Aztec ideographic writing[3]

The correspondence between sign, semantic designation and phonetic realization is unambiguous only in the case of logograms (Fig. 3, "B"). It becomes complicated with homonyms, when the identical phonemic designatum is shared by more than one single semantic designatum. If each of these words had a graphic sign of its own, this is merely a phonemic coincidence (Fig. 3, "F"). This may be due to the fact that some signs can be drawn or recognized more easily than others or that the writer customarily tended to employ only one graphic sign for all homonyms (Fig. 3, "C"). This clearly is the first step towards phonetic writing, but unfortunately Nahuatl possesses very few true homonyms so that phonetic writing by way of homonymy never played an important role in Aztec hieroglyphic writing. This is one of the most striking differences between Aztec and Maya writing.

Aztec writing never developed alphabetic or syllabic writing. (There is only one exception from Colonial times that will be discussed below.) The dominating feature of Aztec hieroglyphic writing was ideographic writing – it has even been questioned whether any phonetic writing existed before the arrival of the Europeans. Nicholson (1973) has presented a thorough discussion of this point. He concludes (1973: 35) that phonetic writing certainly is an autochthonous element of Central Mexican writing systems. There are various types of phonetic writing that can be distinguished following Nowotny's (1959:109–10) well-founded classification (Fig. 4). Besides a great number of defective forms that do not allow a correct reading (except, if the reader "already knows"),[4] two main categories should be distinguished. Phonetic writing is labeled "constitutive" when it conveys the whole information exclusively; it is called "redundant", when it is added to another, mostly ideographically used, hieroglyph in order to avoid misreadings. Most characteristic is a special type of redundant phonetic writing, which makes use of a so-called "phonetic indicator" (in an earlier publication the author coined the term "Intonierende Schreibung" – Prem 1974:529). The phonetic indicator designates only a submorphemic group of phonemes by which the target word can be selected from a number of possible synonyms. Most frequent is an initial phonetic indicator. There is only a very small number of signs (logograms) that were applied as initial phonetic indicators, misleading some authors to speak of incipient syllabic writing. Redundant phonetic writing of a whole word is extremely rare due to the few homonyms in the Nahuatl language.

While phonetic writing in Aztec hieroglyphs was employed in the first place as a device to reduce phonemic ambiguities, the main body of information was transmitted by ideographic writing. The major part of these ideograms, however, consisted of compounds in which two or more individual signs had been joined to designate a new concept. This corresponds very

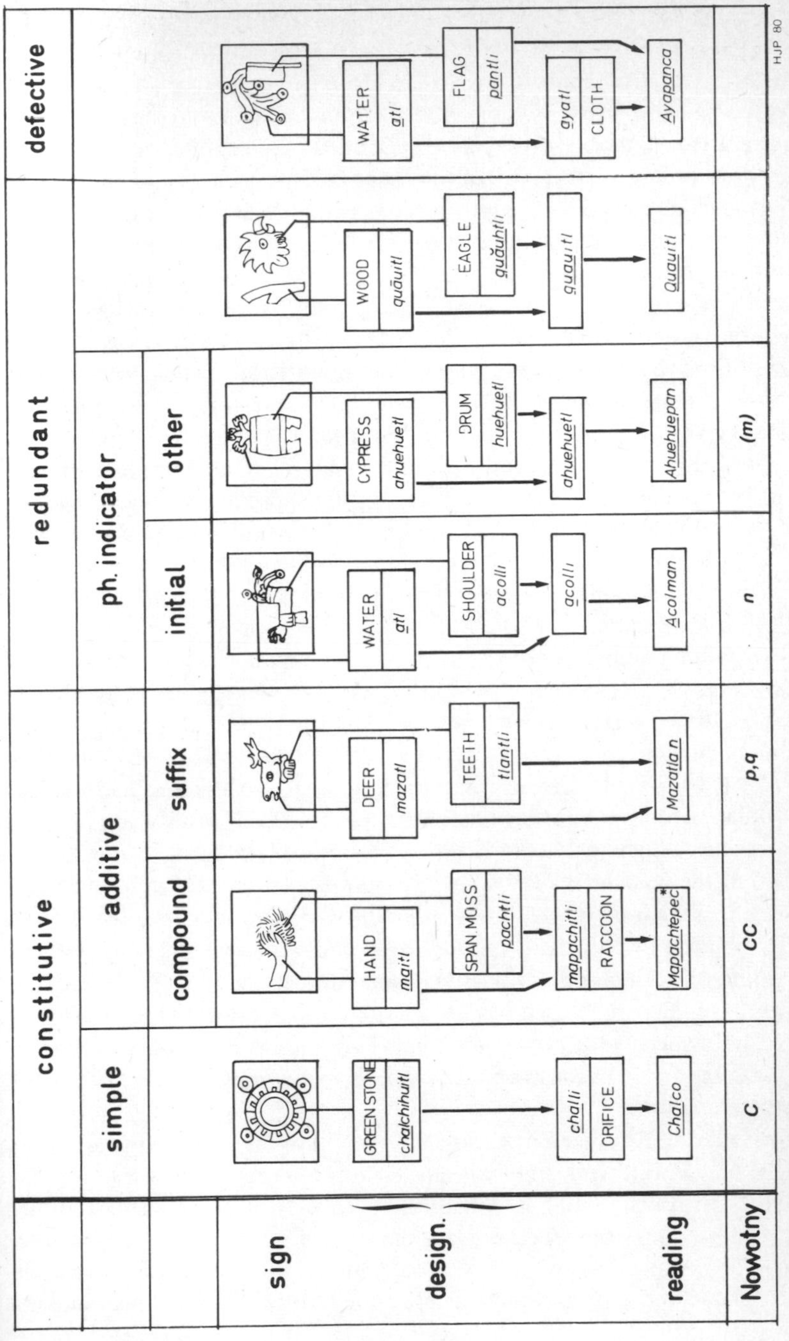

Figure 4. Aztec phonetic writing[5]

neatly to the pattern of word formation by compounding, which is so prevalent in the Aztec language. What has been said already with respect to the individual ideograph, applies also to hieroglyphic compounds: there existed no rules on how to compose (and, equally important, how to read) them. No direction of writing has ever been established. Ideographic compounds – arranged according to graphic conventions (i.e. incorporating, combining or just placing the constituting signs in some spatial relation) – can indeed be read in every possible sequential order (Prem 1979 gives a few examples). Because Aztec writing lacked any method to establish a sequence or another relation between the components of a hieroglyph, the inherent ambiguities of the writing system could not be eliminated. Thus misreadings were not infrequent even by Indians well trained in the native writing system who wrote – after the Conquest, but proceeding from pre-colonial documents – chronicles and other historical works in European characters.

Hieroglyphic compounds, which form the majority of all Aztec hieroglyphs, present yet another problem to analytical study: the problem of etymology. As a rule, in Nahuatl the semantic designatum of a noun is modified when it is compounded with another noun (which is pre-posed). The range of this semantic modification may be quite variable: from a simple genitive-like combination to the creation of a totally new semantic content (a famous example is the compound noun *tzontecomatl*–head, it's components are: *tzontili*–hair and *tecomatl*–jar, itself a compound from *tetl*–stone and *comitl*–once again: jar). If an Aztec scribe decided not to paint the object designated by the compound but those designated by its constituent lexemes (to continue the example: if he drew instead of a human head a jar and a tuft of hair perhaps even adding the conventionalized picture of a cobblestone, often also employed as a phonetic designator): can this writing procedure still be called ideographic? Not, if ideography is used to denote the depiction of the object to be designated. Is it to be termed phonetic? Not, if by phonetic one understands the transmission of an item of phonetic (lexemic) information only without taking into consideration its possible semantic designatum. The procedure just described is characterized by the inclusion of the real or supposed etymology in the associative process of both the writer and the reader. Perhaps it will be necessary to establish a special category of writing and a new term for it: "etymographic".

The reader of the preceding paragraphs may have the impression that Aztec hieroglyphic writing is merely a vehicle conveying ambiguities – and the problem with Aztec writing is, that that is precisely what it is. The structure of the Aztec language, especially the ample use of compounding, favored ideographic writing (as well as "etymography"), the lack of homonyms obviated at least one approach towards phonetic writing. On the other hand the virtuosity that Central Mexican manuscript painters developed in their narrative pictography reduced the necessity for hieroglyphic writing and restricted its actual use. The result was a masterfully applied though imperfect system.

Aztec hieroglyphic writing contained, however, the germ of further development. From a small region in the valley of Mexico, from Tepetlaoztoc near the city of Tezcuco, some documents from early colonial times survived in which phonetic writing was more refined and used almost exclusively. Aubin (1885) who studied one of these manuscripts quite rightly classified this writing system as syllabic. Some 100 elements familiar in Aztec writing were used in Tepetlaoztoc in a form resembling the so-called phonetic indicators. But in this case the whole word had been constructed by this procedure. Even Spanish proper names were written, though inadequately, by means of a sequence of phonetic indicators. Even one of the major flaws of Aztec hieroglyphic writing seems to have been remedied: most of the glyphic compounds are to be read in the same direction – from bottom to top, and the tower-like arrangement of components facilitates the composition demanded of the reader. But even this refined system was doubtless much inferior to the imported European alphabet and did not survive for long.

3. *Classic and postclassic Maya writing*

While two areas of the Maya realm are well represented by writing, documentation on others is scant:
1. the southern lowlands with several thousand monumental inscriptions in stone (and sometimes wood) which were executed from 300–900 A.D. and which treat historical-genealogical matter of strictly local import;
2. the northern part of the Yucatan peninsula, which is represented by three, or possibly four, illustrated manuscripts of calendrical, astrological and augural content. They were executed some time between 1200 and the Spanish conquest after 1540.

There is a major visible contrast between documents written in Maya glyphs and those written in other Mesoamerican systems, such as Olmec, Monte Albán, Zapotec, Mixtec, Aztec etc. Maya glyphs show a high degree of standardization and abstraction. Maya texts are often compact, fairly long, and sometimes completely separated from iconographic information. This hints strongly towards an independent development of the Maya system out of the epi-Olmec Isthmian horizon (Tres Zapotes, Chiapa de Corzo, Abaj Takalik, Miraflores phase of Kaminaljuyú) which we assume to be its direct ancestor. The Maya must have developed their own writing system into a full-fledged script in the incredibly short time-span of 400 years. It represented language exactly and completely, and thus did not develop any further, once this stage was reached at about 400 A.D.

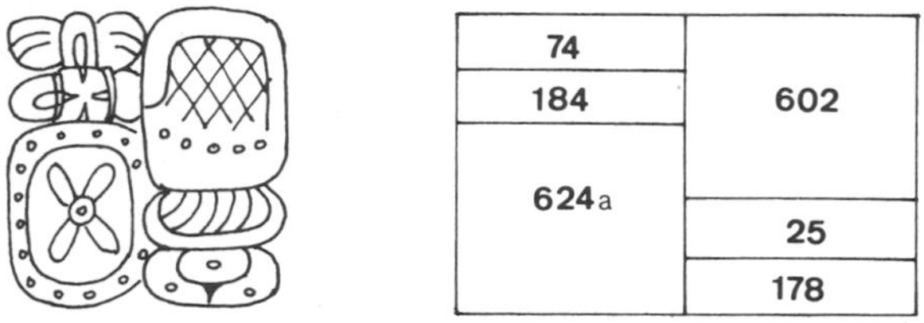

sign*	ideographic designatum	phonemic designatum	type	reading
74		mah	morpheme	mahkina
184		kina	morpheme	
624a	shield	chimal / pacal	lexeme	pacal
602		pah	morpheme	
25		ca	syllable	
178		la	syllable	

* Transcription according to Thompson 1962

Figure 5. Analysis of the personal name hieroglyph "Pacal"

Until recently the linguistic decipherment of Maya writing has suffered from lack of a well defined theoretical framework. Thus highly eclectic and phantastic speculations and claims have discredited this approach for a long time and have overruled serious attempts by scholars like Seler and Kelley. Starting with a publication in 1973 by Lounsbury, more explicit theoretical statements about the nature of Maya writing combined with strictly methodical linguistic attempts in decipherment has brought a break-through which will form the basis for our short discussion. As results are still tentative, a systematic overview cannot be given. Instead we will present some examples highlighting general results.

3.1 *Monumental inscriptions of the southern lowlands*

As an example, we will present the analysis of the name of ruler "Pacal", who reigned in Palenque from 615–682 A.D. (see Fig. 5). The linguistic interpretation is done in terms of the Chol language which prevailed with minor dialect variants (Chol proper, Chontal, and Chorti) in all of the southern lowlands, including the city of Palenque.

According to Lounsbury (1974:ii) *mahkina* is a title applying to lineage-heads, found in early colonial sources of the highlands. We have to revert to this neighboring region because of a lack of pertinent colonial data from Palenque proper. Sign 624a, the picture of a shield, ideographically gives the ruler's name, which was "shield". In Chol there is a choice between two synonyms for "shield", "chimal" and "pacal". Chimal is a Nahuatl-loan word, pacal is derived from an ancient Maya-root. The correct phonemic reading is therefore indicated through addition of syllabically written "paca-l (a)", represented by signs 602–25–178. It is understood, that the vowel of the last syllabic sign (178) "la" is not to be pronounced, thus giving the correct spelling "pacal". With this kind of syllabic writing and some further rules concerning non-distinction between phonetically close phonemes (o/u etc.), and the possibility of suppressing certain "weak" consonants (h, etc.), a syllabic-alphabetic system is established which allows the user to render all possible sequences of phonemes in Maya languages with relative ease, and a high level of precision. Notwithstanding, all known texts preserve a considerable amount of semantic components, often with clearly recognizable iconic qualities, as the image of a shield in our example testifies.

Manuscript-texts from the northern lowlands: Even 500 years later, and in the distant northern parts of the peninsula of Yucatan, the Maya writing system was basically unchanged although confined to a distinct linguistic environment of Yucatec. Yucatec (or Mayathan) along with Chol and some 30 other languages belong to the relatively homogeneous family of Maya languages. They share a great amount of their basic vocabulary, but are significantly different in morphology (verb system). Maya languages have monosyllabic lexemes (CVC) preponderantly, which combine with equally monosyllabic pre- and postfixes to form noun- and verbphrases. Clause structure is fairly variable. We will give two examples of simple clauses, both taken from the postclassic Dresden Codex (Figs. 6 and 7).

Numbers under each text of 4 glyphs indicate distances of days connecting each text with its predecessor, thus forming strings of similar texts, calculated from a common base, in which each text is associated with a different calendar day and states its augury. Both texts have a young goddess as their protagonist. For lack of a firm identification with surviving deity-concepts and decipherment of her name glyph, she has been given the conventional designation G 22 by Zimmermann (1956). Her influence (upon mankind, we assume) is transmitted through augural animals which in Central Mexican mythology are exclusively, in Maya mythology preponderantly, birds. The augury is negative

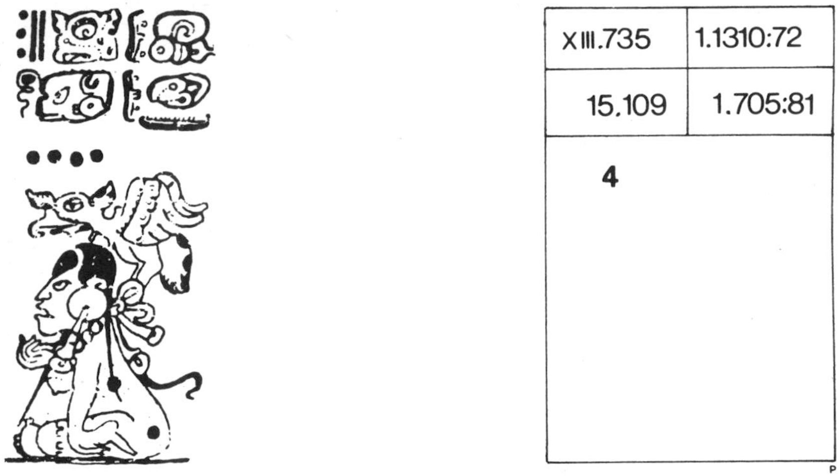

transcribed glyph*	ideographic designatum	phonemic designatum	type	reading	meaning	grammatical analysis
XIII.735	thirteen	oxlahun	lexemes	oxlahun	"13 Muan-bird"	object
	muan-bird	muan		muan		
1.1310:72		u	morpheme			
		mu	syllable	umut	is the augury	verb phrase
		ti	morpheme			
15.109		?	syllable	?	of Goddess 22	subject
	goddess 22	?	lexeme			
1.705:81	?	?		?	(negative)	attribute

* Transcription according to Zimmermann 1956

Figure 6. Analysis of a text from the Dresden Codex.

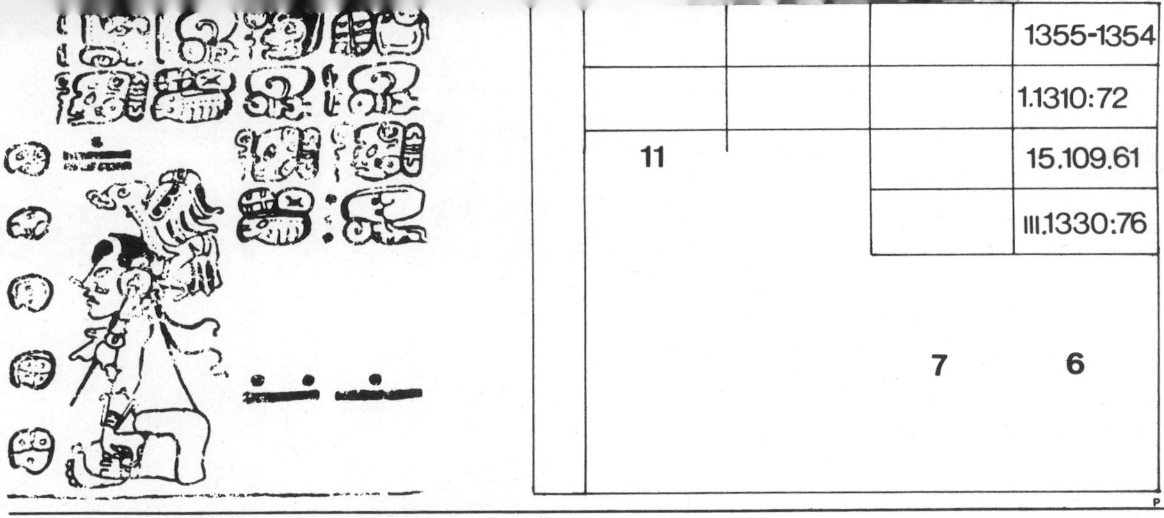

transcribed glyph*	ideographic designatum	phonemic designatum	type	reading	meaning	grammatical analysis
1355–1354		tzu	syllable			
		lu	syllable	tzu-lu	dog	ogject
1.1310:72		u	morpheme			
		mu	syllable	umut	is the augury	verb phrase
		ti	syllable			
15.109.61		?	syllable			
	goddess 22	?	lexeme	?	of Goddress 22	subject
		?	syllable			
III.1330:76		?	?	?	(positive)	attribute

* Transcription according to Zimmermann 1956

Figure 7. Analysis of a text from the Dresden Codex.

in the first example and positive in the second, according to the last glyph of each text.

For their qualifying function these are called attributive glyphs, although these, too, have not yet been deciphered. The textual information is partially visualized below the glyphic text where the young goddess is depicted sitting crosslegged with the augural bird above and behind her head. In our second example the information is conveyed exclusively through glyphs, there being no accompanying picture. This lack of iconographic information, which is fairly common (see for example the companion section preceeding our second example), indicates that Maya writing is a selfsufficient communication system that is not dependant on iconographic information, as is the case in all other contemporaneous Mesoamerican scripts (Mixtec, Aztec etc.).

The construction of hieroglyphs follows the same principle as demonstrated for the name-glyph of Pacal: They are partially ideographic ("13 Muan" and the central section of the undeciphered name glyph of goddess 22), partially syllabic (dog, augury). With these examples in mind, we can make some observations on morphology and syntax. Reading order is from left to right and from top to bottom, on both levels. This sequence is followed more strictly on the text-level, than on the level of single hieroglyphs. In glyph-formation, positioning of a sign is often governed more by aesthetics than by rules of reading order, and moreover, to such an extent that a sign can be doubled just for symmetrical purposes without affecting the reading.

Decipherment of manuscript-texts as compared to monumental inscriptions is much more direct, because some of their contents, later and independently, were transcribed into Latin script. Therefore, we can supply parallel texts to our glyphic examples from the Códice Pérez, where they are contained in a chapter on "the auguries of the days" (Códice Pérez 1949:184–5). Furthermore, we do have an "alphabet" and a few sample sentences furnished by Diego de Landa in his attempt to describe the Maya writing system in 1556. His information is very defective and misleading, however. This is so because of the differing concepts of writing entertained by Landa and his Mayan informant and Landa's inability to elicit the information he was looking for. His alphabet and sentences illustrate only 30 different signs, whereas the Maya system had about 300 fairly common signs in use. For some of them he gives letters as equivalents, although it is now clear that they have syllabic or morphemic, and some even ideographic referents. But once these misconceptions in his description are taken into account, Landa supplies, nevertheless, or confirms selected decipherments. In our examples we have made use of three signs, which were interpreted or are confirmed by Landa (see Fig. 8).

Maya Sign		Landa's value	modern values
T 59		"t"	/ti/
T 25		"c"	/ka/
T 1		"u"	/?u/ or /u/ or /uy/

Figure 8. Examples from Landa's 'alphabet'

3.2 *Language differentiation and hieroglyphic writing*

The question whether language differentiation in the Maya area is reflected through similar differentiation in hieroglyphic writing has not been investigated adequately. The basic unity of classic Maya writing is well established through comparison of calendrical inscriptions from major sites in different regions (especially Copán in the southeast, Palenque in the southwest, Tikal in the centre, and Chichen Itzá in the north).

Assuming that parallels to different languages and dialects spoken in these regions in Classic times are reflected in hieroglyphic writing, we should be able to find major systematic differences between texts from different regions, paralleling for example the t-ch contrast of Yucatan and Chol. And, in fact, the first hints confirming this hypothesis have been identified as we will show by means of the glyphs representing "in his/her house" (Fig. 9). The meaning "in his/her house" is confirmed contextually for both glyphs. The only significant, i.e. emic difference between them is the addition of sign T 59 ('ti') in Copán texts. In the Chol language, which was spoken in a dialectal subdivision in Copán, "in his/her house" is "tuyotot". In Yucatec, which was spoken in the region where we assume the Dresden Codex originated, "in his/her house" is spelled "tuyotoch". Thus the only contrast is in the end-consonant t/ch.

The Copan scribe apparently took the whole glyph in its Yucatecan form, as an ideograph (or as an unanalyzed phrase), thus disregarding the phonemic complement contained therein (T 601), which indicated the ch-phoneme. To indicate the proper reading in his language (i.e. "tuyotot"), he added the sign T 59, as a phonemic complement to the glyph he perhaps knew would otherwise be read "tuyotoch".

4. *A glimpse ahead*

Much research will have to be done to clarify all the details of the Maya writing system, to define deviations and unsystematic components and to investigate glyph-dialectology on a geographical basis. The evolution of the Maya system from its epi-Olmec base in pre-Classic times to the fully-fledged Classic system, and the impact of late (essentially post-Classic) intrusions from Central Mexican systems as well as the apparent decay prior to the Spanish conquest (Codex Madrid, Codex Grolier), will have to be clarified in order to add the important diachronic dimension to our understanding of this intellectual achievement.

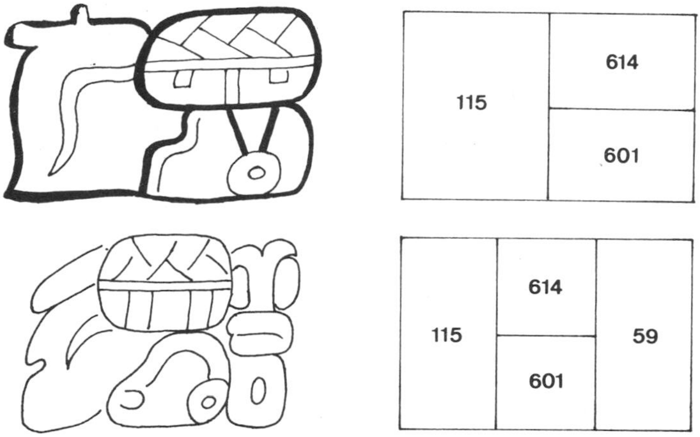

sign*	ideographic designatum	phonemic designatum	type	reading	
115		tu	syllable	tuy	
614	house	otoch	lexeme	otoch	otot
		na			
601		chu	syllable		
59		ti	syllable		

* Transcription according to Thompson 1962

Figure 9. Analysis of regional variations of glyphic expression

Notes

1. The section "Maya writing" was written by Riese.
2. The Indian civilizations of the Andean region (Inca and their predecessors) apparently never developed any form of writing with the exception of a knot-string-notation (quipu).
3. Depending on the type of correspondence between sign, concept (i.e. semantic designation) and expressed word (lexeme) some classes of ideographic writing can be distinguished. "A" represents the elementary category, where unambiguous transmission of information is restricted to the semantic designatum whereas there are more than one phonetic "readings". "B" is the classical example of a logogram. It is open to question whether a semantic designation is implied as well or not. "C" may be the first step towards phonetic writing. Due to the scarcity of true homonyms in the Nahuatl language, only few examples can be cited where

the object depicted by the sign and its semantic information diverge due to a phonetic detour. "F" shows the more frequent case where different semantic designata – all corresponding to the same word and, probably, being etymologically related – are nevertheless represented by different signs. Also combinations of type "C" and "F" occur. "E" demonstrates that – especially in case of deverbative nouns – the same semantic designatum can be covered by more than one sign. Often, the depiction of an action and the action itself are thus interchangeable. Class "C" seems to be non-existent in Aztec ideographic writing.

4. This type has to be called "defective" instead of "elliptical" which seems to imply a conventionalized procedure.
5. Phonetically used signs transmit information that can either be constitutive (being the only vector of transmission for the word or part of the word) or redundant (thus confirming information that has been transmitted by another vector, especially ideographically used signs). "Pure" forms like those shown are rare, compared with forms where different types are combined or where the type is difficult to determine. There is a wide variation of active forms which have in common that their present elements do not suffice for a correct reading.

Most examples show place names; *-co, -tepec, -tlan, -man, -pan* are locative suffixes, *-ca* is the plural gentile noun (denoting ethnic affiliation) suffix corresponding to *-co* locatives. No. 6 is a personal name. The phonetically transmitted information is underlined. Examples 1, 2, 3, and 5 come from the Mendoza Codex, no. 4 from the Matrícula de Tributos, no. 6 from the Matrícula de Huexotzinco and no. 7 from the Historia Tolteca-Chichimeca. In no. 2 the graphic element "mountain" (*tepetl,* denoting the locative suffix) is omitted for the sake of clarity. For each type, Nowotny's (1959) classification is given.

References

Aubin, Joseph-Marius-Alexis
1885 "Mémoires sur la peinture didactique et l'écriture figurative des anciens Mexicains". In *Mission scientifique au Mexique – Recherches historiques et archéologiques; premiere partie, histoire.* Paris.

Bloomfield, Leonard
1950 *Language.* London: Allen & Unwin; New York: Holt.

Codex Dresdensis. Die Maya-Handschrift der sächsischen Landesbibliothek Dresden.
1962 Berlin: Akademie-Verlag.

Codice Perez. Traducción libre del Maya al Castellano.
1949 Ed. Emilio Solis Alcalá. Merida: Liga de Acción social.

Landa, Diego de
1959 *Relación de las cosas de Yucatán.* México: Porrúa.

Lounsbury, Floyd G.
1973 "On the derivation and reading of the 'Ben-Ich' prefix." In Elizabeth P. Benson, ed., *Mesoamerican Writing Systems.* Washington: Harvard University, pp. 99–143.
1974 "Pacal." In Merle Greene Robertson, ed., *Primera Mesa Redonda de Palenque,* Part I. Pebble Beach: The Robert Louis Stevenson School, p. ii.

Kirchhoff, Paul
1952 "Mesoamerica, its geographic limits, ethnic composition and cultural characteristics." In Sol Tax, ed., *Heritage of Conquest.* Chicago: The Free Press, pp. 17–30.

Marcus, Joyce
1976 "The origins of Mesoamerican writing." *Annual Review of Anthropology* 5:35–67.

"Zapotec writing." *Scientific American* 242:46–60.
Nicholson, Henry B.
1973 „Phoneticism in the late pre-Hispanic Central Mexican writing system." In Elizabeth P. Benson, ed., *Mesoamerican Writing Systems*, Washington: Harvard University, pp. 1–46.
Nowotny, Karl Anton
1959 Die Hieroglyphen des Codex Mendoza; der Bau einer mittelamerikanischen Wortbildschrift. *Mitteilungen aus dem Museum für Völkerkunde in Hamburg* 25:97–113.
Prem, Hanns J.
1973 A tentative classification of non-Maya writing systems in Mesoamerica. *Indiana* 1:29–58.
1974 Matricula de Huexotzinco. Edition, Kommentar, Hieroglyphenglossar. Graz: Akademische Druck und Verlagsanstalt.
1979 Aztec writing considered as a paradigma for Mesoamerican scripts. In Barbro Dahlgren, ed. *Mesoamérica, homenaje al doctor Paul Kirchhoff,* Mexico: Instituto Nacional de Antropologia e Historia, pp. 104–118.
Riese, Berthold
"Dynastographische Studien von Copán". (Ms.)
Smith, Mary Elizabeth
1973 *Picture Writing from Ancient Southern Mexico; Mixtec Place Signs and Maps.* Norman: Univ. of Oklahoma Press.
Thompson, John Eric S.
1962 *A Catalog of Maya Hieroglyphs.* Norman: Univ. of Oklahoma Press.
Zimmermann, Günther
1956 "Die Hieroglyphen der Maya-Handschriften." *Universität Hamburg – Abhandlungen aus dem Gebiet der Auslandskunde* 62. Hamburg: Cram, De Gruyter.

TOUSSAINT TCHITCHI et MARC LAURENT HAZOUMÉ

Le développment d'un alphabet national dans une communauté multilingue

Abstract

This essay is an attempt to reveal the objectives pursued by the language policy of the People's Republic of Bénin, a policy which will make possible the liberation of the people from the suffocating hulls of political oppression, cultural and social domination, economic exploitation. The People's Republic of Bénin is a multinational state in which every nationality possesses the right to use its own language in speech and writing and thus to develop its own culture.

Except for Dendi, Fulfulde etc. the country is covered by two great language groups: the Kwa group with Aja, Fon, Gun, Yoruba etc. and the Gur group with most of the northern languages, Ditammari. Waama, Yom etc. Such heterogeneity neccessitates the development of a national alphabet equally suitable for transcribing any of these diverse national languages. The introduction of this alphabet in 1975, while still open to modification, already represents a major step in the solution of problems arising in connection with the use of several languages in a multilinguistic society. At the same time it evidences the state's desire to follow a definite policy of language planning. It will be a motor in the struggle against illiteracy, which is without doubt a brake on development in general and on Bénin society in particular.

1. *Introduction*

La langue est le support et le véhicule d'une culture, et partant, instrument privilégié de communication entre les hommes; l'homme, moteur et facteur du développement, se doit, pour les besoins de sa cause, d'utiliser une langue de communication courante, ne serait-ce que quand il se trouve en "situation nécessaire d'échange"; une des situations nécessaires d'échange se remarque lorsqu'au cours d'une promenade vous rencontrez un ami à qui vous adressez votre salut; à supposer que l'ami vous comprenne, on peut en déduire que vous parlez la même langue, car on dit que "deux personnes parlent la même langue lorsque leurs parlers individuels sont mutuellement compréhensibles dès le premier contact, sans passer par une phase d'apprentissage" (Coupez 1977). L'apprentissage d'une langue peut se situer à deux niveaux: un niveau oral et un niveau graphique; les locuteurs maternels et les locuteurs non-maternels sont concernés par ces deux niveaux.

Tout acte de communication verbale se situe au niveau oral; apprendre à parler sa langue, c'est apprendre à distinguer les objets les uns des autres, c'est imiter la voix des autres; ce qui entre en jeu à ce niveau, c'est bien la perception auditive. Chacun de nous a pu faire cette expérience. Au niveau graphique, on entrevoit l'utilisation du signe écrit; en effet, "le signe écrit est désormais (. . .) une des conditions essentielles du progrès. Le signe écrit a toujours été de tous les temps l'outil permanent en même temps qu'une mémoire renfermant toutes les connaissances à l'action et au développement individuel et collectif de l'homme en société" (Guedou et Tchitchi 1977). C'est dire que la création et l'enseignement d'un alphabet à une communauté linguistique dans une société multilingue est une action scientifique de grande portée politique et idéologique; la prise de conscience des peuples anciennement colonisés atteint un degré tel que l'on considère aujourd'hui celui qui parle une langue autre que la sienne comme étranger à sa propre culture; l'expression est courante en ajagbe, qui dit "mɛ̄ɖē bú yǐ gbè, à nyì é bú yìɖékí"; et assez curieusement, cette citation traduit la pensée habilement exprimée par le feu Président français Georges Pompidou qui savait bien de quoi il parlait lorsqu'il disait à peu près ceci: "qui perd sa langue, perd tout". Donc, la langue, expression orale ou écrite de la pensée, est un véritable outil au service du développement intégral d'une nation.

L'oralité qui caractérise les civilisations africaines doit pouvoir céder le pas à l'écriture, d'où la nécessité pour les linguistes de créer un alphabet pour les langues qui n'en ont pas encore. Ce n'est que grâce à l'écriture que l'on peut sauvegarder l'acquis culturel, social, économique et technologique d'un groupe humain donné; la fixation par écrit du patrimoine culturel d'un peuple milite en faveur des recherches minutieuses en vue de la création d'un alphabet. Mais il ne suffit pas de créer un alphabet; il faudra pouvoir l'utiliser de manière rationnelle en facilitant aux usagers son accès; en d'autres termes, dans la situation actuelle tout chercheur doit connaître les destinataires des résultats de ses recherches; dans cette perspective, la recherche ne saurait être neutre; elle doit s'insérer dans le processus de développement intégral d'un pays. C'est pourquoi le sujet de cette communication doit être envisagé sous plusieurs aspects; l'aspect politique de la question nous paraît d'autant plus important que la politique linguistique d'un Etat plurilingue doit être conséquemment définie en fonction de l'option idéologique de cet Etat; faisant suite à cette politique linguistique nationale, le caractère multinational de la société béninoise nous permettra de dégager le rôle et l'importance d'un alphabet national dans une telle société, les principes et les objectifs d'un tel alphabet; nos propos se devront d'être illustrés par quelques exemples tirés des travaux réalisés par des chercheurs de la République Populaire du Bénin.

2. *La politique linguistique de la République Populaire du Bénin*

La promotion des langues et cultures nationales s'inscrit au Bénin dans une stratégie globale de développement; on note une volonté manifeste de l'homme béninois de se libérer du carcan d'étouffement que constituent l'oppression politique, la domination culturelle, économique et sociale; c'est pourquoi depuis le 30 Novembre 1972, la tendance générale veut que l'on travaille avec acharnement à la sauvegarde et à la réhabilitation de nos valeurs culturelles; sauvegarder et réhabiliter des valeurs culturelles constituent une seule et même entreprise qui requiert une certaine détermination; cette entreprise exige de l'homme qu'il fasse un travail de ressourcement et de fixation de modèles culturels. Fixer les modèles culturels nécessite la maîtrise de l'écriture, et partant la création d'un alphabet comme soutien scientifique de cette écriture; en effet, "convention extérieure aux langues, l'écriture résulte d'une réflexion intellectuelle consciente. Elle est de ce fait accessible aux décisions de l'autorité: l'Etat et l'école peuvent en contrôler intégralement l'usage" (Coupez 1977). L'Etat peut et doit intervenir pour "légiférer" en tenant bien entendu compte des résultats des travaux de recherche en la matière; une décision d'une telle envergure ne doit pas se prendre dans la précipitation. L'école au contraire garantit la survie de l'écriture; elle se maintient, se perfectionne grâce à la pratique quotidienne à laquelle elle est soumise: maîtres et élèves s'en servent à longueur de journée.

La politique linguistique de la République Populaire du Bénin ne souffre d'aucune ambiguité; elle est clairement définie dans le Discours-programme du 30 Novembre 1972 et constitue un soubassement culturel et idéologique du gouvernement en matière de développement de l'enseignement et de l'éducation.

Le Discours-programme constate en effet que

> jusqu'ici, l'éducation et la culture ont été au service de la domination et de l'exploitation étrangères. Ici également s'impose une politique nouvelle d'indépendance nationale qui rompt avec le carcan d'étouffement

> de nos valeurs nationales que constitue l'école traditionnelle. Dans cette optique, il est impérieux d'installer un systeme d'éducation démocratique et patriotique qui permette l'enseignement d'une science et d'une technique modernes au service des intérêts du peuple. Pour cela, il faudra .... revaloriser nos langues nationales, réhabiliter notre culture en l'adaptant aux besoins de nos masses laborieuses, ouvrir notre université à toutes les formes du savoir et à tous les courants contemporains de la pensée scientifique. Elle doit avoir une vocation africaine en même temps qu'universelle et réserver une place privilégiée au brassage des expériences accumulées par les universités soeurs, assurer le développement de la culture populaire en organisant dans les langues nationales l'alphabétisation des masses, facteur essentiel de notre développement.[1]

La volonté politique et idéologique est suffisamment claire. Cet extrait pose implicitement le problème de l'alphabet des langues nationales; la République Populaire du Bénin n'est pas un Etat homogène du point de vue linguistique; l'article 3 de la Loi Fondamentale l'explicite beaucoup plus clairement; cet article dit en substance:

> La République Populaire du Bénin est un Etat unifié multinational. Toutes les nationalités sont égales en droit et en devoirs (...). Toutes les nationalités jouissent de la liberté d'utiliser leur langue parlée et écrite et de développer leur propre culture.[2]

C'est en tenant compte de l'apparente complexité linguistique de notre pays et en essayant d'apporter une solution lucide à la question nationale qu'il faudra appréhender cette volonté politique. Cet extrait de l'article 3 de la Loi Fondamentale montre bien qu'il existe en Afrique Noire en général et en République Populaire du Bénin en particulier tout comme dans bien d'autres pays du monde des majorités et des minorités nationales, et de ce fait, des langues nationales majoritaires et des langues nationales minoritaires; ici l'Etat garantit à chaque nationalité l'utilisation de sa langue parlée et écrite; l'Etat garantit donc le respect, la dignité et la promotion de la langue et de la culture de chaque nationalité. Une telle option politique appelle la mise en oeuvre de moyens scientifiques adéquats qui permettent de cerner de près chaque réalité nationale. Une telle option politique est inhérente à la complexité de la situation linguistique de notre pays. Quelle est cette situation?

3. *La situation linguistique*

La multiplicité des parlers que l'on rencontre au Bénin a fait que le Professeur Pierre Alexandre a classé l'ex-Dahomey parmi les Etats africains à hétérogénéité linguistique. Cette constatation est inhérente à l'inexistence d'un inventaire systématique et exhaustif de ces langues; l'Atlas linguistique de la République Populaire du Bénin pourra éclairer la question des langues nationales au Bénin.

En dehors du dendi (zarma), du hawusa, du fulfulde etc., les autres langues de la République Populaire du Bénin appartiennent à la grande famille nigéro-congolaise définie par Greenberg et se répartissent en deux groupes, à savoir,

– le groupe Kwa pour les langues parlées dans les provinces méridionales du Bénin; elles sont "caractérisées chacune, au plan des constituants nominaux, par un morphème de pluralisation pour tout le stock nominal, avec un système de pronoms réduits" (Nata 1980), parmi ces langues, il faut citer le fongbe, le gungbe, le ayizgbe, le tɔfingbe, le ajagbe, le ede yoruba, le gɛngbe, le wacigbe; soulignons qu'à l'intérieur de ce groupe Kwa on peut distinguer deux sous-groupes: le "groupe [èdé]" se rapportant au yoruba et à toutes ces variantes dialectales, le "sous-groupe gbè" anciennement désigné sous-groupe Aja-Tado, origine hypothétique de la plupart des groupes socioculturels au Sud de notre pays – notons que "èdé" ou "ègbè" traduit le terme "langue", considérée comme le véhicule de la pensée; les glossonymes s'obtiennent de manière très simple; dans le cas du sous-groupe èdé, il suffit d'antéposer le terme èdé au nom du groupe socio-culturel considéré pour obtenir le nom de la langue; ainsi nous avons par exemple ede-yoruba, ede-nago, etc.; en ce qui concerne le sous-groupe gbè, il faut postposer le terme gbè au nom par lequel on désigne le groupe socio-culturel; c'est ainsi que nous avons ayizɔgbè, fɔngbe, gungbe, ajagbe, gɛngbe, wacigbe, etc.,

– les langues du groupe "gur"; elles sont "caractérisées par les classes nominales comme les langues bantu. Ce sont des langues de type complexe, à morphématique différenciée sinon très différenciée pour certaines d'entre elles" (Nata 1980); parmi ces langues, il faut citer le baatɔnu, le waama, le ditammari, le nateni, le biali, le gulmancema, le mbɛlimɛ, le yom, le lekpa, le giseḍa ou ani etc.

Au point de vue formel, ces langues gur se répartissent à leur tour en trois sous-groupes selon la place du morphème de classe dans le constituant nominal. Ainsi donc nous avons:

1. les langues à préfixes (de classes), c'est-à-dire les langues où le morphème de classe est préfixé au radical du nominal, donc les langues où le

constituant nominal (si l'on symbolise par la modalité nominale) est de type:

m – $\sqrt{\text{RAD}}$ – (avec ou sans préfixes dérivatifs)

C'est le cas du giseḍa et du foodo;

2. les langues à suffixes (de classes), c'est-à-dire les langues où le morphème de classe est suffixé au radical du nominal, donc les langues où le constituant nominal est du type:

$\sqrt{\text{RAD}}$ – m (avec ou sans dérivatifs).

C'est le cas du waama, du baatɔnu, du nateni, du lokpa, etc.;

3. les langues à préfixes et à suffixes (de classes) ou langues à modalité nominale discontinue telle que cette modalité se préfixe et suffixe à la fois au radical du nominal. Ce sont des langues où le constituant nominal se présente sous la forme:

m – $\sqrt{\text{RAD}}$ – m (avec ou sans dérivatifs).

C'est le cas du ḍitammari, du mbɛlimɛ et du gulmancema (Nata 1980).

Nous avons tenu à faire cette longue citation pour éviter des répétitions inutiles. Le groupe gur ainsi identifié au Bénin présente des particularités au niveau des glossonymes; les noms de groupes socio-culturels sont nettement différents des noms de langues; c'est ainsi par exemple que les batɔmbu parlent le baatɔnu, les waaba parlent le waama, les gulmanceba parlent le gulmancema, les natema parlent le nateni, les bɛtammaribɛ parlent le ḍitammari, les bɛbɛlibɛ parlent le mbɛlimɛ, les yowa parlent le yom, etc. Bon nombre de ces langues sont utilisées à la radio; certaines font l'objet de presse dite rurale; elles sont toutes des langues nationales, c'est-à-dire des langues dotées d'un alphabet et d'une orthographe plus ou moins harmonisés.

4. *Caractère de l'alphabet national*

La République Populaire du Bénin présente une physionomie linguistique assez variée; cela tient sans doute à l'occupation de l'espace géographique par des peuples venus d'horizons divers; on a donc affaire à une communauté multilingue, comme le cas se présente dans bon nombre de pays en Afrique et dans le monde.

4.1 *Destinataires de l'alphabet*

L'analphabétisme est un fléau social, un frein au développement économique, social et culturel, en un mot, un handicap au développement intégral tout court. La lutte contre l'analphabétisme s'inscrit dans la stratégie globale de développement de la société béninoise.

Les conditions maximales du développement ne sauraient être remplies sans qu'on ait préalablement songé à la destruction systématique du carcan d'étouffement des valeurs culturelles que constitue l'analphabétisme; la mise en oeuvre d'un alphabet national devient une tâche politique et idéologique intéressant tous les secteurs d'activité. Selon notre logique, les premiers intéressés par cette mise en oeuvre ce sont les intellectuels assimilés entièrement ou non, qui pensent lutter au coude à coude avec les masses paysannes et ouvrières en vue de la destruction systématique du vieil ordre colonial et néo-colonial; cette conception qui va dans le sens du progrès vise deux objectifs:

– désaliéner les intellectuels qui jusque-là, à la traîne de l'Europe bourgoise et capitaliste, ont nié et continuent de nier leur propre identité culturelle, en déniant aux langues nationales le rôle de levier qu'elles doivent jouer pour une promotion correcte des valeurs culturelles,

– faire de ces intellectuels des cadres d'alphabétisation au sein des masses paysannes et ouvrières. Mais ces rôles ne sont pas perçus de cette manière-là aujourd'hui; la tâche de la confection d'un alphabet et de sa mise en oeuvre naît d'une prise de conscience d'abord individuelle, et qui plus tard, sans doute embrassera tout le monde.

Les autres destinataires de l'alphabet national sont les autres couches de la population qui, d'une manière ou d'une autre, ne sont pas du tout touchées par le système scolaire en vigueur ou le sont insuffisamment; il s'agit, bien entendu, des masses ouvrières et paysannes; c'est à ce niveau que l'alphabet se doit d'être simple et accessible à tout le monde; il doit en être fait abstraction de l'utilisation des signes diacritiques. Les principes devant être à la base de l'élaboration d'un tel alphabet seront définis en fonction de la situation linguistique nationale et en fonction des objectifs à atteindre; ces objectifs ne sont rien d'autre que l'éradication de l'analphabétisme au sein de la société où il est considéré comme un fléau.

4.2 *Les principes*

La réalité est que "toute proposition d'alphabet doit découler d'une analyse de la situation linguistique du pays où la langue est parlée et s'inscrire dans le cadre d'une planification politique. On peut décrire les situations linguistiques comme simples ou complexes. Une situation linguistique d'un Etat sera dite simple si une seule langue est parlée dans le cadre de l'Etat. On sait que cette situation est rare en Afrique (Rwanda, Burundi, Somali)" (Olasope et Yaï

1975). La République Populaire du Bénin jouit d'une situation complexe; c'est un Etat multinational, avons-nous précisé.

Le souci qui devra guider l'élaboration d'un alphabet est de pouvoir forger un outil permanent de lutte entre les mains de chaque citoyen; un alphabet dans une communauté multilingue doit être un ensemble de symboles judicieusement mis au point pour faciliter l'accès à l'écriture dans une civilisation de l'oralité. L'élaboration d'un seul stock de symboles obéit à une politique linguistique planifiée; un seul stock de symboles pour l'ensemble des langues d'une communauté multilingue, a deux avantages immédiats; cela permet une lecture plus commode des langues d'intercompréhension; cela peut faciliter l'apprentissage d'une seconde langue nationale; c'est donc un souci d'harmonisation en vue de mettre un terme à la "prolifération anarchique d'alphabets et à(l')encouragement objectif du micro-nationalisme" (Olasope et Yaï 1975).

La mise en oeuvre d'un alphabet national "suppose une bonne connaissance de la situation linguistique et la décision éclairée d'investir les ressources intellectuelles que requiert un tel travail". "Cela va sans dire, une telle décision ne se comprend que dans le cadre d'un bouleversement général des structures héritées de la colonisation" (Olasope et Yaï 1975). C'est-à-dire que l'émergence d'un alphabet pour une communauté linguistique donnée doit résulter d'un travail scientifique approfondi. L'un des principes fondamentaux de tout alphabet doit être celui d'un symbole = un son distinctif; dans cette perspective, il y a lieu de résoudre d'abord la question de l'analyse phonologique de la langue considérée et d'appréhender les réalités concrètes de son environnement dialectal. Que faut-il enseigner aux masses paysannes dans ces conditions? Est-ce un alphabet phonologique ou un alphabet phonétique. Du point de vue théorique, l'enseignement d'un alphabet phonologique est recommandé, la phonologie étant le fait d'hiérarchiser et d'ordonner le donné phonétique; le phonème dans ce cas est un signe distinctif non doué de sens; il devient le son utile de la langue – son enseignement doit répondre à une certaine normativité dans la mesure où il existe de manière pertinente dans la langue.

S'agissant de l'alphabet phonétique le problème est plus complexe et est intimement lié à des conditions économiques; en effet, dans une communauté multilingue, l'Etat qui garantit l'utilisation de sa langue à une nationalité donnée doit pouvoir déployer des moyens financiers énormes pour le succès de son action; or, il se fait que ce n'est pas toujours le cas; lorsqu'on entreprend de donner une chance égale à toutes les nationalités par le biais de l'alphabétisation, on ne peut que s'interroger sur la véritable nature d'une telle entreprise. Comment faire pour atteindre un tel objectif – ici, la question de la démarche méthodologique est fondamentale – une méthode fondée sur l'enseignement à l'adulte ou à l'analphabète des sons par lui-même produits est indispensable; un tel enseignement ne peut reposer que sur des donnés phonétiques; c'est ce qu'on a tenté de consigner dans le document de recherche intitulé *Alphabétisation par la Méthode Directe.* La méthode directe "se fonde sur une alphabétisation à la fois sui generis et autogerée tendant à résoudre les problèmes spécifiques d'une communauté donnée".[3] Cette méthode est "incontestablement économique: au contraire de l'alphabétisation traditionnelle, elle n'engage pas des frais d'impression des syllabaires et d'autres matérieux coûteux. Fondé sur le principe du 'Lowema' . . . elle compte sur la motivation et la volonté enthousiaste des paysans pour élaborer et produire eux-mêmes les documents didactiques nécessaires à l'animation du club".[3] Une autre raison qui militerait en faveur de l'utilisation d'un alphabet phonétique est que "dans un Etat à hétérogénéité linguistique comme le nôtre, on ne saurait faire économie de la méthode directe . . . , où alors, il faudra attendre encore plusieurs décennies pour que démarre l'alphabétisation pour certaines nationalités".[3] Ce qui prime dans cette méthode, c'est la spontanéité et cette spontanéité, après réflexion, ne peut se fonder que sur un matériau produit séance tenante. Tout cela ne va pas sans difficulté; la méthode est faussée si au départ, il n'y a pas eu un minimum de travail phonétique: un travail de repérage et d'identification de tous les sons de la langue considérée est indispensable au succès de la méthode.

Mais phonétique ou phonologique tout alphabet doit reposer sur la simplicité. C'est pourquoi tout alphabet doit avoir comme base "une symbolisation unique pour les phonèmes identiques des langues à l'intérieur d'un Etat, une symbolisation unique pour les phonèmes d'une langue parlée dans plusieurs Etats";[4] il faut souligner ici que les auteurs de cet extrait ont lourdement insisté sur une analyse phonologique préalable avant l'établissement de l'alphabet; nous avons cru devoir signaler les conditions de faisabilité d'une telle analyse; mais comment matérialiser l'alphabet phonétique ou phonologique.

Au cours des tentatives de mise en oeuvre d'un alphabet national, des conceptions entâchées d'erreurs peuvent se glisser dans les idées – l'une d'entre elles, l'utilisation des machines à caractères spéciaux est d'ordre beaucoup plus politique et idéologique qu'économique. Une tendance voudrait que l'on plaque les alphabets des langues africaines sur le modèle des alphabets des langues de colonisation. Quelles sont les motivations économiques et idéologiques qui guident une telle démarche? Il faudra sauvegarder la mainmise culturelle sur les peuples colonisés – car "nous devons nous rappeler, disait M. Delage, Inspecteur Général, que le but (de l'enseignement) est moins de sauvegarder l'originalité des races colonisées que de les élever vers nous"; "élever les races vers" l'Outre-mer signifie tout simplement qu'il faut façonner le peuple colonisé à l'image du colon; et c'est la langue, considérée comme instrument privilégié de communication qui servira de lien ombilical entre le colon et le colonisé. Il n'y a donc pas lieu de dire ou de faire croire que les machines à caractères spéciaux sont difficiles à acquérir; la raison économique est que les caractères coûtent réellement cher et c'est pourquoi à chaque réunion d'experts, on recommande l'élaboration d'un alphabet unique pour une sous-région donnée, un alphabet unique dont le caractère essentiel serait la simplicité. C'est ainsi qu'en Août 1975, une réunion organisée sous l'égide de l'UNESCO a regroupé les linguistes venus de Ghana, du Togo, de la Haute-Volta, du Nigéria et de la République Populaire du Bénin. A l'issue de cette réunion, explique le communiqué final, "il en a résulté un alphabet unique à stock ouvert proposé pour toutes les langues de la sous-région". Le communiqué précise par ailleurs que "la nasalisation est différemment symbolisée selon qu'il s'agit d'une langue à syllabe fermée ou d'une langue à syllabe ouverte.

Dans les langues à syllabe ouverte telles que les langues du groupe Kwa, elle sera indiquée par la nasale (n) postposée à la voyelle. Tandis que dans les langues à syllabe fermée comme dans la plupart des langues du groupe voltaïque, elle sera indiquée par le tilde suscrit".[5]

Certaines investigations refutent aujourd'hui l'argument selon lequel les langues du groupe voltaïque sont des langues à structure syllabique fermée, à preuve l'alphabet du ḍitammari et de beaucoup d'autres langues en cours d'élaboration. Ceci pose effectivement la problématique d'une recherche fondamentale avant toute ébauche d'alphabet dans une communauté multilingue.

Cet extrait nous amène vers deux exemples d'alphabet en République Populaire du Bénin: nous verrons l'alphabet des langues aja et ḍitammari.

4.3 *L'alphabet aja*

Le ajagbe est parlé au Togo et au Bénin par environ 400.000 âmes; c'est une langue du groupe Kwa et du sous-groupe "gbè" ou Aja-Tado. Son alphabet se présente de la manière suivante:

4.3.1 *Les voyelles*

Voyelles orales

[a] – àzò, la corne, (horn, cow-, sheep- or goat-)
àtā, la jambe, (leg)

[e] – ētê, l'igname, (yam)
ētā, la tête, (head)

[i] – àbì, la plaie, (wound)
àfǐ, la cendre, (ash or cinder)

[o] – zò, voler (aile), (to fly)
bòmɛ̀, le champ, (field)

[ɛ] – èlɛ̄, ici, (here)
ātɛ̄, le tamis, (sieve)

[ɔ] – èdɔ̀, la maladie, (illness)
édɔ̌, le travail, (work)

[u] – àḍǔ, la dent, (tooth)
àvǔ, le chien, (dog)

ces voyelles se présentent dans l'ordre suivant:

i u

e o

ɛ ɔ

a

Les voyelles nasales

Du fait de ce qui précède, à savoir que la nasalisation est symbolisée par la nasale (n) postposée à la voyelle à nasaliser, nous présentons les voyelles nasales de la manière suivante:

an – [ã] – àkǎn, le charbon, (coal)
àdǎn, la colère, (anger)

ɔn – [ɔ̃] – vɔ̀nvɔ́n, la peur, (fear)
fɔ̀nfɔ́n, le réveil, (awakening)

un – [ũ] – èhùn, le sang, (blood)
èhǔn, le tambour, (drum)

in – [ĩ] – ālǐn, la houe, (hoe)
èfin, le vol, (theft)

ɛn – [ɛ̃] – àfɛ́n, l'erreur, (mistake)
àdɛ̀n, le comportement, (behavior)

N.B. La colonne où la nasalisation est symbolisée par la nasale (n) postposée à la voyelle est conforme aux dispositions du decret No 75–272 du 24 Octobre 1975. Le tilde suscrit à la voyelle est conforme à l'alphabet de l'International African Institute (IAI). Ces voyelles nasales se présentent dans l'ordre suivant

in/ĩ un/ũ

n/~ ɔn/ ɔ̃

an/ã

4.3.2 *Les consonnes*

Les consonnes simples

[b]	–	bàfǒ, le maïs, (maize) byɔse, demander, (to ask a question)
[c]	–	àcǐ, l'arbre, (tree) ècǔ, le fusil, (gun) cùkù, malaxer, (to knead)
[d]	–	èdà, le père, (father) èdě, le palmier à huile, (palm tree)
[ɖ]	–	àɖě, la langue, (tongue) èɖè, l'enfance, (childhood) àɖyí, le savon, (soap)
[f]	–	āf̃, le pied, (foot) èfǔn, le poil, (hair)
[g]	–	àgɔ̌, la réjouissance, (joy) gòdú, derrière, (behind, the back of)
[γ]	–	ēγī, l'araignée, (spider) èγǐ, blanc, (white)
[h]	–	èhǒ, l'argent, (money) àhwà, la guerre, (war)
[x]	–	àxwǎ, le cri, (cry) àxwě, la maison, (house)
[j]	–	èjè, le sel, (salt)

èjì, le coeur, (heart)

[ʒ] – àʒìn, l'oeuf, (egg)
ʒīnflū, l'obscurité, (darkness)

[k] – èkǔ, la mort, (death)
àkɔ̀nnu, la poitrine, (chest)

[l] – ālɔ̄, la main, (hand)
ēlì, le mil, (millet)

[m] – mā, partager, (to share)
āmà, la feuille, (leaf)

[n] – ānā, le pont, (bridge)
ēnɔ̄, la mère, (mother)
nūxū, la parole, (word)

[ŋ] – ŋɔ̄cī, le nez, (nose)
aŋɔ̀, la peinture, (painting)

[s] – esɔ̄, hier, (yesterday)
sà, vendre, (to sell)

[t] – ètǒ, l'oreille, (ear)
tɛ̀n, enfler, (to swell)

[v] – àvà, le grenier, (granary)
vòvò, la liberté, (freedom)

[z] – èzǎn, la nuit, (night)
àzě, la sorcellerie, (witchcraft)

[p] – pɛ̌, mettre hors circuit (jeu de ludo), (to put out)
pɛpɛpɛ, exactement, (exactly)

[r] – dro, vouloir, (to will)
drado, réparer, (to repare)

[w] – wà, faire, (to do)
wema, papier, (paper)

[y] – àyà, air, (air)
yɔ̌, appeler, (to call)

Les digraphes

[gb] – àgbè, la vie, (life)
gbɔ̀n, respirer, (to breathe)

[kp] – àkpě, le remerciement, (acknowledgement)
kpàlíxò, le voisinage, (neighbourhood)

[ny] – nyɔ̀xò, le vieillard, (old person)
nyǐ, être, (to be)

[sh] – shikɔ, la soif, (thirst)
shive, la faim, (hunger)

4.4 *L'alphabet du ɖitammari*

Cette langue, commune au Togo et au Bénin, comme le ajagbe, est parlée par environ 120.000 bɛtammaribɛ. L'alphabet tammari actuellement en cours au Bénin se présente de la manière suivante.

4.4.1 *Les voyelles*

Les voyelles orales

Ce sont:

[i] – ítá, quitte!, (go away!)
fítá, vend, [he] (sells)

[e] – centa, réveille-toi!, (wake up!)
cetá, commence!, (begin!)

[ɛ] – kɛ̀, si, (if)
ɛɛtá, rince!, (rinse!)

[a] – ta, entre!, (come on!)
áà, non, (no)

[u] – kupuku, le chimpanzé, (chimpanzee)
utá, vide!, (pour out!)

[o] – ɖikònnì, la faim, (hunger)
ɖitoò, l'oreille, (ear)

[ɔ] – ɖibòɔ̀, le démon, (demon)
kapɔnta, casser, (to break)

Les voyelles nasales
Ce sont:

[ĩ] – ĩtá, débouche!, (clear!)
pĩ́, saisis!, (seize!)

[ɛ̃] – ɛ̃ɛ̃, oui, (yes)
myɛ̃ɛ̃ka, dans, (in)

[ã] – ãnná, mets!, (put in!)
ɖikãã̀, la houe, (hoe)

[ũ] – ṹũ, ferme les yeux!, (close your eyes!)
mukṹũ, la mort, (death)

[ɔ̃] – ɖikɔ̃́ɔ̃̀, l'os, (bone)
diɔ̃nni, le nez, (nose)

4.4.2 *Les consonnes du ɖitammari*
Les consonnes simples
Les sons consonantiques de la langue tammari sont les suivants:

[p] – opwà, l'hôte, (host)
potá, frappe!, (hit!)

[b] – bɛ́ɛ, dis!, (say!)
bɔ́tá, lapide!, (stone to death!)

[t] – katenkà, la terre, (ground)
mutápɛɛ, la cendre, (ash, cinder)

[ɖ] et [r].

[d] est une occlusive rétroflexe sonore, ou alvéolaire. Cette rétroflexe est une variante contextuelle de la vibrante [r] qui apparaît à la médiane ou intervocalique; [ɖ] et [r] sont donc en distribution complémentaire.

ɖitammari, la langue tammari, (tammar – language);
ɖikori, la perle, (pearl)

[c] – cáaká, mange!, (eat!)
kacɔ́ɔtá, arracher, (to tear up)

[k] – ɖikã̀tri, le marché, (market)
mukɛ̀ɛ, la pêche, (fishing)

[f] – fítá, vends!, (sell!)

kafíıkú, planter,´(to plant)

[s] – ɖìsɔ̀rì, la cachette, (hiding-place)
kasootá, mentir, (to tell lies)

[h] – hã̄nná ou ã̄nná, mets!, (put on!)
muhã̄ã̄ ou muã̄ã̄́, le feu, (fire)

[m] – mumɔmmú, la maladie, (illness)
tamotà, le chien, (dog)

[n] – nanka, demain, (tomorrow)
náká, parle!, (speak!)

[ŋ] – ŋã̄ã̄̀, je mets, (I put)
ŋoó, je râtisse, (I rake)

[w] – muwammù, la chasse, (hunt)
diwɛ̀ɛ, la joie, (joy)

[y] – yà, vois, ([I] see)
ɖiyuu, la tête, (head)

Les digraphes:

[kp] – kp̣eta, ouvre!, (open!)
dikpànni, la guerre, (war)

[nm] – dikunmenni, le matin, (morning)
nm, neuf (9), (nine)

[ny] – nyuu, ma tête, (my head)

Nota: [ny] et [nm] résultent de certaines combinaisons.

- [ny] est une nasale palatale qui résulte de la séquence de la nasale alvéolaire [n] avec la consonne palatale [y] ou la voyelle antérieure d'aperture minima [i].
- [nm] est une nasale labio-vélaire ou vélo-labiale; elle résulte de la séquence de la nasale alvéolaire [n] avec la consonne labiale [w].

4.5 *Les tons en ajagbe et en ditammari*

Le ajagbe comme le ditammari sont des langues à tons, c'est-à-dire des langues où toutes les voyelles de toutes les syllabes de tous les mots sont intonées; ainsi, à l'étape où se situent nos recherches, on a pu dégager des tons ponctuels:

- le ton ponctuel haut noté [´]

- le ton ponctuel bas noté [ˋ]
- le ton moyen noté [–]

Ceci nous donne pour les deux langues:

1. *ton haut*	*ajagbe*		*ditammari*	
	nỳ xó	"le vieillard"	fítá	"vends"
	àk nnú	"la poitrine"	náká	"parle"
2. *ton bas*	wà	"faire"	dīsɔ̀rì	"la cachette"
	àgbè	"la vie"	yà	"vois"
3. *ton moyen*	ēs	"hier"	nm̄	"neuf"
	āf	"le pied	nānkā	"demain"
	nūxū	"la parole	dīyuū	"la tête".

En ajagbe par contre, il existe des tons modulés. On distingue:

- les tons modulés bas-haut notés [ˇ], dans par exemple àdě "la langue",
- les tons modulés moyen-haut notés [˜́] dans par exemple anā́, "le pont".

L'analyse phonologique des différentes langues révèlera le statut phonologique de l'ensemble de ces signes.

Les deux examples d'alphabets sont tirés, le premier du *Nouveau Guide Pratique Aja*, et le second, du *Guide de lecture tammari*, documents publiés par la Commission Nationale de Linguistique.

5. *Problématique de l'utilisation des langues nationales dans une société multilingue – cas de la République Populaire du Bénin*

L'utilisation des langues dans une société multilingue soulève, si elle n'est pas appréhendée avec clairvoyance et discernement, de graves problèmes qui ne manquent pas par conséquent de rejaillir sur tous les secteurs du pays en question.

Les nombreux conflits linguistiques auxquels nous assistons de par le monde sont bien le reflet de l'inadéquation des conclusions envisagées ou même d'une grande démission devant tous ces faits.

Ils ne seront que plus aigus lorsque les critères de choix de tel ou tel parler sont inexistants faute d'études ou de descriptions scientifiques des langues en présence.

La République Populaire du Bénin dont nous nous permettons de décrire la situation est un pays multilingue où la langue officielle demeure encore celle du pays colonisateur.

C'est donc à travers le français que la minorité intellectuelle et les cadres moyens peuvent trouver une raison de vivre. Alors la majorité des populations demeure encore dans un alphabétisme inquiétant.

Nous savons pourtant qu'aucun système politique, qu'aucun plan de développement et plus encore qu'aucune prise de conscience effective ne peut être envisagée si les vrais destinataires que sont ces populations laborieuses demeurent dans une situation de sous-hommes.

Envisager alors un développement culturel, social et économique harmonieux nécessite donc que le problème linguistique trouve dans un tel contexte une solution acceptable.

C'est dans cette perspective que les chercheurs béninois qui ne manquent pas de faire de la linguistique une science au service du développement et partant du devenir même du pays, ont depuis bien des années orienté leurs différents travaux dans cette voie libératrice.

La nécessité ressentie, avant toute chose, d'organiser à Cotonou, sous l'égide de l'Unesco, le séminaire sur la normalisation et l'harmonisation des alphabets existants pour la transcription de nos langues nationales en est une preuve palpable.

Dans cette même optique, et fort heureusement, l'Etat béninois, conscient de l'importance des langues dans notre société et de son rôle dans le processus d'un développement intégral et pour répondre à la nouvelle orientation de sa politique, a solennellement proclamé qu'il faudra assurer le développement de la culture populaire en organisant dans les langues nationales, l'alphabétisation des masses, facteur essentiel de notre développement; il est nécessaire de créer un institut de linguistique chargé de mettre au point les moyens de lever les obstacles à l'utilisation des langues nationales.

Il vient donc d'être clairement exprimé une volonté dont la conséquence immédiate sera le renforcement des institutions mises en place en vue de la recherche linguistique et de la poursuite de l'alphabétisation des populations.

Ces institutions sont: la Commission Nationale de Linguistique, la Section de Linguistique de l'Université Nationale du Bénin et la Direction de l'Alphabétisation et de la Presse Rurale. Chacune à son niveau s'est assignée des tâches précises dont l'aboutissement est nécessairement le développement de la recherche linguistique et l'application des résultats dans le processus de l'alphabétisation.

C'est ainsi que la Commission Nationale de Linguistique joue le rôle de structure de recherche, la Section de l'Université quant à elle s'est assignée la tâche de formation et de recherche également alors que la Direction de l'Alphabétisation se trouve être la consommatrice des résultats de la recherche.

En dehors de sa tâche de description des langues, la Commission Nationale de Linguistique s'est attelée à l'établissement de l'atlas linguistique de la République Populaire du Bénin.

Le travail qui s'inscrit dans la perspective d'un recensement global des langues parlées dans le pays et de leur étude contrastive devra permettre de poser à terme le problème du choix de la langue ou des langues officielles. Et c'est bien ici que nous pouvons parler alors de problématique de l'utilisation des langues dans une société multilingue.

Faire le recensement de toutes les langues parlées dans un pays, établir un alphabet commun pour déterminer des critères de choix, cela suffit-il pour justifier et imposer l'utilisation de telle ou telle langue?

Sans nous situer dans un cas spécifique cette fois-ci, nous pouvons affirmer que tout problème linguistique est un problème politique dont la résolution ne pourra être elle-même que politique. C'est dire que tous les travaux préliminaires, quelle que soit leur importance, doivent être doublés d'une sensibilisation politique poussée pour une grande prise de conscience et une appréhension claire de la valeur et de l'urgence de l'utilisation des langues dans la vie nationale.

Sans cette sensibilisation, la recherche de solution à la question linguistique restera vaine. Ainsi, de la résolution correcte du problème découlera un choix adéquat de la langue ou des langues à utiliser.

En la République Populaire du Bénin, la stratégie, qui découle d'ailleurs de ces différentes considérations, est celle du développement de toutes les langues nationales afin de permettre à tous les locuteurs des dites langues de s'en imprégner par l'écriture et par la mise en valeur de la culture ou des cultures qui en ressortent.

Bien que bilingue dans la majorité des cas, les populations demeurent comme partout ailleurs très attachées à leur langue maternelle et n'auront d'intérêt à accorder à une autre langue que lorsque le travail politique nécessaire aura été fait pour les y intéresser.

Le résultat serait à terme l'encouragement et le renforcement du bilinguisme ou du multilinguisme existant. Cela, sans nul doute est propice à toute tentation de choix. Cette voie dans laquelle ce pays s'est engagé, semble donner satisfaction pour le moment, dans l'état actuel de l'avancement de l'expérience.

Tel est, mesdames, messieurs, l'essentiel de ce que nous pouvons dire de l'expérience béninoise dans le domaine de l'utilisation des langues nationales dans une société multilingue telle que la nôtre.

6. *Conclusion*

Un alphabet est un outil au développement d'une communauté linguistique; car l'écriture et la lecture de toutes les langues pour lesquelles il a été conçu et confectionné ne peuvent pas se réaliser de manière correcte, d'où le caractère simple de cet alphabet qui doit éviter l'usage des signes diacritiques complexes au point de devenir inaccessibles aux locuteurs non scolarisés. Une langue se doit de fournir sa propre écriture, autrement dit, dans une communauté multilingue, l'alphabet national doit être un facteur d'unification de toutes les nationalités s'il est regardé comme un ensemble de stock ouvert où chaque langue pourra puiser des signes distinctifs pour une fixation adéquate de son écriture. L'écriture, qui est une convention extérieure à la langue pour être bien menée, doit être envisagée dans une perspective normative; en écrivant une langue on doit songer à la définition des règles d'une bonne lecture et d'une bonne écriture, c'est-à-dire que lecture et écriture supposent la définition claire et nette des règles orthographiques, des conventions sans lesquelles l'alphabet retenu ne rendra aucun service à la communauté. La lutte pour la création et l'enseignement d'un alphabet national dans une communauté multilingue est politique et idéologique; c'est une lutte pour le développement intégral de l'homme; elle ouvre une perspective certaine à la problématique de l'utilisation des langues nationales dans une telle communauté.

Annotation

1. Extrait du Discours-Programme du Gouvernement Militaire Révolutionnaire – – Cotonou 30 Novembre 1972.
2. Extrait de l'article 3 de la Loi Fondamentale de la République Populaire du Bénin
3. Th. Nata. in Préface à *Alphabétisation par la Méthode Directe* (G. Elwert et T. Y. Tchitchi) – Commission Nationale de Linguistique Cotonou, Septembre 1979, 32 pages.
4. Extrait de la déclaration d'orientation et de politique générale. Travaux de la Commission Nationale de la Réforme de l'Enseignement et de l'Education au Dahomey – Mai 1973. Porto-Novo.
5. Extrait du Communiqué final du séminaire sur la Normalisation et l'Harmonisation des Alphabets des langues de la sous-région.

Références

Coupez, A.
1977 "*La Situation du Virundi*". Communication au séminaire international sur le thème: Langues nationales et enseignement. Bujumbura, 10–14 Octobre 1977 (MS).

Guedou, G. G., et Tchitchi, T.
1977 "*Communication de la République Populaire du Bénin au séminaire international sur le thème: Langues nationales et enseignement*". Bujumbura, 10–14 Octobre 1977 (MS).

Haupt, G., Lowy, M., et Weil, C.
1974 *Les marxistes et la question nationale.* (1948–1914) – Paris: Col. Maspero.

Nata, Th.
1980 "*Contact de langues: lexicologie comparée des constituants nominaux de trois langues gur du Benin septentrional: le ditammari, le mbelime et le gulmancema*". Communication à la IVe Table Ronde des Centres de Linguistique Appliquée d'Afrique Noire Francophone, Dakar, 14–17 Mars 1980 (MS).

Stalin, J.
1975 *Le Marxisme et les problèmes de Linguistique*. Pelain.
Sow, A. I.
1977 *Langues et politiques de Langues en Afrique Noire*. Paris: Nubia.
Tchitchi, Y.T., et Elwert, G.
1979 "*Alphabétisation par la méthode directe*". (document de recherche) – Commission Nationale de Linguistique, Cotonou, Septembre 1979 (MS).
Tchitchi, Y. T.
1976 *Nouveau Guide Pratique Aja*. Commission Nationale de Linguistique Porto-Novo. Février 1976.

Autres Sources

- *Alphabet des langues nationales*. (1976). Commission Nationale de Linguistique. Porto-Novo.
- *CNL-INFO N° 1*. (1976). Commission Nationale de Linguistique. Cotonou, contenant:
- Olasope O. Oyelaran et Olabiyi B. Yaï. *Quelques principes pour l'élaboration d'un inventaire de symboles communs aux langues du Dahomey – Ghana, Haute-Volta, Niger, Nigéria et Togo*. Ifè, Août 1975.
- *Guide de Lecture tammari*. Commission Nationale de Linguistique. Sous-Commission Tammari.
- *Loi Fondamentale de la République Populaire du Bénin*. (1977). Cotonou, Septembre 1977
- *Travaux de la Commission Nationale de la Réforme de l'Enseignement et de l'Education au Dahomey*. (1973). Ministère de l'Education Nationale, de la Culture, de la Jeunesse et des Sports. Porto-Novo, 14–28 Mai 1973.

MICHAEL GIESECKE and GEORG ELWERT

Adult literacy in a context of cultural revolution: Structural parallels of the literacy process in sixteenth-century Germany and present-day Bénin*

Abstract

We compared the process of the development of a culture of writing (Verschriftlichung) in native languages in 16th- century Germany and in present-day Bénin, and found astonishing similarities between these movements.

The causes for these similarities lie in a common social background of cultural revolution and in common techniques of first propagating literacy. In both cases, learner-oriented structures of literacy and "democratic" processes of codification are favored.

As a result of our comparison, we arrive at a new perspective for
- *educational problems with literacy campaigns,*
- *the development of a written form of a standard language, and*
- *the connection between political movements and the fate of literacy campaigns.*

On the basis of experience with literacy policies, we argue for a slower historical growth of standard languages and the inclusion of the masses in this process, as opposed to literacy campaigns planned by professional linguists and controlled by central authorities.

1. *Introduction*

The idea for this paper resulted from discussions between two people whose work would hardly seem to have much in common: An anthropologist-sociologist who, in the 1970's, participated in the movement for adult literacy among African peasants and who encountered an historian-sociologist who was doing research on one of the protagonists of adult literacy in the early stages of the German Reformation. In discussing their work, they were astonished to discover a series of striking parallels between the 20th-century African and the 16th-century German literacy campaigns. The traits the two campaigns have in common at the same time distinguish them from other efforts to teach adults reading and writing. We think that the common elements, which go down even to the level of didactics, are somehow related to the political contexts to which these movements reacted and within which they, as an element of cultural revolution, contributed to the initial stages of language standardization. The projects to which we refer[1] are:

(a) Adult literacy by a peasant self-help group in Ayou/Bénin, and

(b) the method for learning reading and writing without formal schooling, propagated by Ickelsamer in Germany in the early sixteenth century.

We cannot present both projects in detail here. In order to acquaint the reader with them, however, we start off with a documentary section on them.

In our presentation, we shall limit ourselves to a cross-section examination of the obvious similarities of the two literacy movements and, furthermore, will formulate some hypotheses concerning the causes of these similarities.

Thus, we hope to create new insights into the problems of literacy processes in a culture ("Verschriftlichung") in the Third World as well as into the development of standard languages.

2. *Documentation:*[2] *Two cases of non-schooled adult literacy*

2.1 *The "clubs for explaining writing" – Adult literacy through a peasant self-help group in Ayou/Bénin*

Beginning in late 1973, one of the authors took part in a movement for adult literacy initiated by peasants and students and later entirely run by peasants. It started in the village of Ayou in Southern Bénin (or Dahomey, as this West African country was then called).

The peasants lived mostly from maize, which they produced by swidden agriculture (slash and burn agriculture). Formal schooling – which reaches only a minority of the population – is still carried out in French, excluding African languages such as Fongbe and Ayizogbe which are spoken in this region.

In discussions with peasants in the course of the author's anthropological field work as well as in discussions with an organization of students, the idea emerged that a literacy program should be organized, "relying on our own forces", as the then current Dahomean ideology claimed.

Several essential points were defined during this process:

- Peasants do not like to be "treated like children" which easily can be the case when, for example, a teacher or a textbook prescribes the words that are to be learned.
- There is nothing to read. If there is no useful written material (e.g. for economic purposes), it seems quite irrational to afford time and effort to

literacy. Parts of the region had already experienced as many as three literacy movements in the previous 15 years, a farce for the participants, since they could not profit from their efforts. Hence, the idea "we will produce books ourselves" was a necessary requirement for the campaign.

- It seemed obvious that only literacy in native languages helps the peasant to express himself. Other studies have shown that it is easier to learn to write in one's own language and after that to learn a new language than to do both at the same time.
- One should not adopt the repressive way of teaching used e.g. in the Bénin secluded initiation groups called *vodunkpamɛ* ("the voodoo-convent", an institution which is devoted to reforming rebellious and deviant people). This coincides with the sociologists' view that authoritarian schooling of European traditions tends to break down initiative and inhibits the development of a critical spirit.
- One should not adopt the traditional way of transmitting technical and magical knowledge. There, information is handled as "secrets"; it is transmitted either on the basis of reciprocity in the institution of a "special friend" (*xɔntɔn*), or on the basis of pooling in kin-organized groups. This does not achieve the intended snowballing effect of innovation-diffusion which transcends the boundaries of familial and other consumption- and production-oriented groups.
- The traditional culture possesses an association of image and proverbial sentences called "*lŏ-wémà*" (proverb-paper or proverb-letter) which comes close to Freire's idea of the key-word. We called it the key-sentence. Traditionally, any important piece of knowledge is preserved and handed down in the form of proverbs, songs, and stories, whose point is summarized in a proverbial sentence. This is the way the Ayizo accumulate their historical, juridical, and sociological knowledge. Such a proverb can be symbolized by a picture. Very often the association between the proverb and a picture is standardized.

The group had the defined goal of producing its own "*wema*" (book). This was to be a "primer" as well as a propaganda leaflet consisting only of "*lŏ-wémà*". The meetings to teach literacy were at the same time sessions for the production of this "book" (consisting of two pages).

A meeting where a new key-sentence for the primer was selected went on like this:

1. The peasants discuss a problem of progress in its economic and ideological dimensions.
2. They choose a traditional parable which expresses the conclusion of the discussion.
3. They name the point of the parable.

Whenever the peasants had chosen a proverb which seemed sufficiently progressive (*yi nukɔ̀n*) to them, they could draw it so that everybody could recognize it. Then the literate member of the group wrote the words in the phonetic writing system adopted in Dahomey (a version of the alphabet "Africa") below the image, and everyone tried to copy it. Even when the literate ones were not present, the peasants could train themselves since they had the drawing with the sentence (whose words they knew) on the wall or on a poster.

After some words had been learned, it proved to be very useful to write cross-tables of words containing the same letters, starting from a central core. From these tables, they came through "lautieren" ("sounding out")[3] to the identification of individual graphemes.

After the departure of the "initiators", the peasants continued to follow the motto "if there is nothing published in our language, we have to produce it ourselves", producing serigraphic posters dealing with traditional pharmacy.

The original group helped to create new groups. This process of extension was, however, slowed down because of a lack of reading material other than their own. In 1977, the government's literacy campaign reached the region. The campaign consisted mainly in the creation of committees and the training of teachers for literacy by these committees. Of the many members of the original group who already had teaching experience two went to such a seminar in order to become "recognized" teachers. They *failed* because they knew no French . . .! Some time later, the district's coordinator forbade the "savage" activity of the self-help literacy groups.

2.2. *"To learn reading and writing by oneself" – Ickelsamer's nonschooled method in early 16th-century Germany*

Valentin Ickelsamer worked in the "free city" of Augsburg, in Southern Germany. His ideological background was in the "Schwärmer" wing of the German Reformation (which included people such as Schwenckfeld, Karlstadt, and Müntzer) for whom the active integration of the masses into public affairs, the fight against grading systems as part of the university system, etc., were part of a cultural revolutionary impetus. Ickelsamer was a learned scholar and might have become a professional in the education system, but, like others of his orientation, he broke off his studies in favor of political agitation (conceived partly as religious reform).

He advocated through his book *Die rechte weis aufs kuerzist lesen zu lernen* (1527; "The right way to learn reading in the shortest time") and *Ain Teütsche Grammatica – Darauß ainer von jm selbs mag lesen lernen* (1534; "A German grammar – from which one might learn to read for oneself"), a method of learning reading and writing which did not require the use of primers (although Ickelsamer's manuals also included some exercises) and made schools superfluous – but of course did not rule out the help of a literate person (see Müller 1882).

Learning began by isolating phonemes in the current of speech. Then one had to learn the phoneme/grapheme correspondence ("lautieren", or "sounding out"). Wherever the orthography differed from the phonetic principle, Ickelsamer spoke of "faults of our alphabet" ("*mangel vnd faehl vnnsers A be cees*"). He tried to explain this "incorrectness" with etymological and grammatical features.

His target group was the common man ("*gemein man*"), as can be seen from his explicit mention of people of low rank such as woodcutters and shepherds. His goal was the "public good" ("*gemein nutz*"). Everyone should be able to take part in the ideological struggle of his time. To "judge for oneself" ("*selbs vrteilen*"), according to Ickelsamer, requires literacy. Only then, he argued, could the common people read, for instance, God's word and its current interpretations and learn about technical innovations without the oral explanation of an expert.

Until then, reading was not regarded as a general and elementary activity of the culture. It was required only for certain professions. Literate people were educated either in Latin or in one of the German dialects, which could only be used for certain purposes and which did not qualify their readers to participate in a scientific or learned discussion. The method of "lautieren" was invented by Ickelsamer (at least this is the opinion of his contemporary Petrus Jordan, also a schoolmaster).

In didactics and definition of goals and target-groups, he was more radical than others, but, insofar as there was a wave of publications on literacy in German and raising the consciousness of the masses was a goal of all the "Schwärmer", Ickelsamer should be viewed as an element of this movement rather than as an isolated figure. The establishment of the Lutheran orthodoxy – viz., by Melanchthon – after the death of the "Reformator" brought all these efforts to an end; literacy courses ("Winkelschulen") based on Ickelsamer's method were banned after 1545 (Roth 1909).

3. *Initial conditions of the literacy movements in 16th-century Germany and present-day Bénin*

Both movements for adult literacy were part of a greater cultural and political movement; they took place in a period of social transformation. It is necessary to describe these social and communicative conditions. We believe they determined the specific strategy which was followed, in both cases, for adult literacy. The participants' subjective motivation, their appraisal of the situation, the didactical methods, and the instruments used depend on the socio-cultural context.

(a) The *political conditions:*
National identity exists but is poorly developed. The state was either fictitious (sixteenth-century Germany) or is conceived as an alien power (Ayou/Bénin). Various social and political movements with differing ideas concerning the reform of this state exist, but the political structures do not appear stabilized to the people concerned.

Participation of the masses in the organization of economy and politics of the state is minor, but changes and innovations in different realms of society seem possible. There is a widely distributed, though not general, optimism regarding the possibilities of transformation and innovation. There are high rates of illiteracy. Reading and writing are, in fact, knowledge of the powerful ("Herrschaftswissen") or a specific and monopolized skill. Compulsory schooling is either non-existent (Germany) (Engelsing 1973) or not yet in effect (Ayou).

(b) The *socio-economic conditions:*
The organization of experience transmission seems to be one of the most important initial conditions of literacy campaigns. In both movements, experience transmission (one of the necessary conditions for the reproduction and improvement of the masses' life) is done only in face-to-face situations and not by means of the abstract medium of communication, i.e., printed texts. Learning from books is unknown. Knowledge is very often withheld as a secret. The development of institutions and media for learning in abstract situations (school and technical literature) is still in a developmental phase. Teaching is generally done in a foreign language.

The usefulness of reading and writing for general qualification is unclear. Reading and writing in the native tongue are only understood as qualifications for specific tasks. The effort to acquire literacy seems very high compared, for instance, to the economic benefit, because of the lack of literature on many economic subjects and technical issues.

(c) The *communicative and linguistic conditions:*
Even these conditions are similar in both literacy movements. In their beginnings, the linguistic conditions are very bad. There exists no standard language with an oral and a written variety which are universally understood. The official written language understood in all regions is a foreign language (Latin in Germany and French in Bénin) (cf. Giesecke 1979a). No current language on any higher level than that of local dialects exists. Most, if not all, dialects and languages have no written variety.

These circumstances are very important for the learning process: There is no possibility to learn "in school" an already codified and standardized system; this very system has yet to be established through the literacy movement. Thus the movements for adult literacy were, at the same time, movements creating a written language. Both projects had the explicit (Ickelsamer) or implicit (Ayou) tendency to modify the language variety in use, leading to the creation of a common language mediating between different dialects ("*Gemeinsprachbildung*"). In other words, the development of a common language understandable for speakers of several dialects is intended as a compromise. This seems to be related to the political idea of creating a community greater than just a small region.

The movements created their own reading materials. The posters, leaflets, and small pamphlets were at the same time an effort of the movement's members to make their ideas publicly known and to create teaching materials for the newcomers. The first of these results were, in Ayou, leaflets and posters on traditional herbalist medicine and, in Germany, technical literature (cf. Giesecke 1980). The language used in these publications destined for a wider public was in Germany mostly a conglomerate of different dialects and for Ayou in Bénin an Ayizogbe, using many semantical and phonetical elements of Fongbe, the lingua franca of the markets in that region.

The leaflets and posters were the result of the literacy movements. In the beginning, hardly any mass communication in written form existed.

The written varieties of dialects were only used for the very personal uses which demand only handwriting (letters, diaries, and bookkeeping) instead of print.

4. *Motives for the transformation of ways and means of communication through adult literacy*

In order to understand the moving forces of a social movement, one should analyze the perspectives of the people concerned. The question is, what are the goals which motivate people to learn reading and writing?

These questions, of course, cannot be answered in general, and even detailed studies are confronted with considerable methodological problems. Therefore, we shall limit ourselves to a summary of the most important and relatively easily verifiable motives for adult literacy in both movements:

- Both movements have an explicit interest in publishing knowledge which was, until this time, privately monopolized. To make the knowledge public was a political as well as an economical goal. To "nationalize" private knowledge for the use of the community was one major aim.
- The means of mass communication should help the masses to become integrated into the ideological and political affairs of their country.
- The transformation of the traditional forms of transmission of knowledge

and experience seems to be of great importance for the progress and welfare of the society.
- The new – written – form offers the possibility of an autonomous learning process using written sources.

5. *The educational methods*

At this point, a basic presentation of the didactical procedure would be desirable, in order to describe thereafter, in a contrasting analysis, the important similarities and differences of the educational methods.

The didactical method is, however, so complicated in its particulars that such a presentation would go beyond the purpose of this article (see for details Elwert 1979; Giesecke 1979b). We shall confine ourselves here to listing the most important common steps of the didactical procedures:

(a) Both movements start from the assumption the adult literacy can be achieved without schools, and are, in that sense, anti-institutional. The teaching is done in the locally spoken language. This is a part of the didactic principle: "Start with the known and understandable and then proceed to more complicated affairs! " Only if words are already known will the phoneme-grapheme correspondence be analyzed ("*lautieren*"). The correspondence of phonemes to graphemes is first taught in its simplest form. Only later will these correspondences be corrected following criteria of etymology and/or grammatical systematics. The didactic procedures exclude two issues which are often combined with writing systems, viz. (a) orthography as a norm, or even as a subject of teaching, and (b) calligraphy or calligraphic standards.

(b) Both movements insist upon the fact that adult literacy can be achieved without using a primer, but that it is even easier to learn to read and write without the frightening authority of an expert or an expert's book.

The use of pictures in these lectures should be understood not only as a mnemotechnic device (as it may have been intended by the authors) but also as a way of teaching the interpretation of the symbolic language of drawing according to the aesthetic and symbolic standards of that very culture.

Another common element of the didactic devices of both projects is playing with writing, viz. considering it not as something sacred but as something which can be used for one's own pleasure.

We want to call the methods of the two literacy movements "direct methods". One of their particular characteristics is that every pupil is himself, potentially, a teacher of adult literacy.

In principle, this is the same system as that which is used for the transition of knowledge within the family, viz. chain reaction. Other methods of adult literacy are fundamentally distinct from this mode of transmission, because there transmission passes through an anonymous institution – the school. The question remains whether the institutionalization of adult literacy in a larger political community is automatically linked to the fact that the standard language in its written form has to be taught according to standards and codifications. Therefore, training other people to express themselves in this written form may require formal training of the teachers. The link of the direct method to situations where the standard language was still in the making might incline us to this hypothesis. (There are, however, counterexamples, as the form of transmission practiced by the Tuareg in the Sahara, who transmit their writing system "*tifinagh*" only by passing it from mothers to daughters and sons (Rennell of Rodd 1926: 173–174).

It might also be questioned whether a standard language for a wider use necessarily demands formal institutions (like schools) or quasi-institutionalized standard-giving texts (e.g. primers, or the Koran) in order to preserve a necessary minimum of uniformity throughout the community of speakers. If this is not the case, the explanation for the discontinuance of the direct methods and their replacement with more institutionalized and more authoritarian methods could not be explained by the changing linguistic situation of an intensified standardization but has to be brought back to a change in the general societal climate towards activities which are carried out by "ordinary people". This will be discussed in the following section.

6. *The dissolution of the literacy movements*

Both literacy movements using direct methods did not last long and, due to political intervention, came to an abrupt end. Their place was taken by more institutionalized and more authoritarian methods of adult literacy – by schools. The ends of the movements coincided with the ends of the cultural revolutions of which they were a part. After the end of the Peasant War in Germany (*Großer deutscher Bauernkrieg*), the role of leaflets, of non-school learning, and of uncontrolled teaching of the basic ethical values (from the Bible), as an important factor of insurgency was clear to all the old and new political groups. The orthodox wing of the reformation, represented by people such as Melanchthon, became very influential, and institutionalized schools were set up with trained teachers and prescribed textbooks, which emphasised learning the catechism by heart, and regarded reading and writing as a secondary matter (see Roth 1909).

In Bénin, the influence of the rural youth movements which supported adult literacy and the general rise of consciousness among peasants in different parts of the country declined considerably after their banning became effective and some of the leading cadres became progressively integrated into the state apparatus.

In both movements, adult literacy was understood by the protagonists primarily as a tool. For them, literacy was not a "social indicator" which might show the general progressiveness and stage of development of the country; it was an instrument which was to be used in the interests of the cultural revolutionary movement. It was to be used for the production of leaflets, for making public practical knowledge, which had been private in character before, to make it a social force of production. The publication of medical knowledge played an important role in these movements, since they originated from the use-value relevant for the people at the 'basis' who were concerned more with their own quality of life than with more abstract values. The posters and books were "do-it-yourself" books, that is, they were useful for laymen without further oral explication (Giesecke 1979; Giesecke 1980).

With the end of these cultural revolutionary movements, adult literacy by direct method ended, too. From then on, adult literacy took on a schooled form, and the didactic methods were transformed. As a consequence, in the German example, the rate of illiteracy increased.

7. *Some particularities of the "direct method" and the reasons for them*

In this section, we shall discuss some common elements of both literacy movements which distinguish them from those structural settings where a "schooled" method is used to promote literacy. Furthermore, we shall introduce hypotheses concerning the reasons for these distinctions.

First, however, we would like to summarize the common situation that existed at the beginning of the literacy movements: Both movements had their drive in the motivation to transform the existing social, economic, and communicative conditions. The transmission of experience and knowledge was bound to demonstration and the non-institutionalized chain reaction of orality within the family or within the craftshops. There was no general school enrollment and no generally known standard language. The written standard language was part of a foreign language group. Oral communication was based on several dialects of the same language or language group. Reading and writing were restricted up to this point to specific groups for whom they were of professional use.

7.1 *Development of a standard language*

In this situation, adult literacy meant at the same time the development of a written standard language. The impetus to transform the societal conditions based on the integration of the masses, and to produce a setting for democracy, did not allow for the use of a foreign language. Written communication with the possibility of feed-back through dialogue was very limited. Therefore, in order to allow immediate understanding in spite of linguistic differences, there was a need for standardization.

7.2 *Educational situation*

The educational situation was unique. The learners in these adult literacy movements were not only the first producers of written material but also the ones who created the codified language. This occurs only in these types of movements, i.e. at the very beginning of adult literacy. The didactical situation gave the individual participants in such movements considerable freedom of action, because they were not confined to any standards but could create the standards by their own efforts.

In any later situation the pupils not only have to learn to read and write, but they also have to learn the rules of codification, rules of orthography, and so on, which were established by the first transcriptors.

7.3 *Standardization*

In order to achieve general understanding and interregional diffusion of a standardized written language, certain conditions have to be met. Thus the standard variety should not stand as a symbol for any antagonistic or low-status social group. Concentrating on linguistic aspects, we can figure out several norms of standardization:

- The meanings of words have to be standardized in such a way that they are also accessible for someone who does not use a certain word in his own speech. The simplest method of doing this is to fix the meaning by dictionaries.
- The orthography has to become more rigid, since a greater variety of dialects has to be integrated into the standard language.
- A system of punctuation has to be introduced. Since the European forms of writing do not transcribe syntactic tone and stress by means of graphemes (in contrast to the transcription of semantic tone and stress by means of accents or orthographic rules), the punctuation by means of stop, question mark, and so on can partially compensate for this lack of infomation.
- The lack of syntactic tone and stress as vehicles of syntactic meaning in the European forms of transcription necessitates more rigidity in the syntactic structure of the word order within the sentence to allow general understanding.
- The grammar should not vary more than common understanding allows.
- Even more important is the development of stylistic standard forms which

permit the reader to have specific expectations on the kind of information he will get. The limited possibilities for feed-back in written communication necessitate several new forms of style which go far beyond the written monologue of the letters. These new forms have to be learned, and they should be predictable and, as such, understandable for any reader, and therefore they need some standardization.

7.4 *Common base of paralinguistic knowledge*

Indirect communication with an unknown receiver, which is typical under conditions of general literacy (and which was, of course, also the goal of the two movements we analyzed) requires a common base of knowledge including stylistic standard forms, orthography, and so on, as has been said above. The common base of knowledge must have the two characteristics of order and stability. *Stability* is needed to make the effect of any act of communication, especially of printed communication, foreseeable, and *order* is needed to exclude ambiguities and to explore the unknown, starting from the known, without the help of oral communication (by means of reference to learned rules, dictionaries, and so on). Such an ordered space can be produced by a network of institutions which define rules and meanings and guarantee their transmission to the new learners. Part of this network may be institutions that use control and sanctions as part of the learning process. We classify "schools" in this sense as institutions. It is an open question for us whether a common base of knowledge might also be produced by other types of institutionalization. The use of one long text of reference like the Koran in the first stages of Islamized Arab culture is a different form of institutionalization. But when the generally used language develops in areas not covered by the reference text, and when speakers with different languages are included into this linguistic community, the reference text is not sufficient and has to be embedded into a network of schooled institutions, which transmit the meanings of the words and develop (as a by-product of ethics) rules of correspondence between the established standard text and the new realms of life. Another – still untested – hypothesis concerns newspapers in a non-fragmented public community (*Öffentlichkeit*); they might fulfill the function of an institution guaranteeing the common base of knowledge concerning the use of language.

7.5 *Political motives and the link to political movements*

The political motives for the movements were not only to enable the individual to use writing for his own private use, but to develop a national network of communication based on printing. Therefore, it is not just a written language but a standardized written language that is the goal of the movement. This language should be understood by speakers of all dialects and therefore has to mediate between them.

This democratic intention might have been another reason to create the "direct method" of adult literacy. It begins with the assumption that it is sufficient to be a member of the "people" as part of the linguistic community in order to define what has to be learned, and, furthermore, to teach others according to their defined needs, which implies ideas of the emancipation of the individual and equality. These types of adult literacy also reinforce the ideas of emancipation and equality, because the appropriation of an, at that time, unknown competence produces a particular pride in oneself, a consciousness which will be relevant for other self-help activities.

Obviously, a low degree of standardization and codification of language is of great help for these types of movements (even if this were not a necessary condition (an issue which still has to be debated)), because everyone can then become a learner/teacher without mastering beforehand the defined common base of knowledge concerning the notation of language. The more the standardization and codification of the written language is developed, and the more it distances itself from the common language of the learner/teacher, the less the sequence of learning steps can be defined by a pupil and the more every teacher needs specific training. In this respect, things also work the other way around: The more the creation of a standard written language is part of a cultural revolutionary movement where every pupil can start to produce his own "literature", the closer the newly created standard language will be to the language of the masses, thus hindering its transformation into a symbol and instrument for the separation of an elite.

The creation of a standard common language needs to be a mediation process. If not, oppressed linguistic minorities will be created which linguistically are still excluded from participation in the public discussion. The degree to which the common people are able to introduce their knowledge into the body of knowledge which is transmitted through printed material has an important impact on the cultural evolution of society.

7.6 *Counter-reform – politics and didactics*

The linguistic reasons mentioned above (7.5), which make the direct method less plausible for adult literacy in more advanced stages of standard language development, should not allow us to forget that, in the situations discussed in this paper, the direct method was banned for political reasons. But this does not necessarily imply that these movements died because of political reasons, since it might well be that another factor weakened them so that they could not survive political attacks.

We see three aspects of this political fight against the "direct method":

- There is a fight against grass-roots journalism. Not every ("uncivilized") person should be able to express himself in the form of written publications; the self-esteem stemming from this grass-roots journalism of popular leaflets and so on is dangerous far beyond these publications, and it is a dangerous root for any self-organized process.
- The political power needs codified concepts. Those in power want to control the meaning and the connotative field of words in order to control political consciousness. Not everyone should be allowed to define words which fit his purposes, and to give them connotations fitting his goals.
- The equation of teacher with revolutionary has to be broken. The teachers in these movements are seen as (potential) revolutionaries. The fact that the status and the role of the teacher (which had been transmitted only by institutions controlled by those in power) now can be acquired simply through the basic learning process itself threatens the legitimacy of the institutions of those in power.

Since the structure of the mode of acquisition of literacy is as much bound to these political conditions as to the aforementioned communicative conditions, the political motives and reasons can be hidden by "didactics". The resurrection of the institution "school" after the end of the literacy movements thus has a double origin: on the one hand, an interest in political control,[4] and, on the other hand, the necessity to develop and stabilize the standard language. Whether the "school" is a *necessity* for literacy is still an open question.

8. *Differences between the literacy movement in 15th- and 16th- century Germany and in present-day Bénin; Conclusions*

In addition to the striking parallels between the two literacy movements under discussion, we also wish to call attention to some differences.

The major differences are linked to the medium of communication and notation.

(a) In the 15th and 16th centuries, we find a tradition of hand-written literature in the native tongue in Germany. We know of legal documents, recipes, Bible translations, and even fiction (e.g. "*Minnesang*"). Although the number of authors and readers of this literature was very small, we have to note a difference nevertheless, to the situation in Bénin, where a comparable written background does not exist. (For references to the history of native language reading and writing in medieval Germany, see Giesecke 1975.)

(b) With respect to the initial linguistic conditions, the government and the population of Bénin are confronted with a number of more serious problems than were the Germans in the Reformation period: It is true that in 15th century Germany, too, a number of different dialects were spoken; but these were part of language systems with similar structural qualities. In Bénin (as a whole), however, totally different language groups are confronted. The difficulties involved in creating a standard language under these conditions are tremendous.

(c) In 15th century Germany a system of notation, a writing system, is basically in existence. It can be used for the notation of the *"gemein teutsch"*, the German standard language, in the following centuries. The repertoire of symbols which had been developed within the framework of both, the handwritten Latin tradition, and the tradition of literature in the native language in the Middle Ages contained more entries than necessary, and the use had hardly been codified; nevertheless, the authors of the 15th and 16th centuries were able to profit from it. Their task was, first of all, the selection and reduction of the repertoire of symbols. Taking, e.g., the first Gutenberg prints as a starting point, one finds a reduction of approximately two thirds of the symbols within less than a hundred years. The second task was the codification of the writing system and the standardization of the notation method. Syntactic, orthographic, and punctuation rules did not exist in German dialects during the Middle Ages. Ickelsamer did pioneer work in all of these areas. The conditions in Bénin in this respect are also somewhat different. Theoretically, it is possible to choose between totally different notation systems due to the complete, or almost complete, lack of a writing tradition. The choice of writing systems and the regulation of notation can be made by trained linguists according to rational criteria.[5]

A conscious language planning, in contrast to a longer, historical growth of a writing system, has some advantages; it also has disadvantages. One of its disadvantages is, as has already been mentioned, the extensive exclusion of the populace from all processes of standardization. Language is not only a tool for communication, but also the representation system of common knowledge and, furthermore, an important factor for national self-esteem and social integration.

Considering this simple fact and the experience of the literacy movements in 15th and 16th century Germany as well as in Bénin, we plead for a slow historical growth of a standard language and stress the importance of including the masses in this process.

Notes

* We would like to thank Michel Ahohounkpanzon for cooperation in research, Utz Maas for bibliographical hints, and Florian Coulmas, Constance Guhl, and Konrad Ehlich for the clarification of our manuscript – without their contribution the text would not have found its present form.

1. The two movements under consideration are not the only ones which might be labelled "culture-revolutionary". The experiences of the Protestant missionary Frank Laubach (see Medary 1954) and of Paolo Freire (Freire 1971) and the people influenced by him (see Humbert 1975) might also be cited as examples. But we prefer to confine ourselves here to the two cases we have personally analysed and studied in detail.
2. For further information the reader should consult the publications quoted in the bibliography.
3. cf. p. 15
4. Lévi-Strauss (1955: ch. 28) discusses the link of literacy process and domination. We agree with the tendency of the argument, but our material about cultural-revolutionary literacy shows that literacy and domination are not necessarily linked.
5. In fact, they developed a variant of the alphabet 'Africa'.

References

Ayou

Elwert, Georg

1977 "Adult literacy – A case study of a peasant organized experiment". In *Adult Education and Development* (8): 4–6, 8–20, 33–35.

1978 "Animation zur Selbsthilfe – Von Bauern getragene Alphabetisationsgemeinschaften". In B. Engels & U. Laaser, eds., *Die deutsche Bildungshilfe in der zweiten Entwicklungsdekade,* München: Weltforum Verlagsgesellschaft, pp. 353–387.

1979 "Alphabetisation in Ayou – Untersuchung einer bäuerlichen Selbsthilfe-Bewegung". In *Osnabrücker Beiträge zur Sprachtheorie* 12: 109–150.

Elwert, Georg and Tchitchi, Toussaint

1979 *Alphabetisation par la methode directe.* Cotonou: Commission Nationale de Linguistique.

Freire, Paolo

1971 *L'éducation – pratique de la liberté.* Paris: CERF.

Humbert, Colette

1975 *Conscientisation – Expériences, positions dialectiques et perspectives.* Paris: Harmattan.

Sixteenth Century Germany

Engelsing, Rolf

1973 *Analphabetentum und Lektüre.* Stuttgart: Metzler.

Giesecke, Michael

1975 Lesen und Schreiben in den deutschen Schreibschulen des ausgehenden 15. und beginnenden 16. Jahrhunderts. Unpublished thesis. Universität Hannover.

1980 "'Volkssprache' und 'Verschriftlichung' des "Lebens" im Spätmittelalter". In H. U. Gumbrecht, ed., *Literatur in der Gesellschaft des Spätmittelalters.* Heidelberg: Carl Winter pp. 39–70.

1979a "Schriftsprache als Entwicklungsfaktor in Sprach- und Begriffsgeschichte".

In R. Koselleck, ed., *Historische Semantik und Begriffsgeschichte.* Stuttgart: Klett-Cotta, pp. 262–302.

1979b "Schriftspracherwerb und Erstlesedidaktik in der Zeit des 'gemein teutsch' – eine sprachhistorische Untersuchung der Lehrbücher Valentin Ickelsamers". In *Osnabrücker Beiträge zur Sprachteorie* (11): 48–72.

Müller, Johannes
1882 *Quellenschriften und Geschichte des deutschsprachlichen Unterrichts bis zur Mitte des 16. Jahrhunderts.* Gotha: Thienemann.

Roth, Friedrich
1909 Die Maßregelung der Augsburger Schulmeister wegen des Interims am 31. August 1551. In *Beiträge zur bayerischen Kirchengeschichte* 15 (5): 217–227. Erlangen: Junge.

General references

Goody, Jack (ed.)
1968 *Literacy in traditional societies.* Cambridge: Cambridge University Press.

Lévi-Strauss, Claude
1955 *Tristes Tropiques.* Paris: PLON.

Medary, Marjorie
1954 *Each One Teach One: Frank Laubach, Friend to Millions.* New York: Longman.

Rennell of Rodd, Francis
1926 *People of the Veil.* Reprint 1966; Oosterhout: Anthropological Publications.

WERNER WINTER

Tradition and innovation in alphabet making

Abstract

The author uses his experience in the steps taken in the attempt to arrive at a viable writing system for Walapai, a Yuman language of Arizona, to point out the effects of differing backgrounds of linguists and of native users of the language upon preferences shown and choices made in actual alphabet making. It becomes clear that previous experience of the parties involved makes it next to impossible to arrive at solutions that seem optimal to all, and that the best one can hope for is a sensible compromise.

1. It can probably be said without exaggeration that the days when writing systems could be developed as it were *in vacuo* are gone forever. With writing practiced all over the world and within relatively easy reach of every person who might feel the need to convert a hitherto unwritten language into written form, a fully spontaneous solution of the task at hand can hardly be imagined. Any graphic system now developed will thus be radically different from the earliest systems invented by mankind: there will always be not only a relationship between a new writing system and a language, but also one between this system and other writing systems (or at least one other writing system) already in existence. Expressed in terms of units that will serve as the basis of systems, one can say that graphic entities do not only enter a relationship with phonic units, but also one with graphic units (or combinations of units) that belong to other graphic systems.

This statement applies to the orthography developed by a professional linguist just as well as to that designed by a layman. Even if a linguist takes a strictly scientific stance to the effect that the systemically relevant entities of the language to be converted into writing, and only these, should be rendered graphically – that is, if for instance a rigid 'one-phoneme one-grapheme' approach is taken and maintained – even then the linguist will tend not to be at odds with pre-established and widely accepted systems. It is totally inconceivable that a linguist would choose a symbolization of phonemes by arbitrarily devised signs or even by numbers with two digits (which would certainly suffice to identify succinctly and unambiguously the items of any known phonemic system). Instead, he will always have recourse to letters or combinations of letters from accepted alphabets (or perhaps syllabaries). It matters relatively little whether such alphabets are Latin- or Cyrillic-based (or whether a non-Western system is utilized) – all that counts is that even a professional linguist will never completely sever his ties with established conventions. Deviations are, to be sure, found often enough; but they occur when the given inventory referred to turns out to be inadequate for the immediate purpose of rendering the relevant distinctive entities of a language.

2. The most common deviation is the use of diacritics. Some of them have been used for a long time and may therefore be considered part of a given inventory; the macron would be one example. In other instances, linguists themselves may have established a tradition which is now followed – here the use of a colon to mark length could be mentioned. In other cases, one and the same diacritic might be used quite differently by different scholars working with different languages – witness the various values of dotted consonants. Sometimes, traditional signs may be utilized in untraditional ways, a fact which not infrequently leads to considerable difficulties for the non-specialist trying to interpret a written text in phonic terms. The use of *q* as a representation of glottal stop comes to mind, or the rendering of [dz] by *j* in Hübschmann's generally well-reasoned transliteration of the Armenian alphabet (the choice is perfectly logical as *j* for [dz] is to *ǰ* for [dź̌] as is *s* for [s] to *š* for [š] and particularly as is *c* for [ts] to *č* for [tš]; trouble results merely from the fact that noone trained in a Latin-based tradition will identify the Armenian *j* properly: a speaker of English will take it to indicate [dž], a speaker of French, [ž], a speaker of German, [y]).

Only rarely will linguists take recourse to signs that are not even modifications of signs found in established alphabets. The fact that clicks are symbolized in linguistic transcriptions by arbitrarily selected non-alphabetic signs points to an important property of the clicks: they seem so far removed phonically from anything letters can adequately render (the conventionalized spelling of non-phonemic clicks in English provides no argument to the contrary) that the selection of letters would have violated the basic principle of sign choice even more than in the Armenian case just mentioned: A sign should suggest at least some essential properties of the sound it is meant to symbolize – and none of the languages used as points of reference by the linguists first faced with the task of transcribing clicks had adequate letters at their disposal in their respective traditional writing systems.

In a way, the non-letter signs for clicks are of course on a level with the numerical signs referred to a while ago: without explicit instructions as to the phonetic value of a click symbol or of a numerical sign, any attempt at a pronunciation will be mere guesswork. Such signs are therefore innately less practical than letter-based signs: in the case of the latter, at least a crude approximation of the proper pronunciation of a sign sequence can usually be produced, certainly if the reader is familiar with the sign used from an alphabet or alphabets he knows, and if the principle 'one phoneme one grapheme' is not violated. Thus, both the IPA and the Czech rendering of [š] is likely to be identified as 'some kind of [s]', however inadequate this may be for purposes of exact classification and production of the sound in question. Difficulties arise when alphabetic symbols familiar to the reader have been assigned values totally different from those expected: an unsuspecting linguist will be just as much at sea as any layman if he is asked to respond correctly to Amerindianist *q* for glottal stop, Slavicist *x* for the velar spirant, or Hübschmann's *j* for Armenian [dz]. There are of course degrees of unfamiliarity of choices: Slavicist *x* stands a better chance of being properly recognized, or properly guessed at, than *x* in the initial *xh-* of the name of the Bantu tribe *Xhosa* – in the latter case, an uninitiated linguist is just as unlikely to come up with the proper pronunciation (aspirated lateral click) as the German radio announcer whom, just a few days ago, I heard valiantly struggling with an initial cluster [ksh].

Even for a linguist, the implied goal in his choice of transcription is then to operate with a maximum of known entities. He will tend to be explicit about his points of reference, whether it is the IPA alphabet or some other conventionalized system of transcription used by linguists familiar with a particular field of research, or even some particularly adequate standard orthographic system. He would be well-advised to adopt widely accepted conventions – if he expects to be read and understood by more than a small group of fellow specialists.

On the whole, the principle 'one phoneme one grapheme' is likely to be the most attractive one for a linguist. Still, conditions may prevail that may make a deviation from the principle advisable. If the allophonic range of a phoneme is such that the choice of one symbol is highly nonrepresentative for a large number of commonly found allophones, a subphonemic approach may be advisable as long as no overlap with the graphic representations of other phonemes results. On the other hand, a morphophonemic point of reference may be preferable to a phonemic one. If, for instance, there is an area of recurrent variation in the phonetic shape of forms which would require the introduction of several phoneme-based orthographic renderings for several occurrences of the same form, and if this variation could be covered adequately by a small number of realization rules (rules permitting, to be sure, the selection of various acceptable alternatives), then a morphophonemically based transcription is definitely preferable to a phonemically oriented one.

3. Still, the 'one phoneme one grapheme' principle retains its attractiveness for a linguist, certainly as long as he tackles the task of transcribing a language and recording it with a piece of paper and a pencil or a ball-point in his hand. Once he moves beyond this area of maximum freedom of choice, though, he finds himself confronted with reality on a new plane. As long as he just writes by hand, he can choose to select any symbol and any variant of a symbol that he considers maximally adequate for his purposes. As long as the diacritics remain distinctive, he may insert them wherever he wants; he may change the basic shape of letters at will, as long as he is consistent and avoids overlap; he may liberally combine letters from various alphabets; wherever he feels a need for it, he may add nonalphabetic signs, including signs invented for the purpose at hand. But this pleasant state of affairs does not last long; it will at best serve the linguist well for the composition of his first fieldnotes. The moment he decides that his transcribed material should be ready for publication, he has to cope with new conditions imposed on him – possibly very much to his dismay.

The next step in his work will probably be the preparation of a typewritten manuscript. Now all the beautiful signs he may have invented or taken over from alphabets alien to his typewriter turn out to be a nuisance, unless they are readily composable with the help of basic letters and diacritics available on his typewriter. Of course, he can decide to insert all missing letters in the shape developed for the field notes by hand; but any practitioner will be able to predict that this approach is the best way to ensure that there will be omissions or (if the typewritten manuscript is to be the basis for a typeset or composed text) errors of a frequently quite serious nature. So, if the linguist is also a realist, he will part company with his original version of a transcription and devise a new one better suited for the typewriter. A standard keyboard provides him with the raw material for a fairly high, and generally sufficient, number of complex signs which permits him to adhere to the principle 'one phoneme one grapheme' if the notion of grapheme includes all simple letter signs (including upper case ones) with or without superscript, subscript, or adscript diacritics. It is a very common phenomenon that the phonemic inventory of a natural language will be almost exhausted before some of the simple signs have been used; if he is willing to violate the principle that a sign selected should suggest to the reader at least some aspects of its phonetic equivalent, he can usually find a way to accommodate even quite outlandish sounds with the aid of a standard keyboard. An example would be the accepted use of the surplus signs *c, q,* and *x* for the rendering of dental, alveolar, and lateral clicks, respectively, in a language such as Xhosa or Zulu.

If the next step in the publication process is the reproduction of a camera-ready copy, then the linguist's worries are over – anything he has been able to produce on his typewiter will be publishable. The moment, however, that the publication plans involve other procedures, new problems arise. The linguist's typewriter may have been changed to contain some extra symbols, such as a shwa, a digraph *æ,* or square brackets and other auxiliary signs. A composer may not have one or other of these signs, and a seemingly simple process such as turning an *e* upside down so as to get a shwa is not readily manageable. A linguist may choose to disregard such a mundane problem; but he normally does so at a price – quite literally: any deviation from readily available type raises the cost of a publication, and as normal linguists are not only recipients of royalties, but also buyers of books, disregard for practicality tends eventually to hurt them.

Similar problems arise if a book is to be typeset. Long gone are the days when printers would be willing and able to handle any alphabet, be it Latin or one as outlandish as Syriac or Glagolitic. Signs not available can be obtained – again, at a price – but there is, as with the typist preparing copy for the composer, the constant problem that signs deviating from normal signs only by a small diacritic may not be recognized as non-normal by the typesetter. The result is obvious: printer's errors will have to be found and corrected; some will always manage to remain undetected.

Thus, the beautiful freedom of the original transcription by hand will be severely reduced, particularly if noncongruent systems of reproduction, such as typing and typesetting, affect the final product. An experienced author will try to anticipate difficulties and adjust his transcription system accordingly; he may, in doing so, even consider violating the cherished 'one phoneme one grapheme' principle. If, for instance, a language has phonemic aspirated stops but no sequence of plain stop plus phoneme /h/, he may – probably with a feeling of regret – decide to give up writing the aspirated stops with plain consonant signs plus aspiration diacritic and instead put down sequences of plain consonant plus *h* as graphic equivalents of monophonemic aspirates. Likewise, if no sequence of two identical short vowels has to be recorded in a language, the linguist may find a rendering of a phonemically long vowel by a sequence of two plain vowels more appealing than the use of plain vowel plus length mark. Thus, under conditions where no ambiguities arise, the strict 'one phoneme one grapheme' principle (or any of its variants discussed earlier) may be given up; but the requirement that no ambiguities must arise leads to the introduction of a less stringent principle than the original one, namely, that phonemes (or morphophonemes, or allophones) may be rendered by sequences of graphs, provided these sequences do not also serve as a rendering of sequences of phonemes (morphophonemes, or allophones). To give just one example: An interdental spirant may be written *th* as long as no sequence *t* plus *h* is found in the same language. For a linguistically oriented transcription system, bi-uniqueness of individual phonemes and graphemes may thus be too much of an ideal state of affairs, but unambiguity of signs and sign sequences is a requirement that cannot be foregone.

4. I have dwelt on these matters, which are familiar to all of us, after all, to make us aware of the fact that we linguists, too, do not operate *in vacuo*, but in the context of traditions we more or less tacitly accept. We may be more aware of what we are doing than laymen who ponder about adequate orthographies, but we should not consider ourselves freer in our decisions than they are – at least not substantially so. The only significant difference that I can see is that laymen, for reasons still to be discussed, may not feel the need for unambiguity as much as we do – and, as it were, this means less freedom on our side than on theirs.

Before we enter upon a discussion of the layman's interest and his resulting actions, we should note a significant difference between what is the linguist's normal position with respect to a language to be committed to writing and the position of the layman: The linguist will, as a rule, be not a native speaker, but an outsider; in trying to devise a writing system he will generally think of other outsiders (usually fellow linguists) as his target group, and therefore unambiguity and maximum explicitness will be high on his scale of values. If, as happens now and then, he will be asked to devise, or assist in devising, a writing system for a hitherto nonliterate group, he will be inclined to adhere to his scale of values, often overlooking the fact that his new target group has some qualifications which usually neither he himself nor his colleagues will have, qualifications which include a native command of the language to be written, and that, from the vantage point of native command, explicitness and unambiguity may be much less in demand than is the case (rightfully so) within a scholarly frame of reference. An example may clarify the point: A Semitic writing system is quite inadequate from the point of view of an outside linguist (to be sure, even more so from that of an outside layman), but it has served its purpose seemingly to the full satisfaction of the native users of the system – the lack of an indication of a large part of the vowels apparently did not interfere enough with a successful decoding of a Semitic text written in a Semitic alphabet to trigger a change of the system (which of course would be easily enough accomplished, as a full inventory of vocalization devices is available).

A linguist, if he is an outsider, cannot rely on the native speaker's intuition that will make even inadequately spelled passages clear, because the intuition is based on an assessment of forms rendered either ambiguously or not explicitly enough in the context provided through an understanding of preceding (and possibly also following) forms, an assessment which automatically leads to the exclusion of graphically possible, but grammatically or semantically improbable forms. Homographs are a problem for the outsider, but not for the native speaker.

When a linguist and a native speaker get together to discuss possibilities for a new orthography, it is to be expected that there will be disagreement as to how unambiguous the orthography should be. Some features of language apparently seem much less in need of graphic expression to the native speaker than to the outsider. We do not have to look very far for examples. I already mentioned incomplete vocalization in Semitic alphabets; one may add the suppression of the writing of accent in Russian, an accent which is far from being easy to predict and which determines very much the realization of vocalic graphemes. We could spend much time lamenting the redundancies and insufficiencies, often occurring side-by-side, in orthographic systems with a long history. As a rule, it can be said that the native speaker is not seriously impeded in his attempts to decode a written text in his native language. (That he may have trouble in producing a correctly spelled text is a different story.) As this seems to be a fact, it is not surprising that a native speaker frequently will find the linguist's wish to have an unambiguous and preferably widely understood writing system exaggerated – a wish, in his view, that would create problems – because the native speaker, with his recourse to full knowledge about such things as what a particular ambiguously spelled form must mean in a given context, cannot possibly see any difficulty.

5. I said earlier that all of us, whether we are linguists or laymen, are part of groups for which certain graphic traditions are a matter of course. Problems may arise from the fact that a linguist and a layman, in a given case, may not share the same – shall we say – non-professional background (no layman can be expected to have studied the IPA alphabet). What may seem to be a perfectly natural spelling device to the one may seem outrageous to the other – and this goes both ways, although the linguist may usually think he knows best. For the layman, the experience with actually-used spelling systems is allimportant, more important than, say, internal consistency. Thus, someone familiar with English spelling habits may find it perfectly natural that [u:] might be spelled with *oo*, and may need special persuasion to see that such a

solution makes no sense for a language that has both the short and long /o/ in its inventory of phonemes, along with the short and long /u/. It is more the case that the layman may find it hard to see why he should spell [u] with a *u*, the number of instances like *put* where the English *u* is to be pronounced [u] being so small.

A practice-oriented orthography will usually take the native speakers' experience with other writing systems into account rather thoroughly, even though such a decision might hurt a linguist's feelings. The arguments in favor of such a decision are fairly strong: making use of spelling habits acquired earlier to a full extent makes the acquisition of literacy in the native language easier (after all, German dialect texts for the normal reader generally adhere to standard German orthography, even though that may not be an ideal choice for a professional). Transfer of spelling habits, even if done with circumspection, has its drawbacks, though: spelling habits are hardly valid beyond the sphere of dominance of a given written language, and an outsider may be in for some bewildering surprises. Thus, the choice of *j* for [x] and of *x* for [š] in orthographies created by members of the Summer Institute of Linguistics may make very good practical sense for people literate in Mexican Spanish, but the outsider is likely to struggle with words containing *j* or *x* about as much as the radio announcer in Germany did with the *xh* in *Xhosa* – a value [š] for *x* being about as unexpected as a value [lateral click].

6. Looking at the troubles we tend to have with writing systems with a long history behind them, we tend to believe that creating an orthography for a hitherto unwritten language would be without problems; it is not. For history enters the picture here, too. Hardly ever will we be in a position to start from scratch, and if we do, we may not be able to persuade the native speakers that our choice makes really good sense.

Let me illustrate this point with some experiences I had in working with Walapai, a Yuman (and therefore ultimately a Hokan) language of Northern Arizona. I did my first fieldwork, and recorded my first texts, in 1956. Since then, I have been back a number of times for shorter or longer field trips, and, among other things, I served as a consultant to the bilingualism program of the tribe in 1977 and 1978. My first text was ready for publication in 1961, but, for a number of reasons beyond my control, it was not printed until 1966. The text was accompanied by a presentation of the phonemic system; the transcription system I used was, however, morphophonemic (with a short list of realization rules) and too complex to serve as the basis for a practical orthography. My phonemic system was defective inasmuch as it did not recognize labialized velars and postvelars as being different from sequences of velars and postvelars and *w*, and did not include pre-aspirated consonants which seem to contrast with *h* plus consonant. The decision in favor of a morphophonemic rendering (not a natural decision at all for the early sixties) was based on the fact that in certain environments the presence of a vowel could be predicted (historically speaking, its not having been deleted could be predicted), but the coloring of the vowel was conditioned by the environment in such a way that [ə] could alternate with [a] in one environment, with [i] in another, with [u] in a third, and with [i] and [u] in a fourth, and that no rules could be given as to which realization was required when – which meant that one and the same morpheme could, apparently without recognizable conditioning, assume any one of two or even three phonemic shapes (for the principle 'once a phoneme, always a phoneme' would have forced me to assign [a], [i], and [u] to the respective phonemes which are very much present in the language). The series of stops was highly interesting, as it contains a large number of points of articulation: labial, interdental, postdental, prepalatal, palatal, velar, postvelar, glottal. The number of spirants is smaller (which suggests, for instance, secondary origin of the prepalatal and palatal stops); the list of pre-aspirated stops is shorter, too; so is the list of nasals. Labialization appears to be limited to velar and postvelar position, but affects stops and spirants. The stops are voiceless and lenis; so, apparently, are the spirants.

When native speakers of the language first considered writing it, they disliked some of the solutions I had chosen in my published text. They felt, for instance, that lenis stops should be rendered by the signs used in English for voiced consonants (as there is no voiceless/voiced contrast in Walapai, the decision did no harm to the Walapai itself, although in the overall Yuman context, it is the less desirable alternative); typological considerations to the effect that voiced consonants usually, if not generally, imply the presence of voiceless ones of course did not enter the picture. Another argument seemed to be compelling for the native speakers in question, all members of the younger generation: in their own speech, what were pre-aspirated stops (or sequences of *h* and plain stop, depending on the analysis one prefers) in the language of the older generation (which had been the basis of my analysis), had become fortis voiceless aspirates and thereby quite similar to some realizations of English voiceless stops (a parallel development affected *hv-* which became fortis *f-* for these younger speakers). Change had also affected another consonant: in the speech of the older people, the postdental oral consonant was either a flapped or briefly trilled *r*, or a postdental voiceless lenis stop. In the Walapai of the younger people, the lastmentioned variant prevailed, and they took the [r] they encountered in the speech of the older generation to be a marginal phenomenon. In my own choice of a symbol, which was *r*, I was influenced both by what I observed with my elderly informants and by the knowledge that neighboring, closely related languages showed a clear *r* which did not alternate with a postdental *t* or *d*.

The native speaker's inclination to prefer the recent stop variant and to transcribe it with a *d* without diacritic forced them to introduce a diacritic for the interdental stop, while my own orthography managed to do without it. In view of what I said earlier in this paper, I did not, and do not, consider this a trivial point at all. The barred *d*, which the young Walapai chose for the interdental stop, is not available on a normal typewriter; it cannot be composed on anything but very large type; it is a very impractical choice. But for my co-workers, my *r*-choice was not a natural one because they used their own speech as a point of reference and not that of the elderly members of their community. So they did not have the option of getting by with two plain signs, whether they be *t* and *r*, as in my system, or *d* and *r*, as would be possible in theirs, but had to give a diacritic to one of their *d*'s. The regrettable fact that they resorted to a sign complex unsuited for composition on a typewriter has the undesirable effect that, to name just one example, the Tribal Council does not have the possibility of using a standard-keyboard typewriter should it ever decide to publish its notes on the tribal bulletin board in Walapai instead of in English. I therefore presume that the life expectancy of barred *d* will be limited, but that does not detract from the fact that for the time being it is being used and its use is being taught to school children.

Another decision of doubtful linguistic value was that of writing the unstressed-vowel variants *a, i, u* in the same way as the stressed vowels. The problem involved here will become obvious once it becomes necessary for the competing variants mentioned above, to be included in a tribal dictionary – a dictionary which is likely to be produced not too long after my own dictionary becomes available. In my own approach, I will want to avoid the listing of doublets and instead will give instructions for the correct production of variants; the orthography presently in use in school does not provide this option.

In other respects, the decisions of the native speakers and of the linguists could easily be made to agree. Thus, neither of us has any difficulties in rendering long vowels as plain vowels plus colon. The only interesting aspect here is that this practice deviates from that favored by native speakers of neighboring languages, in particular, of the nearly identical Havasupai. Here, a long vowel is always written with a double vowel sign. The motivation behind the decision of the Walapai group adds a very human touch to the overall picture: As for both Walapai and Havasupai a decision was made to write lenis stops with signs for voiced consonants, and as unstressed vowels received the same treatment in Havasupai and Walapai, the use of the colon as a length mark provided a very convenient means for making obvious the fact that the text presented here was a Walapai and not a Havasupai one, a fact frequently not immediately detectable from a mere inspection of the text.

At first glance, we may find such a deliberate attempt at being different, and rather strange, where an identical solution would have seemed advisable from a purely practical point of view; but then, haven't we had different orthographical rules for decades for written German in the various political entities using German as their standard language, and isn't even now a possible decision in favor of retaining capitalization or eliminating it just as much a political decision as one based on linguistic considerations?

For the linguist, the native speakers' decisions are not necessarily optimal, but quite adequate for the cases discussed. More regrettable, from his point of view, but not really surprising, as we have seen, is that in some instances the decisions made obscure existing linguistic contrasts. Thus, whenever no unstressed vowel is recorded, a sequence of velar or postvelar and *w* will not be distinguished from a labialized velar or postvelar consonant: /h^w/ in the word for 'blood', /'əh^w at/ (tribal orthography *hwad*) will be written the same way as the sequence /h/ plus /w/ in *hwak*, the word for 'two'. Furthermore, there is a tendency to interpret the ejectiveness of word-final consonants in such a way that they are classed with the fortis stops, that is, the old pre-aspirated stops; here, a connection is suggested which does not seem to have a sound enough basis for it to be even considered as a possibility.

The violation of the 'one phoneme one grapheme' principle, as manifested by the choice of *th* for /θ/ or of *ny* for /ń/, etc., has a very limited effect upon the convertibility of a tribal text into a phonemic one. The only half-way serious overlap occurs for *gy*, which can represent both the palatal /k^y/ and the sequence /ky/, but a minimal knowledge of morphology will suffice to remove all ambiguity.

On the whole, the tribal orthography and my own show so much equivalence that the question seems inevitable as to why I do not abandon mine in favor of theirs. After all, several of my colleagues have made just that decision. I think that the problem of competing variants of unstressed vowels is so serious for even such a highly practical endeavor as the compilation of a dictionary, that I prefer to stick to my own solution of basic variant plus rule. I also think that the choice of voiced-consonant symbols for the lenis stops is unfortunate in a context of general linguistics, as it might suggest a typological problem where there really is none. All this, of course, does not mean that I would not do such a thing as converting into tribal orthography, say, some of the stories I will publish into tribal orthography, once I have presented them in my own analysis, as only then will they be usable in school and thereby contribute to the preservation of some of the Walapai heritage.

7. In conclusion, let me try to come up with some more general remarks. As linguists, we should remain aware that neither we nor the laymen we encounter in literacy programs are independent of our respective conditions, but that we all have been shaped by them. One advantage – and an obligation results from this advantage – may be that we can be more conscious of what the tradition consists of, of what is indispensable, and where we can yield to our counterpart's point of view. Quite often, a compromise may be possible; sometimes, a dual approach may be inevitable or even desirable. As long as we do not remain convinced that our own solution is the only one possible, we can at least be confident that no major harm will be done.

FLORIAN COULMAS

Writing and literacy in China

Abstract

The Chinese writing system is the most important and successful rival of the alphabet. The peculiarities of this system account for the fact that China has, at the same time, the oldest writing tradition of all countries in the world today and a very high rate of illiteracy. This chapter is an account of the problems involved in achieving general literacy in China. The reform of the Chinese writing system and its possible replacement by a romanized script are important political issues in the Chinese speaking world, most of all in the People's Republic of China. The focus of this account is on three tasks that the Committee for Reforming the Chinese Written Language has set itself to fulfill: (1) the simplification and standardization of Chinese characters, (2) the development of a phonemic orthography, and (3) the nationwide establishment and popularization of a standard language.

1. *The issues*

The Chinese language is often seen through the filter of two traditional misconceptions or prejudices. One concerns the units of that language: It is frequently described as monosyllabic. Individual words allegedly consist of only one syllable. The second misconception is about the writing system which is misleadingly labeled "ideographic". The underlying idea goes back, at least in part, to Leibniz who was fascinated by the Chinese script, because he thought that it came close to what he was looking for, a universal means for the communication of ideas, a *characteristica universalis*. The attempt to understand the efforts and the preconditions of a reform of the Chinese writing system obliges us to get rid of both of these misconceptions.

Chinese has the longest uninterrupted writing tradition of all living languages. The Chinese script has been in use for more than 3000 years, and its beginnings can be traced even further back. In the development of writing systems, logography, the holistic representation of words in a script, represents a relatively early state. Ideographic systems for writing natural languages, on the other hand, never existed, in spite of the occurrence of ideographic elements in many writing systems (such as, e.g., figures, mathematical or logical symbols, etc.). An ideographic system is a system where the representation of meaning is not mediated by a representation of sound, a system, in other words, whose units are not the units of any one particular language. The Chinese language, it is well-known, is split into a number of vastly different, and, to a large extent, mutually unintelligible dialects. Yet, they are all written by means of the same writing system. This fact may well have fostered the assumption that the Chinese script actually has the properties of an ideographic system. However, it is mainly in the phonology that the Chinese dialects differ from each other while being very similar as regards syntax and lexis. Hence the Chinese writing system can be viewed as having ideographic properties within the Chinese speaking world, because the relation between visual sign and meaning is functionally more important than that between visual sign and sound. Nevertheless, the units that are written are linguistic units, not language independent ideas.

The grammatical system of classical Chinese almost invites a confusion of logographic and ideographic writing. Because of the isolating character of the Chinese language every word appears in the same form in every environment. Hence, the principle that there is a character for every meaningful unit and vice versa is not marred by the necessity to represent inflectional or other grammatical morphemes. As pointed out above, the meaningfulness or information load of the characters is much greater than that of the phonetic forms of Chinese words, because the former outnumber the latter by a rate of more than ten to one. Therefore, the assumption that the writing system is ideographic was very suggestive.

In classical Chinese, the relation between word, character, and syllable was predominantly 1: 1: 1. Today, this relationship is more complicated, as the better part of the vocabulary consists of bi- or polysyllabic words in modern Chinese. However, the fact that every character is phonetically realized by a syllable remains unaltered. (Obviously, the inverse does not hold, owing to the unequal number of characters and syllables.) Only very few characters are used as syllabic signs, that is, solely for their sound value disregarding their meaning. The necessity of this practice arises in every logographic writing system once it is used for writing proper names, particularly those of foreign languages. The same holds true for loan words. A small number of characters lack a genuine association with a particular meaning altogether. Thus the characters 垃 and 圾 designate the syllables *lā* and *jī*, respectively. In isolation neither of them has a meaning. Only in conjunction do they represent the word *lājī* which means 'garbage'. All of these cases, where the principle that a character is related to one syllable and one meaning is violated, however, are extremely rare. By and large, Chinese characters constitute a morphemic writing system. The representation of meaning is still the major property of the Chinese script. All attempts to reduce the number of characters to a small inventory of syllabic signs have failed.

Proposals for using a limited number of Chinese characters as a syllabic script have been made periodically since the early 17th century when Jesuit missionaries first came to China. After the foundation of the republic under Sun Yatsen, the efforts to reform the Chinese writing system were increased in order to facilitate its use both for foreigners and Chinese and thus to promote literacy. In 1918, a syllabic system by the name of *dùgīn xǐmǔ* was officially recognized by the government and taught in elementary schools for some time. However, all attempts to overcome illiteracy and facilitate international communication that were made before the founding of the People's Republic in 1949 were to no avail. The difficulties of a writing system which can only be learned at the cost of memorizing thousands of characters over many years have long been recognized and taken into account by progressive educators and politicians. They were always faced with the additional problem that the majority of those competent to carry out a reform of the Chinese written language had little interest in simplifying and hence changing the system they themselves had taken so long to acquire. Many intellectuals and literary men considered the continuity of the tradition as being more important than the spreading of literacy by means of a simpler writing system. For the leaders of the communist party this issue had high priority from the very beginning. As early as ten days after the founding of the People's Republic, a research group was formed which later became the Committee for Reforming the Chinese Written Language (*Zhòngguó wénzì gǎigé wěnyuáhuì*). The importance of this committee became obvious to everyone when it was placed directly under the state council, in 1954.

There are three main tasks that the Committee for Reforming the Chinese Written Language has set itself to accomplish: (1) the standardization and simplification of Chinese characters, (2) the nation-wide establishment of a standard language, and (3) the creation of a romanized orthography. In the sequel, I will deal with each of these tasks in turn. Notice, however, that they are being pursued simultaneously rather than consecutively. The reasons for a parallel approach to all three tasks will become clear in what follows.

2. *Standardization of Chinese characters*

The Chinese writing system is cumbersome and difficult to learn not only because of the large number of characters, but also because for many of them more than one variant is in current usage. This fact is an obstacle for character recognition as well as for lexicographic recording. Character standardization is hence first and foremost a lexicographic task. The number of strokes of which the characters are composed is the crucial principle of their ordering and retrieval in a dictionary. Obviously, then, the standardization of the characters is highly desirable for all kinds of work involving mono- or bilingual dictionaries. Unless there is one and only one standardized variant of every character, the search procedure in the dictionary is unnecessarily complicated, because there is always a chance that a character has to be looked up at several different places in the dictionary.

Because of the large number of characters and their having been used for centuries or millenia, the process of standardization and simplification is a long ranging task that cannot be accomplished at one stroke. The Committee has been working on this task since its foundation, and it is not yet completed. At present, Chinese lexicography is in a state of transition. Many new dictionaries, that have simplified characters as their entries, are provided with indexes including obsolete variants which were simplified or eliminated altogether, in order to make sure that every character can be found. In the long run, non-standard variants should all be eliminated from the written language. Since 1956, when the first standardization scheme was issued, 1055 variants have been ruled out. In the same time, 2238 characters have been simplified.

The simplification of characters is a particular mode of standardization. The basic idea is to reduce graphic complexity and hence facilitate acquisition and usage. The simplification of characters is a major normative intervention in the linguistic practice of the literate Chinese language community. Institutionally, this is clearly reflected by the fact that simplification schemes of the Committee are enacted as precepts by the highest legislative body, the People's Congress. The first scheme which was accepted in 1956 has proved to be successful. The simplified characters included therein are widely used today without, however, having replaced their older variants completely. Old and simplified characters are still found, one next to the other, in non-official writing. The ancient character for *xué* (learn), 學, for instance, can be seen in public announcements at least as often as its simplified version 学. The second simplification scheme whose first version was drafted in 1977 is presently undergoing some revisions. Its implementation can be expected within the next two years.

The simplification of characters is a very complicated process. A number of different factors must be taken into account rather than a single principle. Obviously, one of these factors is redundancy. Whenever a multitude of strokes differentiates a character from all other characters, the number of strokes can be reduced. Reducing the strokes above all serves to facilitate the writing of the respective characters. The desirable changes with respect to production and recognition are not necessarily the same. Rather, every individual simplification has to find a balance for competing requirements. While the reduction of redundancy is highly desirable for the sake of facilitating and speeding up the writing process, it may reach a point where it becomes an additional obstacle in the reading process because too little discriminatory redundancy is preserved. Theoretically, this looks like a straightforward principle, but, in practice, a solution that benefits both the writing and reading process is often hard to find. In order to avoid revisions of the simplifications once they are published, every proposal has to be tried out and carefully checked against the entire system before its final acceptance. As an example, consider the simplified characters 边 and 辺 which were derived from different sources. The differentiating feature can easily get lost in handwriting. Thus, in this case, the two characters were eventually considered too similar and were withdrawn.

Another aspect to be taken into account is typography. The simplification should not yield characters that violate the basic principles of graphic composition. In most cases, characters are simplified by replacing a complex element by a simpler one. If possible, without loosing too much redundancy, multiple occurrence of one element within one character is reduced to one occurrence. Another common strategy is to eliminate parts of characters. The cursive writing which has been cultivated for many centuries provides another guideline for simplification. Thus cursive variants of characters are re-linearized and standardized (cf. for instance the characters for *shū* (book) 书 < 書 or *dōng* (East) 东 < 東).

Simplified characters are published in lists issued by the Committee for Reforming the Chinese Written Language, and their use becomes mandatory thereupon, at least in official texts, newspapers, etc. Somewhat surprising is the fact that even the writing of proper names is changed in accordance with the standardized characters. Mr. Mǎ, who used to write his name with the character 馬, now uses the simplified version 与. This amounts to a reduction of 50% in the number of strokes. Yet, there is an obvious similarity between the two. This kind of similarity between old and new is an important aspect of the simplification scheme. It is aimed at preserving continuity in the Chinese writing tradition, in spite of the reform.

Aside from the aspects mentioned above, there are some numerical guidelines for the simplification. In addition to the first simplification scheme of 1956, only characters with more than 12 strokes should be simplified. Simplification is optional for those with 13–16 strokes. Frequently-used characters with 17–20 strokes as well as those with more than 20 strokes have to be simplified in any event. For every proposed simplification, a detailed justification must be given, including a frequency analysis.

Considering the importance of a normative intervention in the Chinese writing system for any kind of work involving the use of dictionaries, the carefulness and attentiveness with which the simplification and standardization of characters is being carried out is hardly surprising. The eventual result of this work will be a new standard dictionary containing the standardized versions of all characters of common usage, an indication of their pronunciation including the tones, a frequency index, a marking of the order of strokes, as well as the admissible and inadmissible variants.

A sample of traditional (upper row) and simplified characters (lower row) is given below (quoted from Yang 1980: 21).

業	蟲	鐘	漢	後	個
业	虫	钟	汉	后	个

The reduction in graphic complexity is very apparent. In how far these simplifications actually facilitate the use of characters, and what exactly the perceptual and manipulative advantages are remains subject to empirical investigation.

3. *Some problems of romanization*

The technological superiority of the West has often been linked to the alphabet (e.g. McLuhan 1962) which is simpler and more economical than every other writing system. The development of Japan over the past 100 years has more than clearly demonstrated that prosperity and a modern economy can be achieved in spite of a non-alphabetic and highly complex writing system (cf. Coulmas 1980). Yet, in most cases, economic arguments were put forth in favor of a radical solution of writing reform issues; a solution that led Turkey to replace the Arabic script by the Latin alphabet in the 1920s and many other countries to adopt the alphabet as the standard writing system for their national languages. In China, the development of a standardized alphabetic orthography has been recognized as an important task, regardless of whether or not such an orthography should eventually supplant the Chinese script. A replacement of this sort is anything but imminent; and the efforts that are being made in connection with the simplification of characters testify that a hasty adoption of the alphabet as the common writing system is not the policy of the Committee for Reforming the Chinese Written Language. For the foreseeable future, literacy in China will thus be tied to a mastery of the Chinese script. Both, character simplification and romanization, are integral parts of the current writing reform policy in China.

After many years of thorough investigation and deliberation, in 1958, the People's Congress of the People's Republic of China officially adopted the Chinese phonetic alphabet, *hànyǔ pīnyīn,* as the standard system of transliteration for transcribing the Chinese language. With this decision, a chaotic situation resulting from the many coexisting and rivalling transliteration systems came to an end. Since the early 17th century, numerous transliteration systems had been developed and used, often reflecting the orthography of the inventor's mother tongue as much as Chinese phonology. Wherever Chinese proper names or words were to be written alphabetically, a romanization convention had to be developed. The differences between the evolving conventions are due to the many different ways in which orthographies of various European languages make use of the alphabet. Again European missionaries spearheaded the development of regular transliteration systems in order to facilitate their own study of Chinese. Texts using these systems were published long before an autochthonous movement for a phonetic script emerged. At the beginning of this century, Sun Yatsen supported such a movement, and in 1913, the first phonetic script was officially recognized. In this system, Chinese chararacters were used as graphical elements in order to display the distinctness of the Chinese language in its written form. Only in 1927, was a phonetic system using roman letters issued by the Ministry of Education of the Goumindang government. It was based on the phonology of the Beijing dialect which, at that time, was not generally understood throughout the country. Therefore, its geographical expansion and use remained very limited. Another system was developed by emigrant intellectuals during the 1930s in the Soviet Union. On its basis the *hànyǔ pīnyīn* system was created. This system has recently been officially implemented by the United Nations as the standard system of romanization of Chinese names. It has also been adopted by major news agencies and publications.

Hànyǔ pīnyīn constitutes only the first step towards a solution of the romanization problem. As a phonemic system, it lacks those properties that make the Chinese script a relatively appropriate means for coping with Chinese dialect differences. Chinese characters map into speech at the level of morphemes rather than of syllables or phonemes. Hence, even decisive differences in pronunciation of words between the dialects do not impair written communication. Efficient usage of a phonemic writing system, on the other hand, depends on the knowledge of the phonological system of the dialect that is being written and of the rules relating graphemic and phonemic units. Moreover, the standardization of spelling does not insure a standardization of pronunciation, as can be seen from the difficulties that radio announcers with no knowledge of Chinese have in correctly pronouncing names such as, e.g., *Xinhua, Qu Qiubai, Hangzhou Jianqiao, Conghua*, etc. (cf. Wu 1980), to say nothing of the tones. This is not only a problem of international communication, because Chinese learning foreign languages are now susceptible to interferences between different alphabetic orthographies (those of the respective foreign languages and *hànyǔ pīnyīn*). Writing reform thus becomes an issue that cannot be detached from an overall conception of language policy.

An exclusively sound-related writing system is of little value to the person who does not understand the language written by that system. As a consequence, the romanized script will have to be used either for writing each of the dialects or for one privileged dialect only, which then has to be pushed throughout the country as the standard language. Obviously, the first solution would destroy the unity of the Chinese language which the Chinese script served for so many centuries to preserve. The disintegration of the Chinese language community can hardly be the aim of reforming the Chinese written language. Hence, the nationwide establishment of a standard language is a precondition for employing *hànyǔ pīnyīn* as an efficient means of communication. Accordingly, the official promotion of *hànyǔ pīnyīn* is coupled with the promotion of the standard language *putōnghuà* which is based on the Beijing dialect. The use of the *pīnyīn* system for writing other dialects, although theoretically possible, is not planned.

The creation of an alphabetic orthography is a complex task. Its aptness and its deficiencies only become evident when the system is put to use. A theoretically sound and highly coherent system may not meet all of the requirements of the speech community (cf. Winter, this volume). Once the orthography is widely used, some revisions may become necessary. *Hànyǔ pīnyīn* is no exception in this regard. Some of the unsolved problems are discussed in the following:

(1) the spelling of proper names of alphabetically and non-alphabetically written languages. In order to insure unambiguous reference, a uniform convention has to be established. The importance of this point becomes clear in the light of the parallel issue of spelling Chinese proper names. Even more important than the internal regularities of a spelling convention is the very existence of such a convention and the fact that it is universally adhered to,

because all kinds of reference works, such as, e.g., maps, encyclopedias, dictionaries, indexes, etc. are affected. In the following list, the *pīnyīn* spellings of some place names of Chinese towns and provinces are given (in the left column) in contrast to (in the right column) the respective spellings most commonly used before the implementation of *hànyǔ pīnyīn.*[1]

hànyǔ pīnyīn	old spelling
Beijing	Peking
Chongquing	Chungking
Guangdong	Kwangtung (hence Canton)
Guangzhou	Kwangchow
Guilin	Kweilin
Henan	Honan
Hubei	Hupeh
Jiangsu	Kiangsu
Jiangxi	Kiangsi
Nanjing	Nanking
Qingdao	Tsingtao
Shaanxi	Shensi
Sichuan	Szechuan
Taibei	Taipei
Urumqi	Urumchi
Xian	Sian
Xinjiang	Sinkiang

As for the spelling of foreign proper names, two options can be considered: (a) adopting the original spelling, provided that an alphabetic system is used for writing the language in question; (b) representing the phonetic form of the name by means of *hànyǔ pīnyīn.* In the former case, the phonetic realization of the name will often be distorted by Chinese readers; in the latter case, the original spelling will be altered in many instances. Karl Marx, for example, would become 'Marks', according to the latter option. It seems difficult to present convincing arguments that favor one of the options over the other. A decision, however, has to be made. Similarly, a uniform convention for transcribing proper names of non-alphabetically written languages must be adopted.

(2) the writing of imported technical terms. With respect to the incorporation of technical terms of other languages into the Chinese language, the conditions are like those of the spelling of proper names. There is, however, another possibility, loan translation, a procedure that, in former times, was often preferred to the phonetic use of Chinese characters in borrowing words from other languages. As Chinese characters still provide the major means of Chinese written language, this procedure is still made use of.

(3) the representation of tones. Aside from the 26 letters of the Roman

alphabet, *hànyǔ pīnyīn* employs two diacritical marks (¨ , ˆ) and four tone marks (¯, ´,ˇ, `). While some Chinese dialects differentiate up to eight tones, *pǔtōnghuà* has only four. The use of the tone marks is summarized in the following chart.

tone	tone mark	quality
1.	¯	flat high pitch
2.	´	slow rise to high pitch
3.	ˇ	voice drops first and then rises again
4.	`	voice drops sharply starting from high pitch

Theoretically, the use of the tone marks is clearly regulated. In practice, however, their employment varies considerably. In some publications appearing in *hànyǔ pīnyīn*, the tone marks are by and large dispensed with, or limited to those instances where they serve a disambiguating function that is not otherwise fulfilled contextually. The use of the tone marks is tonemic, that is, variations of the realizations of tones that are conditioned by the phonetic environment are not represented in writing. The omission of tone marks in many *pīnyīn* publications seems to indicate that the alphabetic representation of the Chinese language is even less of a problem than it is claimed to be by those arguing in favor of maintaining Chinese characters because of the ensuing confusions that are allegedly bound to be brought about by romanization.

(4) segmentation. When most Chinese words were monosyllabic, there was no reason to introduce any spacing into the writing other than the equal spaces between characters each of which represented a word. This convention was sustained even when polysyllabic words began to form the majority of the Chinese vocabulary. Thus, in modern Chinese writing word boundaries remain unmarked. Thefailuretomarkwordboundariesinalphabeticwritingcreates unnecessary difficulties for the reader, difficulties which can be avoided by the *pīnyīn* spelling convention. Whether a given linguistic entity is grammatically a single word, a compound, or a phrase consisting of several words never mattered in character writing. In isolating languages, the differences between these three kinds of linguistic entities are even more difficult to determine than in inflectional languages that do not lack a morphology.[2] However, despite the absence of a morphology in Chinese, there *are* differences in the grammatical behavior of words, compounds, and phrases. A systematically sound convention for the demarcation of words in *hànyǔ pīnyīn* depends on a thorough analysis of such differences.

(5) homonymy. Owing to the small number of Chinese syllables, homophonous words abound in this language. In the written language there was no

correlate of this phenomenon so far, because, in addition to a phonetic component, each character has a meaning-related component. Graphically, many homophonous words are disambiguated and, therefore, characters often serve as a reference system for clarification. By adopting the alphabet, homonymy in speech will be reproduced as homography on the level of written language. Historically, the problem of homonymy has greatly contributed to the emergence and increase of bisyllabic words in the Chinese vocabulary. Many bisyllabic words consist of two originally synonymous but heterophonous words, the respective second ones of which served as an explanation or clarification of the first. In the course of time, the two words collapsed into one. In this way, the problem of homophony has been reduced considerably. As a matter of fact, it does not constitute a significant obstacle to spoken communication where speaker and hearer, in most cases, share a common context of situation. There are, however, a considerable number of homophonous words belonging to the same word category, such as, for instance, *ai* 'love' and *ai* 'hinder'. While not causing serious problems, they give reason to think of possible improvements of the spelling system. One possibility is to incorporate some morphemic information into the otherwise phonemic system. Thus homophones could be differentiated graphically despite their phonetic identity. This kind of morphemic writing is very common in alphabetic orthographies.[3]

Another interesting possibility to avoid homography is the standardization of dialect variants of homophonous words. The experimental character of the Chinese writing reform and its consequences for the language as a whole become overtly apparent here. Writing reform and the popularization of the standard language intimately interact and mutually influence each other. Some time will pass before *hànyǔ pīnyīn* will begin to exercise an influence on the spoken language. However, the possibilities arising out of the synchronized campaigns to teach *hànyǔ pīnyīn* and popularize *pǔtōnghuà* are clearly visible. While the northern dialects of China are similar to *pǔtōnghuà*, the standard language is identical with none of them. For speakers of southern and western dialects *pǔtōnghuà* is almost as different as a foreign language. The written language has always been rigidly standardized, and the differences between spoken and written language were considerable. For obvious reasons, the standardization of the written language did not pertain to the phonetic forms of words. The implementation of *hànyǔ pīnyīn*, for the first time in Chinese history, introduces a means of unequivocally specifying the standard phonetic form of words rather than vaguely indicating their pronunciation. Once a phonetic writing system is introduced, its orthography sets a standard for the phonetic form of words. At present, it is impossible to make any predictions about the effects that such a measure will actually have on the spoken language at large. The use of a logographic script implies a relationship between spoken and written language as well as an attitude towards language as a whole which, in many respects, are very different from those implied by an alphabetic writing system. The consequences of the transition from one to the other, or rather, of the additional introduction of the latter into the Chinese written language will be highly interesting to observe. The process by which this is brought about is a language policy program of unparalleled dimensions involving as it does the largest linguistic community in the world.

4. *Popularization of the standard language*

For reasons explained above, the implementation of *hànyŭ pīnyīn* as a public means of communication prior to the nationwide establishment of the standard language, *pŭtōnghuà*, is not a sensible proposition. This state has not yet been reached. The level of education among the rural population is still very low, and not even in the cities can a speaker of *pŭtōnghuà* make him/herself understood throughout the country. Neither *pŭtōnghuà* nor the *pīnyīn* writing system are generally known by the Chinese people. The latter even less than the former, which is hardly surprising considering the fact that, as yet, *hànyŭ pīnyīn* is of very little practical value. Publications are scarce, and nobody employs it for private communication. The use of the romanized script was even abandoned for telegraphing after a short test period, because most recipients were unable to decode alphabetically written texts. Thus, for everyone who has but a limited command of Chinese characters there is no motivation whatsoever to learn the *pīnyīn* system and use it. In general, the public seems to associate the use of roman letters with languages other than Chinese and not to recognize *pīnyīn*-written texts as being Chinese at all. New dictionaries tend to be arranged in alphabetical order nowadays, but this is about the only practical use of the alphabet in the Chinese written language to date. Only gradually will alphabetic literacy alter the Chinese written language.

Eventually, however, general knowledge of *pŭtōnghuà* and *hànyŭ pīnyīn* will drastically change the linguistic situation in China. While there are no intentions to establish a uniform standard language at the cost of eliminating the dialects, it is clear that *pŭtōnghuà* will play an increasingly important rôle. It has a privileged position already as regards oral mass media and it will monopolize the use of *hànyŭ pīnyīn*. A text written in Chinese characters can be read aloud in various dialects. Thus produced differences in the phonetic realizations of one and the same text are quite stunning. Nothing like this will be possible when the *pīnyīn* system is used, even though it allows for some variation in the phonetic realization of texts, as does any romanized script. Yet every phonetic realization of an alphabetically written text is mapped onto it in a regular way and hence on any other phonetic realization of the same text. Phonologically unrelated readings of alphabetically written linguistic units within the framework of the grapho-phonemic system of one language are systematically impossible. Thus the privileged status of *pǔtonghuà* will be enhanced by the spreading of *hànyǔ pīnyīn*, as this spelling system is designed to fit the standard language. This effect is, of course, intended rather than merely tolerated by those responsible for the Chinese language policy. In a sense, the written representation of *pǔtōnghuà* by means of *pīnyīn* serves the function of a model for, rather than a copy of, the spoken language. *Hànyǔ pīnyīn* thus becomes a means of specifying and canonizing the norm of the standard language. This is very important, because the written norm will help to prevent the standard language from splitting up in turn into various dialects once it has been established throughout the country. With a language community of approximately one billion this is more than a remote possibility, and the success of the standard language promotion campaign depends, at least to some extent, on the ability to install the romanized script as a guideline of pronunciation. Spelling pronunciation is generally considered as a kind of perversity in the relation between speech and writing. Within limits, the process of creating and promoting a standard language may, however, take advantage of this perversity.

As for the relationship between *pǔtōnghuà* and *hànyǔ pīnyīn* concerning their public usage, the overall political aims of the Chinese government and the Committee for Reforming the Chinese Written Language are difficult to pin down. For some, the universal command of the standard language in the Chinese speech community seems to be the sole precondition for introducing the *pīnyīn* system as a means of communication on a large scale. If, however, the Chinese script were to be replaced by the alphabet very soon, a reform of Chinese characters would not be worthwhile. Many intellectuals frown upon the very possibility of introducing the alphabet into the Chinese written language, maintaining that the cultural heritage of China is inseparable from Chinese writing. This is undoubtedly true, and no responsible person in China argues in favor of giving up the Chinese script altogether.

In China, as in Egypt and Sumer, literacy has always been restricted to a small cast of scribes and literary men. With the exception of Japan, universal literacy was only achieved where an alphabetic writing system was used. Given that one of the aims for reforming the Chinese written language is to achieve universal literacy, the current rate of literacy is a crucial consideration. Unfortunately, no exact statistics are available. As of 1973, an estimate of the U. S. Agency for International Development (AID) puts the literacy rate in the PR China as low as 25%. Today it is bound to be considerably higher, and there is a big difference between the urban and rural population. Still, much remains to be done in order to turn China into a literate country. With respect to romanization this point is important, because the lower the actual literacy rate the more sense it makes to promote literacy by means of the alphabet. No other writing system affords literacy at equally low cost. At present, *hànyŭ pīnyīn* is taught for a short period in elementary school. Otherwise it does not play any significant part in general education. *Pŭtōnghuà* is likewise taught in elementary school, and most lessons are taught in *pŭtōnghuà* in high school. College and university classes are supposed to be taught exclusively in *pŭtōnghuà*. In addition, nationwide and many regional broadcastings use the standard language.

A question quite different from the mastery of *pŭtōnghuà* is the attitude toward this language. Clearly, the standard language favors the northern dialects, and some resentment from speakers of *Wŭ* (Shanghai) and Cantonese can be expected. On the other hand, the standard language is so similar to some of the northern dialects that many of their speakers fail to make an effort to adapt to the standard because they can make themselves understood anyway. Both of these attitudes make interesting topics of sociolinguistic research. To my knowledge, no systematic investigations about them have been carried out to date.

The most important means of spreading the standard language are the mass media. They guarantee a standard pronunciation. However, teachers, who are of course also important agents for promoting the standard, tend to teach in a speech community whose dialect is their own dialect. Therefore, they are more likely to fall back on the dialect or a regionally colored version of *pŭtōnghuà*.

Another important aspect of the national language promotion campaign is the fact that the major Chinese speaking communities outside the PR China have adopted the proposed standard. *Pŭtōnghuà* (also called *guóyŭ*) is taught in Hongkong and Singapore. The standard language taught in Taiwan is also very similar because the majority of the ruling class of mainland Chinese in Taiwan emigrated from northern parts of the country. Hence the prospects are very good that *pŭtōnghuà* will be able to become a common means of communication for the Chinese nation, and thus fulfill the function that Chinese characters have served for the educated for many centuries. The question is what part will the alphabet play in this process and how easily will it be accepted as a means of writing Chinese by the Chinese speech community. The alphabet has scarcely begun to invade Chinese written language, and it meets the firm resistance of a millenial tradition. As yet its effects are hardly visible. The co-occurring part of the reform of the Chinese written language, on the other hand, has already covered some ground. The first scheme of 1956 was well received by the public and the same is to be expected for the second one which is due to appear within a year or two. The fact that both romanization and character simplification are pursued at the same time should not be mistaken as lack of decisiveness or halfhearted policy. Rather, it is a result of the insight that writing reform and language reform in a country with so vast a population as China are processes that take, by necessity, several decades rather than years to complete.

Notes

* My thanks are due to the government of the People's Republic of China and to the Deutscher Akademischer Austauschdienst (DAAD) for funding a fact-finding mission to China for a delegation of German linguists during the summer of 1980, of which I had the privilege to be a member. Many discussions with Wolf Thümmel and Dieter Wunderlich helped me to clarify some of the problems dealt with in this paper. My thanks to them.

1. For a more extensive list see Yang 1980: 26.
2. Inconsistent or arbitrary word demarcations are a common feature of many orthographies. Very often, they merely reflect historical coincidences. *Alright*, for instance, is still considered nonstandard in English spelling, as opposed to *always* or *already*. There is no systematic reason why *radfahren* is considered to be one word in German while *Auto fahren* is spelled as two words. Historically, it is a common word formation process that causes two words to collapse into one. It may take a long time before such a process is reflected in the spelling. Clearly, *beaucoup* has not always been spelled as one word. Considerations of this kind have to be taken into account when an alphabetic orthography is created or reformed.
3. See Bolinger 1946 for an account of "visual morphemes" in English spelling.

References

Bolinger, Dwight
1946 "Visual morphemes". *Language* 22: 333–40.

Coulmas, Florian
1980 "Struktur und Funktionsweise der Japanischen Schrift". In Coulmas, ed., *Zur Semiotik der Schrift.* Themenheft der *Zeitschrift für Semiotik* 4: 361–374.

McLuhan, Marshall
1962 *The Gutenberg Galaxy*. Toronto: University of Toronto Press.

Wang, Willian S.–Y.
1973 "The Chinese language". *Scientific American* 228: 51–60.

Winter, Werner
1980 "Tradition and innovation in alphabet making". *In this volume.*

Wu Wenchao
1980 "The adoption of the Chinese phonetic alphabet as the international standard for romanization of Chinese names of persons and places". *Journal of Chinese Linguistics* 8: 320–22.

Yang Ling
1980 "Reforming written Chinese". *Beijing Review* 33: 19–26.

Part Three.

Psychological aspects of writing

MARGARET MARTLEW

The development of writing: Communication and cognition

Abstract

The process of writing is an integration of skills. Learning to master these skills involves lower order performance factors such as handwriting and spelling becoming automatic so that the writer is free to apply himself to the more demanding levels of the writing process.

The decontextualised nature of written language compared with speech, demands specific intellectual abilities and a greater awareness of language itself. Young children, for instance, can have conceptual difficulties in separating words from the objects to which they refer. Segmentation problems arise in realising that words are built up from smaller elements, and, at the next level in learning, what is an acceptable written sentence. The written sentence offers the child new modes of expression which are both complex and economic. The decontextualised text challenges the child to develop his planning capacities for verbal messages.

The final integration of the various skills involves the application of a variety of cognitive procedures in order to achieve the communicative goals. When mastered, these allow the writer a high degree of flexibility, enabling him to make stylistic adaptations to accommodate the reader and his expectations, and also the particular mode of discourse engaged in. The development of writing may have important consequences for the development of certain kinds of abstract thought, though little research has been done on this influence so far.

1. *Introduction*

Writing has been described as a fragile skill, the last to be learnt and the one that is soonest lost in states of acute disturbances (Chedru and Geschwind 1972). This is attributed to the non-habitual nature of writing compared with speech, and to the large number of components involved: motor, praxic, visuo-spatial and linguistic. These observations highlight the complexity of written language and the fact that while speech is used daily, few, even in literate societies, have to write with such frequency. For many children, practice in writing is a task to be endured at school and avoided whenever possible once freed from the educational system. Writing is not the only great cultural achievement to elicit this response, but the immense importance of writing makes this a regrettable reaction. The importance lies not only in the communicative potential of writing but also because, as Olson (1977a) states, written language is an instrument of enormous power for constructing an abstract and coherent theory of reality.

For many, writing is difficult, and it is not only the novice who finds the task an "intolerable struggle with words and meanings" (T.S. Eliot; East Coker). The experienced writer's problems of translating intended meaning into objective text creates an awareness of difficulty just as the young learner's problems with spelling and punctuation does at a different level. In any writing exercise, the characteristics of the writer, the text or mode of discourse, and the processes or procedures relating the two, affect the level and awareness of the difficulties involved. The mode of discourse and the writer's expectations of the reader are major task variables, the writer's goal being to produce a text that is cohesive, unambiguous and explicit in meeting these goals. The writer brings to the task stored information, both linguistic and experiential, together with certain organisational strategies. These enable him to assess his stored information and translate his retrieved ideas into a symbolic representation that realises his communicative intention. The process of writing is an integration of skills, some of which are automatic in the experienced writer, such as handwriting and spelling. When these lower order skills do not require conscious attention, the writer can focus on higher level cognitive processes such as planning or revising, and can also switch focus between one aspect of the task and another. Young writers have to progress through the various stages of acquiring and integrating these component skills, but at each level various cognitive procedures are applicable. Within these procedures themselves there is a developmental progression, commencing with the ability to recognise and differentiate, to make comparisons and find correspondences. These are essentially extensions of the basic recognition capacities which make it possible to discriminate the letter *A*, for instance, or recognise the spelling of a particular word. Evaluation and correction, procedures for operating on language, are more difficult. These are revisionary procedures with particular relevance for the generation and production of text, which young children find difficult. More difficult, however, is being able to explain and discuss language, to have a metalinguistic awareness of the different levels of the writing process. Young children, for instance, can use words even though they lack the concept of what a word is, confusing it with what it represents.

Learning to write is a long process, one which is possibly never completed. The decontextualised nature of written language necessitates a different order of cognitive operations from those required in spoken discourse. Although writing is deliberately taught and children acquire writing skills through conscious application, the child is not always fully aware of the processes involved. In fact, the act of writing itself probably fosters an awareness of the kind of intellectual activities involved. As a much more analytic and abstract system than spoken language it is conducive to the development of a different order of cognitive operations.

2. *Speech and writing*

There are certain important differences between speech and writing which need to be clearly understood before discussing what develops in writing. Spoken language precedes written language both historically and ontogenetically and the development of writing marks the emergence of differences in both the structure and function of language.

Children come to writing with a good knowledge of how to use spoken language in reciprocal exchanges. Spoken language has a firm basis in social interaction stemming from the development of intentional communication in the pre-verbal period. It is acquired in a highly motivating social context and established as an effective means of achieving communicative goals. Throughout the acquisition period, gesture and context are important adjuncts to communication and young children use them extensively as paralinguistic aids for both interpreting and producing speech (Bates 1976; Bruner 1978; Snow and Ferguson 1977). The sequence of development of spoken language is similar for all children and within the space of a few years they progress with little effort from using only one word at a time to a close approximation to adult grammar.

Writing, however, is consciously acquired in a pedagogical environment, as a private activity, meeting no immediate responses from another person. It involves a greater number of skills and calls for an abstract awareness of language. It is as Vygotsky (1978) puts it, a system of secondary symbolism in which signs replace words, which are, in turn, signs for objects and relations in the real world. Added to this, "the motives are more abstract, more intellectualized, further removed from immediate needs" (Vygotsky 1962).

The essential difference between the two systems lies in the high level of abstraction and elaboration required in written as opposed to spoken language. Writers lack the advantages of prosody, immediate context and reciprocated exchanges. As readers rely solely on what is written, and have to build an interpretation of the writer's intended meaning from the internal relations in the text, the writer has to be explicit and unambiguous, meaning must reside solely in the text (Olson 1977b). This is difficult for young children. While several studies show that young children can be competent communicators in a variety of social situations, they are inadequate when the task is too abstract and they cannot rely on contextual support (Martlew 1979).

The complex quality of written language may mean, in fact, that writing is a separate linguistic function, differing from speech in both its structure and its mode of functioning (Vygotsky 1962). Because writing has permanence, it can be objectified and manipulated as an object. It is a system with its own regularities and conventions, neither being an isomorphic transcription, nor in a formal and conceptual sense, is it speech written down. Reflecting on what is needed to achieve adult competence in writing it is interesting to speculate why there are child prodigies of under 10 years who achieve adult competence in music, chess and mathematics, but not in writing (Steiner 1972).

3. *Writing by hand and by eye*

The development of writing, as an action, requires complex visuo-motor coordination. The highly skilled motor actions required to produce a visible representation of language are extremely demanding. Although the physical act of writing with a pen is not essential for the writing process, in that typing or dictating both necessitate the same awareness of the properties of written language (Gould 1980), motor programs are, however, likely to be related to spelling patterns and to the building up of lists of available words. Motor actions have themselves to be coordinated with visual information, first in the formation of letters and then words. Bradley (1981) also points to the efficacy of simultaneous oral spelling as a method for organising correct motor patterns, linking the visual and auditory modalities through writing. This is a particularly useful method with backward spellers as it enables them to label and differentiate letters, and organise them into appropriate patterns. For the correct motor pattern to be established, it must be organised and practiced. Bradley draws attention to the fact that children who are notoriously bad at spelling have also been observed to have problems with the organisation of their movements.

Writers acquire the ability to integrate individual movements when writing into "a generalized schemata of action which determines the sequence of specific acts" (Lashley 1951). Once this sequence is established it cannot be modified without considerable disruption. Imagine the consequences, for instance, of asking an experienced writer or skilled typist to omit *e* from every *the* in a text. Also, once the motor pattern has been established, the acquired action pattern for producing say the letter *C*, can be generalized; it is not specific to writing just with a pen (Connolly 1975). It is the construction of an action program that is important so that the established patterns of frequently used words can become effectively an automatic process.

Little is known of the pattern of visuo-motor development in writing. Thomassen and Teulings (1979) have tentatively suggested the existence of two semi-independent motor systems; a more primitive one for rapid and non-figurative tasks and the other for more accurate symbolic purposes. The latter they suggest is under some higher level of cognitive control and usually develops between five and seven years.

This suggestion stems from observing the preferred direction for making circles and loops, anticlockwise movements being the preferred direction for accurate symbolic writing. This conflicts however with Hollenbach's (1980) findings, where fast writing adults almost totally eliminated clockwise in favour of anticlockwise movements, a modification adopted by fast writers to achieve speed rather than accuracy.

The discrepancy between these findings needs to be resolved but both indicate that there are different strategies for fast rather than slow writing. Writers are usually aware of the trade-off between speed and accuracy. Writing too slowly, which is inevitable for beginners, restricts the amount of information that can be manipulated in short term memory. The consequences of poor legibility can be detrimental to the writer, however, affecting, among other things, spelling achievement and teachers' assessment of the content of written papers (Graham and Miller 1980).

Writing then, is initially taught, usually in school. Whilst it is a conscious activity it comes to be executed without conscious awareness at the level of a motor skill. The writer is then free to apply himself to the more demanding levels of the writing process.

4. *The concept of word: a problem of segmentation*

Effort and practice is needed to integrate visuo-motor skills for the efficient ordering of letters to produce words. This differs from speech, where biological mechanisms initially facilitate the differentiation of phonetic features (Eimas and Tartter 1979), words being eventually produced without conscious awareness of the mechanics of production. Young children, in fact, are aware of language as meaning units, only later becoming aware of the phonological and syntactic substrata of language (Gleitman and Rozin 1977). Relating the continuously varying acoustic waves of speech to a linear array of discreet symbols obviously presents difficult problems. Gleitman and Rozin suggest that children could avoid these problems initially, when learning to read, by being introduced to the concept of reading via a logographic and syllabic system which is more accessible to them. This has interesting parallels with Vygotsky's (1978) views on the antecedents of written language. He suggests that writing derives from symbolic representation in play and from drawing, which represents a movement from first order symbolism, where drawing directly denotes objects or actions, to the creation of written signs, "the drawing of speech" as he terms it. Children can be encouraged to realise the communicative function of idiosyncratic signs in game situations and then make the transition to the conventional forms of written language.

As words and syllables are more accessible units for young children than phones are, they have difficulty in segmenting speech. Consequently they are frequently inadequate at differentiating sounds and translating them into conventional representations. As children's spelling tends to reflect strategies of applied "sound-to-spelling" rules, problems arise, for instance, where phonemes overlap and affect each other within syllables. Read (in press) found that children younger than six years omitted /m/ in a word like *bump* 40 percent of the time whereas when it occurred at the end of a word, before a vowel (*bum*), it was omitted only 1 percent of the time. Children did not hear these words as being similar. Furthermore, although children may follow certain idiosyncratic phonetic strategies, they are not aware of the significance of the rules they are applying. They can write words with invented spellings following a phonetic strategy but afterwards, they have difficulty in reading what they have written (Read 1975). Even their early attempts to grapple with orthography, however, appear to be rule governed and not random.

It seems, then, that children initially have a limited awareness of the nature and function of manipulating and acting upon sounds and letters. Some children, however, show a surprising ability to reflect on language in this way. Gleitman, Gleitman and Shipley (1972) report the following query about the a/an distinction from a four-year old: "Mommy, is it AN A-dult or A NUH-dult?". Interestingly, this distinction was not apparent in the child's spontaneous speech until two years later. The ability to explicate an awareness of segmentation was not associated with an ability to act on this awareness. Children's limited capacity for differentiating sounds and for evaluating their representations suggests that they learn orthographic conventions without full awareness of the processes involved, but they organise their approach in a rule governed manner. Even though words as units of meaning are more accessible than phones, children have little realisation of what a word is before five to seven years. Typically they define why a word is a word by giving the attributes of the word in question. The word is confused with what it signifies, as can be seen in the following examples:

"Why is pencil a word?"
"Because it writes" (Papandropoulou and Sinclair 1974)

"Why is cow a word?"
"Because it has horns" (Vygotsky 1962)

Children operating under this confusion take longer to recognise function words as words, there being no concrete image to which to relate them. Their reasons for not accepting function words do not seem to follow any obvious pattern. *The,* for instance, received the following responses from children of four to six years: "No people say it"; "It isn't with another word"; "It doesn't sound like one" (Templeton and Spivey 1980). Preschool children also have no real concept of the relationship of the length of the sound of a word to the length of its written equivalent (Rozin, Bressman and Taft 1974). Again, this can result from confusing the word with the designated object. Given a long and short word, such as *caterpillar* and *cat,* children are likely to choose *cat* as the longer word because it refers to the larger object.

Between five to seven years, words gradually begin to have autonomous meaning. Children begin to realise that words are separable from what they represent. Some of their conceptual problems may in part be relatable to coping with indirect reference. The acquisition of words and concepts occurs in contexts where the object, event or relationship is observable and where direct reference associates word and concept. Children find indirect reference difficult until they dissociate words from the things referred to. They then realize that not knowing the name for a particular object or event does not inevitably lead to a breakdown in communication (Baron 1977). The developing awareness of alternative strategies is important at this and all levels of writing because it leads to flexibility in the ordering and reordering of ideas, as well as to lexical and syntactic variation.

5. *What is a sentence?*

The emergence of the concept of 'sentence', particularly an acceptable written sentence rather than spoken utterance, develops gradually over what may be a lengthy period. At one level, this is again a segmentation problem, linked to learning the appropriate use of punctuation and capitalization. There is practically no research investigating the development of children's awareness of the significance of these specifically written conventions. There is, however, an interesting example of an unusual awareness of the need for a punctuation symbol in a six-year old (Gleitman, Gleitman and Shipley 1972). This can be seen in the following example where the child invented one for herself:

Child (writing): They call Pennsylvania Pennsylvania because William Penn had a (Penn) in his name.
Mother: Why did you put those marks around the word Penn?
Child: Well, I wasn't saying Penn, I was just talking about the word.

Punctuation is a system for demarcating boundaries, initially adopted in a haphazard manner, particularly during the period when children are beginning to combine their ideas into extended *and* sequences. Despite the range of signs, punctuation is extremely limited in scope when compared with prosodic features in spoken language. Although the question mark is acceptable in formal written language, other marks, such as underlining for emphasis, or exclamation marks are reserved for more informal texts. Prosodic features have to be either written into the text, if for instance a point needs to be emphasized, or counteracted if the writer's meaning is dependent on them. This emphasizes the decontextualized nature of writing; meaning cannot be marked by paralinguistic devices as it can be in speech.

In spoken language, even very young children can recognise whether words are combined into meaningful units or not, that is whether they cohere as well-formed, or deviant, utterances. Gleitman, Gleitman and Shipley (1972) found some two-year olds could provide a non-random differentiation of sentences on this basis and there was a particularly dramatic increase in explanations between five and seven years. Children were asked to assess the grammatical acceptability of sentences by playing a game with the experimenter:

Adult: How about this: *know the answer* (1)
Child: That's the only way to say it, I think.
Adult: The only way to say what?
Child: *You better know the answer*!
Adult: How about this one: *I am eating dinner* (2)
Child: Yeah, that's okay.
Adult: How about this one: *I am knowing your sister* (3)
Child: No: *I know your sister.*
Adult: Why not *I am knowing your sister* – you can say *I am eating your dinner.*
Child: It's different! (shouting) You say different sentences in different ways! Otherwise they wouldn't make sense.

It is apparent from this section of dialogue that this seven-year old child could evaluate sentences (2) and (3) and accept or correct them as required. The response to (1) is interesting. It is accepted because it can be attached to another segment of a spoken sentence. Adopting the criterion of acceptability as applying to spoken sentences persists into written language for a considerable time. In observations made recently in Sheffield on the awareness of acceptable written sentences by poor writers aged between sixteen to seventeen years, we found a 91 percent error rate for familiar expressions in spoken language such as *Two pints of bitter, please* or *Ten green bottles standing on a wall*. The usual reason given for acceptance, particularly for descriptive noun phrases (*a bright red skirt*), was that they could have been answers to questions (*What did you buy*?). Some who did recognise that certain constructions would be inappropriate sentences in a written composition gave reasons which showed they confused *sentence* with truth value. For instance, a reason given for *students sitting on the stairs* being an unacceptable sentence was that it was wrong for students to sit on the stairs. The phrase was given contextual reality.

Children can, and of course do, produce sentences in both spoken and written language without being able to analyse their performance. From an early age they are aware of the interchangeability of elements and will practice juxtaposing words and phrases (Weir 1962; Clark 1977). Indeed it is possible that early sentence formation is based on word order and juxtaposition strategies, and that children only perform transformations in the concrete operational period when they are capable of relating two structures and performing reversible operations (Ingram 1975).

One way to discover whether children are using complex sentences in an adult manner in the early stages of acquisition is to examine the occasions when they were not used but could have been. Children's early stories provide useful examples. Initially, ideas are loosely connected and may not even be in the correct temporal order. Between four and six years, children begin to connect their ideas usually by the frequent use of *and*. When relative clauses emerge, the most common pattern is the reduced relative with *named* or *with* phrases (Ingram 1975);

"Once there was a kitten named Cindy".
"Once there was a big scary man with lots of faces".

Following this, information begins to be combined more economically, the diffuseness of *and* conjunctions being replaced by more complex constructions. This reflects some knowledge of embedded sentences and the transformations that reduce them (O'Donnell, Griffin and Norris 1967).

As writing is conducive to economy of expression in a way that speech is not, does writing encourage the development of complex syntax? Ingram (1975), referring to the difficulties that linguists have in eliciting complex structures from informants of unwritten Indian languages, claims that it does. As children gain more experience as writers and become more aware of the economy effected by using complex syntax, the structure of their written language should become observably more complex than their spoken language. This development seems to take place between nine to thirteen years (Hunt, in press) and Loban (1976) notes a plateau in oral language at about thirteen to fifteen years, this coming a year later in written language.

Experienced writers effect economy in writing by condensing a number of related ideas around a central topic. Less experienced writers are unable to reduce and consolidate in this way. The different approaches can be seen in just two examples of responses to a passage Hunt (1970) devised as a sentence-combining exercise:
Original passage:

> Aluminium is a metal. It is abundant. It has many uses.
> It comes from bauxite. Bauxite is an ore. Bauxite looks like clay. . .
>
> (1) Aluminium, which is a metal, is abundant. It has many uses and comes from bauxite. Bauxite is an ore that looks like clay. . .
>
> (2) Aluminium, an abundant and useful metal, comes from bauxite, a clay-like ore.

Examining the relationship of intelligence to this ability, Hunt found correlations between IQ measures for older children but not for younger ones. Nineteen year olds in the high IQ group were able to consolidate their ideas significantly more than the low IQ group.

Obviously a high level of conceptualization is needed to operate on language in order to complete this particular exercise in an optimal manner. However, it is difficult to assess whether practice in sentence-combining exercises of this kind can qualitatively effect the development of writing. Putting emphasis on surface characteristics makes it possible for the writers to focus on structural organisation without having to select and organise their own ideas. Complex sentences can be created however by encouraging students to structure their own ideas around a given topic (The cat sat on the mat).

> The big, silky, black, green-eyed cat, layed on the middle of the blue mat which was in front of the fireplace.

> Out of habit, our neighbours bedraggled looking ginger tom cat, sat drowsy and content on the warm old mat in the bright sunshine.

> This morning Peters big, black, fluff, cat, sat lazely on the big, red, wooly, mat, beside the blazeing fire all snuged up and not a care in the world.

These sentences would not win any literary prizes but were collected from sixteen to seventeen year old poor writers of below average intelligence who did not perform well on sentence combining exercises. Hunt (in press) in fact has demonstrated that these exercises can accelerate syntactic complexity by as much as two years. After twenty-eight months, however, his control group had caught up with his experimental group but an interesting difference remained. The sentence combining group were significantly more confident about their ability to write, and more of them claimed that they enjoyed writing.

The complexity of sentences is due as much to their conceptual difficulty as to their structure. Several studies suggest there is a very gradual development in children's understanding of the logical implication of linguistic representation (Katz and Brent 1968; Sternberg, in press; Ackerman 1978) but the relationship between written language and general cognitive development remains unclear (Scribner and Cole 1978; Rosenthal 1979). Young children fail to see the logical implication of language. Instead they assimilate sentences into what they know and expect (Olson and Nicholson 1978). They do not fully understand how sentences are being used. For instance, when shown a picture of red dots and asked "Does the picture show that the dots are not red", adults will answer "No, *it* doesn't" whereas children reply, "Yes, *they* are". The children have ignored the embedding construction and therefore fail to work out the literal meaning (Hildyard and Olson 1980). Where adults treat sentences as logical propositions, children treat them as descriptions of known events. As Olson (in press) points out, in written language meaning falls primarily upon semantic structures. The rules of syntax and the meaning of words have to be explicit because they cannot be negotiated as they can in interpersonal exchanges. Children's understanding and mastery of linguistic representation gradually develops to conventionalising in written language the relationships previously expressed as contextually bound to situations.

6. *Text as message*

Effective writing fulfills certain minimal conditions in terms of internal cohesiveness and intelligibility for a distant reader. The writer's goal is to plan, organise and translate his ideas into a symbolic form appropriate to a particular mode of discourse and suitable for the anticipated reader. This involves the writer in a series of complex procedures which should be applied at each stage of the writing process.

Initially, in planning what to write, the writer has to consider what relevant knowledge he has on a topic. This has to be retrieved from long term memory or gathered from external material, then structured to satisfy the needs of the material itself, the type of discourse and the expected reader. During the planning operation, the procedures of differentiating, selecting, evaluating and revising ensure that the operation produces the appropriate material. The plan has then to be translated into a linguistic representation, again with the writer selecting and evaluating particular syntactic and semantic structures to achieve his communicative purpose, and revising and analysing in view of what has already been written or is planned to follow. Writers vary in their approaches to writing (Wason 1980) but experienced writers can pre-plan, plan and execute this plan, switching their attention from the immediate sentence to other selected focal points. In other words their high level of skill gives them flexibility. They are free to concentrate on whatever aspect of the task they choose.

Children's problems with composition arise from several sources. First, their level of skill in any of the component processes may not be fully developed so there could be interference from lower level skills intruding into higher level cognitive operations. It is, for instance, difficult to retain complex plans in short term memory when impeded by slow writing or the need to think carefully about spelling. Second, children may not be able to integrate these skills adequately which limits their ability to switch focus and attend to different aspects of the task while writing. Initially they tend to concentrate on one thing at a time. Third, the number of procedures and the extent to which they are applied between planning the operation and its production is limited. For instance, even when information has been retrieved from long term memory children may fail to be adequately selective or evaluative particularly with regard to communicative goals.

Children's early compositions are relatively unplanned and bear an immediate relationship to their own experience and oral expression. These first attempts are generally stories, factual narratives about concrete objects and events which closely resemble transcribed speech. Before children can begin to use written language for more general purposes, they have to sever this link which associates writing with the language of stories (Britton 1981). One of the most difficult problems children then encounter is that of finding sufficient information on a topic to both begin and sustain a piece of writing. Unlike spoken discourse, where new ideas can be triggered off and incorporated into the conversation by mutual exchanges, the writer has to provide his own internal stimuli in order to gain access to stored information. Without these external prompts, children are unaware of what they know, and find the retrieval processes difficult. They are unable even to make decisions on which topics they know a lot or a little about (Bereiter and Scardamalia 1979).

Children benefit from procedural support which can help them to generate text. Appropriate assistance at the pre-planning stage can facilitate the initial elaboration of ideas. For example, Bereiter and Scardamalia (1979) found that when children listed words rather than ideas they almost doubled their overall output and tripled the number of uncommon words they used. Listing words, it was suggested, made it possible for children to address their memory stores at a suitably high level, avoiding the direct search for details which constrained output when ideas were listed. Children can also be encouraged to write more, even when they claim to have exhausted their knowledge of a topic. Bereiter and Scardamalia discovered that even minimal prompts ("Can't you think of something more?") could be extremely effective. Rather than relying on these external aids, however, children have to develop their own internal procedures for generating and elaborating ideas.

Generating text in this associative manner assists production but neglects the strategies needed for planning and organising a cohesive text. Pre-planning not only provides a global framework but also indicates the appropriate semantic and syntactic structures. Unplanned discourse can show a reduction in syntactic complexity as well as less economy in organisation (Kroll 1978; Ochs 1979).

Pre-planning, however, even with a written outline of this plan as a mnemonic aid to refer to while writing, does not invariably mean that the writer sustains an awareness of his overall goals. To do this, the writer has to alternate the focus of his attention during the time he is writing between the various procedures of evaluating, revising and editing. By doing this, he can monitor and check that the text being produced does not deviate beyond acceptable limits for the particular discourse and anticipated reader's expectations. The complex organisational skills required to write in this way do not develop until quite late, children finding revision and correction particularly difficult (Scardamalia, in press). Novice writers tend to plan locally (Flower and Hayes 1980), poor writers showing an absence of any goal related planning. They write as though engaging in an oral discourse.

Language based in oral discourse is unlikely to show indications of sustained planning. Indeed, in conversations it would be maladaptive to plan too far ahead as no one participant is in total control. Speakers monitor and adapt their plans continuously in response to both verbal and non-verbal feedback from whoever they are talking to. Even children as young as four years of age can adapt their way of speaking to different listeners (Shatz and Gelman 1973; Maratsos 1973), situations (Menig-Peterson 1975) or invented characters (Martlew, Connolly and McCleod 1978). However, in experimental situations, where children below eight years have been called upon to give precise descriptions without the aid of contextual cues, their messages are inadequate. Either children fail to decentre from their own egocentric viewpoint (Glucksberg, Krauss and Higgins 1975) or they do not make essential comparisons and fail to evaluate ambiguous messages (Asher and Oden 1976). It is also possible that children do not realise that messages convey meanings so they have no basis for differentiating a good message from a poor one (Robinson and Robinson 1976). Young children therefore have difficulty in communicating without the assistance of contextual support even in spoken discourse. Written language increases the cognitive requirements of the task, consequently audience awareness develops later in writing than in speech. The extent of children's ability to maintain an awareness of their reader is unclear. Children of twelve were found to differentiate their ways of writing persuasive arguments by using more complex syntax for a teacher than a friend (Crowhurst and Piche 1979). Fifteen-year olds, however, showed only mediocre evidence of adaptation when writing for three audiences (known hardly at all; not very well; very well) on a persuasiveness measure, and evidence of syntactic differences was unclear (Rubin and Piche 1979). The only difference to emerge in stories written by thirteen-year olds for adults as opposed to children was that they used more abstract nouns when writing for adults (Martlew 1978).

In all these studies, adults appeared to alter the way in which they wrote so as to take account of their reader. However, there may be some doubt as to whether all adults can change their way of writing as readily, and seemingly automatically, as they can their way of speaking. Martlew (1978) found that over a third of the adults writing stories for children, wrote very short, condensed versions. Further examination showed there was no differentiation for their reader on any measures except one. This was the same as that found in the thirteen-year olds' stories; they used more abstract nouns in stories written for adults. Interestingly, the eleven-year olds showed an awareness of the need for adaptation but an inability to sustain it. Almost 90 percent began their stories for children, but not for adults, with the conventional opening "Once upon a time".

Some adults may fail to maintain an awareness of their reader for reasons which are different from those of young children. Writing is a solitary occupation in which the writer must develop his or her own idiosyncratic style. Habitual ways of writing for one reader, notably the teacher, encourages the development of written text which serves to fulfil the requirements that text should be autonomous, but it can then lack flexibility. Stylistic habits should be modifiable if the writer is to ensure the interest and understanding of his reader. For some adults, it may be difficult to change their established ways of writing, particularly in certain modes.

7. *Conclusions*

The ability to write allows us to be contributing members of a literate society. As Olson (1977) has put it "speech makes us human and literacy makes us civilised". The primary purpose of writing is to communicate, but the importance of writing lies as much in the consequences it has for the writer as for the reader. The complex skills and processes and their integration, which have to be developed in writing, may have important implications for cognitive development. A high level of abstract conceptualisation is involved in writing which entails the individual in translating both experience of the world and imaginary events into autonomous text. The writer must restructure his thinking to meet the demands of convention and explicitness demanded in writing, for without this, the meaning intended would not necessarily be the meaning communicated. Spoken language, as a shared, negotiated enterprise, does not require this objective awareness. Speakers do not need to operate on experience in a formal and abstract manner.

The extent to which writing is involved in and, in part at least, is responsible for the development of abstract thought is not clear. It is unlikely to control all aspects of intellectual performance (Scribner and Cole 1978) but it may well affect the way we construct "context-independent abstract thought" (Greenfield 1968). More attention should be devoted to exploring the interaction between the development of writing and cognition generally, particularly as this has important implications for the way writing is taught.

References

Ackerman, B.P.
1978 "Children's comprehension of presupposed information: logical and pragmatic inferences to speaker belief." *Journal of Experimental Child Psychology* 16: 92–114.
Asher, S.R. and Oden, S.L.
1976 "Children's failure to communicate: an assessment of comparison and egocentricism explanations." *Developmental Psychology* 12: 132–139.
Baron, N.S.
1977 "The acquisition of indirect reference: functional motivations for continued language learning in children." *Lingua* 42: 349–364.
Bates, E.
1976 "Pragmatics and sociolinguistics in child language." In D. Morehead and A.

Morehead, eds., *Language Deficiency in Children.* Philadelphia: University Park Press, pp. 411–463.

Bereiter, C. and Scardamalia, M.
1982 "From conversation to composition: the role of instruction in a developmental process." In R. Glaser, ed., *Advances in Instructional Psychology, Vol 2.* Hillsdale, New Jersey: Lawrence Erlbaum Associates, pp. 1–64.

Britton, J.
1981 "Learning to use language in two modes." In N.R. Smith and M.B. Franklin, eds., *Symbolic Functioning in Childhood.* Hillsdale, New Jersey: Lawrence Erlbaum Associates, pp. 185–197.

Bradley, L.
1981 "The organisation of motor patterns for spelling: an effective remedial strategy for backward readers". *Developmental Medicine and Child Neurology* 23: 83–91.

Bruner, J.
1978 "From communication to language: a psychological perspective." In I. Markova, ed., *The Social Context of Language.* New York: John Wiley, pp. 17–28.

Chedru, F. and Geschwind, N.
1972 "Writing disturbances in acute confusional states." *Neuropsychology* 10: 343–353.

Clark, R.
1977 "What's the use of imitation?". *Journal of Child Language* 4: 341–358.

Connolly, K.
1975 "Movement, action and skill." In K. Holt, ed., *Movement and Child Development.* London: Spastics International Medical Publications, Heinemann, pp. 102–110.

Crowhurst, M. and Piche, G.L.
1979 "Audience and mode of discourse effects on syntactic complexity in writing at two grade levels." *Research in the Teaching of English* 13: 101–110.

Eimas, P.D. and Tartter, V.C.
1979 "On the development of speech perception mechanisms and analogies." In H.W. Reese, ed., *Advances in Child Development and Behaviour, Vol. 13.* New York: Academic Press, pp. 155–193.

Flower, L.S. and Hayes, J.R.
1980 "The dynamics of composing: making plans and juggling constraints." In L.W. Gregg and E.R. Steinberg, eds., *Cognitive Processes in Writing.* Hillsdale, New Jersey: Lawrence Erlbaum Associates, pp. 3–30.

Gleitman, L. and Rozin, P.
1977 "The structure and acquisition of reading." In A.S. Reber and D.L. Scarborough, eds., *Towards a Psychology of Reading.* Hillsdale, New Jersey: Lawrence Erlbaum Associates.

Gleitman, L., Gleitman, H. and Shipley, E.F.
1972 "The emergence of the child as grammarian." *Cognition* 1: 137–164.

Glucksberg, S., Krauss, R. and Higgins, E.T.
1975 "The development of referential communication skills." In F. Horowitz, ed., *Review of Child Development Research, Vol. 4.* Chicago: University of Chicago Press, pp. 305–345.

Gould, J.D.
1980 "Experiments on composing letters: some facts, some myths and some observations." In L.W. Gregg and E.R. Steinberg, eds., *Cognitive Processes in Writing.* Hillsdale, New Jersey: Lawrence Erlbaum Associates.

Graham, S. and Miller, L.
1980 "Handwriting research and practice: a unified approach." *Focus on Exceptional Children* 13: 1–16.

Greenfield, G.
1968 *"Oral or written language: the consequences for cognitive development in Africa and the United States."* Paper presented at the symposium on Cross-Cultural Cognitive Studies, Chicago.

Hildyard, A. and Olson, D.
1980 "On the comprehension and memory of oral versus written discourse." In D. Tannen, ed., *Spoken and Written Discourse.* Hillsdale, New Jersey: Ablex, pp. 19–33.

Hollenbach, J.M.
1980 *"An oscillation theory of handwriting."* Mimeo, M.I.T.

Hunt, W.K.
1970 "Syntactic maturity in school children and adults." *Monographs of the Society for the Research in Child Development.*, No. 134.
(in press) "Sentence combining and the teaching of writing." In M. Martlew, ed., *The Psychology of Writing: A Developmental Approach.* Chichester: John Wiley. pp. 99–125.

Ingram, D.
1975 "If and when transformations are acquired by children." In P. Dato, ed., *Developmental Psycholinguistics: Theory and Application.* Georgetown University Press: Georgetown University Round Table on Language and Linguistics, pp. 99–127.

Katz, E.W. and Brent, S.B.
1968 "Understanding connectives." *Journal of Verbal Learning and Verbal Behaviour* 7: 501–509.

Kroll, B.M.
1978 "Cognitive egocentrism and the problem of audience awareness in written discourse." *Research in the Teaching of English* 12: 269–281.

Lashley, K.S.
1951 "The problem of serial order in behaviour." In L.A. Jeffress, ed., *Cerebral Mechanisms in Behaviour.* New York: John Wiley, pp. 112–166.

Loban, W.
1976 *Language development: Kindergarten through Grade Twelve.* (Research Report No. 18) Urbana, Ill.: National Council of Teachers of English.

Maratsos, M.
1973 "Non-egocentric communicative abilities in pre-school children." *Child Development* 44: 697–700.

Martlew, M.
1978 *"Writing for the reader: a developmental study."* Paper given at the International Conference or Social Psychology and Language, Bristol.
1979 "Young children's capacity to communicate." In K.J. Connolly, ed., *Psychology Survey No. 2.* London: Allen & Unwin, pp. 110–127.

Martlew, M., Connolly, K.J. and McCleod, C.
1978 "Language use, role and context in a five year old." *Journal of Child Language* 5: 81–99.

Menig-Peterson, C.L.
1975 "The modification of communicative behaviour in preschool aged children as a function of the listener's perspective." *Child Development* 46: 1015–1018.

Ochs, E.
1979 "Planned and unplanned discourse." In T. Giron (ed.), *Syntax and Semantics, Vol. 12: Discourse and Syntax.* New York: Academic Press, pp. 51–80.

O'Donnell, R.C., Griffin, W.J. and Norris, R.C.
1967 *Syntax of Kindergarten and Elementary School Children: A Transformational*

Analysis. Research report No. 8. Urbana Illinois: National Council of Teachers of English.

Olson, D.
1977a "Oral and written language and the cognitive processes of children." *Journal of Communication* 27: 10–26.
1977b "From utterance to text: the bias of language in speech and writing." *Harvard Educational Review* 47: 257–281.
(in press) "Writing and literal meaning." In M. Martlew, ed., *The Psychology of Writing: A Developmental Approach.* Chichester: John Wiley, pp. 41–65.

Olson, D. and Nickerson, N.
1978 "Language development through the school years: learning to confine interpretation to the information in the text." In K. Nelson, ed., *Children's Language, Vol. 1.* New York: Gardner Press, pp. 117–170.

Papandropoulou, I., and Sinclair, H.
1974 "What is a word? Experimental study of children's ideas on grammar." *Human Development* 17: 241–258.

Read, C.
1975 "Lessons to be learnt from the preschool orthographer." In E.H. Lenneberg and E. Lenneberg, eds., *Foundations of Language Development, Vol. 2.* New York: Academic Press, pp. 329–346.
(in press) "Orthography." In M. Martlew, ed., *The Psychology of Writing: A Developmental Approach.* Chichester: John Wiley, pp. 143–162.

Robinson, E.J. and Robinson, W.P.
1976 "The young child's understanding of communication." *Developmental Psychology* 13: 328–333.

Rosenthal, D.A.
1979 "Language skills and formal operations." *Merrill Palmer Quarterly* 25: 133–145.

Rozin, P., Bressman, B. and Taft, M.
1974 "Do children understand the basic relationship between speech and writing? The mow-motorcycle test." *Journal of Reading Behaviour* 6: 327–334.

Rubin, D.L. and Piche, G.L.
1979 "Development in syntactic and strategic aspects of audience adaptation skills in written persuasive communication." *Resarch in Teaching English* 13: 293–316.

Scardamalia, M. and Bereiter, C.
1983 "The development of evaluative, diagnostic and remedial capabilities in children's composing." In M. Martlew, ed., *The Psychology of Writing: A Developmental Approach.* Chichester: John Wiley, pp. 67–95.

Scribner, S. and Cole, M.
1978 "Unpackaging literacy." *Social Science Information* 17: 19–40.

Shatz, M. and Gelman, R.
1973 "The development of communication skills: modifications in the speech of young children as a function of the listener." *Monographs of the Society for the Research in Child Development 38.*

Snow, C.E. and Ferguson, C.A.
1977 *Talking to Children: Language Input and Acquisition.* Cambridge: Cambridge University Press.

Steiner, G.
1972 *Extraterritorial: Essays on Language and Linguistics.* London: Faber.

Sternberg, R.J.
1979 "Developmental patterns in the encoding and combination of logical connectives." *Journal of Experimental Child Psychology,* 28: 469–498.

Templeton, S. and Spivey, E.M.
1980 "The concept of word in young children as a function of level of cognitive development." *Research in the Teaching of English* 14: 265–278.

Thomassen, A.J.W. and Teulings, H.L.
1979 "The development of directional preference in writing movements." *Visible Language* 13: 299–313.

Vygotsky, L.S.
1962 *Thought and Language.* Cambridge, Mass.: M.I.T. Press.
1978 "The prehistory of written language." In M. Cole, V. John-Steiner, S. Scribner, and E. Souberman, eds., *Mind in Society: The Development of Higher Psychological Processes.* London: Harvard University Press, pp. 105–119.

Wason, P.
1980 "Specific thoughts on the writing process." In L.W. Gregg and E.R. Steinberg, eds., *Cognitive Processes in Writing.* Hillsdale, New Jersey: Lawrence Erlbaum Associates, pp. 129–137.

Weir, R.H.
1962 *Language in the Crib.* The Hague: Mouton.

EMILIA FERREIRO

The development of literacy: A complex psychological problem*

Abstract

The paper focuses on the cognitive processes involved in the understanding of the writing system. It is shown that very young children approach this socio-cultural object with a set of suppositions that are completely foreign to the alphabetical system. These suppositions are not received from outside; they constitute constructions emanating from the children themselves, built-up in contact with a literate environment, but not in imitation of it.

Examples from 3 to 6 year old French- and Spanish- speaking children are used to illustrate the main trends of this development. The paper may be considered as an overview of several experimental studies carried out with Piaget's method of critical exploration, and reported in detail elsewhere.

1. *Introduction*

One of the basic principles of genetic psychology, as stated by Jean Piaget, is that, in order to understand complex processes of thought, it is necessary to follow their development in the child. I have attempted to apply this Piagetian principle to the comprehension of the writing system.

Traditionally, the development of literacy is considered to be a learning process similar to the acquisition of a complex skill. As a school subject, it is considered to be an instrumental acquisition, not an acquisition of knowledge. However, written symbols, in so far as they are socially constituted objects, can be regarded as objects of the external world and, as such, may become objects to think about. Children living in an urban environment constantly encounter written texts on all kind of objects: books and newspapers, toys, shirts, tins and boxes, calendars and street signs, television sets, posters, etc. We know that in many other fields, children don't wait until their first school year to start thinking about complex problems, their ideas of "easy" and "difficult" problems being often quite different from those that guide pedagogical decisions.

As regards knowledge of the writing system, the problem, as in other cognitive domains, is not only to identify the activities that can be considered as the starting point of the development under study, but also to comprehend in what sense they are the constitutive elements for the next step in development; in other words, to establish a sequence that is not only chronological, but developmentally ordered, and thus constitutes a psycho-genetic progression. In the present study, pre-reading and pre-writing behaviors have accordingly been considered not as a kind of masquerade of an adult activity, but as indicators of internal activities through which the organization of the object of knowledge is taking place.

A child who makes an approximate correspondence between sounds and letters may have spelling difficulties, but he is already functioning within the alphabetic system of writing. In order to understand how he has reached this point, it is necessary to understand also those children who, for example, have started to use the alphabet, but who do not see any need for two words starting with the same sound to also start with the same letter. We also need to understand the conceptions that are at work even earlier, such as with those children who use unconventional signs but organize them in a linear order that is very different from the order of elements in a drawing.

In this paper some general results will be reported, obtained with children 4 to 6 years old, belonging to very different cultural milieux (middle-class and shanty towns) who spoke Spanish as their mother tongue, and middle-class French-speaking children.[1]

2. *The text and the picture*

In the domain under discussion, one of the first problems children must solve is the differentiation between two kinds of graphic representation: pictures and texts. When they start behaving as 'scriptors', they already distinguish between what they see as a drawing and what they see as a piece of writing (waving line, or series of straight or circular strokes about which they say "it is written", "j'ai marqué", etc.). When starting to behave as readers, children have to understand what the two systems represent. Initially the text and the picture are merely two objects that can be found in the same physical space. It may well be realized that in one case the elements are marks, and the child may even call them "letters" or "numbers", without yet understanding that they are symbolic objects and that, in spite of perceptual differences, there is something in common between the marks and the pictures.

The next step is characterized by the establishment of a link between the text and the picture: according to the child, one can find in the text the names of the objects represented in the picture. The distinction between written text and pictured objects is orally made clear by a subtle differentiation: the indefinite article is kept for the identification of the picture, and the name without article for the text (e.g.: "un pato" (a duck) in answer to the question "what is drawn there?", and "pato" (duck) in answer to the question "what is written here", in the text close to the picture).

At this level, it does not matter whether the text is composed of one or two lines, or of one or several segments. Only later will the child take into account the objective properties of the text, once he has learnt to make use of the picture to anticipate the content of the text. In order to maintain the necessary distinctions, some children make a semantic difference between "reading" and "telling" a story. They rely on the physical basis of both activities: one "tells" the story about the picture, and one "reads" it in the text. These two activities do not have the same result, nor do they originate from the same part of the page.

The next step is made when children take the objective properties of the text into account in order to adjust the anticipation of meaning they made on the basis of the picture. Now, the first characteristics of the text which the children start noticing are the number of lines, and the length or quantity of segments in a single line. Only later will qualitative differences between the letters themselves be taken into account, once the child is able to interpret the quantitative (or at least quantifiable) characteristics (such as number of lines or segments). This means that, for instance, looking at a picture with several objects, and at a text with several segments, children will try to make the name of each object in the picture correspond to a segment of the text; they will easily interpret a single object and a text composed of a single segment, but will find it difficult to interpret a text of several segments that goes with the picture of a single object.

In the children's behavior, two further considerations are at work: they think that a segment must be composed of a minimum number of letters if it is to represent the complete name of one of the objects in the picture; and they make a distinction between what is actually written and what may be read. We shall consider both problems immediately after the two illustrative examples given below.

(a) Leonardo (5 years old) deals with a picture representing a composite scene: there is a child rowing in a boat, a fish in the water, a tree on the bank, and other elements. The text is composed of five segments, two of them being only two letters long (*Raúl rema en el rio*, i.e., Raul is rowing on the river). Going from right to left, Leonardo "reads":

"pescado" (fish) in *rio*
"bar-co" (boat) in *el en*
"nene" (child) in *rema*
"árbol" (tree) in *Raúl.*

He thus makes a one-to-one correspondence between the elements in the picture and the segments in the text, but using both two-letter segments together (*en el*) for a single complete name; at the same time, he takes into account the separation between the two shortest segments, proposing a syllabic separation ("bar-co") for the one word they are supposed to mean.

(b) Erik (5 years old) deals with a picture representing only a duck in the water. The text is composed of three segments: *el pato nada* (i.e. the duck is swimming). We ask him what the text says, and he answers: "Duck", pointing to the entire text. We ask him: "How did you figure it out?" and he explains: "Because the duck is swimming," pointing to the picture. We then ask him: "So where does it say duck?" He points to the last segment of the text (*nada*) and immediately adds: "and here the water", pointing to the rest of the text (*el pato*). We ask: "So, what does it say all together?" and he answers: "Duck is in the water. The duck is gone into the water" ("Pato está en el agua. El pato esta metido en el agua.") Erik thus makes a clear distinction between what is actually written in the text (only "duck" and "water") and what can be read from it (a complete sentence).

To take into account the properties of the text and, at the same time, to adjust the anticipation of meaning to the hypothesis that only nouns are written, children make various attempts, one of which is to try a one-to-one correspondence between segments of the text and syllables of the word. For instance, for the three segments of *el pato nada*, several children proposed "pa-ti-to" (little duck). When syllables are made to fit segments of the text, all segments are treated as equivalent, regardless of their actual length; the number of letters of a segment is taken into account only when the reference is to words, because for the child, there is a condition that must be fulfilled: a complete word cannot be written with less than a given minimum number of letters – usually three.

Only later do children take into account the length of the entire text in order to decide whether it is sufficient for a sentence or only for a single word; usually children are able, at this point, to use a few letters as cues to adjust the anticipation of meaning made from the picture. For instance, Laura (5 years old), dealing with a picture of a man smoking a pipe and a text of only one word (*pipa*, that is pipe), thinks that "papá" is written, using the initial *p* as a cue. She refuses to agree that the text could be read as "papá está fumando" (daddy is smoking) because "it is very short and it is not enough" ("Es muy chiquito y no alcanza").

3. *Criteria for "readability"*

Children are able very early to classify letter-like materials. This is confirmed in two recent papers. Lavine (1977) used as graphic variables pictoriality, linear-horizontal orientation, variety, and similarity to Roman letters (conventionality). She also used multiplicity as opposed to singularity (six characters opposed to a single one). She presented a series of cards, using the following instruction: "if it has writing on it, if it is writing, it goes in this box" (p. 91). Children from 3 to 5 years old were tested. She concluded that "discrimination of the pictures from writing is already complete at age 3" and that "children's criteria for writing do include (. . .) linearity, multiplicity, and variety" (p. 92). However, even if "children by age 3 perceive writing as a linear varied series", a single capital letter – she did not present cards with single numbers – was accepted as "writing" by more than 70% of children within each age group (p. 94).

In another study, Pick, Unze, Brownell, Droydal and Hopmann (1978) asked children from 3 to 8 years of age "to say which cards had words and which ones did not" (p. 671). They presented only upper-case letters – some cards also showed misorientated letters – with variations in the number of letters from one card to the next (one letter as opposed to "short" strings of 4 to 5 letters, and to "long" ones of 12 letters). Pre-school children were very sensitive to the differences in the number of letters: single-letter cards were considered as non-words; moreover, "between the younger and older nursery school children there was a decline in the acceptability of single letters as words" (p. 672).

From the beginning of our research in 1975, we also used a classification task, but with a different instruction: Which cards are good for reading? (i.e., which ones are "readable"). We did not ask children to read the cards, but only to determine whether the cards showed what is necessary for a reading act. Ambiguous as it is, this instruction nevertheless elicited a striking behavioral consistency among children. Our material differs from the sets used by the authors just mentioned in that we used not only the contrast between singularity/multiplicity of characters, but also the full range of variation between one and six. This allowed us to determine not only that multiplicity is an important criterion for pre-school children, but also which is the critical number of characters they demand for readability. Our procedure differs also in that we asked for justifications after the classification task was completed, using contrasting pairs of cards when necessary to elicit answers.

Thus, we found that a mininum number of characters and internal variety are important characteristics of a "readable" string. A card with the same letter repeated four or five times is rejected, because "it is always the same one, it cannot be read", and a card with one or two graphemes – even if they are real letters – is also rejected, because "there must be several ones". Even if children often find it difficult to make explicit the "how many" of the "several ones", their classification shows that the critical number is three (actually, the minimum number of characters demanded for readability is 3 ± 1).

Let us note that such demands for variety and specific multiplicity of characters may occur before the correct naming of letters and numbers, and may also occur before the recognition of individual letters. But it is interesting to note that those demands may still be maintained after the identification of individual characters and may even determine the naming of the letter. For instance, Sandra, 5 years old, accepts as readable the card with EA written on it, because "it is an *e* an *a*", but immediately afterwards rejects the card with only a E, "because it is a number" ("c'est un chiffre").

Cursive writing may be identified as writing, but nevertheless may not be considered as "good for reading"; children explain that those are "letters badly made", or that it is a "scribble" (the "scribble" – "griboullage", in French, or "mamarracho", in Spanish – is something just on the border between writing and drawing).

When a piece of cursive writing shows repeated letters, it is often considered as a mere drawing (a series of *m* becomes "sea waves" or "a little river", etc.). We did not use cards with drawings, but some with pseudo-letters which the children considered as unfinished drawings. For instance, the grapheme Q was thought of as "a bull's head", "it's daddy, the eyes are missing", "it looks like a rabbit", "there are cat ears", "it's like a alarm-clock", etc. All those utterances are justifications for rejecting the grapheme as a letter; the similarity of a grapheme with a drawing *never* leads to a justification for accepting a card as "good for reading".

The global denominations used to characterize a group of cards may vary (although they are rarely used fortuitously): "letters", "numbers", "marks". There is a denomination term that almost never occurs: "words" (we only heard it twice, used by 6 year-old children); another one takes its place: "names" ("noms", in French; "nombres", in Spanish). This strongly leads us to think that children keep the term "word" for speech, and that they look for another term to designate the groups of letters one can read. But at the same time, the term "name" is related to hypotheses about the parts of an utterance which are actually written, as we will see next.

4. *The relationship between reading and the written text*

Thus far we have considered the problems of one-to-one correspondence which children face when interpreting the written text in connection with a picture. Let us now turn to another problem of correspondence, which arises when a text without a picture is read aloud by an adult. (cf. Ferreiro 1978). What kind of correspondence do children make between the segments of a normally written sentence and the parts of the corresponding utterance? Which of the many possible analyses of an utterance will the child choose? Children may accept that the graphemes shown are a representation of an utterance, but the uttered sentence is also, from a certain point of view, a single unit (of intonation, of meaning, a complete syntactic structure), whereas the text shows blanks, it is segmented. For adults, the blanks separate words, but what meaning do children attribute to them?

We have pointed out that, at a certain developmental level, when interpreting a text close to a picture, children expect only nouns to be represented. Exactly the same expectation occurs when children interpret the reading aloud by an adult of a complete sentence. Confronted with various sentences children face the same problem: if only nouns are represented, why are there so many segments in the text? Children may solve the problem in several ways: they may ignore the blanks, leave some segments without interpreting them, or introduce other nouns which have something to do with the meaning of the utterance, even if they were not uttered.

Here are some examples.

(a) A 4 year old child is shown the sentence UN CANARD NAGE (i.e. a duck is swimming), and after he heard and repeated the sentence he answers the questions: "Did I write duck somewhere?", by pointing to the last word (NAGE). We then ask "What is written here?", pointing to the first word, and he answers: "It's the water" ("c'est l'eau"). We ask the same question pointing to the remaining segment (CANARD) and he answers first "I don't know", and then "also the water" ("aussi l'eau").

(b) Another 4 year old girl answers our first question ("Did I write duck somewhere?") by pointing to the first word (UN), but she adds, as a justification for her pointing to a short segment: "ducks are very small" ("les canards sont tout petits"). She then comes spontaneously to the second segment (CANARD) and explains: "this is the water" ("ça c'est l'eau"). We then ask what is written in the remaining segment (NAGE) and she answers: "it is also the water" ("c'est encore l'eau").

Dealing with the sentence PAPA LANCE LE BALLON, Yves (4 years old) thinks that "ball" is written in the last segment, and "daddy" in the first one; but then trying to figure out what is written in the middle of the text, explains to us that LANCE "is also daddy, and this and this (LE BALLON) is all ball, it is all the letters for ball" ("et puis ça et ça c'est tout ballon, c'est toutes les lettres pour ballon").

Children of this level usually find it rather easy to interpret the written segments in a sentence such as MAMAN PREPARE TROIS GATEAUX or MAMA COMPRO TRES TACOS (mummy is making three cakes, or mummy bought three tacos, "tacos" being a popular Mexican food), because there are as many written segments as objects referred to in the utterance. For instance, according to a 4 year old girl, "mummy" is written in the second segment (PREPARE), TROIS is "the cake", GATEAUX is "a big cake' and MAMAN is "also a cake" ("encore un gateau").

It is important to note that, when asked "what does it say all together?" (pointing to the entire text), children who gave us those answers have no trouble in repeating the entire sentence correctly. They feel no contradiction in saying that the verb is not included in the writing while nevertheless reading the text as a complete utterance; they also feel no contradiction in saying that other nouns are written, while not introducing them into the reading of the entire text.

Ricardo (4 years old), working with the segments of MAMA COMPRO TRES TACOS, makes the following interpretations, from left to right: "mummy", "tacos", "table", "meal", but these two new nouns don't appear in his reading of the whole text united: obviously, tacos are to be eaten, and you eat them at a table. Others introduce other new nouns, which are also omitted in their reading of the whole text like "shop" or "money", which are obviously thought of because to buy tacos you need to go into a shop and take some money with you. And so on.

This kind of answer is typical of a conceptualization completely foreign to the adult's conceptions of writing. Children do not consider the writing system as a representation immediately related to the formal aspects of speech. At the same time, children make a distinction between what is actually written and what could be read; for them, the reading of a complete sentence may be drawn from a text where not all the words of the uttered sentence are necessarily written. Written texts are not considered as graphic representations that mirror the spoken utterances, but as a system of symbols, somehow, but not directly, related to spoken language: one can say things from what is written, but in order to move from the written text to an actual utterance a process of reconstruction is thought to take place. The great majority of pre-school children have this view on written texts, even if they no longer give the kinds of answers just mentioned. A great step forward is made when the child assumes that the verb can also be represented in writing (or, more precisely, when the child supposes that not only the objects referred to, but also the relation between them, can be represented graphically). However, it does not immediately follow that the verb can be represented as an isolated segment. Because the verb represents a relation (e.g. "to eat" implies an "eater" and "something eaten"), the child has great difficulty in admitting that it can nevertheless be written as an isolated unit.

After the verb is credited with an isolated representation, children face the problem of the representation of articles. For pre-school children, articles are not considered to be real "words" (Berthoud-Papandropoulou 1980). Moreover, when written, they do not comprise enough letters to be "for reading". Using sentences like PAPA LANCE LE BALLON, PAPA PATEA LA PELOTA, LA NENA COMPRO UN CARAMELO, UN CANARD NAGE, UN PAJARO VUELA, etc., we saw advanced pre-school children finding the position of the nouns and verb without difficulty, but not of the articles. These children repeat the complete sentence, but when dealing with the meaning of each one of the segments, they leave aside the two-letter ones ("here it says nothing", some of them explained); they either propose to cross them out, or they suggest joining them with the major units, or, finally, they interpret the two-letter segment as a syllabic fragment of one of the major words of the utterance (a frequent solution). For instance:

LA becomes "pe" of "pe-lota" or "ne" of "ne-na";
UN becomes "ca" of "ca-ramelo", or "pa" of "pá-jaro", etc.

Such answers were given by children 6 years old, or close to that age. The distinction between what is actually written and what could be read is still maintained. The rules and restrictions of oral language (which a child of that age applies with ease) are not immediately transposed into rules governing a written text.

This suggests that the linguistic competence of children cannot be directly geared to their literacy development without a certain meta-linguistic awareness. Only a limited number of pre-school children are able to find the correct place for each uttered word, using two basic assumptions of our system of writing: that all the uttered words are written and that the ordered parts of the text can be put in correspondence with the ordered words in the uttered sentence.

Children face similar problems of one-to-one correspondence concerning the interpretation of the component parts of a written word. In order to understand the meaning attached to the letters composing a written word, it is necessary to look at the written productions of children themselves.

5. *The construction of writing*

Let us now briefly characterize the main steps followed in the evolution of spontaneous writing. By "spontaneous" writing is meant the writing children produce outside any systematic training. Obviously, children pick up information from their environment, but the information provided by the milieu is always processed by them through their own conceptualizations of the writing system. One piece of information provided by the milieu is the repertory of letters; but the preference that children manifest for capital letters, even in a country (Argentina) where the "school type of writing" is cursive, is very striking. Middle-class children receive another piece of information from their milieu, i.e., the writing of their own names; but the interpretations they give of this piece of writing are very surprising.

In tasks where children are asked to decide on the "readability" of a text, they use criteria that cannot be provided by their social environment (for instance, the criterion of a minimum number of characters) as was mentioned before. Further manifestations of the internal nature of children's hypotheses about the writing system need to be taken into account.

Four-year-old children usually write linearly ordered series of graphemes similar to letters or numbers. When they try to write different nouns, the results may look strikingly similar (particularly if the child is using wavy lines). These similarities in the results do not trouble the child, because at this level the 'scriptor's' subjective intention is considered more decisive for the interpretation of the result than its objective graphic properties. If the child's intentions had been different, the 'scriptor' considered the written results to be different, even where the graphic similarities were striking. For instance, we showed Sandrine (4 years old) how to write COQ in French, and then asked her to write "poule" (hen) and then "poussins" (chicks). For each word proposed she rewrote the same graphic series –COQ– but, nonetheless, did not agree that one might read "poule" (hen) anywhere else than in the place where she had intended to write it, nor did she agree with this for any of the other words.

In order to ensure a stable interpretation, children at this level often resort to drawing. This does not mean that drawing and writing are confused with each other; the function of the drawing is only to make quite sure that what was intended to be written was actually written.

When children at this level use separate signs, two important characteristics, which anticipate the following level, begin to appear: the child tries to avoid repeating the same letter twice (or more than twice), and tries to keep a constant number of letters. The few systematic variations we noticed in the number of letters used do not depend on the length of the chosen word, nor on the opposition between a word and a sentence, but on quantifiable differences among what is referred to. For instance, "elephant", when contrasted with "butterfly", may be written with more letters.

If any correspondence is to be made, it is between the written noun and certain properties of the referred object, and not between the noun and its corresponding sound pattern. For instance, according to Gustavo (4 years old), "oso" (bear) must be written with more letters than "pato" (duck), "because it is a larger name than duck" ("porque es un nombre mas grande que el pato"). Valeria (same age) spontaneously writes down her name, with six letters, and then says she is going to write down the name of her father with "long letters, because daddy's name is long" ("des longs lettres, parce que le nom de papa il est long", although both names happen to have the same number of letters and syllables). She then writes down the same letters she used for her own name, but larger (see Figure 1.)

Figure 1. (Valeria, 4 years old)

The letters are the same, but arranged in another order, because Valeria already belongs to the next level, where such a correspondence with the properties of the referred object may still be found, but whose main characteristics lie elsewhere: to be able to read different things, children at this level think that there must be an objective difference in the written text.

When children of this second level already have a wide repertory of letters at their disposal, they change one or several letters when making a new piece of writing (but keeping the number of letters unchanged). On the other hand, it is striking to see how children who have a restricted repertory of letters at their disposal manage to solve this problem. Constrained by two purely internal demands (to keep to a minimum number of letters, and not to repeat the same letter twice), they discover that by changing the linear order of the same elements, they obtain different wholes (see Figures 2 and 3).

The reading of what has just been written, till then global, starts to change: children look for a correspondence between the parts of the piece of writing and the parts of the word they wanted to write. After a long and laborious search for such sound correspondences, the child will come to the next step: the syllabic hypothesis according to which every written letter corresponds to a syllable of the word.

At the beginning of the syllabic period, children adapt their reading to what they have just written: if the number of letters exceeds the number of syllables in the word, they allow themselves to repeat the same syllable twice running, or to miss a few letters. Little by little, the correspondence is made more rigorous: a single letter for a single syllable, without repeating syllables nor leaving letters uninterpreted (see Figure 4). The syllabic hypothesis progressively also starts to guide the writing, and helps the child to foresee the number of letters that must be marked down before one starts writing.

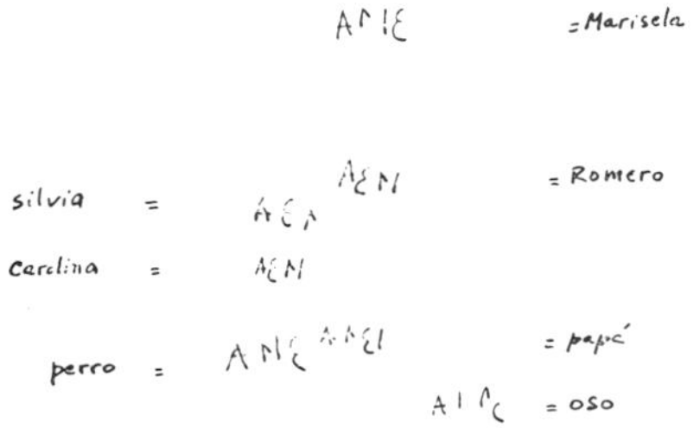

Figure 2. (Marisela, 4 years old)

Figure 3. (Romina, 4 years old)

At this point, new problems arise. How should one write monosyllabic words? With one letter, according to the syllabic hypothesis. But with only one letter "one cannot read" (according to the hypothesis of the minimum number of letters for readability). Thus the child, after having unsuccessfully tested several ways out of the difficulty, will discover that one has to abandon the syllabic hypothesis, and replace it by an analysis which goes beyond the syllable. Children will not change their minds overnight, because they, as scientists do, cling to their hypotheses and are not ready to abandon them at the first obstacle.

At this level, other conflict sources are added to the purely internal conflict we have just sketched. They are the models proposed by the milieu, and among them, the child's name, in its conventional spelling, is the most impor-

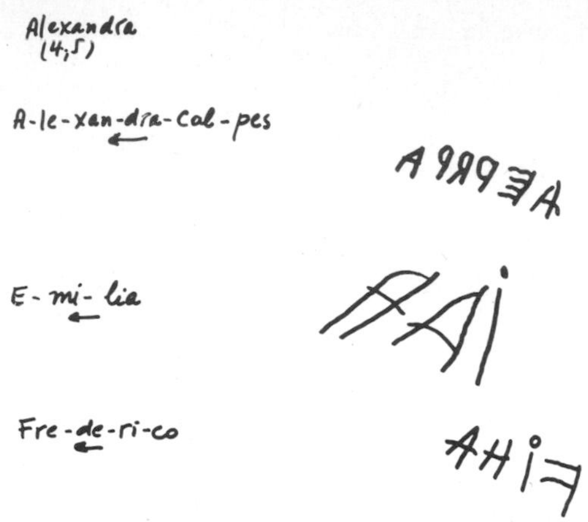

Figure 4. (Alexandra, 4.5 years old)

tant of all. The first name, together with other names, will help to give the letters relatively stable sound correlates (the child usually gives the initial letter of names a sound corresponding to their first syllable). But the total writing of the name is "unreadable" according to the syllabic hypothesis. Some children try compromise solutions: reading the first name and the family name in the same piece of writing, so that every letter may be interpreted syllabically.

According to the data we have now collected, it is apparent that this double source of conflicts (conflicts between the results obtained from different internal principles, and conflicts between the child's conceptualizations and the objective properties of written samples and of adult's reading and writing practices) helps children in their understanding of the internal nature of the system of representation of language that society has created.

From now on, the child is ready to understand the internal rationality of the system, while accepting the arbitrariness of the representation itself. Only at this point do spelling difficulties start.

The general trends of the development we have described lead us to the following conclusion: to understand the nature of the writing system, children re-construct it internally. This re-construction has many aspects in common with other psycho-genetic processes (such as, for instance, the comprehension of the number system); it also presents many epistemological problems, mainly those related to the history of writing systems and to the individual's re-construction of an already established system.

Notes

* This article is based on a paper presented to the Conference "Beyond Description in Child Language", Nijmegen (Netherlands), June 1979.

1. The examples quoted here come from four different research projects carried out with the following groups:
   80 children from 4 to 6 years old (Buenos Aires Argentina)
   30 children from 6 to 7 years old (Buenos Aires, Argentina)
   55 children from 4 to 5 years old (Geneva, Switzerland)
   90 children from 4 to 6 years old (Monterrey, Mexico)
   Further projects are at present being pursued in Mexico, with grants from the Ford Foundation and the Spencer Foundations.

References

Berthoud-Papandropoulou, I.
1980 *La réflexion métalinguistique chez l'enfant.* Thèse No. 79 Université de Genève. Genève: Imprimerie Nationale.

Ferreiro, E. and Teberosky, A.
1979 *Los sistemas de escritura en el desarrollo del niño.* México: Siglo XXI.

Ferreiro, E.
1977 "Vers une théorie génetique de l'apprentissage de la lecture". *Revue Suisse de Psychologie* 36 (2): 109–130.
1978 "What is written in a written sentence?. A developmental answer". *Journal of Education* 160 (4): 25–39.

Lavine, L.
1977 "Differentiation of letterlike forms in pre-reading children". *Developmental Psychology* 13 (2): 89–94.

Pick, A.D., Unze, M.G., Brownell, C.A., Drozdal, J.G. Jr., and Hopmann, M.R.
1978 "Young Children's Knowledge of Word Structure". *Child Development* 49: 669–680.

DAVID R. OLSON AND ANGELA HILDYARD

Literacy and the comprehension and expression of literal meaning*

Abstract

In this paper, the relation between semantic structures, possible worlds and speaker's meanings is offered as an explanation of the differences between casual meaning, literal meaning, indirect meaning and metaphorical meanings. Casual meanings result when contexts are treated as invariant and the semantic structure is altered in determining a speaker's meaning; literal meanings result when semantic structures are held invariant and context or possible world is altered in determining that meaning, and indirect and metaphorical meanings result when both semantic structures and contexts are taken as invariant and the meaning is altered to a marked form. These altered relations between semantic structures and contexts in the determination of meaning are used to account for some of the peculiarities of written language and for the difficulties associated with becoming a skilled writer, namely the problem of learning how to build those possible worlds stipulatively, specified by "the very words" preserved in a written text.

1. *Introduction*

According to Webster, 'literal' means "according to the letter or verbal expression; not figurative or metaphorical; following the letter or exact words; not free (a literal translation)". Four assumptions underlie these definitions.

First, literal meanings have a special relation to the wording, the surface structure of language "according to the letter or verbal expression". That is, literal meanings seem to imply or presuppose a device for the preservation of the very words, or as we shall say, for the preservation of what was said.

Second, literal meanings suggest a particularly close tie between the form of the expression and the intention expressed by that form, between what is "said" and what is "meant". This relationship between what is said and what is meant is sometimes taken to be so direct that it bypasses the need for context in computing the speaker's meaning. Hence, such language has been referred to as decontextualized speech (Greenfield 1972; Greenfield and Bruner 1969), disembodied speech (Donaldson 1978) or as language in which "the meaning is in the text" (Olson 1977). However, all these descriptions are misleading in that if context is irrelevant, such meanings become equivalent to linguistic meaning. As we shall see, this assumption is not warranted. Hence, although we wish to preserve the spirit of that distinction, we shall make it by specifying the various roles that context plays in determining *any* meaning, whether casual, literal, indirect, or metaphorical and we shall have to do this by adding an analysis of speaker's intentions or speaker's meanings.

Third, literal meanings have an obvious etymological relation to literacy: We may expect that literal meanings have some particular or favored relation to written language. Written language, we shall argue, is a means of preserving "the very words", the surface form of an expression, and its preservation puts new demands on both the processes of comprehension and production of written language, demands having to do with the management of literal meaning.

Finally, the definition of 'literal' suggests that all three of these aspects are interdependent – that if one preserves the very words, one also preserves the literal meaning of those words and that the primary instrument for this preservation is written language. All these assumptions deserve more careful scrutiny and their consideration forms the basis of this paper.

2. *Assumptions underlying literal meaning*

2.1 *The preservation of "the very words"*

2.1.1 Verbatim recall

Since literal meaning is presumed to depend upon the preservation of the very words, let us first consider what means are available for preserving the very words. The most fundamental means is to preserve the sentence surface structure in working memory during the course of understanding speech. Sachs (1967) and Jarvella (1971) have shown that the surface structure of an utterance is preserved in working memory until a meaning is assigned. Once meaning is assigned to a constituent, the exact words are dropped from memory, and a new constituent is assembled. Jarvella, for example, had people listen to a prose passage, interrupted them every so often and asked them to write down as much of the immediately preceding passage as possible. The subjects tended to recall verbatim only the constituent on which they had been operating; the sentence preceeding the constituent was recalled only as gist. The "very words" were lost after processing and only the meanings were stored in long term memory. Such meanings could, of course, be given expression but often in new words, that is, as gist. Bransford, Barclay and Franks (1972) too, showed that in the recall of semantically related sentences, subjects are frequently unable to differentiate the sentences which were actually presented from those which expressed semantic relations implicit in those sentences. This same point is nicely illustrated in Seleskovitch's (1978) discussion of the processes involved in interpreting from one language to another at international conferences. She argues that it is impossible to translate directly from one language into another: "Interpreting could never consist of a mere word-for-word translation from one language to another . . . between the time the interpreter hears a message and the time he re-expresses it in another language, he must have carried out the essential process of analyzing its meaning" (p. 84).

The verbatim surface structure of an utterance, then, is briefly stored in working memory during which time an analysis of the constituents must be completed. Secondary analysis or reanalysis of the sentence is difficult, thus problems of assigning alternative "readings" to an utterance rarely arise, although, of course, it is quite possible to re-examine and re-interpret the meanings which were extracted before the original sentence was lost from working memory.

2.1.2 Direct quotation

Is it ever possible to retain the surface structure for longer than this brief period? It would appear that there may indeed be some means, such as direct quotation and various oral mnemonic devices, including verse, song, and rehearsal. Let us examine these possibilities in more detail.

By the use of direct quotation, the speaker purports to have preserved not only a set of meanings but also the surface structure of their expression. Moreover, speakers generally know when they are paraphrasing and when they are directly quoting although there are frequent arguments both as to whether or not, in fact, A said "x" and if s/he did, whether or not s/he meant "y" and so on. Whether one preserves the very words or simply the gist may depend in part on the context. A politician will usually be very careful to preserve the very words because those words will determine both the implications and loopholes. Hence the secretary to presidential candidate Ronald Reagan had to offer the disclaimer: "The Governor's words do not always reflect his total meaning" (*The Globe and Mail,* February 27, 1980). In other social situations it may be more to the raconteur's advantage to preserve just some of the words. In most cases, however, memory for form appears to be tied to memory for meaning, and substantial parts of the surface structure may be lost, as this example shows:

> 'Get away from here, you dirty swine,' she said.
> 'There's a dirty swine in every man,' he said.
> 'Showing your face round here again,' she said.
> 'Now, Mavis, now, Mavis,' he said.
> She was seen to slam the door in his face, and he to press the bell, and she to open the door again.
> 'I want a word with Dixie,' he said. 'Now, Mavis, be reasonable.'
> 'My daughter,' Mavis said, 'is not in.' She slammed the door in his face. (p. 7)
>
> [Later, Mavis retells the incident].
> 'You could have knocked me over,' [Mavis] said. 'I was just giving Dixie her tea; it was, I should say, twenty past five and there was a ring at the bell. I said to Dixie, "Whoever can that be?" So I went to the door, and lo and behold there he was on the doorstep. He said, "Hallo," he said. I said, "You just hop it, you." He said, "Can I see Dixie?" I said, "You certainly can't," I said. I said, "You're a dirty swine. You remove yourself," I said, "and don't show your face again," I said. He said, "Come on Mavis." I said, "Mrs. Crewe to you," and I shut the door in his face.' (p. 11, Muriel Spark, *The Ballad of Peckham Rye.* New York: Penguin, 1963).

We may note that the gist of the conversation is preserved and also many of the forms of expression, particularly the colorful ones "dirty swine" and so on. Yet, overall, the wording is altered somewhat, perhaps in order to enhance the status or role of the speaker, or perhaps because of limitations in memory. "Get away from here, you dirty swine" becomes "You're a dirty swine, remove yourself". And "Now, Mavis, now Mavis" becomes "Come Mavis" and so on.

There are forms of language, though, where the surface structure and specific words form an indispensible component of the meaning, for example, the punch line of a joke, a well-timed retort, a command and the like. Several studies (e.g., Kintsch and Bates 1977; Keenan, MacWhinney and Mayhew 1977; Bates, Masling and Kintsch[1]) have shown that the delayed recall of these language forms may be quite robust. Kintsch and Bates, for example, found that even after five days, subjects recalled the surface forms for jokes and asides even if they could not for topics and details. Keenan et al. found subjects were able to distinguish target sentences from true paraphrases for such forms as figures of speech, mock insults, and jokes. Bates et al. found that memory for surface form was particularly good for "marked" forms, that is, those forms which are more informative or more novel. In addition, they suggested that surface form reflects pragmatic aspects of meaning rather than the more semantic or propositional aspects of meaning. Hence, surface form is more likely to be remembered in ordinary conversational language than in laboratory text. If meaning is construed broadly to include both pragmatic and logical components, then it is impossible to determine if the surface form is being generated from that underlying meaning or whether the surface form has in fact been stored. More sensitive recognition measures (Jacoby[2]) suggest that form is indeed preserved over substantial intervals. But again it is unlikely that such forms can be mentally scanned, or "re-read" as they would be if they were currently available in working memory or could be retrieved from a written document or long-term memory.

This memorability of certain forms of language has, of course, been picked up and exploited in sayings, aphorisms, proverbs, slogans, verse, song, and so on, yet another indication of the preservation of "the very words". As Havelock (1976) and others have shown, this memorability is at the basis of the oral tradition, an archival form which is particularly important in non-literate societies.

In oral societies and, to a lesser extent, in our own, important cultural information is "stored" for re-use in formalized speech including poetry and ritualized speech. These devices permit the recall of discourse structures much longer than a single expression, indeed sometimes of immense length. At first sight, such memory appears to preserve language verbatim, that is, on a word by word basis. More careful analysis has shown, however, that this is not the case. Lord (1960), J. Goody (1977), and Finnigan[3] all found that the recall is not verbatim recall but reconstruction from a scheme or formula on each occasion of performance. Thus, if a transcription of the poem was made on two occasions, the two performances would not be identical although, to be sure, they might be extremely similar and thematically identical. Finnigan, in her studies of oral poetry of the Limba of Sierra Leone, wrote:

> I discovered that when I was told that two stories were 'the same', this statement meant something other than that the exact words were the same. When I asked a Limba assistant to elucidate the words I could not catch fully while trying to transcribe taped stories, he could not be made to understand that I wanted the *exact* words on the tape. As far as he was concerned any comparable phrase with roughly the same meaning would do (p. 9).

J. Goody (1977) adds:

> . . . exact repetition, as both Parry and Lord were well aware, seems more

> characteristic of the written transmission of written literature than the reproduction of oral verse . . . But even the most standardized segments of oral sequences never become so standardized, so formulaic, as the products of written man. Reproduction is rarely if ever verbatim (p. 118).

Long term oral memory for language, then, is rarely word for word, verbatim memory; indeed, both Lord in his study of the oral poets of Yugoslavia and Goody in his study of the LoDagga and the Gonja noted that there was no word for *word,* but only for a "bit of speech" which could apply equally to a sound, a morpheme, a sentence, or a theme. Further, Francis (1975) found that when children in our society first learn the word "word" they use it to refer to a bit of print not a bit of speech.

As with direct quotation so, too, with other oral language devices: It seems that primarily the meaning is preserved along with some aspects of the surface structure of the expression. The extent of the preservation of the expression, whether key words or the entire utterance, depends upon the importance of those words to the particular meanings expressed. Rarely, if ever, do these oral devices preserve the words in a verbatim fashion. Indeed, Goody (1977) has suggested that recall in an oral culture is better construed as reconstruction from a set of meanings by means of a set of formulae for generating expressions. Verbatim recall, on the other hand, is based upon the notion of an "original" of which each reproduction is a "copy", that original being stored somewhere in written form. Writing is an instrument par excellence for preserving "the very words" and for making possible the re-reading and re-analysis of those words. The somewhat unique power of writing in preserving "the very words" would explain, in part, the association of writing with literal meaning. The other source of the association can be traced to the somewhat unique relation to context of written language, the second assumption of literal meaning.

2.2 *The role of context in literal meaning*

2.2.1 Sentence meaning and speaker's meaning

Let us turn now to the issue of the role played by context in literal meaning. Basic to traditional analyses of the role of context in literal meaning is Grice's (1957) theory of meaning intention. Following the linguistic convention of distinguishing sentences as linguistic objects from utterances of those sentences in particular contexts by particular speakers, Grice first differentiated the sentence meaning, the meaning that a sentence may have in any context, from the speaker's meaning, the meaning that the speaker intends to express by means of that sentence. Ordinarily, the sentence meaning is the conventional way of expressing a speaker's meaning. But, as Grice has shown, what the sentence means is often somewhat different from what a speaker intends by that sentence. This is particularly apparent in the case of indirect meaning or implicatures of which Grice (1975) has identified two forms, conversational implicatures and conventional implicatures.

To account for conversational implicatures Grice introduced a set of Conversational Maxims which are used as guides by a listener and a speaker for the interpretation of any particular sentence in any particular context. The general principle, which Grice called the Cooperative Principle stated that one should make one's conversational contribution such as is required, at the stage at which it occurs, in accord with the accepted purpose or direction of the exchange in which you are engaged. In being cooperative, speakers observe the following maxims:

Quantity:	Make your contribution as informative as required.
Quality:	Do not say what you believe to be false.
Relation:	Be relevant.
Manner:	Be perspicuous, that is, avoid obscurity, ambiguity, prolixity and incoherence.

These maxims, as suggested, inform a listener how to construct a speaker's meaning on the basis of sentence meaning and context. By means of the maxims, the listener may derive additional inferences which are determined neither by knowledge of context alone nor on the basis of the relation of that sentence to that context. These additional features are conversational implicatures. Thus, if the speaker says, "He's a fine friend" in the context of having been deserted, the sentence violates the Quality maxim, from which the listener may infer that the sentence is being used sarcastically. The speaker's meaning is in fact the opposite of the sentence meaning.

Karttunen and Peters (1975) have attempted to integrate the second type of implicature, conventional implicature, within the logical framework of model theoretic semantics. According to Grice, an implicatum is an implicature which is derived from what was said but is not logically entailed by that expression. Conventional implicatures are those implications which are derived from the choice of the specific words themselves. They are, Karttunen and Peters have suggested, equivalent to the pragmatic presuppositions which are induced by such words as *fail, manage, again, even,* and the like. To use one of Karttunen and Peters' examples, if a speaker says

(1) John managed to find a job.

he "... commits himself to the view that it isn't easy to find a job, or at least not easy for John" (p. 2). In saying that sentence the speaker warrants the implicature that the job was difficult to find, although this is not what the speaker actually or literally said. Hence, even if the implicature is false, the speaker would not have said anything false. "The truth of (1) depends solely on whether John actually found a job, the rest is a conventional implicatum to which the speaker commits himself by using the word *manage*" (p. 2). However, that boundary may not be as strict as suggested above. If, in fact, it was easy for John to find the job, then by uttering sentence (1), the speaker has uttered a sentence which is false. The speaker and the listener are aware that the word *manage* carries certain meanings and that these are implicated each time the word is used. Nonetheless, truth/falsity rests primarily on the truth of the complement.

Ordinarily, these pragmatic presuppositions or conventional implicatures define the "common ground" of discourse, "the set of propositions that any participant is rationally justified in taking for granted" (p. 3). That is, conventional implicatures are not introduced by the sentence alone, but ordinarily are previously established as part of the common ground of the discourse; they are part of the context of the utterance.

Although the differentiation of what was meant (i.e., conventionally and/or conversationally implied) from what was said is critical to an analysis of literal meaning, it may lead to two tempting but incorrect theories of literal meaning. The first is that literal meaning is synonymous with sentence meaning (what was said) and so is its timeless, context-free linguistic meaning, the Fregean "sense" of the sentence (Grice 1957). But the literal meaning of a sentence cannot be the "sense", for literal meaning is meaning in a particular context. Consider an argument between two children A and B:

(2) A: I'm bigger than you.
(3) B: I'm bigger than you.

These two sentences have the same linguistic meaning, or sentence meaning, or as we shall say later, they have the same semantic structure, but they have opposite literal meanings which we could express as:

A: bigger (A, B)
B: bigger (B, A).

The two sentences map into their contexts differently, they determine different truth-conditions and therefore they have different literal meanings.

The second possible but incorrect theory concerns the conflation of the verbatim memory of "the very words" with the literal meaning of what was said. As we have seen, even literal meaning depends upon context, hence recall of the surface form of the language is not equivalent to the literal meaning. Yet the preservation of the very words, however briefly, is a necessary condition for the computation of literal meaning. Moreover improving the preservation of the wording, as in the case of writing, may be conducive to the computation of the literal meaning.

Two recent papers, one from speech act theory (Searle 1975, 1979) and the other from model-theoretic semantics (Bierwisch[4]), help to clarify the relationship between sentence meaning and speaker's meaning and the role of context in deriving one from the other. Searle (1975, 1979) calls upon the Gricean distinction of what is said from what is meant to help account for two non-literal uses of language, metaphor and indirect speech acts. In neither of these cases, Searle argues, does the literal meaning of the sentence correspond to what the speaker meant by the sentence. In the case of a metaphoric utterance, such as "John is a chicken", a listener may know that John is not literally a chicken but rather has some of the secondary properties associated with chickens, such as cowardice. And in the case of an indirect speech act, such as the teacher's comment "Someone is talking", a child may know that the teacher is not merely describing a situation but requesting silence (Sinclair and Coulthard 1975). In order to understand these "indirect" devices in which what was "said" and what was "meant" diverge, it is necessary to consider the case in which the relationship is direct, that is, literal meaning.

Literal meaning, as we pointed out above, does not correspond to linguistic sentence meaning but, rather, to an utterance spoken by a particular individual in a particular context on a particular occasion in such a way as to determine a set of truth conditions. Searle points out that some contextually dependent elements, which call attention to particular features of the context, are explicitly marked in the sentence in the form of indexical elements, definite descriptions and the like. Background assumptions or knowledge of the world which is not marked in the semantic structure of the sentence may also form the basis for the determination of the set of truth conditions. "Thus even in literal utterances, where speaker's meaning coincides with sentence meaning, the speaker must contribute more to the literal utterance than just the semantic content of the sentence, because that semantic content only determines a set of truth conditions relative to a set of assumptions made by the speaker, and if communication is to be successful, his assumptions must be shared by the hearer" (Searle 1979, 95–96). That is, sentences have meanings *in contexts* and that interdependence of sentences and contexts in the determination of truth conditions is central to a theory of literal meaning. It is a relationship which has been spelled out in more detail in Bierwisch's[5] model theoretic analysis of meaning.

2.2.2. Possible worlds

Bierwisch is more explicit in his handling of sentence meanings, contexts or possible worlds, and speaker's meanings. He too begins his analysis by adopting the linguistic assumption that the semantic structure of a sentence is not to be identified with the meaning of the utterance of that sentence in a particular context. According to Bierwisch's view, an utterance meaning (including the reference of an expression) depends jointly on semantic structure (the sense of an expression) *and* the context. Furthermore, Bierwisch points out that the semantic structure generally fixes a set of semantic presuppositions, a set of conditions that a possible context must meet in order to yield an utterance meaning. We may note that this corresponds to Searle's point that the literal meaning of an utterance depends upon unexpressed knowledge of the world and to Kartturnen and Peters' analysis of the common ground of a particular conversation or discourse. In the utterance (2) above, for example, the context must contain an addressee internally represented as the extension of the term "You", a speaker internally represented as the extension of the term "I", and A and B must actually possess some sizes which can be compared. These contexts or "possible worlds", together with the sentence meaning, make up the utterance meaning (or speaker's meanings or speaker's intentions). If a possible world does not satisfy the semantic presuppositions of the sentence, that is, if the sentence does not have an appropriate context, no utterance meaning can be derived from it (p. 14). Bierwisch adds a final concept. Not only does he claim that an utterance meaning is a certain state of affairs belonging to a possible world, he suggests that "an utterance is, in a sense, an instruction to modify a given context *W* [possible world] . . . thus the thought expressed by an utterance is a change in the structure of a mental state" (p. 15).

We have therefore, three components in our analysis of meaning:

(semantic structure) + (possible world) → (meaning).

Formally, a semantic structure is a function from a context into a set of truth conditions. For our purposes we may say that a sentence meaning is a function from a possible world into a speaker's meaning or intention, a state of affairs asserted as true by the speaker or requested by the speaker and so on. These three components are all we will need for our consideration of literal meanings. The semantic structure is what is preserved in "the very words" or at least in the linguistic structure of the sentence; the speaker's meaning (or intention or utterance meaning), is what the speaker attempts to express or communicate by means of that expression; and the route from the sentence to the speaker's meaning is via the context or possible world.

Let us enlarge briefly on this last point. A context, in a traditional sense, is only roughly equivalent to a possible world. A context implies an actually occurring spatial and temporal state of affairs. A possible world on the other hand implies a set of presuppositions in terms of which a sentence is related to a meaning whether that set is physically given or only stipulatively assumed. A possible world, then, may in the normal case be the spatial and temporal context, but in other cases it may be an imagined, hypothetical or even counter-factual world. Kripke (1972) states: "A possible world is given by the descriptive conditions we associate with it . . . Possible worlds are *stipulated*, not discovered by powerful telescopes" (p. 267). This is a somewhat stronger sense of possible world than that employed by Bierwisch and others but it adds an important consideration. In the ordinary case, the possible world is the known, assumed and shared perceptions, beliefs, feelings and expectancies that make up the context which in turn serve as the presuppositions of the sentences expressed. We will call this ordinary possible world *W* (or sometimes, simply the real or assumed world). In the extraordinary case, we are talking about possible worlds in the Kripke sense, that world specified by a set of stipulative descriptive conditions such as those represented by conditionals, counterfactuals and so on. Kripke continues, "What do we mean when we say 'In some other possible world I might not have given this lecture today'? We just imagine the situation where I didn't decide to give this lecture or decided to give it on some other day. Of course, we don't imagine everything that is true or false, but only those things relevant to my giving the lecture; but, in theory, everything needs to be decided to make a total description of the world" (p. 267). As mentioned, such possible worlds are stipulated, and the semantic structure of the sentence is the principle, if not the only means available for stipulating a possible world. That is, the context or possible world, *W*, is created on hearing or reading the sentence rather than being simply in *W* and being presupposed by the sentence. Such stipulated possible worlds we shall refer to as *PW* (or sometimes simply as a possible world).

What then is literal meaning? We have identified literal meaning with a speaker's meaning, not with a sentence meaning. Miller and Johnson-Laird (1976) make the same point: "Perhaps we should say that there is no such thing as the literal meaning of a sentence, only the literal meaning that a given listener places on a given utterance of it" (p. 704). All meanings, literal or otherwise are speaker's meanings. What then is special about the literal meaning?

Within the family of speaker's meanings, it is worth contrasting literal meaning with casual meaning as well as with such indirect meanings as indirect speech acts and metaphor. In casual speech, a sentence *S* is fitted into its context, *W*, such that the presuppositions of *S* are assumed to correspond to the shared properties of *W*, and *S* together with *W* determine the speaker's meaning *M*; in a formula, $S + W \rightarrow M$. In casual speech, the weight is thrown on to *W*, in the determination of *M*, thereby making allowance for some degree of vagueness and imprecision in *S*; any wording will do, a wink is as good as a nod if *W* is well established. Hence, in the case where *S* corresponds closely to *W*, we may question the attribution of literal meaning: Literal meaning clearly occurs only when *M* is constructed primarily on the basis of *S*. If *S* and *W* are closely aligned, it is difficult to decide if the listener has constructed literal meaning or casual meaning. It is only when the presuppositions of *S* do not correspond to *W*, and the listener is required to construct *PW* in order to determine *M* that one has a clear case of literal meaning. This view differs from Searle's (1979) in that he takes literal meaning as the unmarked case and contrasts it with indirect speech acts and metaphor as marked cases. We suggest, rather, that casual speech be taken as the unmarked case and that literal, indirect and metaphorical speech all be treated as special cases.

2.2.3 The relationship between the sentence, the world and the meaning of that sentence in the world

Let us spell out in more detail the possible relations between *S*, *W* and *M*. Our suggestion is that it is the form of the relation between *S* and *W* which determines whether *M* is casual, literal, indirect, or metaphorical. When *S* and *W* are incongruent, either the marked form of *M* results or *W* is revised to *PW*. Indirect speech acts and metaphorical speech are examples of the former marked form of *M*, what we shall call *M′*. Such marked forms occur when *S* is incompatible with *W* and when *W* is taken as invariant. To accommodate the incongruity of *S* and *W*, *M* is reworked into *M′*. That is, these marked forms are the result of a revision of the meaning *M* of *S* while preserving the presuppositions in *W*. To revisit Searle's example, if someone says:

(4) John is a chicken

S cannot be applied to *W* to yield *M* because *S* violates *W*, the shared knowledge that John really (in *W*) is a person. That is, *M* violates the Gricean maxim of quality, hence one must compute a new speaker's meaning *M′*, the metaphorical meaning that John is a coward.

Similarly, if someone says:

(5) Your hand is on my knee

and *S* in fact corresponds to *W*, the resulting *M* is true but redundant. Hence, it fails to respect the Gricean maxim of quantity. Again then one may derive a new meaning *M'*, the indirect meaning that the listener should remove her hand, and so on.

Note that in the above cases, *W* is invariant and *S* is invariant and in the case of a mismatch, *M* is revised to *M'*. In the case of literal meaning, on the other hand, if a mismatch occurs, the realignment between *W* and *M* runs in the opposite direction. Rather than keep *W* invariant and revise *M* to *M'*, one operates on *W* to produce *PW*, a possible world stipulated by *S*, and to which *S* may now be applied to yield *M*, the literal meaning of *S* in the possible world *PW*. This proposal is similar to Bierwisch's point that an utterance is an instruction to modify a possible world. In the simplest case, the sentence applied to the given context *W*, adds to that context to produce *W'*. All sentences which are genuinely informative have just that effect, they add to our knowledge of the world or at least to the topic of conversation. But to transform *W* into *W'* by means of an utterance is vastly different from its transformation from *W* to *PW*, a stipulated possible world determined by *S*, rather than presupposed by *S*. This latter is the clearest case of literal meaning, and, as we shall argue presently this is the case that is most closely associated with literate competence.

3. *The conceptual basis of literal meaning: Literal meaning and literacy*

We have examined the ways in which context is utilized in understanding sentences, or as we have put it, how sentences map contexts into intentions. These alternative relations between sentences and contexts are summarized in Table 1. All meaning, *M*, assumes a context or possible world and a semantic structure; the important theoretical point is whether *S* or *W* are taken as invariant in determining that meaning. In casual meaning, the context *W* is taken as invariant, and one glosses the semantic structure from *S* to *S'* in order to compute a meaning *M*. A well known example is Piaget's young subjects who, when faced with a collection of three ducks and two rabbits and asked if, "Are there more ducks or animals?" apparently, gloss the question to the more regular form "Are there more ducks or rabbits?" and answer "More ducks." Another example comes from Donaldson (1978) who discovered that when children were shown a collection of four cars only three of which were in the garages, they apparently glossed the question "Are all the cars in the garages?" into the simpler question "Are all the garages full?" and answered "Yes".

In literal meaning, it is the semantic structure *S* which is taken as invariant and the context which is altered, either by adding some information to *W* to produce *W′*, or by constructing a possible world having the properties stipulated by *S*. For Piaget's question, for example, the child must imagine a world in which there really are two disjoint collections one of ducks and one of animals which can then be compared. Or again, to understand the sentence "John is a chicken" literally, one must imagine a world in which John really is a chicken (he is just wearing a human disguise).

Table 1. Some relations of sentences and contexts in the determination of meaning

S	+	W	→	M
semantic structure or linguistic meaning or sentence meaning or sense		knowledge of the world or knowledge of context or possible world		intended meaning or speaker's meaning or utterance meaning or reference

Varieties of M

Casual meaning. (W is invariant) $S \rightarrow S'$ $S' + W \rightarrow M$	Piaget: S : Are there more ducks or animals? → S′ : Are there more ducks or rabbits? Donaldson: S : Are all the cars in the garages? → S′ : Are all the garages full? Hildyard (Blue dots): Does the picture show that the dots are not red? Dots are red? Blue – Yes it does. No they're not.
Literal meaning. (S is invariant) $S + W' \rightarrow M$ $S + PW \rightarrow M$	John is late (when he is often late). Are there more rabbits or animals? John is a chicken (really).
Indirect speech act and metaphor. (S and W are invariant) $S + W \rightarrow M'$	John is a chicken. You have more than me. I hear talking.

Finally, indirect speech acts and metaphor require that both the semantic structure *S* and *W* are taken as invariant but some part of the cooperative principle is violated. In such cases the listener would preserve *S* and *W* but compute a marked or indirect form of meaning. These indirect forms have been more carefully distinguished by Searle (1979).

The progressive development from casual to strictly literal meaning, may help to clarify the stages children pass through in their comprehension and production of utterances and, later, written discourse. In the earliest stages, the child may know *W* and know what the speaker intends, that is *M,* and on the basis of these two s/he may work out the semantic structure of *S.* Several writers have suggested that this is the means whereby a child learns the language (Olson 1970; Macnamara 1972; Nelson 1974) although the point is often abbreviated to saying that the child knows the meaning intention and uses that meaning to crack the linguistic code or, even more elliptically, to say that the child uses the context to learn the language. From our perspective, all three parts are relevant, a semantic structure, a possible world, and a meaning intention.

At the earliest stages of language acquisition, then, the meaning intention *M,* may be identified with the semantic structure, as when a young child thinks that the word "Rabbit" is the proper name for a particular rabbit (cf., Oviatt 1979). Later s/he learns that the semantic structure is a means of mapping varying contexts into particular meanings but the determination of what features of *M* are captured by the semantic structure *S* is not clear, hence the well-known phenomenon of over-generalization. As the child becomes more sophisticated linguistically, which is to say that s/he has control over the various semantic (and pragmatic) structures of *S,* s/he can see that in certain contexts, certain meanings can be expressed by, and only by, certain semantic structures. Hence, whereas earlier a young child may take an *S* which by adult standards is appropriate to *W,* not as an invitation to revise *W,* but simply as an overextension of *S,* leaving *W* intact, at a later stage s/he will insist on the use of a particular *S* in *W* to represent *M.* Thus Bowerman (1977) provides several examples both of young children calling a crescent of spinach a "moon" and, somewhat later of rejecting an *S* when there is a more appropriate *S* available for expressing *M* in *W* ("That's not dripping, that's running" in reference to a leaky faucet). Neither of these cases, however, provide evidence for literal meaning that is of the use of *S* to alter *W* to *W′* or from *W* to *PW.* That is, earliest utterances appear to be redundant with their contexts rather than informative.

Later, we find increasingly clear indications of the comprehension and expression of literal meanings as children no longer come to regard *W* as simply invariant, and begin to use utterances to add information to *W* if that information is compatible with *W* or can be anticipated on the basis of their knowledge of *W.* Finally, children not only revise *W* on the basis of *S* but can imagine a possible world in which *S* could be used to mean *M.* That is, when the child can hold the semantic structure *S* and operate upon *W* to produce a possible world *PW* in order to recover the meaning *M* literally intended by the speaker, we have clear evidence of the child's comprehension of literal meaning *M* of *S*.

But note that such operations require the preservation of *S*, the semantic structure expressed by "the very words". Hence, literal meaning although not uniquely tied to literacy is facilitated by the device so effective in the preservation of those words, namely, written language. Reading and, more importantly, writing force the individual to take stock of what is intended and how that intention might be captured unambiguously by means of a particular surface form in that context. Unlike speech, in which the speaker can alter a surface form mid-sentence if the listener appears to be misunderstanding, the written message is assumed to be in an appropriate form once it has been forwarded to the reader. It is the writer's task to ensure that the reader can extract a nod even if a wink was specified in the surface form. That is, the writer must ensure that any reader can take the linguistic structure of the sentence, apply that structure to a context and come up with the meaning that was intended even if this entails modifying an existing context or occasionally creating a new context.

In learning to read, the child must come to know the particular structure of the written code as well as the relationship between that structure and the meanings expressed by it in particular contexts. In learning to write, the problem is extended one step further. Not only must an appropriate surface representation be found for the expression of an intention, but also the context in terms of which that surface structure is understood, must be created by the writer to assure the correct interpretation. Whereas in much of oral language, a shared context can simply be assumed, in writing an additional burden falls on the writer. Whether through reminding the reader of the context or more importantly through stipulatively specifying a context, the writer must consciously manage the context or possible word in which that sentence can be taken as an expression of the intended meaning. In written language, then, "the very words" are used to specify both the semantic structure and the context, which, together, specify the intended meaning.

Let us now examine in detail the relation between the children's acquisition of literate skills and their sensitivity to literal meanings.

3.1 *Developmental studies*

3.1.1 Negation

There are several important stages in the child's mastery of negation. The one of concern here, however, is that which marks an altered relation between the semantic structure of the sentence *S* and the knowledge of the context *W* in determining the utterance meaning *M*, the meaning that the listener/speaker assigns to that sentence in that context. As we shall see, the meaning assigned by an adult is, in some cases, markedly different from that assigned by a child. We have argued generally that if the presuppositions of *S* correspond to the listener's knowledge of *W*, a sentence meaning *M* can be readily assigned and, in the case of literal meaning, serve as the basis of altering *W* to *W′* or to *PW*.

What are the presuppositions for the use of a negative? Strawson (1952, p. 18) has argued that "The standard and primary use of *not* is specifically to contradict or correct; to cancel a suggestion of one's own or another's". Wason (1972, in press) has shown the experimental consequences of these presuppositions in the comprehension of negation. In Wason's example, for the sentence "The train wasn't late this morning" to count as appropriate negation, it must falsify the preconception of the listeners that the train is usually late. That is, ordinarily the negative denies what is asserted as *W* or what is presupposed in *W*.

The use of negation in direct commands or prohibition makes even clearer the role of presuppositions which actually correspond to *W*. To say "Don't put your finger in the light socket" presupposes a world in which the child is about to put his/her finger in the socket. Similarly, "Let's not go to the movies" presupposes a *W* in which the speaker and listener had the intention of going to the movies. Negatives like any other linguistic form are interpreted in terms of the possible world in which they are uttered. The world or context appropriate for a negative is that of a state of affairs which the negative explicitly denies. Wason has demonstrated this point by showing that subjects can more easily understand "The circle is not blue" if all the other circles were blue. The possible world in this case is one consisting largely of blue circles, that general characteristic being denied in this particular case. As Wason and Johnson-Laird (1972) pointed out, "the step of recovering the supposition goes unnoticed because it has already been processed as part of the context of the utterance" (p. 39).

Some developmental studies have helped to clarify the role of the context, the shared world *W*, in children's comprehension and production of negation. Roy Pea[6] has recently shown that for very young children, "no" first serves the "don't" function of rejecting an offer. Only later does "no" come to serve the "no" or "not" function of expressing truth-functional judgments, that is, for denying the truth of an utterance. Such truth-functional negation is meta-linguistic in that it denies the truth of an assertion, not of a referent. In a typical case reported by Pea, the experimenter, pointing to an apple asks: "Is that a biscuit?" and the two-year-old child replies with a denial: "No, apple". Volterra and Antinucci (1978) have described this denial function of negation in terms of presuppositions. The presupposition is the belief presumed to be held by self or other in *W* which is then denied by the child. When a 16 month old child says "gone", an implicit negative, on seeing a match go out, the child negates the presupposition "the flame is present" which s/he and the listener had taken to be in *W*.

The use of such presuppositions is relatively straightforward in cases where one either affirms a true description or denies a false one. If shown a cat (W_{cat}) and then asked if it is a cat (S_{cat}), the presuppositions in *W* match *S* and the child affirms *S*. If asked if it is a dog (S_{dog}), the presuppositions in *W* do not match *S* and the child denies *S*. It is not clear in such cases if the child actually constructs a literal meaning for *S* which is then matched against *W* or if the only meaning constructed is determined by *W* and the child then simply affirms true descriptions and rejects false ones. We prefer the latter description but know of no compelling evidence on the matter. Regardless of how that issue is decided, it is important to note that if we use even a lax criterion for literal meaning, namely, that the listener revise his knowledge from *W* to *W′* on the basis of *S*, neither assent nor simple denial constitute cases of the comprehension of literal meaning *M* of *S*.

The most critical case involves the use of a true negative description, such as, given a cat, W_{cat}, the child hears the assertion, "It's not a dog". As pointed out earlier, the use of a negation presupposes a state of affairs denied by the negation. But the child has no reason to suppose that s/he would have seen a dog. Hence, the sentence does not deny a presupposition stored as part of *W*. When these presuppositions are not met, that is, not represented in *W*, three interpretative strategies are possible:

1. ignore the negative particle;
2. alter *S* transformation or deletion to *S′* which has presuppositions congruent with *W*: The resulting *M′* we may call casual meaning or glossed meaning;
3. alter *W* to *PW*, a possible world meeting the properties presupposed by *S* (or in some cases those stipulated by *S*). Specifically, faced with "It's not a dog" the child could imagine a *PW* in which he could have been expecting a dog and the negative statement correctly denies that presupposition. It is this resulting meaning we have called the literal meaning of *S*.

In an attempt to uncover the use of context in the construction of the literal meaning of negative and affirmative expressions, Angela Hildyard[7] presented 5 and 8 year old children with pictures showing a collection of either red or black dots. After the children had examined a picture, they were asked a question of the following form: "Does the picture show that the dots are not black (red)?". The percentage of these questions correctly answered by children at these two age levels (and a group of 11 adult graduate students added for comparative purposes) is shown in Table 2.

Table 2. Percentage of correct responses given by children to true and false negative sentences

Question	Display	Question Type	% Correct K	Gr. 2	A
Does the picture show that the dots are not black?	Red dots	TN	25	65	100
Does the picture show that the dots are not red?	Red dots	FN	27	73	100

First, we may note that both of the young groups of subjects have difficulty with the true negative, the sentence which violates their presuppositions, but for the Kindergarten children, the effect is calamitous; their responses are not at chance but far below chance (cf., de Villiers and Flushberg 1975). What comprehension strategy are these young subjects using and how does that strategy change as the child advances to the second grade and on to adulthood?

We can account for the contrasting performances of the youngest children and those of the adults by hypothesizing that children and adults are interpreting the question in systematically different ways, the answers to which coincide for some of the questions and differ on others. What are these questions? First, it appears that the children simply abandon the embedding clause "Does the picture show that . . . " and judge a modified embedded clause. This is indicated by the fact that the youngest children's answers "Yes" and "No" are correct of the dots but not of the pictures. The strategy can be illustrated as follows: If asked "Does the picture show that the dots are not black?" and shown a picture of red dots, older children and adults tend to answer "Yes" with the implicit continuation ". . . It does". Asked the same question, however, the youngest children respond "No" with the implicit continuation "They're red". That is, the children are responding to the embedded proposition but they appear to have deleted the negation from that clause. Similarly, when asked "Does the picture show that the dots are not red?" and shown a picture of red dots, the adults respond "No (it does not)" while the children respond "Yes (they are red)".

Such a strategy would predict that given affirmative questions of the form "Does the picture show that the dots are black" and shown a picture of black dots, the adults would respond "Yes (it does)" while the children would respond "Yes (they are)". Of course, in this case both responses would be correct. Similarly for the false affirmatives: responding either on the basis of the embedding or the embedded clause will result in the response "No".

We interpret these data as evidence that the youngest children gloss S to S' in constructing the meaning ($S' + W = M_1$). Thus, the child's strategy has two parts:

1. Gloss the statement/question into an underlying proposition by means of deleting the embedding construction "Does the picture show. . . " and by deleting the negative particle "not" to form S'.

2. Then compare the sentence to the values W, if they correspond, affirm it; if they differ, deny it.

These stages, however, presumably are not independent, as the values in W may determine how the sentence is glossed. For our purposes, the critical fact is that in working out the meaning M of S in W, the child preserves W, glosses S to S' on the basis of W, and then affirms or denies S'.

It is worth noting, too, that the child does not completely assimilate S to W, as s/he may have done earlier in, say, overgeneralization, assuming that if the dots are black the speaker must have meant that the dots were black. Rather, the child preserves the most critical constituents of S as S' in constructing the meaning M_1.

By eight years of age, children give evidence of adopting the adult strategy and begin to answer the negative questions as adults do, disagreeing with the sentence that the dots are not black when in fact they are, and agreeing with the sentence that they are not red when they are black. This is achieved partly by retaining those constituents of S, the embedding construction and the negative particle, that they had previously ignored. However, children continue to have particular difficulty with the true negative at Grade 2, a difficulty that does not disappear even in adulthood (Wason 1972, in press). What does an adult-like performance require? Recall that true negatives ordinarily deny a presupposition which is shared in W. That is, if ordinarily the dots were red and a black one unexpectedly appeared, it would be appropriate to state, "The dot is not red", a true negative. But in this study, there was no established presupposition in W that the dots ordinarily were red. To get the item correct, a listener would have to *create* the presupposition, that ordinarily the dots are red, on the basis of the statement, and then deny that presupposition. That is, for the true negative, the presupposition for the denial is not already established in W, and the child must stipulatively, on the basis of S, imagine a PW in which ordinarily one sees red dots. Having imagined this PW, s/he can look at the picture of the black dot and affirm that the dots are not red. The stipulative creation of a PW on the basis of S, we take as firm evidence of the construction of the literal meaning of S, evidence that first appears in a few children at Grade 2.

3.1.2 Complex verbs

A second ground for examining children's comprehension of literal meaning is that of certain complex verbs known as implicatives and factives. These complex verbs contain two sentential components which together make up the semantic structure of the sentence (Karttunen 1971, 1973; van Fraassen 1968). The first is the implicative which either asserts or negates the complement of the sentence; the second is the conventional implicature discussed earlier which is equivalent to the pragmatic presupposition of the sentence. To illustrate, consider the following sentences:

(6) John forced Mary to shut the door.
(6a) Mary shut the door. (Implicative)
(6b) Mary did not want to shut the door. (Conventional implicature)
(7) John forgot to shut the door.
(7a) John did not shut the door. (Implicative)
(7b) John was supposed to shut the door. (Conventional implicature)

Both implica*tives* and implica*tures* follow from the sentence, albeit in somewhat different ways. Implicatives follow from the sentence by formal entailment: if one is true the other is necessarily true. Conventional implicatures, on the other hand, follow from the sentences by means of the cooperative principle; although the implicature does not strictly follow from the sentence, the speaker commits himself to the truth of the implicature by the use of that particular expression (cf., Karttunen and Peters 1975). Ordinarily, the conventional implicature corresponds to a presupposition existing in W prior to hearing or reading the sentence.

Note that with these complex verbs it is possible to construct the meaning, M, for both of the constituents either on the basis of the semantic structure S or on the basis of the context W. Frequently, S corresponds to W and we cannot differentiate the grounds for constructing M. It is possible, however, to set up situations where S does not correspond to W and hence, to determine whether S or W is the primary determinant of M. If W is invariant, S will be glossed to S' which will result in the casual meaning M_1 ($S' + W \rightarrow M_1$). If S is invariant, W will be transformed to PW which will result in the literal meaning M. Let us examine these meaning components in the following sentence:

(8) John forced Mary to eat the worm.
(8a) Mary ate the worm. (Implicative)
(8b) Mary did not want to eat the worm. (Conventional implicature)

In this case, the implicative of the sentence does not correspond to W, hence, to construct the meaning M for the implicative, the listener must revise W to PW, a possible world in which humans eat worms ($S + PW \rightarrow M_{impl.}$). The conventional implicature does correspond to W, hence the construction of the meaning M for this component does not require any revision in W ($S + W = M_{con. imp.}$).

Conversely, it is possible to devise sentences in which the conventional implicature does not conform to W while the implicative does, as in the following:

(9) John forced Mary to eat the tasty ice cream.
(9a) Mary ate the ice cream. (Implicative)
(9b) Mary did not want to eat the ice cream. (Conventional implicature)

Here, the implicative is congruent with W ($S + W \rightarrow M_{impl.}$) while the conventional implicature is not. In order to construct the literal meaning for that component, the listener would have to revise W to PW, a possible world in which Mary dislikes ice cream ($S + PW \rightarrow M_{con. imp.}$).

For both 8 and 9 it is essential to create a possible world which is different in some important way from the ordinary or presupposed world in order to extract one of the components of the meaning, M. But what if, as we argued above, children have difficulty in revising W to PW? If they cannot, they are left with the possibility of holding W invariant, and glossing S to S' to produce casual meaning M_1 ($S' + W \rightarrow M_1$). Thus instead of asserting that Mary ate the worm, the implicative correctly derived from S in PW, the child may assert that Mary did not eat the worm, a meaning derived by holding W invariant and glossing S to S'.

Following upon Macnamara, Baker and Olson's (1976) study of children's comprehension of complex verbs, Hidi and Hildyard (1979) and Hildyard and Hidi[8] collected children's answers to questions which queried the implicatives and conventional implicatures of complex verbs which were either congruent or incongruent with children's knowledge of the world. Seven different verbs were used (force, make, pretend, forget, manage, get, to be surprised) having sentence complements which were either positive, neutral or negative *vis-à-vis* children's knowledge of the world. To illustrate, the verb *force* was used in the following three ways:

(10) John forced Sandra to shut the door. (Neutral)
(10a) Sandra shut the door. (Implicative)
(10b) Sandra didn't want to shut the door. (Conventional implicature)
(11) Sandra forced John to fall off his bike. (Negative)

(11a) John fell off his bike. (Implicative)
(11b) John didn't want to fall off his bike. (Conventional implicature)
(12) Sandra forced John to eat the tasty ice cream. (Positive)
(12a) John ate the tasty ice cream. (Implicative)
(12b) John didn't want to eat the ice cream. (Conventional implicature)

Note that if the complement is congruent with the world, *W*, the conventional implicature is not, and vice versa.

Sixty children ranging from 5 to 10 years of age, drawn from three grade levels (Grade 4, Grade 2, and Kindergarten) were tested for their ability to derive implicatives and conventional implicatures from the set of sentences described above. The neutral versions were given first and the order of the positive and negative sentences was counter-balanced. Children were first tested on the implicatives. After hearing a sentence, subjects were asked a Yes/No question on the implicative, following which they were asked a Yes/No question on the conventional implicature. After the second question they were asked to provide a rationale for their response.

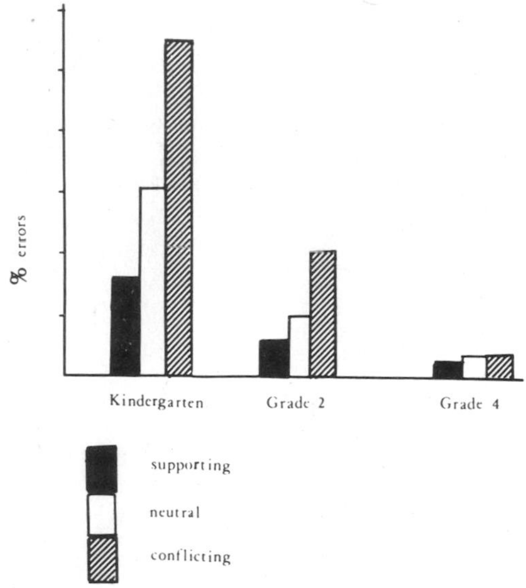

Figure 1. Children's performance on the implicatives (at three grade levels).

First, let us examine children's performance on the implicatives. Figure 1 shows that there are striking differences between the three grade levels. By Grade 4, children made few errors regardless of the congruity between the semantic structure *S*, and the knowledge of the world, *W*. In terms of our analysis, the child preserves *S* and, if necessary, transforms *W* to *PW* in order to construct the literal meaning *M*.

Grade 2 children had more difficulty with some complement types than with others. When the implicative was congruent or neutral *vis-à-vis W*, they made few errors. When they were incompatible, they had more difficulty. In terms of our analysis, Grade 2 children have some difficulty in holding *S* invariant and altering *W* to *PW* in order to arrive at the literal meaning *M*. They had little difficulty, however, transforming *W* to *W'*, that is, in using *S* as an instruction to add to their knowledge of the world.

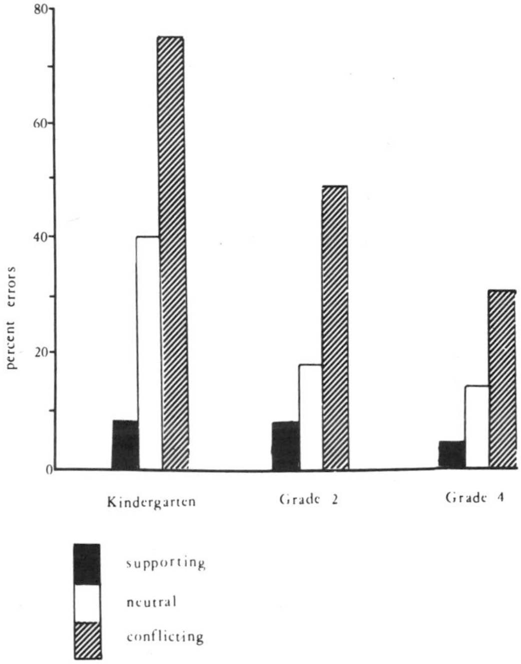

Figure 2. Children's performance on conventional implicatures (at three grade levels).

Not surprisingly, the Kindergarten children made a substantial number of errors in all sentence types but most importantly, their performance on implicatives fell to chance levels on items in which their knowledge of the world, *W*, ran counter to the implicative component of the sentence *S*. That is, these young subjects appeared to be unable to use *S* stipulatively to revise *W* to *PW* in the construction of the literal meaning *M*. Instead, for over 50% of the time, they answered the question on the basis of *W* rather than on the basis of the stipulative *PW*.

The children's performance on conventional implicatures shows a similar but even more marked pattern. As Figure 2 shows, the children made many more errors on the conventional implicatures than they had on the implicatives. That is, it is easier to revise *W* to *W′* or to *PW* on the basis of *S* when that revision is called for in the implicative than when it is called for in the conventional implicature. It will be recalled that these conventional implicatures are what in other contexts are called the presuppositions of the sentence, and as we saw in our analysis of negatives, sentences which violate their presuppositions are extremely difficult for children.

As with the implicatives, there are significant changes with grade level in children's ability to construct a meaning for a sentence which is contradictory to their knowledge of the world. For sentences with conventional implicatures which are congruent with knowledge of the world, there are only slight differences between the youngest and the oldest children. When those implicatures conflict with knowledge of the world the errors are substantial, ranging from 30% for the Grade 4 children, to 49% for the Grade 2 children and up to 76% for the Kindergarten children. Put simply, when *S* and *W* conflict, the youngest children overwhelmingly use *W* rather than *S* as the basis for their response.

Since the children were asked to justify their responses to those implicatures, their comprehension strategies can be examined more precisely. The responses were broken into 4 categories, as follows:

1. rationale derived from the semantic structure of *S*;
2. rationale derived from conventional knowledge *W*;
3. rationale derived from an imagined but not stipulated possible world *PW′*;
4. rationale derived from *W* or *PW* to justify an incorrect "I".

"S" is a response based upon the literal meaning *M* of the sentence *S* in *W′* or in the stipulatively determined possible world *PW*. "W" is a response based upon *W*, the child's existing knowledge of the world. "PW′" is a response based upon a possible world, but a possible world not stipulatively defined by the semantic structure of the sentence. "I" is an incorrect response based upon either existing knowledge *W* or an imagined but unstipulated possible world *PW′*. Examples of each of these response types are as follows:

(11) Sandra forced John to fall off his bike.
(11b) Did John want to fall off his bike? (Conventional implicature)

S – No, because you said that Sandra had to force him.
W – No, because noone likes to fall off a bike.
PW′ – No, because he fell off yesterday and really hurt his knee. and his mum said that if he fell off again she would get mad.
I – Yes, because he wanted to be able to stay home from school.

The results of these analyses are shown in Table 3.

Table 3. Justification of responses to conventional implicatures

	S	W	PW′	Incorrect[I]
Kindergarten				
Supporting	38	31	23	8
Neutral	33	1	24	41
Conflicting	12	1	11	76
Mean	28	11	19	42
Grade 2				
Supporting	63	21	9	8
Neutral	64	3	16	18
Conflicting	45	1	4	49
Mean	57	8	10	25
Grade 4				
Supporting	88	5	3	4
Neutral	82	3	1	14
Conflicting	68	0	2	30
Mean	79	3	2	16

S = response based on the literal meaning *S* (in percentages)
W = response based upon *S* in *W* (in percentages)
PW′ = response based upon a possible world derived from *W* not *S* (in percentages)
I = Incorrect response based on *W* or *PW′* (in percentages)

The development of an adult-like comprehension strategy can be seen clearly. Reliance upon the semantic structure *S* as grounds for the response is shown as the "S" response category, that is the response in which children explain their answer by appealing to the sentence rather than to their knowledge of the world or to some unstipulated possible world. Grade 4 children gave such explanations about 80% of the time, Grade 2 about 60% of the time and the Kindergarten children about 30% of the time. Even in the majority of cases in which the youngest children got the item correct, they did so not by an appeal to *S* but by an appeal to their prior knowledge of the world or to some imagined but unstipulated possible world. The most striking aspect of the data, then, is the progressive development of the ability to hold the semantic structure *S* invariant in constructing a literal meaning *M* even if it requires the revision of *W* to *W′* or to *PW*, and while, by Kindergarten age, 50% of the children can do that for implicatives, it is only in Grade 2 that 50% of the children can do that for the conventional implicatures.

If we recall that conventional implicatures are equivalent to the pragmatic presuppositions discussed in the analysis of negation, the findings of these two studies are remarkably parallel. The presupposition for a true negative was not given by *W* but had to be constructed as a possible world on the basis of *S* just as is the case for the conventional implicature of the sentence containing a complex verb. In both cases only 25% of the Kindergarten children succeeded with the task and some 60% of the Grade 2 children succeeded with it. Thus the study of the implicatures, like the study of negation, indicates that children readily comprehend sentences in which the presuppositions of the sentence correspond to their knowledge of *W*; when the two are incongruent, the children tend to hold *W* invariant while glossing *S* to *S′* and thereby construct not the literal meaning, *M*, of *S* but rather a meaning of *S′*. With development and/or with schooling in a written language, children become increasingly adept at preserving *S* and revising their knowledge of the world in order to construct a literal meaning.

3.1.3 Inferences

Finally, let us consider the role of knowledge of the world, *W*, in the drawing of logical inferences. Before we examine any specific problem, it is important to differentiate two quite different ways in which the term "inference" is used; these two uses correspond precisely to the different uses of *W* that we have discussed. Logical or formal inferences are those which are based upon explicitly mentioned premises; to draw the inference upon the basis of an implicit premise is, from this point of view, not a logical inference but an enthymeme. In terms of the framework we have developed here, a logical inference is based upon a literal meaning and a literal meaning requires the stipulative construction of a possible world on the basis of the sentence $(S + PW \rightarrow M)$.

The second use of the term "inference" is in reference to the drawing of a valid conclusion from *S* in a previously established *W*, the knowledge of the world shared by the speaker and hearer. These inferences have been called "pragmatic inferences" (Harris and Monaco 1978; Hildyard and Olson 1978). While such inferences are valid with respect to the shared knowledge *W*, which has been derived both from *S* and from the Cooperative Principle, pragmatic inferences cannot be said to follow from the literal meaning of *S*. In a simple case, if one reads:

(13) The policeman drew his pistol and fired. The thief slumped to the floor.

one could pragmatically infer that the thief was shot by the policeman. Indeed, if that were not the case, the speaker would be intentionally misleading by violating the Cooperative Principle. Yet the inference cannot be attributed to the semantic structure of the sentence and hence it is not a "logical" inference. The inference is based not strictly on *S* but on the shared knowledge of the world *W* ($S' + W \rightarrow M_1$). That is, *S* is glossed to S′ on the basis of *W* with the result that the listener takes the intended meaning *M* to be something of the form:

The policeman shot the thief.

Under normal circumstances, these two forms of inference are congruent, but they may be pulled apart by experimental means in order to determine children's reliance upon the literal meaning of *S* as opposed to their reliance upon *W*.

In one study (Hildyard 1979), 48 children in Grades 1, 3 and 5 were asked to draw inferences from stories having the logical form:

A is in front of B
B is in front of C
D is behind C

and they were required to draw the following inferences:

A is in front of C
B is in front of D
A is in front of D

Six different predicate pairs were employed (in front/behind, before/after, on top/under, earlier/later, more/less, bigger/smaller) each of which was used to specify the relations between four objects or events. These logical relations made up the basic framework for six different stories.

In line with our preceding argument, children should readily compute the literal meaning of *S* when *S* is congruent with *W* and hence draw the appropriate logical inferences; when *S* is neutral or counterfactual with regard to *W*, the child should have severe difficulty in computing the *PW* stipulated by *S*. As a result s/he will fail to draw the appropriate logical inferences. To test this hypothesis, the logical relations were presented in three different contexts. A *congruent* context was established by embedding the transitive relations in short stories in which the transitive orderings were motivated by known properties of the related objects. A *neutral* context was established by embedding the transitive relations in a story in which those orderings were not motivated by such properties. A *counter-factual* context was established by stipulatively specifying a transitive ordering which violated the known properties of the related objects. Excerpts from the sample stories are as follows:

Congruent: One day the animals decided to have a race to the old hut in the jungle . . . The giraffe with his long neck was able to see the best path to the old hut. The giraffe arrived before the elephant. The elephant was so big he was able to trample on anything that got in his way, so the elephant got there before the lion . . .

Neutral: It was circus time again . . . at the start of the show they had a parade. There were some clowns dressed in funny costumes. The clowns were in front of the elephants. Behind the elephants was the lion tamer. He was wearing a black suit and carried a whip. . .

Counter-factual: One morning Sammy got up in a rush . . . He jumped out of bed and quickly got dressed . . . He found his thick brown coat and put his coat on before his jacket . . . He looked for his thick yellow sweater. Sammy put his sweater on after he put on his jacket . . .

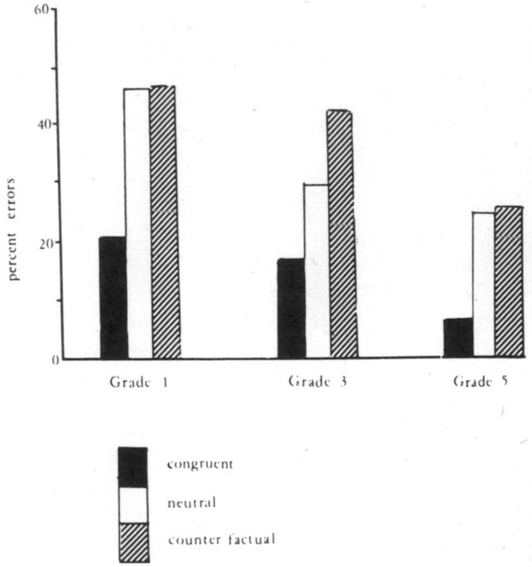

Figure 3. Percentage of errors in identifying logical relations in three different contexts (at three grade levels).

The stories, six of each type, were read to the children at the three grade levels. The percentage of errors as a function of the three types of context for each grade level is shown in Figure 3. As this Figure shows, there are both significant grade and context effects. When the inferences can be drawn jointly from *S* and *W*, as in the congruent context condition, even the youngest children were relatively successful. Maintaining the same set of semantic structural relations and altering context *W*, however, has dramatic consequences on the drawing of inferences. These effects are particularly large for the youngest children. For Grade 1 children (approximately 6 years old) performance in the neutral and counter-factual conditions falls to chance. By Grade 3, children begin to show some competence with the neutral context but with a counter-factual context performance is not far above chance. Only for Grade 5 children (11 years of age) is performance in the neutral and counter-factual conditions handled competently, but even here performance is far from perfect. Again, then, young children can draw valid inferences from statements only as long as those statements are congruent with children's knowledge of the world *W*. But if *W* is neutral or contrary to those sentences, children begin to succeed only by Grade 3, and become reasonably competent only by Grade 5. These are the inferences which are based upon the literal meanings of the sentences in the stories. That is, these inferences require that the listener has some means of preserving the semantic structure of *S*, and of constructing a possible world *PW* stipulated by *S* in the derivation of the literal meaning *M*. This is the form of competence that appears to develop only when the child is well into the school years and perhaps, only under the impact of schooling in a literate society.

4. *General discussion*

In this paper we have considered some of the ways in which the context, which we described in terms of knowledge of the world *W* or a possible world *PW*, enters into the comprehension and production of the meaning *M* of a sentence *S*. We have argued that such varieties of meanings as casual meanings, literal meanings, indirect meanings and metaphors are varieties of "speaker's meanings", that is, speaker's intended meanings of utterances. In this view, sentences *per se* do not have meanings; rather sentences in contexts have meanings, in our formula, $S + W \rightarrow M$. The larger part of the argument had to do with the varying relations between semantic structures of the sentence and the knowledge of the world in the construction of those meanings. Our claim was that in ordinary conversational discourse and particularly in children's speech, the context was the predominant factor in constructing the meaning and the sentence would be glossed either to mean less than it "said" or to mean more than it "said". In the case of literal meaning, on the other hand, the meaning corresponds, in some sense, to what is said. However, we have tried to show that the simple equation of what was "said" and what was "meant" is misleading. Even in the case of literal meaning, the meaning is not equivalent to what was said, to the "linguistic meaning" or semantic structure, but rather as in other cases of meaning, to a sentence in a context. For literal meaning, this context is the possible world stipulated by the sentence. The studies presented above have shown, that children have difficulty understanding sentences in which the presuppositions of the sentence fail to correspond to the context and which therefore require the stipulative construction of a possible world as the means of arriving at the meaning of the sentence.

Three final points require further comment. First, we have not given any detailed analysis of the structure of *W*, the knowledge of the world or the context that is required in the determination of the meaning of a sentence. Although that topic has come in for a great deal of recent study in terms of scenarios, frames, scripts, discourse grammars, and the like, we shall merely suggest how we think that topic could be developed to suit the purposes of an analysis of speaker's meanings. The context, variously referred to as knowledge of the world, knowledge held in common by the participants in the dialogue or discourse, the world of discourse, and so on, we take to be not only the information previously established by the discourse but also all of that knowledge which can safely be assumed to be held in common by the participants and to which they may appeal if discourse fails. This includes both commonsense knowledge, immediate contextual knowledge, knowledge of the language and of ways of speaking. It is the body of knowledge which is presupposed and updated in the light of each contribution to the discourse. Even a possible world, which by definition is not held in common in *W*, is, if successful, introduced into *W* stipulatively through the sentence. Furthermore, a possible world is not simply built from nothing. It, too, is built upon the shared prior knowledge *W*. In a possible world, all the properties of *W* are assumed to be held intact, except those stipulatively given in the sentence. Thus, if a speaker said that on Mars people have three eyes, it would be assumed that in this possible world, eyes were still used for seeing, that Martians count eyes the same way that we do and so on. Hence, a possible world stipulated by a sentence is not simply a semantic structure but rather a world having the properties of the ordinary world, modified on the basis of those specific properties stipulated by the sentence.

The second point is the converse of the first. If possible worlds are merely those worlds stipulated by the sentence, would it not be possible to simplify the theory, dispensing altogether with the notion of possible world, and say that literal meaning is simply sentence meaning. As we mentioned above, it is difficult to note any outstanding differences between the semantic structure of the sentence and the possible world stipulated by the sentence. For example, any inference that follows from one appears to follow equally from the other. Indeed, one of the long-standing disputes in psycholinguistics is the extent to which semantic structures can be explained by recourse to knowledge of the world or of possible worlds as opposed to the view that possible worlds and speaker's meanings generally can be explained by reference to semantic structures. Our present strategy is to adopt the view that a meaning intention is *always* a combination of a semantic structure and a possible world, and it is impossible to have an adequate theory of meaning which ignores either component.

Third, several writers have advanced arguments similar to those presented herein, but from somewhat different perspectives. As mentioned at the outset, cognitive psychologists in general have been impressed with the ways that sentences are assimilated to knowledge schemata and developmental cognitive psychologists in particular have noted the ways in which children disregard aspects of the semantic structure of sentences in their attempt to recover the intended meaning. With development and/or schooling they gain competence with more formal, "decontextualized" meanings appropriate to more formal contexts and more formal registers of language. Perhaps we can best summarize our views by suggesting a compromise between two major types of explanation offered for development. The first and oldest is the theory of abstraction, that children come increasingly to be able to imagine more abstract possible worlds as the grounds for their reasoning. In this view, development is essentially conceptual development. The alternative is that children become increasingly capable of constructing meanings which are more closely tied to what, in fact, was said. Development, in this view, is essentially linguistic. In our view, these two dimensions are inextricably interdependent. Prior to shooling, children have both the ability to use their language and they have the ability to imagine possible worlds; what happens with development in a schooled/literate environment is the ability to imagine those possible worlds stipulatively specified by sentences. Those worlds frequently depend on "the very words" preserved by means of written language. They are the worlds opened up by texts.

Notes

* We are deeply indebted to the Spencer Foundation for their financial support.

1. Bates, E., Masling, M. and Kintsch, W.
   1977 "Recognition memory for aspects of dialogue." *Program on Cognitive Fac-*

tors in Human Learning and Memory Report No. 69. Boulder, Colorado: University of Colorado, Institute for the Study of Intellectual Behavior.

2. Jacoby, L. "Personal communication", 1979.
3. Finnigan, R. "Literacy and literature." Mimeo, 1979.
4. Bierwisch, M. "Utterance, meaning and mental states." Mimeo, 1980.
5. Bierwisch, M. "Utterance, meaning and mental states." Mimeo, 1980.
6. Pea, R.D. "The development of negation in early child language." In D.R. Olson ed., *The Social Foundations of Language and Thought: Essays in Honor of Jerome S. Bruner.* New York: W.W. Norton, 1980, pp. 156–186.
7. Hildyard, A. 1973 "Children's comprehension of negation." Unpublished Master's thesis. Toronto: University of Toronto.
8. Hildyard, A. and Hidi, S. "Implicatives and implicatures of complex verbs: A developmental study." In preparation.

References

Bransford, J.D., Barclay, J.R. and Franks, J.J.
1972 "Sentence memory: A construction versus interpretive approach." *Cognitive Psychology* 3: 193–209.

Bowerman, M.
1977 "The structure and origin of semantic categories in the language learning child." Paper prepared for the Symposium on *Fundamentals of Symbolism.* New York: Wenner-Gren Foundation for Anthropological Research.

de Villiers, J.G. and Flushberg, H.B.T.
1975 "Some facts one simply cannot deny." *Journal of Child Language* 2: 279–286.

Donaldson, M.
1978 *Children's Minds.* Glasgow: Fontana/Collins.

Francis, H.
1975 *Language and Childhood: Form and Function in Language Learning.* London: Paul Elek.

Goody, J.
1977 *The Domestication of the Savage Mind.* Cambridge: Cambridge University Press.

Greenfield, P.
1972 "Oral and written language: The consequences for cognitive development in Africa, the United States, and England." *Language and Speech:* 169–178.

Greenfield, P. and Bruner, J.S.
1969 "Culture and cognitive growth." In D.A. Goslin, ed., *Handbook of Socialization: Theory and Research.* Chicago: Rand-McNally, pp. 633–657.

Grice, H.P.
1957 "Meaning." *Philosophical Review* 66:377–388.

1975 "Logic and conversation." In P. Cole & J.L. Morgan, eds., *Syntax and Semantics. Vol. 3: Speech Acts.* New York: Academic Press, pp. 41–58.

Harris, R.J. and Monaco, G.E.
1978 "The psychology of pragmatic implication: Information processing between the lines." *Journal of Experimental Psychology: General* 107: 1–22.

Havelock, E.
1976 *Prologue to Greek Literacy.* Toronto: Ontario Institute for Studies in Education Press.

Hildyard, A.
1979 "Children's production of inferences from oral texts." *Discourse Processes* 2:33–56.
Hildyard, A. and Olson, D.R.
1978 "Memory and inference in the comprehension of oral and written discourse." *Discourse Processes* 1: 91–117.
Hidi, S. and Hildyard, A.
1979 "Four-year-olds' understanding of pretend and forget: No evidence for propositional reasoning." *Journal of Child Language* 6: 493–510.
Jarvella, R.J.
1971 "Syntactic processing of connected speech." *Journal of Verbal Learning and Verbal Behavior* 10: 409–416.
Karttunen, L.
1971 "Implicative verbs." *Language* 47: 340–358.

1973 "Presuppositions of compound sentences." *Linguistic Inquiry* 4: 256–260.
Karttunen, L. and Peters, S.
1975 "Conventional implicature in Montague grammar." Presented at the First Annual Meeting of the Berkeley Linguistic Society, February 15, 1975, Berkeley, California.
Keenan, J., MacWhinney, B. and Mayhew, D.
1977 "Pragmatics in memory: A study of natural conversation." *Journal of Verbal Learning and Verbal Behavior,* 16 (5): 549–560.
Kintsch, W. and Bates, E.
1977 "Recognition memory for statements from a classroom lecture." *Journal of Experimental Psychology: Human Learning and Memory* 3: 150–168.
Kripke, S.A.
1972 "Naming and necessity." In D. Davidson and G. Harmon, eds., *The Semantics of Natural Language.* Dordrecht: Reidel, pp. 253–355; 763–769.
Lord, A.B.
1960 *The Singer of Tales.* (Harvard Studies in Comparative Literature, 24). Cambridge, Mass.: Harvard University Press.
Macnamara, J.
1972 "The cognitive basis of language learning in infants." *Psychological Review* 79: 1–13.
Macnamara, J., Baker, E. and Olson, C.E.
1976 "Four-year-olds' understanding of *pretend, forget* and *know:* Evidence for propositional operations." *Child Development* 47: 62–70.
Miller, G.A. and Johnson-Laird, P.N.
1976 *Language and Perception.* Cambridge: Cambridge University Press.
Nelson, K.
1974 "Concept, word and sentence: Interrelations in acquisition and development." *Psychological Review* 81: 267–285.
Olson, D.R.
1970 "Language and thought: Aspects of a cognitive theory of semantics." *Psychological Review* 71(4): 257–273.
1977 "From utterance to text: The bias of language in speech and writing." *Harvard Educational Review* 47: 257–281.
Oviatt, S.L.
1979 "Qualitative change in the language comprehension of 9–17 month old infants: An experimental approach." Unpublished doctoral dissertation. Toronto: University of Toronto.

Sachs, J.S.
1967 "Recognition memory for syntactic and semantic aspects of connected discourse." *Perception and Psychophysics* 2: 437–442.

Searle, J.
1975 "Indirect speech acts." In P. Cole and J. Morgan, eds., *Syntax and semantics, Volume 3: Speech Acts.* New York: Academic Press, pp. 59–82.

1979 *Expressions and Meaning: Studies in the Theory of Speech Acts.* Cambridge: Cambridge University Press.

Seleskovitch, D.
1978 *Interpreting for International Conferences: Problems of Language and Communication.* Washington: Pen and Booth.

Sinclair, J.M. and Coulthard, R.M.
1975 *Towards an Analysis of Discourse: The English used by Teachers and Pupils.* London: Oxford University Press.

Spark, M.
1963 *The Ballad of Peckham Rye.* New York: Penguin.

Strawson, P.F.
1952 *Introduction to Logical Theory.* London: Methuen.
The Globe and Mail. February 27, 1980.

van Fraassen, B.
1968 "Presupposition, implication and self reference." *Journal of Philosophy* 65: 132–152.

Volterra, V. and Antinucci, F.
1978 "Negation in child language: A pragmatic study." In E.O. Keenan, ed., *Studies in Developmental Pragmatics.* New York: Academic Press.

Wason, P.C.
1972 "In real life negatives are false." *Logique et Analyse* 57–58: 19–38.

1980 "The verification task and beyond." In D.R. Olson, ed., *The Social Foundations of Language and Thought: Essays in Honor of Jerome S. Bruner.* New York: Norton, pp. 28–46.

Wason, P.C. and Johnson-Laird, P.N.
1972 *The Psychology of Reasoning.* London: Batsford.

DANNY D. STEINBERG AND HELEN HARPER

Teaching written language as a first language to a deaf boy*

Abstract

This paper reports on a project to teach speech-based language and literacy to a profoundly deaf boy entirely by means of written language, without the mediation of speech or sign. The subject was a two year old American boy living in Hawaii. The child was taught to interpret written English by his family at home based on the guidance of the authors. He was 2 years 5 months old when teaching began.

The results show that after 15 months or less, the boy learned to interpret the meaning of 414 written words and 242 phrases and sentences and has begun to read simple books.

It is concluded that significant language knowledge can be acquired by deaf children solely on the basis of written language. Because written English is being learned by a deaf child who has no knowledge of its sound system, it is further concluded that written English may be acquired as a morpheme-based system similar to Chinese, despite its original sound-based design.

1. *Introduction*

As a group, the deaf have a low amount of speech-based language knowledge and literacy. ("Speech-based language" here refers to the language of hearing persons.) Research shows that the average reading level of deaf persons graduating from high school does not exceed that of hearing children in Grade 4 of elementary school (Wrightstone, Aronow and Moskowitz 1963; Lane and Baker 1974; and Furth 1966, 1971; Nakano 1970; Steinberg, Yamada and Takemoto 1977). An adequate degree of language knowledge particularly as it relates to the reading and writing of speech-based language is fundamental, if all deaf persons are to become independent and contributing members of society.

At present, in teaching language to the deaf, two basic approaches are used. One is the *Oral* approach which teaches language through the production of speech. The other is the *Manual* approach which teaches language through body signs. Teaching programs for the deaf use one of these approaches or a combination of the two. This latter combination approach, which is a relatively recent innovation, is called *Total Communication.*

Unquestionably, both of the basic approaches, oral and manual, have been effective in the teaching of language. Through the oral approach, deaf persons have learned to produce and understand speech, and through the manual approach, deaf persons have learned to produce and understand signs. However, because not all deaf persons respond to the oral approach, particularly those whose hearing impairment is great, some other means for providing them with speech-based language is needed. Then, too, some of the deaf who learn sign language also fail to acquire sufficient knowledge of ordinary language. One principal reason for this is that knowledge of sign language may not directly provide one with knowledge of speech-based language. The degree of correspondence with respect to syntax, in particular, may be very low especially where a natural sign language such as American Sign Language (ASL) is involved. For example, such important constructions as those which concern pronominalization (*The boy sang then he danced*), complementation (*The boy wants to go*), relativization (*The candy which the boy bought was sticky*), question formation (*Did the boy sing? Is the boy happy?*) and negation (*The boy did not sing. The boy is not happy.*) are treated very differently in English and ASL. It is because English and ASL are such distinct languages that knowing one provides no great aid in learning the other. While some recent sign-language systems have been designed to correspond more closely to the structure of speech-based language, e.g., *Signing Exact English* for English, it has not as yet been determined how beneficial both systems might be for the learning of speech-based language. Then, too, the signing community is not in agreement with respect to accepting such systems.

Concerning the combination of Total Communication approach, there is at present no clear evidence as to its effectiveness in the acquisition of speech-based language knowledge and literacy. However, because some learners may not respond well to the oral component of that approach and because there may be little direct transfer to speech-based language from the knowledge of sign language, some learners may not acquire a sufficient amount of speech-based language knowledge and literacy. To the extent that Total Communication programs involve a written language component, e.g., reading, such a situation may be ameliorated.

1.1 *Written language as a solution*

Given that a portion of the deaf population has problems in acquiring speech-based language and literacy through the mediation of speech or sign, it is proposed that such knowledge be acquired through the *direct* learning of speech-based written language.[1] The essential idea is that the basic written forms of a speech-based language, its words, phrases and sentences, be acquired through a direct association with objects, events, and situations in the environment. Then, just as hearing children learn language by associating the speech sounds which they hear with environmental experiences, deaf children would learn language in a similar way, but through an association of written forms with environmental experiences. Deaf children would, as a result, acquire essentially the same vocabulary and syntax of speech-based language as hearing children because, as linguists have long noted, in many written languages, such as English, virtually all the vocabulary and syntactic structures which appear in speech also appear in writing, e.g., pronominalization, question formation, passivization, complementation, etc. Differences which have been noted regarding syntax are more of a quantitative rather than qualitative nature, e.g., there is a greater demand in expository writing (but not conversational writing) for passive constructions but a lesser one for sentences ending in a preposition. Clearly, there is but one basic grammar operating in both mediums of expression. This being so, there is no reason not to regard written language as a complete language, much the same as that based on speech and sign, which also gives it the possibility of being acquired as a first language.[2]

In our view, written language should be taught to deaf children *in addition* to their receiving instruction in speech or sign. It is essential that all children be given the opportunity to learn speech and sign. The teaching of written language, however, would ensure that all children would have the opportunity to acquire a level of speech-based language and literacy that is sufficient for obtaining gainful employment in a highly developed technological society.

1.2 *Theoretical guiding considerations*

For the learning of written language by the deaf, four theoretical considerations serve as guides. These are that (1) the non- sound environment can provide a sufficient conceptual foundation for learning written language, (2) the understanding of written language provides the necessary foundation for the production of written language, (3) vocabulary is best acquired by meaningful whole word learning, and (4) syntax is best acquired by inductive learning. Each of these considerations is now discussed.

The non-sound environment provides a sufficient conceptual foundation

In order to deal best with this topic, let us first consider the situation for hearing persons in the acquisition of language. Before such persons learned language, speech sounds conveyed no ideas to them. Meaning had to be acquired. In considering how this might occur, it is clear that simply the hearing or saying of speech sounds is insufficient. For, no matter how many times one hears or says the speech sounds "neko," for example, one would not know that such sounds signal *cat* (in Japanese). What a learner requires is some other environmental experience that provides a clue to meaning. It is essential, therefore, that some object, situation, or event be experienced in conjunction with the speech sounds. Of course, once a certain amount of language is learned, the meaning of new words may be conveyed entirely through speech. Ultimately, however, the source of the meanings of the words used in such speech descriptions will be traced to some non-speech environmental experience that is essential to the formation of concepts.

Since deaf children experience the same non- sound environment as hearing children, they acquire similar concepts relating to that environment. (Only concepts based on sound, e.g., music, noise, bird calls, etc., are denied the deaf, just as visually based concepts are denied the blind.) These are the concepts that could then be associated with writing to provide meaning for that stimulus. Thus, the non-sound environment will provide a sufficient conceptual foundation for the deaf to learn written language. The medium of speech or sign is not essential to that process of acquisition.

Written language understanding provides the necessary foundation for production

Again, in order to deal best with this topic, let us consider first the situation for hearing persons. In acquiring language, hearing persons learn to understand speech before producing it, with the exception of a few words or phrases. Children are not able to utter words or sentences meaningfully until they first have had the opportunity to hear and understand the words and sentences which others have spoken. Interestingly, while the presence of the ability to utter the speech sounds of words may not indicate language knowledge (as in the case of parrots and children who merely imitate what they hear), the absence of that ability may not indicate a lack of language knowledge. Parents commonly observe and researchers on hearing children have found (Huttenlocher 1974; Sachs and Truswell 1976) that speech production lags behind speech. This is not to say, though, that other factors besides the requirement of understanding do not contribute to the lag in production. They do. For a production capacity is not exhibited immediately after understanding is acquired. Speech production also requires, for example, the development and training of motor skills so that the muscles affecting the speech articulators can be brought under intentional control.

The primacy of speech understanding is demonstrated very dramatically in hearing persons who have a defect in the capacity to produce speech. Those with cerebral palsy, for example, may understand everything that is spoken to them yet be unable to formulate an utterance themselves. One of the authors had the opportunity to become intimately involved with such a case in Japan, that of a three year old mute-hearing girl (Steinberg and Chen 1980). This girl could understand what was said to her and was normal in all respects except the ability to produce speech. She was even taught to read. Such cases clearly illustrate that language learning as it relates to speech may occur without speech production.

As far as the deaf child learning written language is concerned, we would expect a similar dependence of production on understanding. In this case, however, production would consist of the perceptual-motor skill of writing while understanding would consist of the meaningful interpretation of writing. Because the motor skill which is needed to control a writing implement takes longer to develop in children than the motor skill required for speech, a greater lag in writing production may be expected as compared to speech production. This is unfortunate, for deaf children could benefit from such a means of production during their early years.

Vocabulary acquisition: Meaningful whole word learning

Ideally, written language should be learned in the same natural manner as hearing children learn spoken language. That is, children learn it at home by being exposed to users of the language. They should not have to be given special language instruction, and their parents should not have to receive special education on language teaching. Unfortunately, because it is not practical for written language to be used as a means of communication around the home, deaf children will not have the opportunity to learn that way. That being the case, it is necessary to introduce some degree of artificiality into the learning situation. Naturalness, however, should be striven for as much as possible so that language learning occurs incidentally, through the course of everyday activities. The teaching of vocabulary and syntax will be considered in that light.

Once a deaf child begins to acquire concepts, that child is ready to acquire the written labels for those concepts. While one could argue that the teaching of phrases and sentences should occur prior to the teaching of individual words, the position which will be taken here is that, in general, individual words should be taught first. It seems simpler for a child to learn single words which relate to concrete objects than to learn whole phrases and sentences which relate to entire events or situations. For, not only are phrases and sentences more difficult to remember because of length, but determining their meaning may be an extremely complex task, particularly if the meanings of component words are not known. Phrases and sentences may be introduced for learning just as soon as a stock of single words adequate for their construction (principally nouns, verbs, and adjectives) is learned.

Given that the goal is first to teach individual words, the question arises as to what the best method might be. Four basic methods are possible in this regard: (1) Teach whole words only; (2) Teach a number of whole words, then teach letter discrimination; (3) Teach a particular whole word and then the discrimination of its component letters; and (4) Teach letter discrimination, then teach whole words. It will be argued here that the first of these methods, teaching only whole words, is the best and should be adopted. The other methods are listed in descending order of optimality. Two reasons are offered for this position, naturalness and ease of learning.

Naturalness

When hearing children learn speech words, they learn them as wholes; e.g., the word *cat* is pronounced as a whole for the child, i.e., /kæt/. The child is never explicitly taught the component sounds of words, viz., phonemes or syllables. Parents do not run through inventories of phonemes or syllables and they do not train their children on those sounds. Rather, they say whole words like *cat*, *cats*, *grandma*, *push*, *pushed*, and *strong* and leave it to the children to make the segmentation on their own, through an analytical process that is traditionally termed "induction." Morphemes are discovered in a similar fashion. Parents do not tell their children that in making plurals and possessives, for example, the sounds /s/, /z/, and /ɨz/ are used: /s/ being used for words ending in unvoiced consonants, e.g., *cats*, *Rick's*; /z/ for words ending in voiced consonant or vowel, e.g., *dogs, toes, Bob's;* and /ɨz/ for words ending in a sibilant, e.g., *watches*, *Chris's*. The fact that children produce words which they have never heard before, such as *mouses*, *comed*, and *breaked* is evidence that they learn by themselves to segment and substitute sounds. Since evidence shows that the analytical and conceptualization processes of hearing-impaired children do not differ from those of hearing children (Furth 1971), deaf children may be expected to be able to distinguish the shapes of the individual letters of the alphabet and to identify the morpheme components of words in the course of learning whole written words, according to the same analytical process. As a matter of fact, the research with deaf children which will be reported on later in this paper demonstrates that deaf children may learn to read without any prior alphabet training. There is no need, therefore, to teach letters to deaf children. The letters will be learned by induction through the learning of written words. This is an important consideration because, as the next section shows, learning to identify individual letters by direct instruction is not easy for children to do.

Ease of learning

Although a word is longer and more complex than any one of its individual component parts, research evidence on the learning of reading indicates that the learning of whole words is easier than that of letters. In an experiment with hearing American nursery school children, it was found that words were learned twice as fast as letters, e.g., the words *dollar*, *old*, and *chase* were learned faster than the letters *c, t,* and *n* (Steinberg 1978; Steinberg, Kushimoto, Tatara, and Orisaka 1979). Similar results are found for Japanese nursery school children where complex Chinese characters representing words, e.g., 海 (*umi*: sea) and 買う (*kau*: buy) were also much faster to learn than less complex *kana* symbols such as い (/ī/ as in *meet*) and へ (/he/ as in *hello*), which represent syllables which are largely without meaning (Steinberg and Yamada 1978–9; Steinberg, Yamada, Nakano, Hirakawa, and Kanemoto 1977). In an interesting variation of these basic experiments, a different group of children was presented the same written items but the speech names for the words were reversed with the letters or syllables. Thus, for example, written *a* was called "dollar," and written *dollar* was called "a," in the English experiment. In the Japanese experiment, the Chinese character 海 was called "he" (no meaning) and the kana was called "umi" (sea), for example. The results in both experiments were similar, the writing form which was called by a word speech name was learned twice as fast as that called by a letter or syllable speech name. These findings demonstrate that the type of writing script and its degree of complexity play only a minor role in learning. Rather, what is important is what is presented along with the script. If what is presented is something meaningful, like a speech word, the item will be learned quickly. If it is not meaningful, like the name of a letter or syllable, the item will be learned slowly. In applying this principle to the situation of deaf children where the children do not have knowledge of meaningful words, a more primary meaningful stimulus such as an object or a picture of an object should be presented. Thus, if a written word may be associated with a cookie, a chair, or a picture of a dog, the child will not experience great difficulty in learning the written items. To the extent that the associated stimulus is not very meaningful, a scratch on a table perhaps, the written word will be much more difficult to learn.

Insofar as the introduction of abstract words is concerned, no special principles need be followed. Just as the hearing child learns the meaning of abstract words by first learning concrete words, so, too, will the deaf child acquire abstract words in the same way. Adults intuitively know when and how to introduce abstract words. They do not need to be told to introduce concrete words first. Then, too, there is ample research evidence which shows that the language which parents use when speaking to their children is selected to assist language learning. In the initial stages of language learning, parents generally talk about what is happening in the immediate environment and not about abstract remote objects and events (Slobin 1975; Phillips 1973). The speech they use is highly simplified, typically consisting of short simple sentences (Snow 1972; Garnica 1977) and a simple and restricted vocabulary (Seitz and Stewart 1975). Repetition and rephrasing is also very common (Snow 1972; Kobashigawa 1969; Brown and Bellugi 1964). There is good reason to suppose, therefore, that the intuitive sense which parents employ for the selection of language items in speech will also be used for language items in writing.

Abstract words should be learned through context, which is the way hearing children learn such words. Such words as *idea*, *pretty*, *like*, *wish*, *because*, and *but* are best learned in the context of environmental experience. They cannot be explained adequately. Furthermore, the language that is used in explaining the meaning of such words is not likely to be understood by a person who is just learning language. Thus, a necessary condition for learning abstract words is that they be used in a relevant environmental context. A teaching program should make an effort to provide such a condition for learning.

Syntax acquisition: Inductive learning

Just as hearing children learn the syntax of speech-based language without being taught, through the exposure to phrases and sentences in a meaningful context, so, too, may we expect deaf children to learn the syntax of written language in the same way. Parents of hearing children do not instruct their children on syntactic rules. Rules about pronominalization, complementation, and relative clauses, for example, are learned by children on their own. Parents do not present such sentences as 1. *John sang and then danced*, 2. *John sang and then he danced*, and 3. *John sang and then John danced*, and tell their children something like. "Now, Mary, when you have conjoined sentences and the subject of the first sentence is identical and refers to the same entity as the subject of the second sentence, you may, optionally, delete or pronominalize the subject of the second sentence."[3] Such an attempt to teach syntactic rules directly to children (in the rare instance that a parent would be able to formulate such a rule!) would be ridiculous. For such explanations would not be understood, even if the simplest of language were used. Understanding would fail for three main reasons: 1. the syntax of the sentences which comprise the explanation would be largely unknown, as would their interrelations; 2. a relatively high level of intellectual maturity is required, since what is being discussed is highly abstract; and 3. the meaning of abstract words and metalinguistic terms such as *conjoined*, *subject*, *sentence*, *optional*, and *pronominalize* must be known, as must any simplified equivalents of these concepts. Only advanced speakers of a language with a mature abstract intellectual capacity could benefit from grammatical explanations. Since hearing children could not learn the syntax of their language in this way, yet they do learn most of the syntax of their language before reaching kindergarten age (Slobin 1979; de Villiers and de Villiers 1978), clearly, they are able to do so through their own process of analysis. As long as children are exposed to phrases and sentences along with meaningful environmental stimuli, they will naturally search for regularities and similarities in the language, formulating rules which underlie those data. That being the case, in "teaching" syntax to deaf children, instructors should not attempt to offer explanations. Rather, what they should do is to provide adequate exposure to language and environmental stimuli in as natural and interesting a way as possible such that children have the opportunity to learn by themselves, through induction.

1.3 *Purpose of this study*

In order to apply the above theoretical framework to the actual teaching of written language to deaf children, a teaching program was formulated and introduced to a deaf child. The remainder of this paper will be concerned with describing the results of that endeavor.

2. *Method*

2.1 *The subject*

The subject is an American boy named Konrad,[4] who was 2 years 5 months when the program began. He is congenitally deaf, having over 90 db loss in his better ear. Both of Konrad's parents are also deaf. They communicate with one another through American Sign Language (ASL). Konrad's father knows ASL and some written English while Konrad's mother, who was raised in Japan, learned ASL after her arrival in America about five years ago. She understands no spoken English and very little written English. Konrad is taught English mainly by his paternal grandmother. She is hearing and lives together with them. Her native language is English and she knows Japanese. Details on the background of the subject and his family is summarized in Table 1. It might be noted that the family volunteered to participate in the project. They received no remuneration or other material inducements.

Table 1. Subject and family characteristics

	Konrad
Sex	M
Age at Program Beginning	2 yr. 5 mo.
Hearing Loss in Better Ear	Over 90 db
Hearing Loss Onset	Congenital
Etiology	Unknown
Birthplace	U. S. A.
Ethnicity	Japanese
Hearing	
– Father	No
– Mother	No
– Grandmother	Yes
Education	
– Father	Intermediate School for the Deaf
– Mother	Intermediate School for the Deaf
– Grandmother	Elementary
Occupation	
– Father	Sewage Worker
– Mother	Homemaker
– Grandmother	Homemaker
Language Knowledge	
– Father: English speech	No
American Sign Language	Yes
– Mother: English speech	No
American Sign Language	Yes
– Grandmother: English language	Yes
American Sign Language	Some

2.2 *Procedure*

A four phase teaching program (described in the next section) was introduced to the family by the authors at weekly and monthly meetings. The purpose of the meetings was to provide and demonstrate teaching activities, to explain the goals of the research, to receive feedback, and to guide the adults in their endeavors. Home visits to the family were made by the writer and assistants for the purpose of determining the workability of the teaching activities, of verifying the child's progress, and for filming their achievement. All teaching, however, was done by the family.

The parents kept records of the child's progress, listing all new items learned (words, phrases, and sentences). They were also encouraged to keep a diary. A written word, phrase, or sentence was considered learned if, when the written item was shown to the child, the child was able to indicate its meaning through some relevant behavior. This could be done by pointing to objects or pictures, by using gestures, or through any other behavioral means. Speech and sign language were accepted if it had already been established that the meaning of the items in those mediums was known. So as to guard against correct responses being obtained by chance, the child was required to give a correct response to the target item on two different occasions, with other written items being presented between the two occasions.

2.3 *The teaching program*

The deaf child may be systematically taught written language on the basis of a four phase system which has been formulated to embody the learning principles and ideas which have been discussed previously. The four phases of the teaching system are: 1. word familiarization, 2. word identification, 3. phrase and sentence identification, and 4. text interpreting. Each phase is ordered in such a way that a preceding phase serves as a prerequisite for the succeeding one, although prior phases may be continued along with the succeeding phases. Games and activities are designed for each of the phases. The program can be applied by parents in the home or by teachers at school.

There are two teaching instructions which are common to all phases. One concerns speaking and signing. Whenever a written word, phrase, or a sentence is presented to the child, it should be spoken aloud or signed as well. In this way, the child may benefit from any residual hearing and can learn signs. The other instruction concerns pointing to written items. Whenever possible, the instructor should point to the written words in a left to right fashion (underneath the word, so as not to block it). In this way, children will get used to the idea that words are to be perceived in that direction. The children, too, should be encouraged to point in a similar fashion.

In the description which follows for each of the phases, there is a specification of aims, some illustrative activities, and an indication of duration.

2.3.1 Phase 1: word familiarization

The purpose of this phase is to acquaint the child with the forms of written words and to make the child aware that different written words relate to different objects. The child is not taught, however, which particular written word is associated with which particular object. That learning is reserved for the next phase – word identification.

As a first step, words are written on cards and are attached to familiar objects or pictures in all the rooms that the child frequents. The cards are placed at the child's eye level wherever possible. The instructor points to the object, e.g., *television*, and then points to the written word while saying or signing what is written on each card. In this way, the child comes to realize that different written words are associated with different objects. Just seeing cards on an incidental basis will aid the child in learning to identify written words on his or her own.

In conjunction with the word cards around the room, games may be played. The instructor may write the name of a word on a separate card, e.g., *refrigerator*, give it to the child, and, without indicating what is written on it, require the child to find which other card in the room matches it. This task does not require that the child memorize the written word, but only compare two written forms, both of which are present. By doing this, the child learns to inspect written words and look for their differentiating features.

Word familiarization games and activities should be continued until the child can identify a written word without the presence of any clue. (This feat is called identification and is described in detail in the next phase.) The length of time required will generally depend on the age of the child. A one year old may require a number of weeks before being able to identify a first word, while a two or three year old might need only a week or less. Individual differences are to be expected, as with hearing children in language learning.

2.3.2 Phase 2: word identification

In this phase, the child learns which particular written words are associated with which particular objects. The difference between this phase and the preceding one is that this one requires the use of long-term memory. Here the child must store a particular written configuration and remember what particular object it represents. No clues are given as in the familiarization phase.

In one activity, some word cards that had been placed on objects in a room are removed. The child is then required to replace the cards on the appropriate objects. (A piece of transparent tape is attached to the card.) In another activity for older children, a play-store game, objects for sale require appropriate word cards as money for their purchase, with child and instructor taking turns in the role of shopper and storekeeper.

Once the child begins to identify the written words for objects around the room, most of which will be nouns, then other types of entities are identified, particularly actions, qualities, and states, e.g., the actions (*run*, *kick*, *give*), the colors (*red*, *yellow*), and the states (*happy*, *cold*). In this way verbs and adjectives are introduced. Function words such as prepositions, conjunctions, and articles would not be introduced. They would appear only in the context of phrases and sentences, in the next phase.

Since there is virtually no end to acquiring vocabulary, this phase is continued even after phrases and sentences are introduced. However, phrases and sentences may be introduced when the child has acquired some nouns, verbs, adjectives, or adverbs, e.g., *car* and *red*, so that phrases or sentences can be formed with them, e.g., *the red car*.

2.3.3 Phase 3: phrase and sentence identification

This phase is similar to the preceding one of word identification, except that larger linguistic units are dealt with. The goal is for the child to read the largest basic linguistic unit, the sentence, of which words and phrases are components. As much as possible, phrases and sentences are to be composed of the single words that had already been learned, since too many unknown words may cause frustration and make learning difficult.

Phrases such as the *red car*, and sentences such as *Diana fell*, could be introduced as soon as some of the main component individual words are learned. It is best not to create phrases and sentences for their own sake, however, but to make them fit the events and situations which occur in the immediate environment. *Diana fell* would be of great interest if it indeed were the case the Diana was a person known to the child and the child had observed that she fell.

Phrases and sentences should include all types of words, including the functional morphemes such as prepositions, inflections, and articles. Thus, if *The dogs are barking* is the appropriate sentence, it should not be reduced to *Dog bark*. The presence of such function items provides the opportunity for their learning. The event or situation in the environment will provide the child with the necessary conceptual basis for determining their meanings. The teaching of words, phrases, and sentences, however, should be continued even when the next phase of text interpreting is introduced. This is necessary in order to provide the child with a variety of language, for books can cover only a limited number of life situations.

2.3.4 Phase 4: text interpreting

Text involves the largest meaningful written linguistic unit, consisting as it does of a sequence of two or more sentences that are semantically and syntactically related to one another. (The prior phase dealt only with sentences in isolation.) Learning to interpret text may be the most interesting of all activities for the child, since there is an excitement which a story can generate that isolated words, phrases, and sentences cannot. It is the purpose of this phase to provide the child with the knowledge and skill that will enable him or her to interpret text fluently.

Just when text teaching should be introduced on a serious basis is difficult to say. Some knowledge of words, phrases, and sentences is certainly required so that proceeding through a book is made casy, but what this amount should be is difficult to determine. We would estimate that 50 words and 20 phrases and sentences might suffice, depending on the simplicity of the items in the book. In addition, the child should have reached the stage where he is beginning to understand novel sentences that involve a substitution of word classes. Thus, given that a child has learned the meaning of *boy* and of *The girl jumped*, the child should be able to comprehend *The boy jumped* without ever having seen this sentence before. Until such a level of knowledge is attained, text interpreting might be too difficult a task.

Books for the child can be custom-made or store-bought. Each has its advantages. The custom-made book can be composed directly of vocabulary which a child knows. Then, too, the child can help in its making. On the other hand, while the store-bought book may not have a completely appropriate vocabulary or syntax, or may deal with unfamiliar concepts, such books are very attractive and do stimulate and broaden a child's interest. Clearly, both types of books are valuable and worth using.

In teaching text, the instructor should first survey the book, so that new vocabulary items might be explained beforehand where possible. In covering the text, the instructor should point to the text sentence by sentence, trying to indicate, as they go along, the ideas involved by referring to the illustrations. The child should then be encouraged to do the reading on his own, also pointing as he goes.

Activities which do not involve books but involve text may also be introduced. For example, stories with as few as two or three sentences may be composed, e.g., Story A: 1. *Sara dropped the egg*. 2. *It landed on the dog*, or Story B: 1. *Harry was riding a bicycle*. 2. *He hit a rock*. 3. *The bicycle turned over*. Each sentence of a story may be written on a card, along with a corresponding picture. One activity could be for children to arrive at the order of sentences that forms the story. The pictures on the cards could later be removed as the child comes to understand the meaning of the sentences. Such an activity fosters in the children an awareness of order and the semantic and syntactic interrelations of sentences.

As the child progresses linguistically and intellectually, so too should such advancement be reflected in the books he/she is given. Selections should be carefully made for the child until such time as he/she is able to make suitable selections on his/her own. It should be noted that although this phase is concerned with the teaching of text from books, it is *not* recommended that the introduction of books wait until this phase is reached. The child can enjoy and learn much about books long before the serious teaching of content is begun.

3. *Results*

The overall results are as follows:

Number of single words learned	414
Number of phrases and sentences learned	242
Total number of items	656
Age at inception of instruction	2 years 5 months
Duration of instruction	15 months
Average daily instruction	30 minutes

Thus, we see that to date Konrad has learned a total of 656 items, of which 414 were single words and 242 were phrases and sentences. A summary of the words, phrases, and sentences which were learned according to month and

Table 2. Results for Konrad: Summary of words, phrases, and sentences learned

Month	Noun	Word class Verb	Adj.	Other	Total words	Total phrases & sentences	Total all items
1	54	5	11	0	70	10	80
2	24	7	2	2	35	19	54
3	37	6	11	13	67	30	97
4	22	14	4	5	45	23	68
5	44	12	9	1	66	37	103
6							
7	13	5	4	1	23	1	24
8	9	5	1	3	18	21	39
9	18	5	1	2	26	20	46
10	9	0	1	1	11	11	22
11						17	17
12	11	3	2	2	18	10	28
13	9	6	0	2	17	13	30
14	8	2	1	1	12	15	27
15	3	1	2	0	6	15	21
Total	261	71	49	33	414	242	656
Percent	63.04	17.15	11.84	7.97	100.00		

items which Konrad has learned is shown in Tables 3 and 4. The items are listed exactly as they were written for the child. (The high frequency of non-

Table 3. Results for Konrad: Listing of particular words learned

Month	Noun	Verb	Adjective	Other	Total
1	airplane, apple, ball, banana, basketball, bath, bear, bed, bell, bird, boat, bus, Calvin, car, chair, chopstick, cup, doll, drum, ear, Eiko [mother], elephant, eye, flower, fork, football, frog, hair, house, Jo-Ann, Konrad, Ken [father], lion, Lori-Ann, milk, monkey, mountain, mouth, nose, orange, rice, Ritsu [grandmother], room, Scott, soap, spoon, table, telephone, tree, tricycle, turtle, wall, window, xylophone	jump, kick, pedal, run, walk	big, black, blue, brown, green, orange, pink, purple, red, white, yellow		70
2	balloon, bat, beach, birthday, book, bucket, cake, candles, cow, crayon, duck, eagle, giraffe, grandmother, helicopter, milk, newspaper, picture, present, shell, slipper, train, umbrella, vase	ate, blow, buy, go, play, stop, swim	cold, round	no, yes	35
3	alligator, baby, basket, boy, butterfly, candies, cap, catsup, corn, crab, crackers, doctor, eel, flour, girl, jello, kangaroo, lobster, mirror, morning, mosquito, night, octopus, onion, pan, pencil, pillow, potato, raisins, salt, *Scissor, tissue, toilet, towel, whale, worm, zoo	help, laugh, learn, put, shower, teach	fat, good, heavy, hot, light, soft, thin, wet, fast, slow	eight, eleven, everyday, five, four, nine, one, seven, six, ten, three, twelve, two	67

4	bank, box, button, cat, children, church, clothes, cousin, dinner, dishes, friend, fun, Gay, hat, lizard, owl, party, rain, sumo, teeth, toothpaste, we	bark, bring, brush, burn, catch, drink, eat, exercise, get, grow, heard, help, let's, wash	afraid, dark, lazy, tired	sometimes, *To-day, *to-gether, *tomorro, *Yesterday	45
5	back, beans, bee, bread, butter, eye, glass, finger, floor, gold, hand, honey, leg, letters, life, light, mailman, money, moon, motorcycle, necklace, needle, noise, park, policeman, pounds, riding, sand, sea, seal, seed, sky, smoke, spider, stamps, star, steps, stomach, sun, tea, they, whispers, wind, wing, zipper	buzz, flies, follow, save, scratch, shake, sweep, throw, weigh, win, wink, write	cheery, some, sharp, short, sick, strong, stuck,	up	*etc
7	Disney, Donald Duck, happiness, joy, ladder, *Matches, Mickey Mouse, Pluto the dog, puppy, Santa Claus, straw, trampoline, world	climb, dare, decorate, shivers, visited	colorful, spooky, wonderful, wooden	away	23
8	animals, August, Japan, she, trip, what, who, whom, wish	bought, enjoyed, invite, rode, took	beautiful	how, when, why	18
9	batter, Carne, glove, Halloween, he, him, Jack o' Lantern, laundry, lemonade, mango, mask, pitcher, raincoat, rubbish, sink, treat, trick, yard	could, hit, made, need, trim	naughty	only, so	26

Table 3. *(continued)*

Month	Noun	Verb	Adjective	Other	Total
10	*Chameleon, *Flag, Friday, insects, Monday, *Pole, Saturday, Sunday, tails		American	many	11
12	accident, alphabet, damage, eve, *Fireworks, monkey, myself, promise, sentences, street, watch	heard, study, works	dangerous, poor	across, slightly	18
13	fingers, gasoline, judo, legs, oil, squeegee, station, toes, Valentine	bought, hop, practices, received, skip, wipe		left, right	17
14	bakery, city, family, fruits, meat, playmate, vegetables, week	stayed, trim	whole	each	12
15	bicycle, parrakeet, speech	imitate	frightened, scared		6
Total					414

* Indicates deviant spelling, capitalization, or syntax.

Table 4. Results for Konrad: Listing of particular phrases & sentences learned

Month	Phrases	Sentences	Total
1	big bear, brown monkey, green frog, little bear, yellow lion	*how old are you?, *kick the ball, *open the door, *pedal the tricycle, *water the plant	10
2	old shoes	*balloon is round, *birds are flying, *Cows gives milk, *Father blow the balloon, *Father goes to work, *Grandmother birthday, *Grandmother Ritsu open the present, Konrad ate the cake, *Konrad blow the candles, *Konrad color the picture with crayon, *Konrad play with Scott, Konrad saw the cow, Konrad swam and the water was cold, Konrad went to the beach, Konrad will go to school, *Mother buy crayon for Konrad, Mother is home, Where is your slipper?	19
3	Apricot Nector, brown sugar, Good bye, Good morning, Good night, Guava jam, pineapple juice, thank you, Vienna sausage	*alligator will bite, *butterfly is pretty, *everyday I take a bath, Father colored the eggs, *help me, How many cups are there?, *Kangaroo hops, *Konrad laugh, Konrad put flowers for grand father, *Konrad put the eggs in yellow basket, Konrad saw the rabbit and chicks, *Konrad sleep in big bed, Konrad went to Ala Moana shopping center, Konrad went to the book store, Konrad went to the doctor, May I have the napkin, My pillow is soft, *Pick up, *sit down, *stand up, *whale is big	30
4		Father and Konrad swam in the pool, Grandmother goes to church, *I am afraid of dark, I drink my milk, I had fun, I help mother wash the dishes, I like to learn, I played with the children, I wash my face, *Konrad brush his teeth, *Konrad catch the ball, Konrad gave flowers to Grandmother, *Konrad has cat bank, *Konrad has new hearing aid, Konrad heard the airplane, Konrad saw a black cat, *Konrad went to Cousin Gay birthday party, Lets eat, rain makes flowers grow, Scott is my friend and my cousin, *sometimes I get lazy, We all had dinner together on Mother's day, *where is the owl?	23
5	bubble gum, Post Office	*At night Konrad see's moon & stars, *bees buzz buzz, *Cat has wiskers, Father is strong, *Grandmother has eye glass on, *I am afraid of spider,	37

Table 4 (*continued*)

Month	Phrases	Sentences	Total
		I am very hungry, I blow my bubble gum, I have big blue buttons, I have ten fingers, I help mother sweep the floor, *I like to play on the sand, I saw the smoke, I walk up the steps, *I went to the sea life park, *honey is sweet, Konrad can wink, Konrad is lonesome, *Konrad plant the bean seed, *Konrad saw the policeman riding motorcycle, Konrad spread butter on bread, Konrad was sick, *Konrad weigh 25 pounds, Konrad will ride the school bus, Konrad will save money, *Mother has gold necklace, *Mother went to Post Office to buy stamp, *Mail man brings letter for us, Scott and Lori went to Kona on the big airplane, *sometimes I feel sad, *sometime my zipper get stuck, The airplane flies up in the sky, The sun gives light, The wind blows in my window, They are growing	
7	shopping center		1
8	All my cousins	*Did you enjoyed the trip?, Grandmother bought (The Eye Book) for me, How many candles are you going to put on your cake?, How old are you going to be?, I am going to be 3 years old, *I am going to put 3 candles & I will blow, I rode on the big airplane, *I rode on the train it was fun, I took a trip to Japan, I went to Ueno Park, I wish to learn, Konrad when is your birthday?, Konrad where did you go?, My birthday is August 12, 1976, She will teach me how to read, There I saw all kinds of animals and beautiful birds, *Whom do you like to invite for your happy birthday party, *Would you like to have birthday cake?, Yes I did, *yes I like to have a cake	21
9	washing machine	Father and I played baseball, *Father trim the mango tree, *Father will carve a Pumpkin and will make it to Jack O Lantern, *Good Children don't throw things, He was a pitcher, I could hit the ball, *I help him pick all the rubbish, I need a raincoat when it rains, I was the batter, I will wear a mask, *It almost Halloween, It was a hot day so we made lemonade, *Konrad always throw things on the floor, *Mother wash dishes in the sink, Mother will buy me a raincoat, Only naughty children	20

		throw things on the floor, *We have lemon tree in our yard, *When my clothes get dirty Mother laundry in Washing machine, *With my Cousin Loriann, Scott and I will go treat or trick to house to house	
10	50 stars, *13 strips	I don't go to school Saturday and Sunday, I go to school Monday thru Friday, *I see American Flag on the Pole, Our flag has 50 stars and 13 stripes, *The color of our Flag is red white and blue, *They eats insects, They have long tails, *They turn colors green to brown and brown to green, *We have many chemeleon in our yard	11
11		*A friend gave me a bubbles, Father climb up the ladder, *For Xmas Grandma gave me trampoline and miniture wooden train, *Dont dare play with matches, *I blow the bubbles, I drink my juice with the straw, *I have Xmas tree at home, *I help decorate the tree, *I would like very much to go to Wonderful World of Disney, *My balloon fly away, *My cousin Scott has puppy dog, The train is very colorful, There I will be able to see Mickey Mouse, Donald Duck and even Pluto the dog. *When I am afraid I shivers, *When it get real dark it spooky, *Xmas is joy and happiness for me, *I visited the Santa Claus at shopping center	17
12	Happy New Year	Father had an accident poor father, *he bang his car into a pole, I can write my name myself, *I have learn all my alphabet by sign, I promise to study and try to learn more words and sentences, *It is the year of Monkey, *It is very dangerous when you dont watch even going across the street, *on New eve I watch and heard the fire works, *The car is sighty damage	10
13		*Althogether I have ten fingers, *Althogether I have ten toes, Father bought gasoline and oil at the gas station, *Father practice judo, I have five fingers on my left hand, I have five fingers on my right hand, * I have five toes on my left feet, *I have five toes on my right feet, I have two legs, I received Valentine cards from my friends, *I will like to ride the	13

Table 4 (*continued*)

Month	Phrases	Sentences	Total
		pony on the Merry Go round, *The boy wipe the car window with the squeegee, *With my two legs I could hop, skip walk and run	
14	barber shop, drug store, pet shop	*At the shopping center there are drug store, bank bakery, shoe store, Pet Shop barber Shop and many others, *From school we went to the zoo on city bus, I also went to the shopping center, I didn't go to school one whole week, *I go to the barber shop to have my hair trim, I stayed home, *I was lonesome I didn't have no playmate, *I went to the super Market with my family, It was spring vacation, *Mother bought meat Vegetables, and some fruits, *They are four seasons in each year, Winter, spring, summer and autumn	15
15	bird cage, front tooth, *Ten Apples on Top	Are You My Mother?, Go dog go, He lost his front tooth, He was hurt, *I could read this book fairly well with sign, I like to imitate others, I received 3 books from Dr. Danny Steinberg, I was frightened, I will work hard and try to learn to read in speech, My cousin Scott fell from his bicycle, *My friend gave me a parrakeet, The big dog came near me	15
Total			242

* Indicates deviant spelling, capitalization or syntax.

the grammatical class of words is shown in Table 2. A listing of all of the standard English usage accurately reflects the usage of English in the family.) Separate tables are shown for words and for phrases and sentences. A breakdown is provided by month, and, for the words, by grammatical class. As might be expected, the items learned at a particular time often involve a similar theme. For example, many of Konrad's items in Month 2 center around a birthday celebration, e.g., *balloon*, *birthday*, *cake*, *candles*, and *blow* (in

Table 5. Books interpreted by Konrad with representative text

Month	Title	Representative Text
10	*The Cat in the Hat Dictionary* P. D. Eastman	candy. Chocolate candy. good. Good dog. Bad dog.
11	*Hop On Pop* Dr. Seuss	UP PUP. Pup is up. MOUSE MOUSE. Mouse, on house.
	Let's Eat Gyo Fujikawa	hamburger. apple. drumstick. Can you eat with chopsticks?
12–13	*Ten Apples Up on Top!* Theo. Le Sieg	Seven apples up on top! I am so good they will not drop.
	The Bike Lesson Stan & Jan Berenstain	See? This is what you should not do. Now let this be a lesson to you.
	The Spooky Old Tree Stan & Jan Berenstain	A spooky old tree. Do they dare go into that spooky old tree?
13–14	*I'll Teach My Dog 100 Words* Michael Frith	The first six words I'll teach my pup are *dig a hole* and *fill it up*!
	The Big Honey Hunt Stan & Jan Berenstain	We ate our honey. We ate a lot. Now we have no honey in our honey pot.
	The Eye Book Theo. Le Sieg	My eyes. His eyes. I see him. He sees me.
	Go Dog Go! P. D. Eastman	Big dog. Little dog. A dog over the water. A dog under the water.
15	*Will You Please Go Away Now, Marvin K. Mooney* Dr. Seuss	Just go. Go go. I don't care how. You can go by foot. You can go by cow. Marvin K. Mooney will you please go now.

Note: All books are published by Random House Inc. in their Beginner Books or Bright and Early Books series, with the exception of *Let's eat* which is published by Zokeisha, Japan.

Table 3) and *Grandmother birthday*, *balloon is round*, *Konrad blow the candles*, and *Konrad ate the cake* (in Table 4).

Insofar as Phase 4 – text interpreting – is concerned, Konrad read his first book 10 months after the program began. These first books, it should be noted, were very simple, generally consisting of single words with a few phrases and sentences. Books with more complex text were introduced as time went on. A list of books and some of the representative text is shown in Table 5 for Konrad. Konrad has truly acquired a love of books. He enjoys visiting libraries and bookstores and he enjoys reading his own books alone at home. It is expected that he will acquire a significant amount of written language on his own in this way.

The learning of written language may have indirectly stimulated interest in sign language for Konrad. Whereas he knew only 15 signs when the program began, he has now become as knowledgeable in sign as he has in written language. (At the time that the project began, the parents did not attempt to teach and expose Konrad to sign language. Apparently, they had been advised against its use by some deaf educators.) At the encouragement of these authors, his parents taught him the signs for the words he was learning through writing. As it has turned out, it is apparent that sign language and written language can be used to assist in the acquisition of the one from the other. It is interesting to note that Konrad's mother who is from Japan and who knew little English (written or spoken) when the program began, has learned written English language along with Konrad. It is reported that Konrad learns more quickly than his mother and sometimes assists in teaching her items!

In general, the speed of acquisition on the part of Konrad has increased with cumulated learning. Now he can remember a word with just one or two presentations, whereas at the beginning stages of the project such items required much more exposure. Such a phenomenon is undoubtedly similar to the accelerating rate of acquisition in speech for hearing children. New speech words are learned rapidly once the basic principle that writing symbolizes meaning and a stock of words have been learned.

4. *Conclusions*

The results of this study show that significant language knowledge can be acquired by a deaf child directly through the medium of writing. Undoubtedly, a greater amount of language knowledge could have been learned had more time been devoted to the child, since the average of 30 minutes daily which the child received is far less exposure than he needs and could benefit from. A nursery school program could provide the necessary exposure and allow the child to learn more.

The written language teaching program is one that is particularly suitable for application by parents of young deaf children in the home. During their child's formative early years at home, parents could provide written language input and a substantial amount of written language knowledge could be acquired in this way. In such cases where written language knowledge is acquired but speech and sign-based language is not, written language would serve as the child's first language.

Because Konrad began to acquire sign language along with written language after he began to acquire written language, this case cannot be considered a pure test of the concept of a written language as a first language. However, other research in progress with other children both in the U.S. and Japan (Steinberg, Harada, Tashiro, and Yamada 1982) supports the validity of that conception.

The results also show that deaf children who have no awareness of speech can learn to interpret writing even when the writing is based on a system that has its origin in speech units such as the phoneme or syllable. What the deaf subjects, particularly the English learners, have done is to treat those systems as a morpheme-based system such as Chinese. The morpheme, as represented by a set of letters, e.g., *cat*, is their primary symbolic unit. The individual letters which form a morpheme unit, e.g., *c*, *a*, and *t*, have no symbolic value for them as they do for hearing readers, where they represent speech sounds. (This situation for the deaf is analogous to the one for hearing readers where the strokes — and  have no relevant symbolic value alone until they combine in the numeral (and morpheme) of five, 5.) It may be concluded, therefore, that language may be learned through a writing system, even when the original basis of its systematicity is disregarded.

Notes

* We are indebted for the referral of the subject to Ms. Beverly Matsuwaki of the Leeward Health Center and Ms. Caroline Kanabida of the Family Health Services Division of the City and County of Honolulu.

We would like to thank the University of Hawaii Research Council (Grant No. G-79-350-F-728-B338) for their assistance in financing this research.

1. When the research was initiated, we were not aware of anyone who had proposed this idea. Just recently (June 1980), however, Prof. R. Conrad of Oxford University drew to our attention a paper by Lenneberg (1972), who proposed that research be done to teach language to the deaf through the writing system. The rationale which he offered was essentially the same as ours. Perhaps the only difference in views involved Lenneberg's thinking that 3 or 4 years of age was the earliest that written language could be introduced. We have introduced written language successfully to a 2 year old (as this paper shows) and we believe that written language should be introduced even from birth – for that is when hearing children begin to be exposed to language stimuli.

Recently, too, we came across a paper by Lado (1976) which seems to suggest that written language could be learned by the deaf without the medium of speech. However, because the paper is unclear on certain critical points, we are unable to make a definite determination.

As far as empirical research in which written language is actually taught as a first language is concerned, we are aware of none except that reported in this paper. Lenneberg appears not to have done any before his untimely death. Lado's research with his own hearing-impaired daughter, which began in the 1960's (Lado 1972), involved the medium of speech, while Söderbergh's work with deaf children (Söderbergh 1976) involved the medium of sign. While there is a great deal of similarity in ideas and practical teaching methods among Lenneberg, Lado, Söderbergh, and ourselves, there is no doubt at all that these were arrived at independently. Many of the ideas for the present study stemmed from the work that the first author and and his wife did in teaching reading to their (hearing) infant son beginning in 1964. That research was first reported in Steinberg and Steinberg (1975).

2. Whether written language is regarded as a dialect of spoken English or a separate language depends on the criterion one applies. If one regards differences in phonology as being crucial, then Spanish and Portuguese are different languages, for, while having very similar syntax and vocabulary, they have dissimilar phonologies. The same is true for Dutch and Standard German. There are many other such cases. On the other hand, if differences in phonology are not considered crucial, then Cantonese and Mandarin, for example, can be regarded as dialects of the same language, since they share essentially the same syntax and vocabulary.

   Whatever criterion is applied, there is no question that written language (or dialect) is a complete language. It has a syntax and a vocabulary (like spoken language) and it has a means of expressing such knowledge, an orthographic component (unlike spoken language, which has a phonology). The orthographic component would include a stock of symbols (letters, punctuation marks) for the construction of words and would also include rules for the production, e.g., left to right directionality, spacing, capitalization, morphographemic changes (pluralization, possession), etc.
3. Deletion accounts for sentence #1, pronominalization accounts for sentence #2, and the optional no-change accounts for sentence #3. The operations of deletion and pronominalization apply only to the second conjoined sentence, since *Sang and then John danced* would be ungrammatical, as would *He sang and then John danced* if *he* was meant to refer to the same person who was doing the dancing (John).
4. The name of the child as well as the name of his family have been changed throughout in order to protect the privacy of those persons.

References

Brown, Roger and Bellugi, Ursula
1964 "Three processes in the child's acquisition of syntax." *Harvard Educational Review* 34: 133–151.

de Villiers, Jill G. and de Villiers, Peter A.
1978 *Language Acquisition*. Cambridge: Harvard University Press.

Doman, Glen
1964 *How to Teach Your Baby to Read*. New York: Random House.

Furth, Hans G.
1966 *Thinking without Language*. New York: Free Press.
1971 "Linguistic deficiency and thinking: Research with deaf subjects, 1964–1969." *Psychological Bulletin* 76, 1: 58–72.

Garnica, O.K.
1977 "Some prosodic characteristics of speech to young children" *Working Papers in Linguistics* (22): 11–72. Ohio: Ohio State University.
Huttenlocher, Janellen
1974 "The origins of language comprehension." In R.L. Solso, ed., *Theories in Cognitive Psychology*. Potomac, Md.: Lawrence Erlbaum Associates.
Kobashigawa, B.
1969 "Repetitions in a mother's speech to her child." *Working Paper No. 14.* Berkeley, California: University of California.
Lado, Robert
1972 "Early reading by a child with severe hearing loss as an aid to linguistic and intellectual development." *Georgetown University Papers on Languages and Linguistics* 6: 1–6.
1976 "Early reading as language development." *Georgetown University Papers on Languages and Linguistics* 13: 8–15.
Lane, Helen S., and Baker, Dorothea
1974 "Reading achievement of the deaf: another look." *The Volta Review* (November): 489–499.
Nakano, Yoshitatsu
1970 "Chookaku no shoogai. (The hearing impaired)" In N. Okamoto, ed., *Hattatsu no shoogai to kyooiku: Jidoo shinrigaku kooza Volume 10.* Tokyo: Kanekoshobo.
Phillips, J.R.
1973 "Syntax and vocabulary of mother's speech to young children: age and sex comparisons." *Child Development* 44: 182–185.
Sachs, J.S. and Truswell, L.
1976 "Comprehension of two-word instructions by children in the one-word stage." *Papers and Reports on Child Language Development* 12: 212–220. Department of Linguistics, Stanford University.
Seitz, Sue and Stewart, Catherine
1975 "Imitations and expansions. Some developmental aspects of mother-child communications." *Developmental Psychology* 11: 763–768.
Slobin, Dan I.
1975 "On the nature of talk to children." In Lenneberg, E.H. and Lenneberg, E., eds., *Foundations of Language Development: A Multidisciplinary Approach*, Volume 1. New York: Academic Press, pp. 283–298.
1979 *Psycholinguistics* (2nd ed.). Glenview, Illinois: Scott, Foresman.
Snow, Catherine E.
1972 "Mothers speech to children learning language." *Child Development* 43: 549–565.
Söderbergh, Ragnhild
1971 *Reading in Early Childhood.* Stockholm: Almquist and Wiksell.
1976 "Learning to read between two and five: some observations on normal hearing and deaf children." *Stockholm Universitet: Institutionen for Nordiska Spraak*, Preprint No. 12.
Steinberg, Danny D.
1980 "Teaching reading to nursery school children." Final Report. Office of Education, U.S. Department of Education, Grant No G007903113. 1980, pp. 1–72.
1978 "Why children can't read: Meaning the neglected factor." Paper presented at 86th annual meeting of American Psychological Association, September 1, 1978, Toronto, Canada.
Steinberg, Danny D. and Shing-ren Chen
1980 "A three year old mute-hearing child learns to read: The illustration of

fundamental reading principles." *Dokusyo Kagaku* (Science of Reading), 24 (4): 134–141. Also in *Working Papers in Linguistics* 12 (2): 77–91, University of Hawaii, 1980.

Steinberg, Danny D., Harada, Michic, Tashiro, Michiko, and Yamada, Akiko
1982 Issai no sentensei chōkaku shōgaiji-no mojigengo shūtoku. [A one year old Japanese congenitally deaf child learns written language.] Chōkaku Shōgai [Anditory Disorders] 376(7): 22–46 and 377(8): 16–29.

Steinberg, Danny D., Kishimoto, Kayoko, Tatara, Naoko, and Orisaka, Ritsuko
1979 "Words are easier to learn than letters." *Working Papers in Linguistics* 11 (1): 121–132.

Steinberg, Danny D., and Oka, Naoki
1978 "Kanji to kana moji no yomi no gakushuu – kanji gakushuu no yasashisa ni tsuite (Kanji is easier to learn to read than kana)" *Shinrigaku Kenkyu*, (Japanese Journal of Psychology) 49 (1): 15–21.

Steinberg, Danny D., and Steinberg, Miho T.
1975 "Reading before speaking." *Visible Language* 9: 197–224.

Steinberg, Danny D., and Yamada, Jun
1978-79 "Whole word kanji are easier to learn than syllable kana." *Reading Research Quarterly* 14: 88–89.

Steinberg, Danny D., Yamada, Jun, Nakano, Yoko, Hirakawa, Seiko, and Kanemoto, Setsuko
1977 "Meaning and the learning of kanji and kana." *Hiroshima Forum for Psychology* 4: 15–24.

Steinberg, Danny D., Yamada, Jun, and Takemoto, Shinsuke
1977 "Rooji no gengo shuutoku (The language acquisition of deaf children)." *Chokaku Gengo Shoogai*. (Language Disorders and Hearing Disorders) 6 (3): 117–125.

Terman, Louis M.
1918 "An experiment in infant education." *Journal of Applied Psychology* 2 (3): 219–228.

U.S. Office of Demographic Studies.
1972 *Further Studies in Achievement Testing of Hearing Impaired Students: United States, Spring, 1971. Data from the Annual Survey of Hearing Impaired Children and Youth.* Series D, No. 13, Washington, D.C.: Gallaudet College.

Weeks, Thelma
1980 *Encounters with Language. Early childhood literacy.* Rowley, MA: Newbury House.

Wrightstone, J.W., Aronow, M.S., and Moskowitz, S.
1963 "Developing reading test norms for deaf children." *American Annals of the Deaf* 108: 311–316.

HARTMUT GÜNTHER

The role of meaning and linearity in reading

Some preliminary data from experiments in tachistoscopic word recognition and letter cancellation

Abstract

Evidence is presented from a tachistoscopic word recognition experiment that the exclusion of meaning as the primary cause for the so-called Word Superiority Effect by Baron and Thurston 1973 is faulty. Attention is drawn to some very interesting positional effects. Further data showing the interaction of meaning and linearity stem from letter cancellation experiments. It is argued that the controversially debated questions of what the perceptual units in the reading process may be and if a phonetic stage exists in the reading process are beside the point, since what matters in reading is not the identification of the linguistic signal, but the sense that can be made out of the material.

1. *Introduction*

In this paper,[1] I shall try to provide some evidence in support of the supposition that a model of the reading process must be a unitary one. It is maintained that whenever a person perceives written material, he looks for meaning, that is, he tries to make sense out of it. The concept put forward here strictly denies the rather common point of view that in reading, people first detect features, then groups of letters, etc., building a mental representation of the linguistic signal, and then, in a second step, derive the conceptual meaning from this internal representation of the signal. Rather, the reader goes down from the level of conceptual meaning only if necessary, that is, if some problem in the construction of meaning is encountered.

I am fully aware of the fact that I am not the first to propose such a point of view. Henderson (1977), reviewing the literature on word recognition, cites several sources. The terms *Gestalt* and *Analysis-by-Synthesis* come especially to mind. However, there is a difference. In Gestalt-psychology – which was, after all, not very interested in language – in addition to analysis-by-synthesis-models it would always be maintained that first the signal is identified as a signal, and only afterwards does a transformation of the identified signal into meaning take place – an operation which, in my view, is neither necessary nor possible in many cases.[2]

In the following, I shall report some results from two recently performed experiments which were designed to give some support to this point of view.

2. *An experiment in tachistoscopic word recognition*

2.1 *The problem*

Because of the very close control of external variables, the analysis of word recognition after tachistoscopic presentation has been conceived of as a very powerful tool for the investigation of the question "How do we perceive written material" from Cattel's first experiments until the present time, see Henderson (1977) for a review. The most prominent finding was the so-called "Word Superiority Effect" (WSE): In general, after tachistoscopic presentation, words are recognised better (that is, quicker or more accurately or both) than single letters or letter strings which do not form words. In our theoretical framework, the explanation for this effect is straightforward: Words are recognised better because they have meaning. There are, however, several experimental results which apparently contradict this statement, since a similar effect was found in many experiments when pseudowords and nonwords were presented. Pseudowords are letter strings which have no meaning, but which are pronounceable because they conform to the orthography of the language – as opposed to nonwords, which are not pronounceable and have no meaning. However, though both of them have no meaning, pseudowords are generally better recognised than nonwords. Moreover, Baron and Thurston in 1973 seemed to be able to prove that the whole WSE was entirely due to the factor of orthographic wellformedness, since they found in their experiments better recognition of words and pseudowords as opposed to nonwords, but not the slightest tendency for words to be better recognised than pseudowords. I shall not report the discussion of their results in the psychological literature here (see Manelis (1974) in particular, where the attempt was made to demonstrate that this failure to find a WSE when comparing words and pseudowords was probably due to some extent to the whole experimental setting). From a linguist's point of view, the explanation as to why this happened seems straightforward. Consider, for instance, the stimuli used in Experiment 1 of their study of the category words:

CARS	CARS	BLED	BLED
CANS	CART	BRED	BLEW

BARS	CANS	FLED	BRED
BANS	CANT	FRED	BREW

It can be seen that more than 2/3 of them are inflected – CARS is the plural of CAR, BLEW is the past tense of BLOW, etc. Linguistically, however, inflected forms are marked with respect to basic forms – that is, forms we find in a lexicon. Inflected forms are morphologically derived and hence, in a linguistic sense, more complex than basic forms.[3] Furthermore, the domains of inflected forms are generally sentences and texts, whereas in isolation, basic forms are expected. In tachistoscopic experiments, however, stimuli appear in isolation! In the following experiment, the aim was to demonstrate that basic forms are better recognised than inflected forms in such a task.

The second point investigated was the difference between pseudowords and nonwords. The hypothesis was that all stimuli that are not words or word forms (which bear meaning) would be recognised according to the linear left-to-right-structure of German orthography; that is, the more to the right the deviant letter sequence occurs, the better the recognition of the stimulus. Under this hypothesis, pseudowords were considered as nonwords with a zero occurrence of a deviant letter sequence.

2.2 *Experiment*

2.2.1 Method[4]

Stimuli

There where six categories of stimuli, cf. the following sample:

W	WF	PW	NWE	NWM	NWB
WEIHE	TOBTE	SIBIT	FENTP	FEJHO	TLBTU
REIHE	TOSTE	BIBIT	FUNTP	FUJHO	TLSTU
WEISE	LOBTE	SIBIE	LENTP	LEJHO	LLBTU
REISE	LOSTE	BIBIE	LUNTP	LUJHO	LLSTU

W means "words in their basic form", in the following often simply referred to as "words". WF are (inflected) word forms. PW are pseudowords. NWE are nonwords where the deviant letter sequence occurs at the end of the stimulus, NWM are nonwords with the deviant sequence in the middle, and in NWB, the deviant letter sequence occurs at the beginning of the stimulus. The set of the 96 stimuli consisted of 16 W, 16 WF, 32 PW, 14 NWE, 6 NWM, and 12 NWB, constructed as in the sample shown.[5]

2.2.2 Procedure

The projection time was individually determined for each subject by using 18 stimuli of similar structure, which were not contained in the stimulus set used in the experiment. The time was adjusted such that subjects correctly reported 60-70% of the letters in the correct position, and was held constant during the experiment. Most subjects improved slightly during the session, some became slightly worse. The mean time of stimulus presentation was 90 msec (minimum: 75 msec, maximum: 120 msec). Mean of correctness was 67% (minimum: 62%, maximum: 72%).

Subjects looked first at the masking field, which consisted of three rows of seven X's typed over O's, followed by the stimulus, which was followed again by the masking field. The inter-stimulus interval was 7 seconds. Subjects were asked to write down what they had seen on a prepared sheet of paper. Blanks were allowed. Subjects were asked to fill in single letters in the appropriate position. They were asked to use the noise of the automatic slide-changing as a signal to end the writing down and to look at the screen again. The interval between the beginning of the noise and the next stimulus was 2 seconds.

Stimuli were presented in 4 blocks with 24 stimuli each; there was an interval of 1 minute between blocks. The masking field remained on the screen during the pause. The categories were evenly distributed between the blocks. Within blocks, the categories were randomly distributed. Each stimulus was presented only once during the session.

Stimuli were presented by an electronic projection tachistoscope, type EPT 4a (Fa. ZAK, Simbach), on a screen which was 2 m away from the subject. Letters on the screen were 8 cm high, the length of the stimulus was 36 cm. All subjects reported that they could see the stimuli well. All had normal or corrected to normal vision. Stimuli had been printed first on white paper by an electric IBM typewriter, font "prestige elite 72", which were in turn xeroxed onto transparent material.

2.2.3 Subjects

4 females and 7 males took part in the experiment. They were students or members of staff of the Institut für Phonetik und Sprachliche Kommunikation der Universität München, aged between 23 and 43 years. Individual differences concerning the variables under investigation were not observed.

2.2.4 Results

Figure 1 displays the percentage of completely identified stimuli in each category (mean = 22%). A one-way analysis of variance shows that the differences are highly significant ($F_{(6,70)} = 16{,}06$; $p<0{,}001$). Duncan's test of

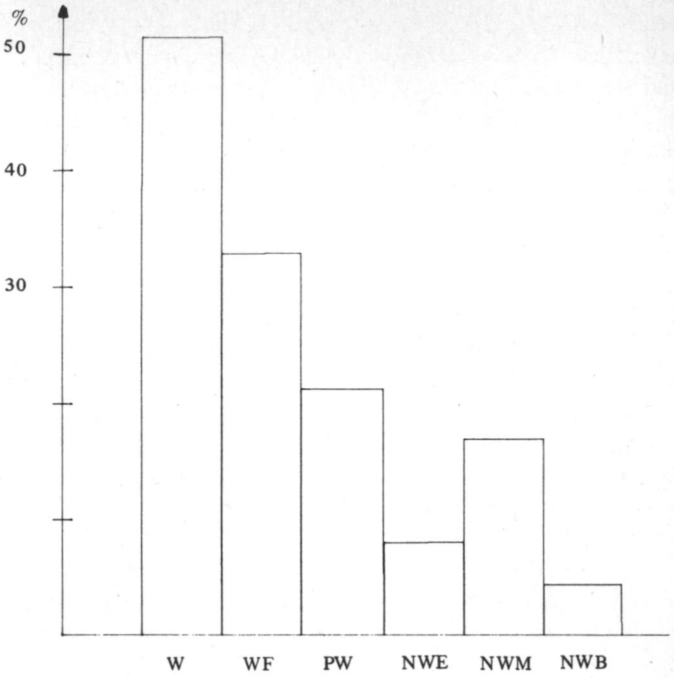

Figure 1. Correctly identified stimuli

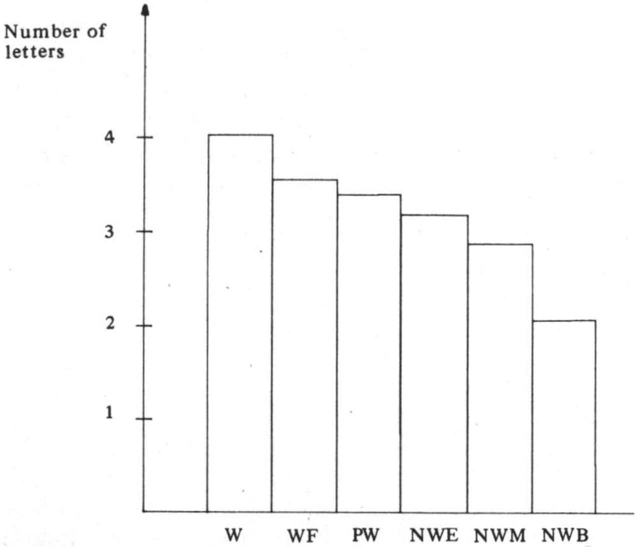

Figure 2. Mean number of correctly identified letters

the differences of means (Clauss and Ebner 1977: 317ff.) reveals that W is better recognised than all other categories, WF is better recognised than all remaining categories except for PW, PW is better recognised than all remaining categories ($p<0{,}01$). In between the remaining nonword-categories, no statistically significant differences have been found.

Figure 2 displays the mean number of letters correctly identified in position per stimulus for all six categories. Again, the difference between the categories is highly significant (across stimuli: $F_{(6,893)} = 34{,}92$; $p<0{,}001$; across subjects: $F_{(6,70)} = 26{,}07$; $p<0{,}001$). Duncan's test reveals that all differences between the categories are statistically significant ($p<0{,}01$) except for the difference between WF and PW ($p>0{,}05$).

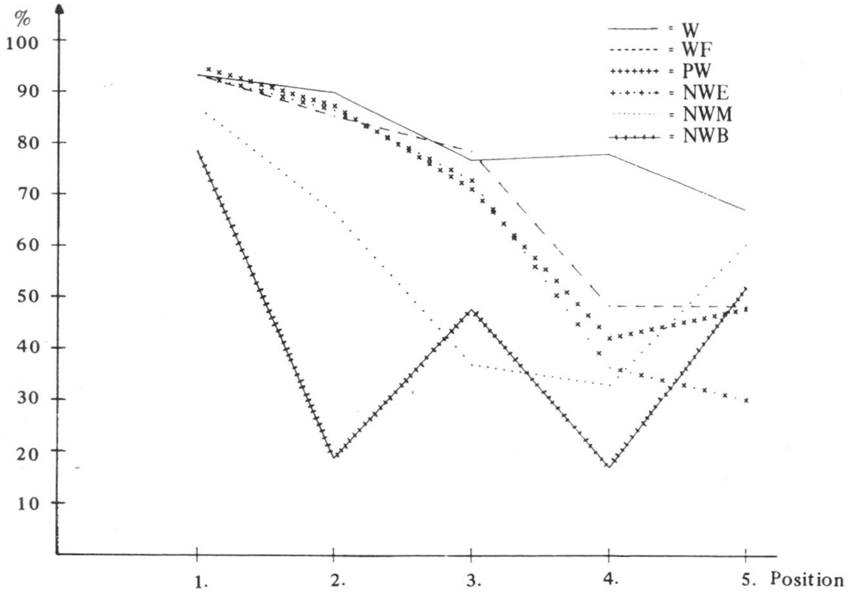

Figure 3. Positional effects

Figure 3 displays the percentage of correctly identified letters in positions 1 to 5 for each category. A two-way-analysis of variance (Clauss and Ebner 1977: 322ff.) shows the following results:

Positions:	$F_{(4,350)} =$	129,78; $p<0{,}001$
Categories:	$F_{(6,350)} =$	37,18; $p<0{,}001$
Interaction:	$F_{(24,350)} =$	8,99; $p<0{,}001$

From figure 3, the following points should be noted in particular:
- The difference of W to all other categories seems to be nearly entirely due to the fact that the letters in positions 4 and 5 are recognised better than in all other categories.
- Virtually no difference can be found between WF and PW.
- The curves for NWM and NWB differ quite clearly from all others: They fall more steeply at the beginning, reach the lowest points of all curves, and ascend quite steeply from position 4 to 5.
- Only the curves for W and NWE are falling from position 4 to 5.

2.2.5 Discussion

From Figures 1 and 2, we can see that the hypothesis concerning the difference between words and word forms is clearly confirmed: Basic word forms are recognised much better than inflected word forms. Concerning the positional hypothesis, we can safely maintain that Figure 3 is more a graphical version of it. That is, NWE differ from PW only in the poorer recognition of the letter in fifth position. NWM shows the lowest scores for position 3 and 4, as predicted by hypothesis, and NWB has the lowest scores of all, as expected (the unexpected peak in position 3 is presumably artifactual).

In the light of these results, it can be said that Baron and Thurston's (1973) failure to find a difference between words and pseudowords is simply the consequence from their failure to take into account the difference between words and word forms. This, however, blows their whole argumentation against meaning as the main reason for the WSE. On the other hand, unfortunately, we ourselves were not able to prove the opposite directly – namely, that meaning is in fact the primary reason for the WSE –, since we established a sound difference between words and word forms, but no statistically significant difference existed between the recognition of word forms and pseudowords. Since, however, word forms do have meaning, this result itself could be used as a counter argument against our conviction that meaning is the main reason for the WSE.[6]

That this would be a wrong interpretation has already been indicated by our initial hypothesising. From our results, we do not argue that the human nervous system processes basic word forms generally better than inflected ones. If this were true, the reading of normal texts in English or German would be more difficult than reading ungrammatical ones containing only basic forms, which is clearly not the case. What we claim is this: The observed superiority of words as against word forms occurs just in this experimental setting. Here – presumably in quite a contrast to the process of normal fluent reading –, the task of the subject is to identify stimuli and letters of stimuli. In such a situation, as pointed out already, the subject expects meaningful material in basic forms. By this token, we can now also explain our finding that the better recognition of words as compared with pseudowords and nonwords is nearly entirely due to the better identification of the letters in positions 4 and 5. In basic word forms, a feedback from the recognition of the meaning of the stimulus helps later identification of the letters of the stimulus; such a feedback is lacking in pseudowords and nonwords. By the experimental setting, such a feedback is hampered in the case of inflected word forms, hence, these are more poorly recognised than basic forms, but are definitely better recognised than nonwords.

It should be stressed that this is not a certain variety of what has become known as the "sophisticated guessing theory", being debated in such a lively fashion in cognitive psychology lately. We do not claim that subjects are more likely to arrive at words than at pseudowords when guessing from an incomplete internal image of the signal. Rather, it is maintained that from the subject's attempt to grasp meaning out of the stimulus instead of identifying its component letters – to put it somewhat differently: to find known patterns which make sense to him –, he is after the fact able to reconstruct the signal's identity on the basis of the meaning drawn from it.[7]

There are three more comments to be made on these results. First, the interpretations just given should remind us to be rather cautious in using data from this experimental technique alone, when we attempt to model the reading process in general. Second, we can see by now why the question "What are the perceptional units in the reading process", being debated controversially over and over again during the last 20 years, cannot be answered in a simple way. In different tasks, different subjects use different strategies, even if in all cases subjects are confronted with written materials. Common to all these situations is the aim to make sense out of it – and there is different sense in different situations. Even in one single task – i.e. tachistoscopic word recognition – words make sense in terms of lexical or conceptual meaning, whereas pseudowords make sense in terms of orthographic pattern, etc. Finally, it should be stressed that our results concerning the linear structure of language do not provide any kind of evidence for a serial processing model of the reading process. It is, first, quite clear that such a concept would not fit into our theoretical frame. Furthermore, it must be understood that the fact that written language is linearily organised from left to right (in our culture), and that people are aware of this fact, does not imply that the perception of written language mirrors this fact.

3. *Evidence from letter cancellation experiments*

It seems convenient to continue by turning to another question which is still debated quite controversially in reading research, that is, the question of whether the reading process *principally* entails a phonetic stage. The general argument for such a stage goes somewhat as follows. Language is learned phonetically. Hence, what a child has to learn when learning to read and to write is simply some translation rules which transform visual images to phonetic representations; from this point onwards, written language is processed in the same way as speech. It is obvious that from our theoretical point of view, such a view is untenable, because there are no mental representations of the signals as signals (!) anyway, neither in writing nor in speech.

We have already offered an explanation for the superiority effect of pseudowords as opposed to nonwords which is based on orthographic regularity rather than on a phonetic stage in the process of recognising written material in tachistoscopic experiments – an effect which is quite often said to provide evidence in favour of a phonetic stage in the reading process. Nevertheless, it seems appropriate to turn to another experimental technique in investigating this point closer since we ourselves have just argued for being cautious in constructing models of the reading process from one type of experimental observation only. One of the most often cited papers when the question of a phonetic or phonological stage in the reading process is concerned is Corcoran 1966. In a letter cancellation task – subjects were asked to cancel every instance of the target letter ⟨e⟩ in an English text –, Corcoran found that subjects tended to overlook far more tokens of the target letter which are silent – as in *HOUSE* or *LIFE* – than instances, where it is pronounced – as in *SET* or *SEAT.* He concluded, that this happened because a spoken ⟨e⟩ can be detected both in the visual and the phonetic search, whereas silent ⟨e⟩ cannot be detected in the phonetic search for lack of a phonetic correlate.

However, Smith and Groat (1979), using a similar procedure, could find no difference whatsoever in the cancellation rate of what they called "syllabic" ⟨e⟩ and other instances of ⟨e⟩, whereby the former category is nearly identical with Corcoran's non-silent ⟨e⟩. In discussing this finding, Smith and Pattison (1980) convincingly argue that Corcoran's and others' results of a higher cancellation rate for non-silent ⟨e⟩ is mainly due to the fact that "these investigators did not properly control for all the other variables that affect cancellation performance" (p. 4) as position, morphemic structure, etc.

Similar results were obtained in my own experiments, which are reported in full in Günther (1980a). First, no difference between the cancellation rate of ⟨e⟩ in the digraph ⟨ie⟩ and other instances of ⟨e⟩ are found – however, the digraph ⟨ie⟩ is the only instance of ⟨e⟩ in German where ⟨e⟩ is truly silent (its only function is to signalise the length of the preceeding ⟨i⟩). Second, also in the case of the target letter ⟨h⟩, no difference in the cancellation rate of those instances where ⟨h⟩, is truly silent in German (i.e. the occurence in the digraph ⟨th⟩ and some instances of the so-called "Dehnungs-H", see Günther 1980a for details) and those instances where it is definitely spoken (i.e. word-initial or occuring before a full vowel) was found.[8] Hence, we may cautiously conclude that the evidence brought forward by Corcoran and others (cited in Smith/Pattison 1980) has to be checked against the contradictory data just mentioned. No proof is available at present in this paradigm that the reading process necessarily entails a phonetic stage.

In the following, I wish to report some more interesting results of my experiments. First, however, I wish to dispense with one general objection against letter cancellation experiments. One might argue that this task – like, perhaps, tachistoscopic word recognition – has, in fact, nothing to do with reading, being, as some people put it, a purely visual task. From a theoretical point of view, Smith and Pattison (1980), provided some convincing arguments against this objection. In Günther (1980a), I tried to give some empirical evidence for the salience of this paradigm as a tool for investigating the reading process. I prepared a situation in which subjects encountered a nonsense text. It was manufactured out of the text used in the condition for the target letter ⟨h⟩ just mentioned by interchanging vowels and consonants in the appropriate positions. The result is a syllabic and somewhat language-like structure, as shown in the following example:

German text: Wenn Menschen heute irgendwohin verreisen
Nonsense text: Wust Masnchit huena ermisdwohet vurraenis

From this sample, one can easily understand the technique used to obtain the nonsense text: ⟨s⟩ was replaced by ⟨n⟩, ⟨g⟩ by ⟨m⟩, ⟨n⟩ by ⟨t⟩ or ⟨s⟩, ⟨e⟩ by ⟨i⟩, ⟨u⟩, or ⟨a⟩, etc. Precaution was taken that the overall distribution of the 26 letters of the alphabet in German texts was preserved in the nonsense version. Now, one result we had obtained with the target letter ⟨h⟩ in some pilot studies and also in the experiment reported here (Günther 1980a) was the observation that the target ⟨h⟩ in the digraph ⟨ch⟩ – pronounced [ç] or [x] according to the surrounding letters – was overlooked far more often than any other token of the target letter. On the other hand, when a single ⟨h⟩ was followed by a full vowel, which is the only instance where ⟨h⟩ has a direct phonetic correlate in German, it was cancelled far more often than any other type of ⟨h⟩.[9] The nonsense text, however, was prepared in such a way as to reflect these properties of the German version. Hence, every instance of ⟨h⟩ followed by a full vowel in the German text was also followed by a full vowel in the nonsense condition, and all instances of ⟨ch⟩ remained unchanged as well.

Nevertheless, the results in the nonsense-condition were quite different from the results obtained with the German counterpart. First, no difference between all types of ⟨h⟩ (esp. pronounced ⟨h⟩ vs. ⟨ch⟩) could be found. Also, no positional effects of the type reported below could be detected. Third, and most important: Subjects failed to cancel far fewer instances of ⟨h⟩ in the nonsense-condition than in the German one (approximately 2/3 less). These results can be interpreted straightforwardly. In letter-cancellation-tasks with language materials, reading occurs inspite of the fact that the task required of the subject is quite different. That is, the grasping of meaning out of the written material is disrupting in relation to the task to be performed. This disruption disappears, when the text is not written in a language known to the subject. Besides the fact that these results rather strongly underline the fruitfulness of letter cancellation tasks for the investigation of the reading process, they also seem to provide strong evidence in support of the theory of reading put forward in this paper. Even if asked to identify only letters and not to read the text (this was explicitly one of the conditions investigated by Smith and Groat (1979)), people nevertheless do read the text, and the results of the task directly reflect their reading behaviour, which is primarily oriented towards meaning.

Furthermore, this is shown by some (though *post hoc*) results of my study. Most researchers in the field (e.g. Corcoran, Smith and Groat, Smith and Pattison, and others) found strong positional effects in their data. Comparing these findings with the above reported tachistoscopic experiment, a parallel can be observed: The more to the left the position of the target letter within a word, the higher is the cancellation rate. This tendency holds for 3 out of 4 target letters used (U-tests across items, $p<0,01$), but only in German texts: No positional effect whatsoever was observed in the nonsense condition. This is clearly similar to the curve we observed in Figure 3 for the correct identification of the letters in positions 4 and 5 in words. Concerning the cancellation experiments, the explanation for this finding seems clear: In this task, the subject is reading, hence, he is seeking for meaning. However, letter scanning – essential for the task of cancelling – operates generally from left to right in real time. Hence, the meaning might be clear very soon, making the identification of single letters or whole words unnecessary. Since – and different from word recognition tasks – the meanings to be detected here are not lexical meanings of single words but of higher units, no feedback from the identified meanings back to the signal occurs, hence cancellation rates for nonsense-texts are higher than for normal ones.

Such an explanation seems to be further supported by the following two findings. First, in words where the target letter occured more than once, there was a highly significant tendency to overlook the last instance of the target more often than any of the others (U-tests across items, $p<0,01$).[10] Again, this result was obtained in all four conditions with German materials, but not in the nonsense text! Our explanation of this result would be that the identification of the meaning signalled by the sequence of letters forming a word-form may be much quicker than the scanning process in order to cancel letters – hence the tendency to overlook the last instance of the target.

Second point: Several investigators in this paradigm found that the definite article *THE* in English attracted far more omissions then any other word in these studies (see Smith and Pattison (1980), for references). Similar results were obtained in our studies. In all conditions using German texts, the target letter is overlooked in function words far more often than in others – function words being words which are not nouns, verbs, or adjectives/adverbials.

One characteristic of function words, however, is their redundancy in very many cases; therefore, we can again explain our finding by the meaning-principle. Two points, however, are particularly interesting. First, it is definitely not the usual shortness of these words which is responsible for this result, because neither did short content words receive a similarily high cancellation rate, nor was a short-word-effect observed in the nonsense condition. Second, it is apparently not simply the categorial status of these words which is causing this effect. This is indicated by the fact that the target letter in the same function word in the same text was overlooked by nearly every subject in some place, and overlooked by no subject in another place. Moreover, whereas pooling data over all instances of the German preposition *IN* resulted in an extremely high cancellation rate for the target ⟨n⟩, the preposition *AN*, which is very similar in meaning, frequency and function in German attracted no single error in this text. I would strongly suspect that a closer investigation of the cancellation rate for ⟨e⟩ in the English definite article *THE* would reveal that there are also cases where *THE* is cancelled more often than expected.

4. *Final remarks*

I do not wish to draw too many conclusions from the preceding discussion: however, I wish to stress some points again. It seems to me that the results reported here, though somewhat preliminary, have shown that questions such as "what are the perceptual units in the reading process" or "is there a phonetic stage in reading" are wrongly posed. There is not one reading process, but several strategies which are used differently by different people in different situations. Especially the demonstration of a superiority effect of words as opposed to word forms is a case in point. Hence, the perceptual units of a person who reads a detective story are presumably different from the units used by the same person looking at advertisements, and different units again might be involved when that same person serves as a subject in a tachistoscopic experiment. The subject may in some cases rely on a phonetic representation of an unknown word when reading, and he is presumably not doing so when reading abbreviations, etc.

This does not mean, however, that it is wrong to call all these instances "reading" in a general sense. What the subject is doing is always the same: He tries to make sense out of what he is seeing. As pointed out above, the sense is different in different situations.

Finally, as already indicated in the sub-title of this paper, most of what has been argued here is preliminary. What has been made plausible (hopefully) to a certain extent in this paper has to be proven by more solid evidence. This shall be our concern during the next few years. However, I am rather optimistic about this point, because times seem to be changing: Big red question marks are put on all those simple computer analogies which consider the reader as a thumb machine, sampling features in order to get letters in order to get representations of letters in order to form representations of words in order to get meanings in order to be able to act in this world which is, after all, dominated by the acting of human beings most of whom are – readers.

Notes

1. This is the revised version of the paper I read at the Bielefeld-conference. I am grateful for the bunch of critical comments brought forward in the discussion.
2. It seems to me that this point of view shares many features with the "Pattern-Analysis-Model" put forward by Paul Kolers in this volume. However, since I only listened to the oral presentation and discussion of his paper at the Bielefeld-conference, I cannot go into a detailed comparison here.
3. Peter Eisenberg rightly pointed out to me that this is, strictly speaking, not generally true. For instance, the present tense infinitive of German verbs – which is the form of verbs we find in a lexicon – is as complex as other forms of the paradigm, consisting of a stem and a suffix, etc. That this form is considered to be the citation form of the verb is a rather arbitrary decision of the grammarians of the past. However, this does not touch our point that it is considered as the basic form by ordinary people, who expect this form and not another one when occurring in isolation. There is furthermore some sense in some of these decisions, because in many cases, the basic form (that is, the leading form in the paradigm, or the form we find in a lexicon) is indeed morphologically, at the surface, less complex than other forms of the paradigm (cf. the singular-plural-distinction, the comparative and the superlative in adjectives, etc.).
4. Full details are given in Günther 1980b.
5. The different number of stimuli for each category has several reasons, which are discussed in Günther 1980b.

6. Danny Steinberg and Dorli Kegel (personal communication) both suggested that the use of more subtle statistical methods would presumably reveal that the difference between WF and PW is statistically significant as well as the other differences (using a more adequate model of the two-way analysis of variance and an analysis of trend). According to my hypothesis, I would also suspect that there is such a difference. However, as an inspection of Figure 3 shows, the curves for WF and PW are more tightly connected and more similar than any others in the diagram, which to me is a more interesting result than a possible significant difference in the total scoring between WF and PW. Furthermore (as sketched in Günther 1980b), there seem to be also some differences in the recognition of different types of pseudowords, which should be taken into account when comparing WF and PW. Hence, I decided to leave a closer investigation of this topic for later experimentation.
7. It should be mentioned that this interpretation of our results goes somewhat parallel to the theorizing of Johnston (1978), who held that the WSE is primarily due to the fact that the information available after tachistoscopic presentation simply vanishes more rapidly in pseudowords and nonwords.
   Because of the results of Johnston (1978), it seemed safe, furthermore, to discuss these results here already before trying to replicate them in a forced-choice-paradigm, which was not possible at that stage for technical reasons.
8. It is quite astonishing that nearly all investigations of the reading process in this paradigm always and only use the letter ⟨e⟩ as target in English texts. As Philip T. Smith pointed out to me (personal communication), this is primarily caused by the fact that the letter ⟨e⟩ in English serves very many different functions and that it occurs quite frequently. However, it seems to me that it would be wise to use other letters as well to check if the results achieved by using ⟨e⟩ as target would be obtained also when using other targets. One particularily interesting case would be the targets ⟨t⟩ or ⟨h⟩ in English: Would we find also a lower cancellation rate in the definite article *THE*, which was found in many investigations using ⟨e⟩?
9. At first glance, this result looks like an argument for a phonetic stage, since ⟨h⟩ in ⟨ch⟩ might, in a certain sense, be called 'silent'. That this is not a sensible interpretation is discussed at length in Günther 1980a.
10. It is important to note that this is not the case for double occurrences of the target letter (as in *BEE*, *SEEN* in English the target ⟨e⟩). In these cases, as observed also by Smith and Groat (1979), things are quite different: Subjects generally tend never to miss the target in these cases. Whereas Smith and Groat assume that this is a rather visual effect, I strongly suspect that this effect is due to the fact that double occurrences of letters generally serve definite linguistic functions. However, this point needs to be clarified by more experimental work.

References

Baron, Jonathan and Thurston, Ian
  1973 "An analysis of the word superiority effect." *Cognitive Psychology* 4: 207–228.

Clauss, Günther and Ebner, Heinz
  1977 *Grundlagen der Statistik.* Frankfurt: Deutsch. Reprint of the 2nd edn.

Corcoran, D.W.
  1966 "An acoustic factor in letter cancellation." *Nature* 212: 658.

Günther, Hartmut
  1980a "Letter cancellation experiments and the reading process – a pilotstudy." *Forschungsberichte des Instituts für Phonetik und Sprachliche Kommunikation der Universität München (FIPKM)* 12: 23–44.
  1980b "Linguistische Einflußgrößen beim 'Word superiority effect' – eine Pilotstudie." *FIPKM* 12: 45–64.

Henderson, Leslie
1977 "Word recognition." In N.S. Sutherland, ed., *Tutorial Essays in Psychology, Vol. 1.* Hillsdale: Erlbaum, pp. 35–74.

Johnston, James J.
1978 "A test of the sophisticated guessing theory of word perception." *Cognitive Psychology* 10: 123–153.

Manelis, Leon
1974 "The effect of meaningfulness in tachistoscopic word perception." *Perception & Psychophysics* 16: 182–192.

Smith, Philip T. and Groat, Anne
1979 "Spelling patterns, letter cancellation, and the processing of text." In P.A. Kolers, and M. Wrolstad and H. Bouma, eds., *Processing of Visible Language, Vol. 1.* New York: Plenum, pp. 309–326.

—. and Pattison, H.
1980 "Models for letter cancellation performance and their implications for models of reading." Typescript.

PAUL A. KOLERS

Polarization of reading performance*

Abstract

The prevailing opinion regarding research on literacy emphasizes the semantic component of text processing. Experiments directed at analysis of the role of the graphemes suggest that pattern-analyzing operations directed at the graphemes may carry a significant portion of the overall burden of literacy.

1. *Introduction*

The word *reading* applies to a range of phenomena, from the anesthetized mind that finds itself twenty pages farther into a book but without any sense of having read the intervening material, to conscious and deliberate struggling with the printed text, to the complete immersion of the self in the matter being read. Underlying all reading is the fact that a relation develops between a nervous system and the marks on the page, a relation which changes from the stumbling problem-solving of the novice to the skilled and efficient processing of the expert. The prevailing view holds that this relation is to some semantic or informational representation of the content of the text, and is supported by psychological theories of semantic relations, semantic networks, and the like (Smith 1978). An alternate view emphasizes a development in the pattern-analyzing or pattern-processing capabilities that people bring to their encounters with text.

2. *Polarization of information in graphemes*

I shall support this latter view by describing some properties of textual materials that are important to reading, and some properties of the reader that affect performance, based on research I have carried out over the past several years. I will show first how texts themselves are polarized and so

Figure 1. A model alphabet designed for rapid and clear reading

impose limitations on performance, then how readers are polarized or functionally biased in their performance. The main point of the paper is that a proper analysis of the skills that make reading possible reveals a means-dependency in reading; this dependency, moreover, is often obscured by research that actually places too great an emphasis upon the semantic processing of the text.

Let us begin with the alphabet. The letters of Figure 1 are taken from a standard alphabet developed at the US Bureau of Highways for its directional signs guiding high-speed traffic. The letters were designed to be visible at a distance and in a quick glance. The face is now widely used throughout North America and in some parts of Europe as well, testifying to its success. We might consider it a standard alphabet, exemplary with respect to ease of reading. It is almost unpleasant, therefore, to perform surgery upon the alphabet, except that doing so has some beneficial consequences.

The surgery is intended to seek the source of the information in the alphabet. Our ordinary phenomenological experience is that all parts of an object are equally represented in our perception of it. When we look at a person's face, or out of the window at a scene, or at a printed letter, we have the sense of a whole, of a Gestalt, all the parts of which are seen equally well, especially when they are in central vision. Our friend's nose, eyes, and ears seem to contribute equally to our identifying our friend, and surely the left and right sides of our friend's face are equally informative. It comes as something of a surprise, then, to discover that not all parts of a letter contribute equally to its identity. Figure 2 reveals the consequences of cutting away the right half of each letter. Notice the number of ambiguities that doing so creates, for example, the number of *C*s and *F*s that the alphabet suddenly possesses. Contrast those results with the consequences of cutting away the left side of the letters, as in Figure 3. There are still some ambiguities – particularly *J, K* and *O* – but on the whole many fewer than in Figure 2. Our phenomenological experience that information regarding a letter's identity is distributed homogeneously throughout the letter clearly is not correct. Information regarding identity is polarized; the right halves of letters contain more information regarding letter identity than the left halves. (The argument can be extended to upper and lower halves, but with some complication: the lower half of upper case letters and the upper half of lower case letters contain more identifying information than the remainder (Kolers 1969). One can see this easily by blocking off the upper or lower half of a line of print.) The simple conclusion is that different parts of letters can contribute differentially to identification or recognition.

Polarization of information is not restricted to the letters of our Roman alphabet. Informal tests with Hebrew, whose alphabet shares an ancestry with the Roman but which is read leftwards, reveals that the left halves of

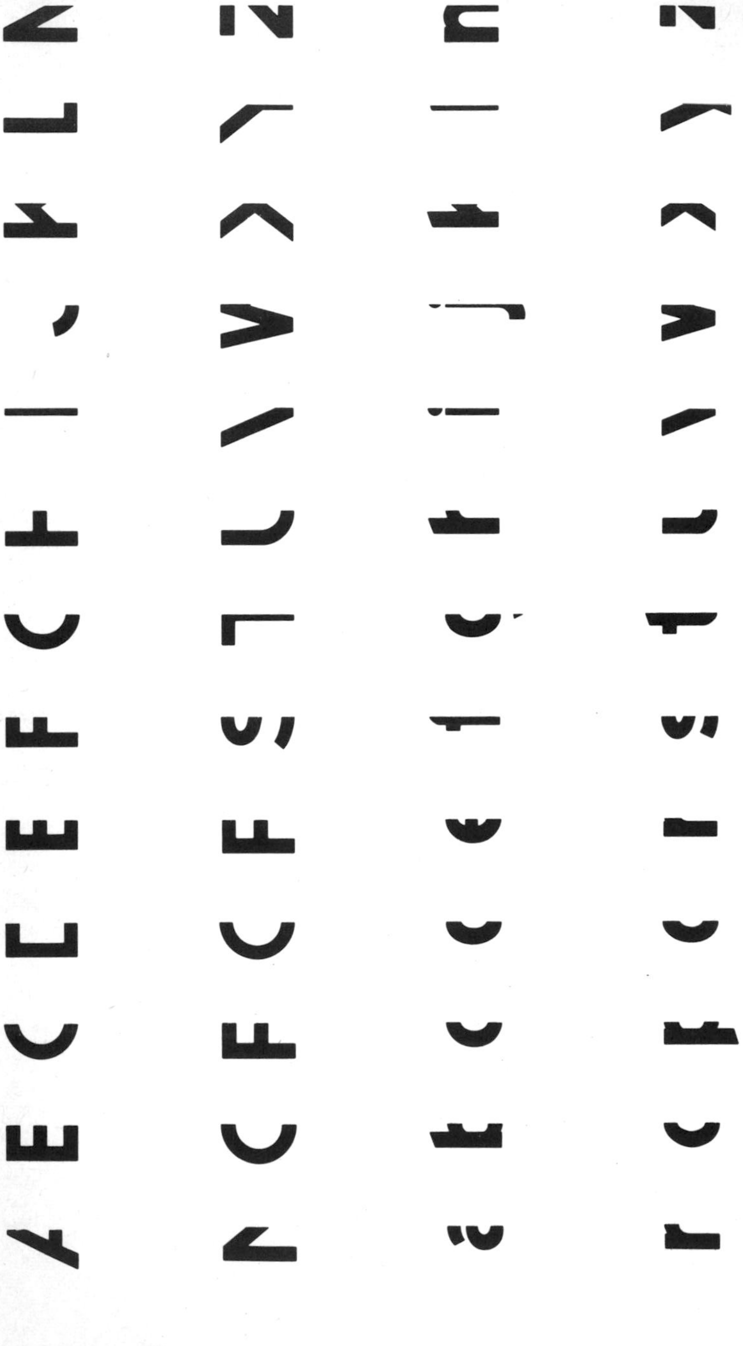

Figure 2. The alphabet of Figure 1 with the right halves of the letters removed

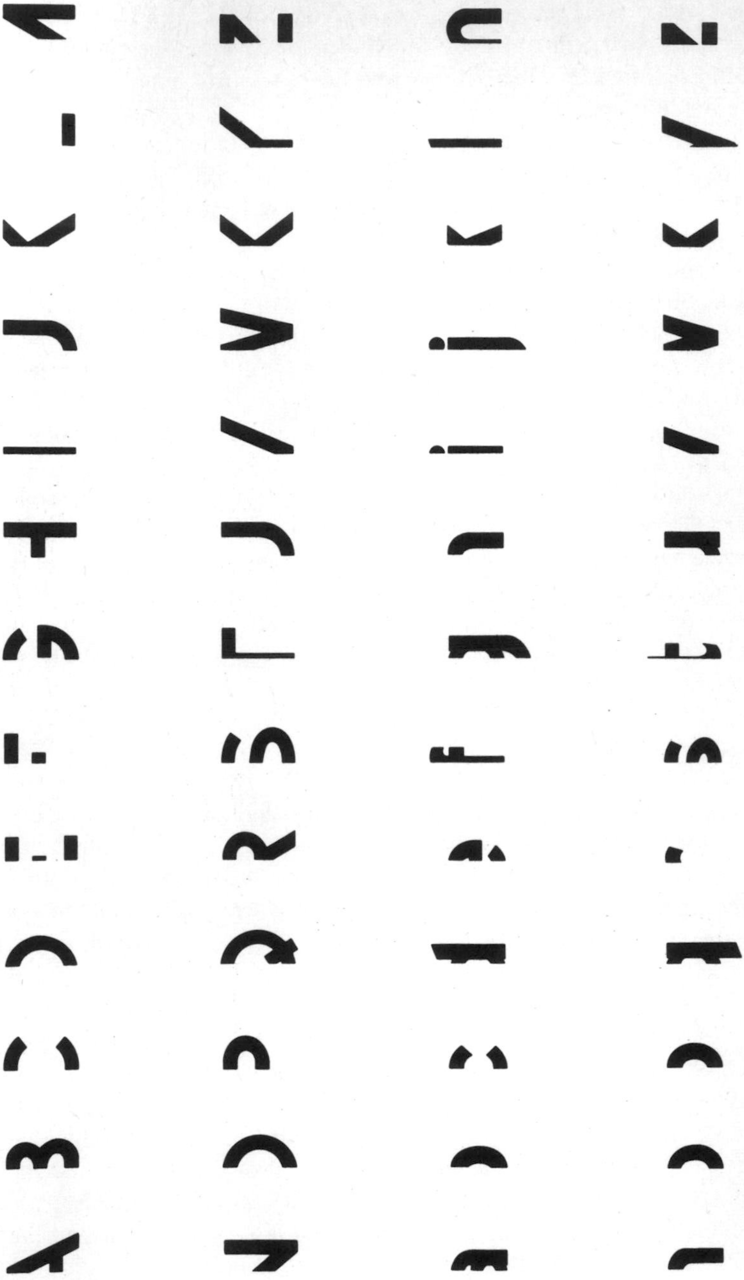

Figure 3. The alphabet of Figure 1 with the left halves of letters removed

Hebrew letters are more informative than the right. In classical Chinese, the characters were written in columns which were read from top to bottom. Chou (1930) reported that the left side and lower half of Chinese characters were the more informative.[1]

Reading is accomplished, of course, not with a stationary but with a moving eye. The inhomogeneity in placement of identifying information tends to favor the part of the character farther away from its beginning: the right half of the rightward-read Roman character, the left half of the leftward-read Hebrew, the bottom half of the downward-read Chinese. One might conjecture that this is a necessary fact of writing. A character has to begin in some place and beginnings are more likely to be similar than later developments are. (Any gardener knows how much harder it is to tell weeds from flowers when they first show through the earth, for example.) But this is not a satisfactory account, for it is known from other sources that the first letters of a word are more important to its recognition than are interior letters (Huey 1908, Chap. 4), whether they are displayed in a tachistoscope (Bruner & O'Dowd 1958) or are items in a crossword puzzle; and the first words of a sentence are worth more in getting the sense of the sentence or in allowing for misreading (Kolers 1970).[2] It is not certain, therefore, why individual characters should have this opposite property of polarization. The polarization seems to be significant for recognition, however, as I shall discuss below.

2. *Polarization in direction*

Performances are polarized also. English is normally read rightwards, but this is a matter of convention, not of necessity. The first two samples of Figure 4 are connected English discourse, in normal orientation in the first sample, and in reversed orientation in the second. The second sample, that is to say, forms a coherent English sentence when it is read leftwards. In an experiment, college students read pages of such texts both rightwards and leftwards. Leftwards reading of the first sample produced nonwords such as "dilav si yteixna fo tnacidni", leftwards reading of the second sample produced the coherent sentence beginning "A strong case can be made", whereas rightwards reading of the second sample produced nonwords. As expected, the upper sample was read more quickly rightwards than leftwards, but the very same fact was found for the second sample also, the students reading "ton seod sriaffa. . . " more quickly than "A strong case can be made. . . ". Hence the familiar skill of reading rightwards was more influential than the meaning of the sequences in affecting speed of performance.

```
If we wish to be certain that our indicant of anxiety is valid,
how should we proceed?  A direct approach is to ask people to
introspect on their anxiety, to report verbally how much anxiety they
```

```
ton seod sriaffa fo etats gniyfsitas eht taht edam eb nac esac gnorts A
eht tahw enimreted lliw rehtar tub ,nrael lliw lamina eht tahw enimreted
   eriuqca lliw slamina taht deugra sah tsigolohcysp enO .od lliw lamina
```

```
Presented experimental the the order in the defense were to booklets
do in for the with witnesses and the had six prosecution the for
twelve which six manipulated.  Recent that were most followed favoring
```

```
Mgiikehhbr chupn ni Issseo sian rrm aip drt aehtoao he bwtr
asco aseoab r or coh ete erai fna slson iqinls doe Emtu
adnee eoee.  Eneoh sap rooolef tc etahbg aaseki dh ds ssord
```

Figure 4. Four samples of text, read leftwards and rightwards

The third and fourth samples were created in order to test this polarization of direction of reading even farther. The third was made from coherent text by misordering its words; thus, a single sentence can be found between *Presented* and *manipulated.* In this test, the students always read whole words, rightwards or leftwards, reading "booklets to were defense" in the leftwards direction, for example. Here, too, the speed of reading favored the rightwards direction. The polarization can be brought out even more clearly with the fourth sample, in which only the letter frequencies and word lengths of the

Table 1. Time taken to read the four texts illustrated in Figure 4 (minutes)

Sample	Direction	
	Rightwards	Leftwards
Normal	1.28	9.96
rM	5.72	6.91
Scrambled	1.76	2.10
Pseudowords	5.54	9.44

original text were preserved in the computer-scrambled output. The students were able to read these nonsense texts almost twice as fast in the familiar rightwards direction as in the unfamiliar leftwards direction. The time scores are displayed in Table 1.

3. *Orientation of objects*

It is well-known that orientation of objects is important to their recognition; not only material objects, but people too are more readily recognized in their familiar orientation (Rock 1973). The fact is true also for letters, although their orientation interacts in an unexpected way with direction of reading. Students were requested to name pages of letters aloud, rightwards or leftwards, the samples composed of separated letters in one of the four orientations illustrated in Figure 5. The three marked M, I, and R are 180-degree rotations of the sample marked N, as mirror reflections around the vertical axis (M), inversion around the horizontal axis (I), or rotation in the plane of the page (R). Even when they were naming letters one at a time the students named the letters of N more rapidly rightwards than leftwards, a finding consistent with the reading times of Table 1. The same was true for M and for the inverted letters of I. The letters of R, however, were named more rapidly leftwards than rightwards, as can be seen in Table 2. The explanation proposed that to recognize misoriented letters students were required to alter a pattern-recognition routine which assessed features of the stimulus that were relevant to their identification; that planar rotations were a second "natural" orientation for the human visual system; that direction of scanning was integral to recognition; and that recognition could be accomplished either by transforming the orientation of features selected from samples and matching them to normal representations, or by transforming representations and matching them to misorientated samples (Kolers & Perkins 1969). (The notion of matching and the implied notion of orientation of an internal representation are used only in the sense of logical requirements of operations carried out. No implication of pictures in the mind is intended.)

The scholar of printed language will appreciate that the leftwards reading of R, like the leftwards reading of M, has historical ancestors in the boustrophedon of the pre-classic Greeks (Guarducci 1967). I think one might conjecture that, when literacy was not as practiced a skill as it is nowadays, the polarization of direction of reading was likely to have been markedly less, and rotated scripts were perhaps less difficult to read than they are now. Some of these relations of direction and orientation were explored with connected discourse.

Table 2. Time taken to name the letters of Figure 5 (minutes)

Orientation	Direction	
	Rightwards	Leftwards
N	4.65	5.66
R	7.16	6.72
I	7.96	8.55
M	7.06	7.20

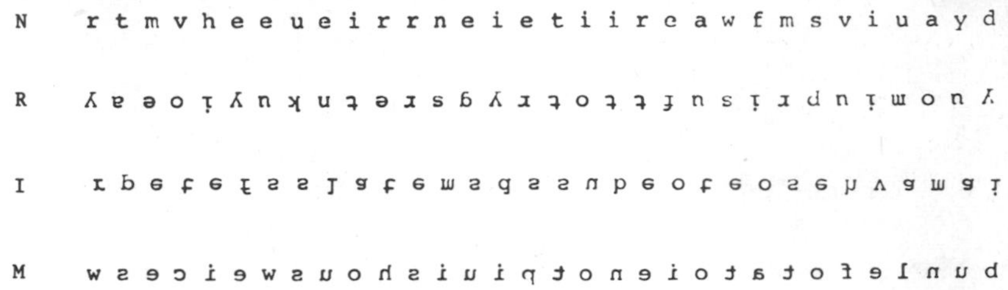

Figure 5. Four orientations of alphabetic letters

The upper four samples of Figure 6 are textual forms of the letters shown in Figure 5, and the lower four add the transformation of rotating each letter around a vertical axis through the letter, symbolized by *r*. Students read one page in each of these eight transformations on each of eight days, the order of reading properly counterbalanced. Some simple model of performance might suppose that the rightwards-going samples were read more quickly or that the upright samples were read more quickly, or that all of the transformations on N were read in equal amounts of time. No such simple notions accommodate the data. Samples N, rN, and R were read the quickest, whereas samples M, I, and rR were among the slowest (Kolers 1968).

Perhaps it will be appreciated that geometrically the eight samples of text can be regarded as a group formed by the operation of three binary variables. For example, inversion (I), mirror reflection (M), and letter reversal (r) can in proper combination yield all eight samples of the text. There are in fact 28 sets of three binary operators whose combination produces the eight samples of text. I have examined them all and none of them accommodates the data perfectly. Below I will discuss some work directed at the nature of the mathematical structure of the data.

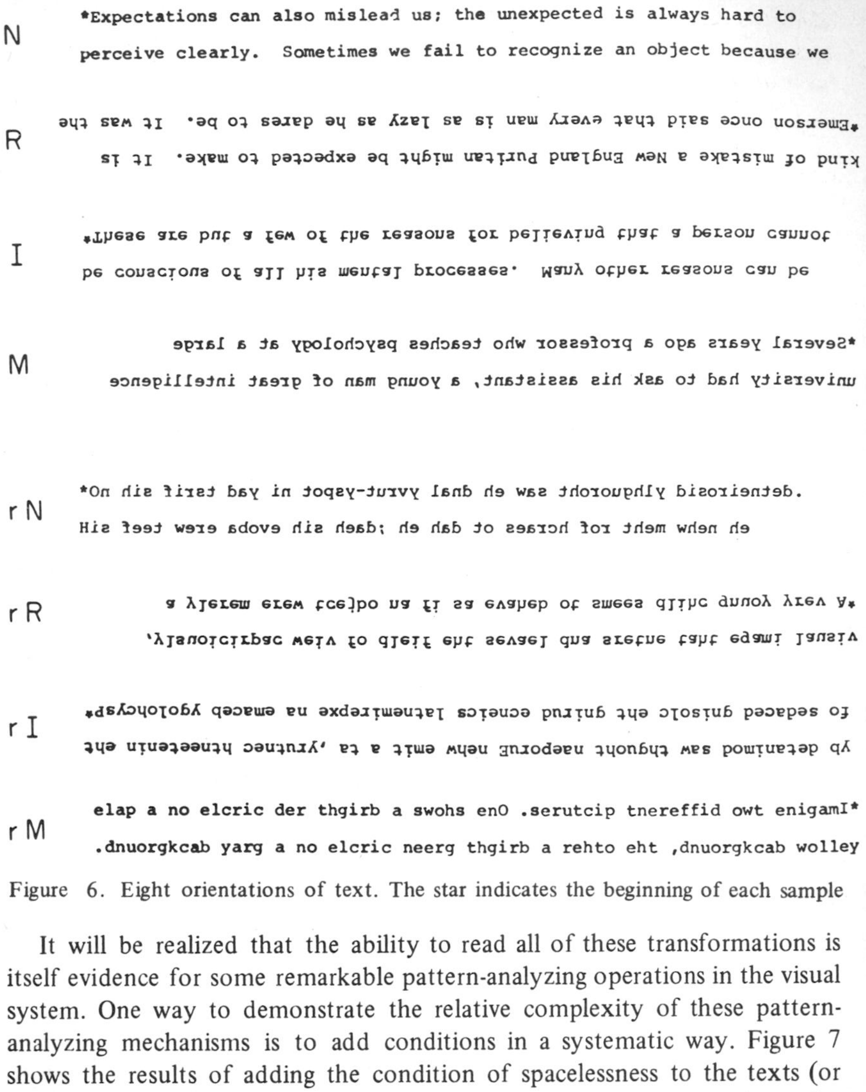

Figure 6. Eight orientations of text. The star indicates the beginning of each sample

It will be realized that the ability to read all of these transformations is itself evidence for some remarkable pattern-analyzing operations in the visual system. One way to demonstrate the relative complexity of these pattern-analyzing mechanisms is to add conditions in a systematic way. Figure 7 shows the results of adding the condition of spacelessness to the texts (or subtracting space). Of course, for centuries texts were written continuously, not only in Greek and Latin, but in Hebrew and Aramaic as well (as the Dead Sea scrolls reveal). Presumably it was part of the reading process to segment the continuous visual signal subjectively, much as it is part of the process of understanding speech to segment the continuous auditory signal subjectively. The skill is not well preserved among modern readers, however, at least so far as reading English is concerned. Many curiosities of perception result from faulty segmentations with the texts of Figure 7. The main point here, however, is only to compare reading time for geometrically transformed text with and without segmentation; for the purpose, students read eight pages of each of the transformations of connected text.

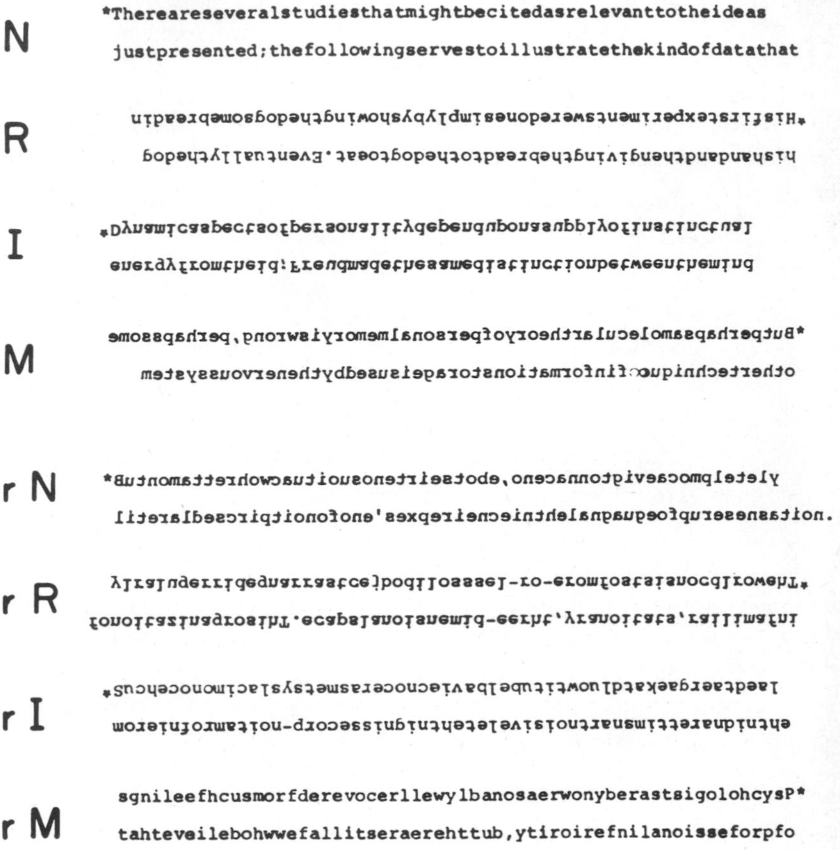

N
*Thereareseveralstudiesthatmightbecitedasrelevanttotheideas
justpresented;thefollowingservestoillustratethekindofdatathat
R
I
M
r N
r R
r I
r M
sgnileefhcusmorfderevocerllewylbanosaerwonyberastsigolohcysP*
tahteveilebohwwefallitseraerehttub,ytiroirefnilanoisseforpfo

Figure 7. The same orientations as in Figure 6, but without interword spaces

The data of Table 3 show the time taken to read the eighth page of text in the two formats. Some slowing down of reading occurs even for normally oriented text; the actual difference is about 60 percent in time. (The comparisons are between two different groups of subjects drawn from a common population of undergraduates.) The actual increment in reading time varies from that value up to 223 percent for R, almost a four-fold difference. Whereas the times range from about 3.69 minutes per page for rN to 8.88 minutes per page for rR, a little more than 140 percent difference for the transformed-spaced text, they range from 11.2 to 17.5 minutes per page for spaceless text, an increase of only about 50 percent. (The actual trend seems to be that the percentage increments, N excepted, are inversely related to reading time for spaced text, the largest increments, 204 and 223 percent, occurring for the most quickly read transformations.) Moreover, the order of difficulty of the transformations of spaced text, measured by the time taken to read them, is only partially preserved in the order of difficulty of the spaceless text. This shows, in still another way, that geometrical operators do not affect readability of the texts uniformly: transformations affect the samples differentially. To put it another way, the mathematical structure of the stimuli is not preserved in the behavioral responses produced by students reading them.

Table 3. Time taken to read spaced or spaceless text (minutes)

Text	N	rN	R	rR	I	rI	M	rM
Spaced	1.46	3.69	4.54	8.88	6.42	7.03	7.73	8.11
Spaceless	2.33	11.20	14.67	17.52	16.23	14.79	15.74	14.88
Difference (%)	60	204	223	97	153	110	104	83

A search for the behavioral structure motivated an experiment in which separate groups of students were practiced in reading a single transformation and then in reading samples of all the transformations. The idea underlying this enterprise was that reading single transformations tapped special skills of the visual nervous system, and these might be identified by their interaction with the other samples. That is to say, practiced on a particular task and then tested by different but related tasks, a person's ability to perform the related tasks might reveal some of the constituents required for the task practiced on. When a number of different tasks were presented, as in the present case, a complex, multi-dimensional factoring of the tasks seemed possible.

For the purpose, seven groups of eight students each read 25 pages in a single one of the seven transformations shown in Figure 6, and then read two pages in each of all eight samples, all reading and testing being appropriately counterbalanced. In their initial reading, the students of each group read different pages of text, but for the test on all eight samples they all read exactly the same pages. Table 4 shows the amount of time required to read a page of the test transformations as a function of the training transformations. The tests are arrayed as columns; the training groups make up the rows. The bottommost row shows that on average the tests differed in the amount of time needed to read them, a two-fold difference, N excepted, from 3.24

minutes for rN to 6.52 for I. The values within columns show, in turn, that the time required to read any single text transformation depended upon the training transformation that had been read. The smallest difference, for M, ranges from 4.38 to 6.58 minutes per page, 50 percent. The largest difference occurs with I, 175 percent.

Table 4. Reading time on test as a function of training (minutes)

	Tests								
Training	N	rN	R	rR	M	rM	I	rI	Training average
rN	1.52	2.32	6.75	8.73	6.40	6.96	8.44	7.99	6.14
R	1.54	4.32	3.54	7.25	6.58	6.08	7.58	6.28	5.40
rR	1.44	3.33	4.05	4.13	5.89	5.42	4.87	6.42	4.44
M	1.44	3.20	4.56	7.18	4.38	5.63	8.90	7.91	5.40
rM	1.37	3.68	4.63	7.25	5.75	3.57	7.62	7.92	5.22
I	1.34	2.96	2.91	4.44	4.89	5.63	3.23	4.25	3.71
rI	1.34	2.88	3.11	5.25	5.32	4.77	4.97	3.08	3.84
Test average	1.43	3.24	4.22	6.32	5.60	5.44	6.52	6.26	

Not only do the reading times depend upon training, the effect of training has some consistency, as is shown by the rightmost column. Training on rN led to the longest test times overall, and training on I to the shortest. In a series of computations attempting to find a mathematical structure for the data, two sorts of findings emerged (Kolers & Perkins 1975). One is that the structure of the scores for naming letters is different from the structure of the scores for reading. Whatever the degree of dependence of reading upon letter recognition, the pattern-analyzing operations of the two tasks are not the same. The second is that a fair approximation to the results is obtained by assuming that rotation of the letters and their sequential ordering are active operations that the visual system engages in, and that mirror reflection of characters, as in rN and M, creates a condition of visual instability or ambiguity. The main finding of the enterprise has been that characters are not all alike, and that training in literacy induces specific polarization of the visual system.

These results raise the question of whether it is possible to generate a set of principles to guide the formation of writing systems; whether, for example, characters might be so shaped as to distribute their informational load better, and whether speed and efficiency of reading might be affected thereby. It is commonplace to worry about the rules of orthography as they affect reading, and many nations alter the spelling of words to bring spelling into line with current pronunciation. I raise a parallel question here to ask whether the actual formation of characters can be put to principled test. I should think the answer would be positive.

The motive for my research has not been to study the relative merits of modified or augmented typography, however, but to study the role of pattern-analyzing operations in reading and understanding. In some circumstances, the evidence has supported the conjecture that notions of semantic memory and semantic processing may be irrelevant; that the pattern-analyzing operations themselves may carry a semantic load (Kolers 1979). Rather than pursue that argument here, I would discuss some other results related to the recognition of letters and words, particularly the role of graphemic analysis as important to literacy. As in the foregoing, a conclusion to be drawn from the work is that letter recognition and reading tap different skills; in fact, reading cannot even be properly conceptualized in terms of the processes associated with the recognition of aggregations of individual letters. Of course this point has been made many times, sometimes in the context of rejecting notions that reading consists in the straightforward translation of graphemes to phonemes (Kolers & Katzman 1965), sometimes in other contexts (Frith 1979). Here the argument is made in terms of the differences in the pattern-analyzing operations that the two tasks implicate.

4. *Letters and words*

The debate between proponents of the whole-word and of the analytical approach to acquiring English literacy has become almost notorious (Chall 1967); certainly it has been going on for a very long time, and with depressingly similar arguments over the years (Mathews 1966). One group advocates learning to read by emphasizing the whole word, the visual Gestalt, in analogy to the way that, it is thought, one learns to recognize a chair, a face, or any other object of the visual environment. Another group emphasizes learning the printed symbols for the sounds of words. The first group argues that visual perception is a synthetic, not an analytic activity; that we recognize a chair, say, as a whole and not as an assemblage of components such as arm, seat, back, and the like. The second group points out that words are not such objects of the natural environment but are man-made symbols; moreover, that the written language serves the function only of representing the spoken language. The closer one can make the correspondence of written to spoken, they say, the better the writing system and the more easily reading will be learned. These two views were put to test in a simple experiment and both were found wanting.

The test consisted of comparing the effect on subsequent reading of practice at naming letters versus practice at reading words (Kolers & Magee

1978). One group of students read 15 pages of connected English text in the unfamiliar typography illustrated as I in Figure 6. A second group named the letters of the very same pages after they were scrambled into a first-order approximation to English. So both groups had identical visual experience of the letters in 15 pages of text. As a test, the two groups then read 10 pages of connected inverted discourse, I, and then named one page of inverted letters. The times for the three performances are shown in Fig. 8, the first 15 pages comparing time to read against time to name letters, the next 10 pages comparing time to read as a function of prior practice, and the twenty-sixth page showing the time to name a page of letters.

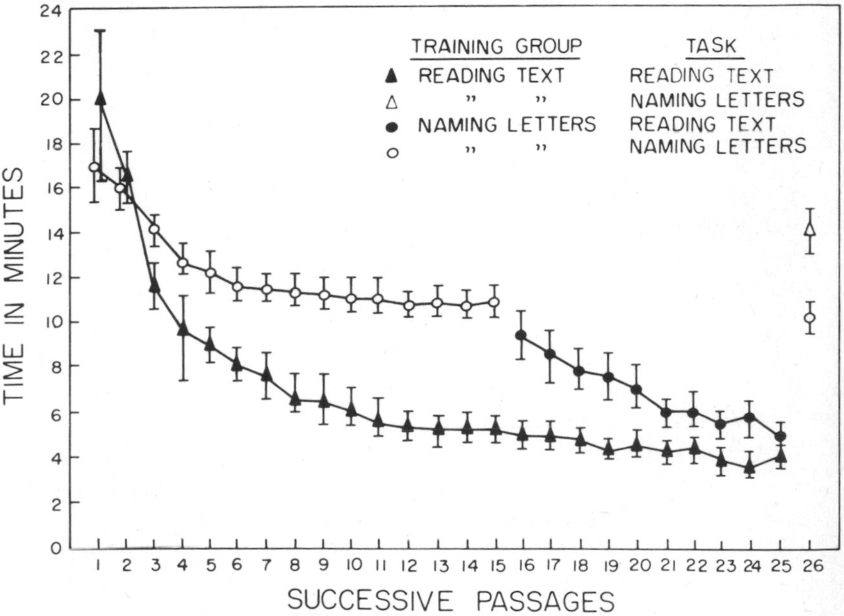

Figure 8. Time to read text and name letters following practice on reading or naming letters

One can see that the students acquired a letter-naming skill quite rapidly and that it approached an asymptote far more rapidly than the reading skill of the second group did. Moreover, the letter-naming skill transferred only somewhat to reading. (Translating the curve for the letter-naming group along the abscissa shows that the effect of 15 pages of naming letters on reading is about the same as 4 pages of practice reading text.) When the students then named letters, the group that had named letters as practice carried on at the same speed they had attained before the interruption of reading 10 pages of text, whereas the students who had only read text named letters at about the speed the first group had attained after one or two passages of letter naming.

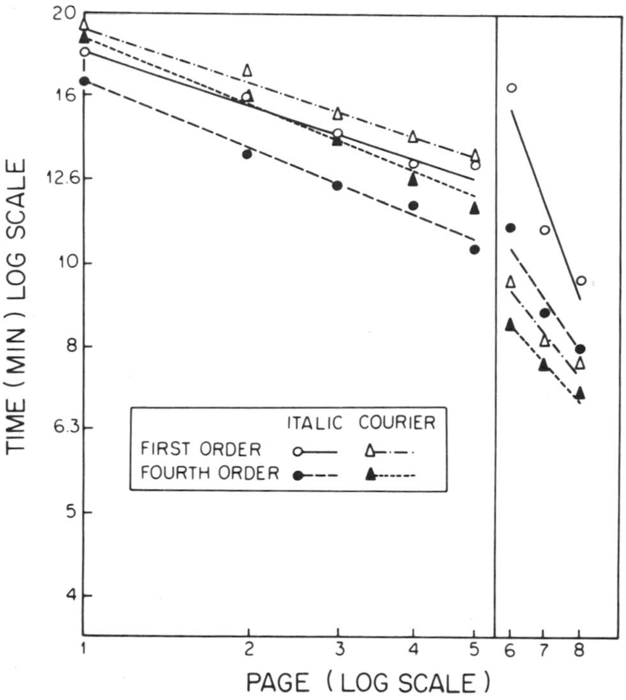

Figure 9. The data of Figure 8 displayed as logarithms

The curves of Figure 8 can be regarded as hyperbolas or power functions, and logarithms are a convenient way to treat time scores. Hence the relations can be seen a little more clearly in Figure 9, where the logarithm of time has been plotted against the logarithm of page number. The straight lines reveal both a steady percentage increase in speed with practice (decrease in time taken), and differences between the groups in test performance. Thus, reading is good practice for reading, but provides poor practice for naming letters. Naming letters is good practice for further letter naming, is impervious to improvement by reading, and provides some transferable practice to further reading. To put it another way, in reading words people are not particularly sensitive to the letters making up the words, and inducing people to attend to the letters is only moderately useful for increasing skill at reading. The results suggest that letter naming and reading – by extension, phonics versus whole-word approaches to literacy – tap significantly different pattern-analyzing operations. They are related but are not included in each other, so it is not possible that training with either one alone would wholly actualize the other. In respect to pedagogy, therefore, arguments regarding whole-word versus phonics as the basis of acquiring literacy are pointless insofar as the two tasks exercise different skills.

The pattern-analyzing operations are directed at the visual signals themselves, at the graphemes. I do not mean that the semantic content is irrelevant to reading; of course it is not. In fact the semantic content often aids in deciphering obscure, ill-formed, or ambiguous letters. I do mean to say that pattern-analyzing operations directed at the graphemes may themselves carry a considerable portion of the interpretation of the signal that is commonly assigned to a semantic component. This is brought out in still another study.

Again university students named letters as practice for reading, but this time the letters formed either first-order or fourth-order approximations to English (Kolers, Palef & Stelmach 1980). A computer program transformed connected English discourse to create the ordered approximations page by page. Hence, the students received identical exposure to individual letters, although in one case the letters were distributed as first-order and in the other case as fourth-order approximations to English. Fourth-order approximations are, of course, orthographically and lexically closer to English than first-order approximations are. As an additional condition, the two orders of approximation were presented in each of two different typographical styles, the familiar IBM Courier illustrated earlier and an italic. Examples of the two approximations and the two typographical styles appear in Figure 10. After naming the letters either in italic or in Courier, in first-order or fourth-order approximation, each of the four groups of separately practiced students then read three pages of text printed in Courier.

One can see on the left side of Figure 11 that fourth-order approximations were named a little more quickly than first-order approximations, and that letters in italic were named a little more quickly than corresponding sequences of letters in Courier. Transfer from practice at naming letters to reading was far greater for the Courier-trained group than for the italic-trained group, however. But even more interesting is the finding that the two groups trained on Courier – first order and fourth order – were not reliably different from each other. Thus the main finding is that transfer of training was greater along lines of visual pattern than along lines of orthographic or lexical influence. (The lexical factor was not without influence; it helped the readers trained with fourth-order italic to read Courier faster than the readers trained with first-order italic. Relatively speaking, however, visual pattern

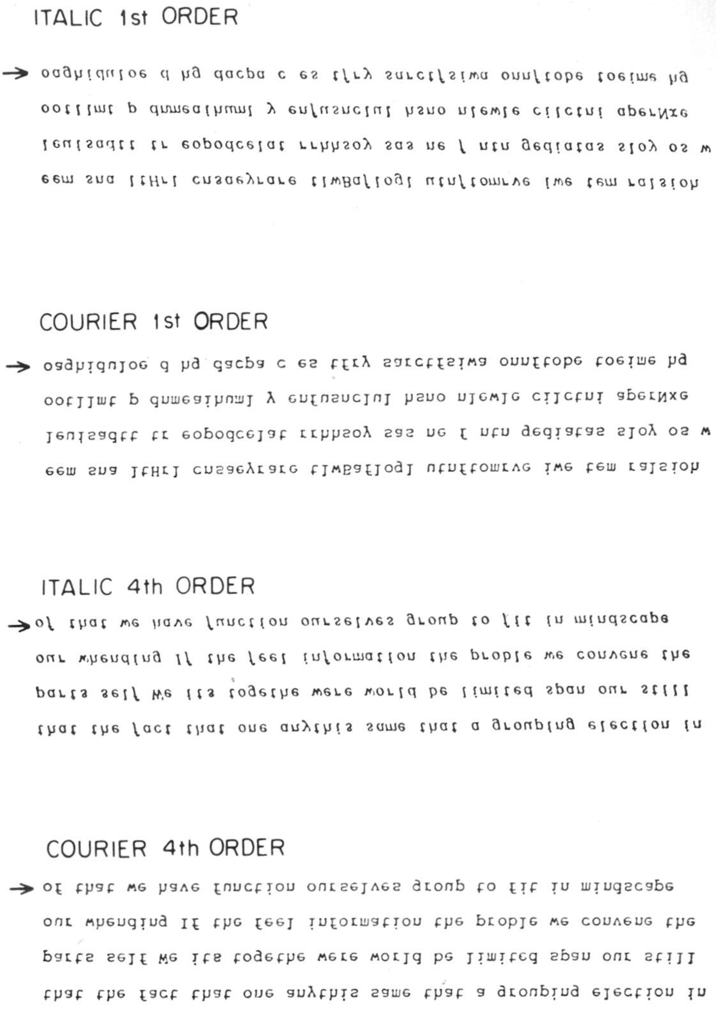

Figure 10. Two typographies, Courier and italic, and two orders of approximation to English, first-order and fourth-order

training on the typographic sequence was of more benefit than orthographic experience.) Presumably, semantic factors were important in enabling the students to name fourth-order letters faster than first-order; seeing fragments of words aided later reading, accounting for the better performance by the fourth-order groups. But these semantic or lexical factors are secondary, apparently, to the pattern-analyzing operations directed at the characters them-

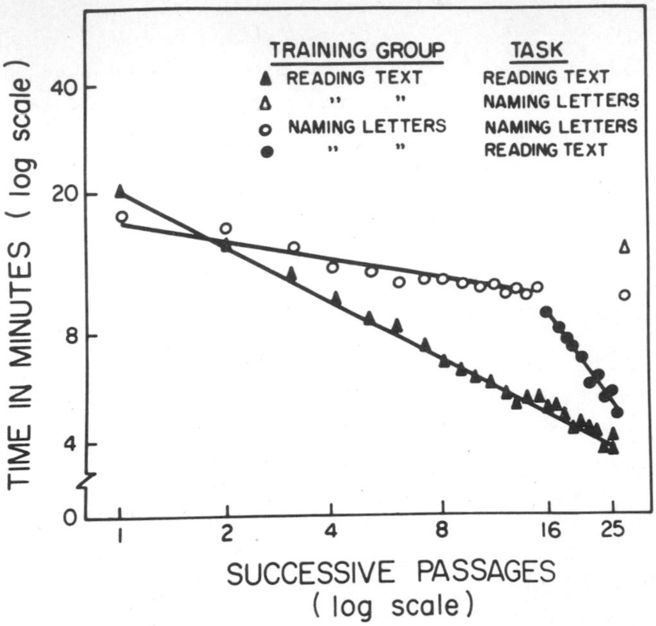

Figure 11. The logarithm of time as a function of the logarithm of page, using the texts of Figure 10

selves, the very shapes on the page that actualize or instantiate the letters. This is shown by the fact that naming letters in Courier is better practice for reading Courier than is naming letters in italic, even though the students could name the italic letters faster than the Courier letters initially.

5. *Conclusion*

The semantic component is usually assumed to be the main one for literacy. Children in school are taught to "read for meaning", are encouraged to restate and paraphrase what they have read, to interpret it, carry it forward, and so on. Without in any way intending to imply that the semantic component is irrelevant, I wish to point with my research to the fact that, in acquiring signs and symbols, the visual system is engaged in very particular forms of pattern analysis that result in visual skills. As is the case with many performances, skills are specific, not general-purpose achievements. To put it another way, I emphasize the relation that develops between a visual nervous system and the marks on the page, and would speak of literacy in terms of the pattern-analyzing operations that must be carried out to achieve it. Moreover, as the last experiment especially has suggested, the operations are not independent of the symbols on which they are exercized; they are not content-free but always content-specific operations. Indeed, for human processing of symbols, it may even be the case that one cannot usefully distinguish between operations and contents on which they are carried out, for both are part of a single pattern-analyzing process.

Notes

* Preparation of this paper was supported by Grant A7655 from National Science and Engineering Research Council Canada.

1. Although I report results only for vertical and horizontal midline surgery, other cuts are also possible. Left and right diagonals, at least of English, Hebrew, and Chinese are particularly informative cuts, as K. Ehlich (personal communication) has also noticed.
2. R. Harweg pointed out that the influence of beginnings of words may have a morphological rather than a perceptual basis. In languages such as Welsh or Hebrew, whose morphological structure is different from that of English, the bias toward the beginning of words may be less.

References

Bruner, J. S. and O'Dowd, D.
1958 "A note on the informativeness of words." *Language and Speech* 1: 98–101.
Chall, J. S.
1967 *Learning to Read: The Great Debate.* New York: McGraw-Hill.
Chou, S. K.
1930 "Reading and legibility of Chinese characters, II." *Journal of Experimental Psychology* 13: 332–351.
Frith, U.
1979 "Reading by eye and writing by ear." In P. A. Kolers, M. E. Wrolstad and H. Bouma, eds., *Processing of Visible Language 1.* New York: Plenum, pp. 379–390.
Guarducci, M.
1967 *Epigrafia greca.* Roma: Istituto Poligrafico dello Stato.
Huey, E. B.
1908 *The Psychology and Pedagory of Reading.* New York: Macmillan. Reprinted, Cambridge, Mass.: MIT Press, 1968.
Kolers, P. A.
1968 "The recognition of geometrically transformed text." *Perception & Psychophysics* 3: 57–64.
1969 "Clues to a letter's recognition: Implications for the design of characters." *Journal of Typographic Research* 3: 145–168.
1970 "Three stages of reading." In H. Levin and J. Williams, eds., *Basic Studies on Reading.* New York: Basic Books, pp. 90–118.
Kolers, P. A. and Katzman, M. T.
1966 "Naming sequentially presented letters and words." *Language and Speech* 9: 84–95.

Kolers, P. A. and Magee, L. E.
1978 "Specificity of pattern analyzing skills in reading." *Canadian Journal of Psychology* 32: 43–51.
Kolers, P. A., Palef, S. R., and Stelmach, L. B.
1980 "Graphemic analysis underlying literacy." *Memory & Cognition* 8: 322–328.
Kolers, P. A. and Perkins, D. N.
1969 "Orientation of letters and their speed of recognition." *Perception & Psychophysics* 5: 275–280.
1975 "Spatial and ordinal components of form perception and literacy." *Cognitive Psychology* 7: 228–267.
Mathews, M. M.
1966 *Teaching to Read.* Chicago: University of Chicago Press.
Rock, I.
1973 *Orientation and Form.* New York: Academic Press.
Smith, E. E.
1978 "Theories of semantic memory." In W. K. Estes, ed., *Handbook of Learning and Cognitive Processes, Vol. 6: Linguistic Functions in Cognitive Theory.* Hillsdale, N. J.: Erlbaum.

Index of subjects

Index of names